Praise for *Helen of Troy*

In her witty, scholarly and wide-ranging study Laurie Maguire explores the deep contradictions inherent in the myth of Helen of Troy. Though she was held to be the most beautiful woman of antiquity, there is no agreement about the specific details of Helen's beauty. For the majority of writers, whether historical or literary, her appearance is essentially a blank, to be filled in – or not – by the imagination of aftercomers. And though she was celebrated for having triggered major military activity – her face launching those 'thousand ships', a phrase interestingly re-spun in modern times – she is herself essentially passive, a victim of rape and/or abduction. Yet, as Professor Maguire shows in the excellent chapter entitled *Blame*, Helen has often been viewed as culpable even in her passivity. Shakespeare, for instance, linked her closely to the morally wavering Cressida. In addition to the 'Faust' legend in its various renditions, Helen's mysterious presence is also discovered in Victorian and Modernist fiction, as well as in contemporary poetry – above all Derek Walcott's epic *Omeros* – in contemporary fiction, including graphic novels, and in film. Often silent and virtually invisible, Helen reveals herself, in Laurie Maguire's richly original examination, as a potent and enduring figure in Western culture.

Katherine Duncan-Jones, University of Oxford

Laurie Maguire's *Helen of Troy* is a book about a myth. It honours the myth's elusiveness that lies in its recurring, and perhaps obsessive, repetition. The book shuns the temptation to trudge through variations on a theme or impose false teleologies and avoids, above all, any attempt to close the story down by explanation or interpretation. In the process it reveals the mixture of anxiety and desire with which we encounter stories and the different stories we make out of their omissions and absences. This work requires an astonishing depth of learning combined with a pitch-perfect ear for language that embodies in its etymology and associations the linguistic connectedness and half-heard echoes that make up the Helen story. It reveals the resonances of knowing and telling, the shudder that is always both fearful and erotic, along with the truth of all myths that beauty vanishes as soon as hands (or words) are laid upon it. Like Helen herself this story cannot be grabbed at or tied down but Laurie Maguire has achieved the intellectual and literary control that allows us to look at it and understand something of its power – which goes some way to explaining the power of literature itself.

Kate McLuskie, University of Birmingham

– What's her history?
– A blank, my lord.
(Shakespeare, *Twelfth Night*)

Imagine that you are hungry for the truth, like everyone always was and is and will be. And imagine that all you have is stories.
(Mark Haddon, *A Thousand Ships*)

Helen of Troy: From Homer to Hollywood

Laurie Maguire

A John Wiley & Sons, Ltd., Publication

This edition first published 2009
© 2009 Laurie Maguire

Blackwell Publishing was acquired by John Wiley & Sons in February 2007.
Blackwell's publishing program has been merged with Wiley's global Scientific,
Technical, and Medical business to form Wiley-Blackwell.

Registered Office
John Wiley & Sons Ltd, The Atrium, Southern Gate, Chichester, West Sussex,
PO19 8SQ, United Kingdom

Editorial Offices
350 Main Street, Malden, MA 02148-5020, USA
9600 Garsington Road, Oxford, OX4 2DQ, UK
The Atrium, Southern Gate, Chichester, West Sussex, PO19 8SQ, UK

For details of our global editorial offices, for customer services, and for
information about how to apply for permission to reuse the copyright
material in this book please see our website at www.wiley.com/wiley-blackwell.

Library of Congress Cataloging-in-Publication Data

Maguire, Laurie E.
  Helen of Troy : from Homer to Hollywood / Laurie Maguire.
    p. cm.
  Includes bibliographical references and index.
  ISBN 978-1-4051-2634-2 (hardcover : alk. paper) — ISBN 978-1-4051-2635-9
(pbk. : alk. paper)   1. Helen of Troy (Greek mythology) in literature.   I. Title.
  PN57.H4M34 2009
  809'.93351—dc22

                                                                  2008047932

A catalogue record for this book is available from the British Library.

Set in 10/12.5pt Sabon by Graphicraft Limited, Hong Kong

1   2009

Contents

List of Illustrations

Preface

This is a literary biography of Helen of Troy. It is not a historical life of a Bronze Age princess or a study of mythology; it is not an account of Troy or an exploration of the ancient world. It does not consider whether Helen of Troy had a historical existence or was a mythical figure. My subject is the literary afterlife of the woman we know as Helen of Troy, the beautiful Queen of Sparta whose elopement with (or abduction by) the Trojan prince Paris led not only to a ten-year war and the downfall of the greatest civilization the East then knew (Priam's Troy) but to 28 centuries of poetry, drama, novels, opera, and film.

Helen's story has been told and retold in almost every century. My study begins in the eighth century BCE with Homer's *Iliad*; my most recent texts are plays and novels published in 2006. My interest throughout is not in Helen's life but in literary depictions of that life: how literature deals with her beauty, her personality, how it blames her or tries to rescue her from blame, how it deifies her or burlesques her; in short, how it represents her.

In Goethe's *Faust*, Faust conjures up a simulacrum of Helen for the Emperor, then later, impulsively, reaches out to seize her. Commenting on this episode, Alexander Gillies cautions:

> A mere image cannot, however, be imperiously turned into reality as Faust wishes, simply by his laying hold upon it. Other means are required if he is to gain Helen. Egotistic impetuosity will need to be replaced by . . . understanding of her whole environment and historical context, from which she must not be disengaged, as she is disengaged here. (1957: 120)

Gillies's critique applies to any scholar wishing to understand Helen of Troy in literature. Because she appears in so many texts in so many periods, it is tempting to home in on the "Helen episodes." But one cannot understand women in epic without understanding men (or epic); one cannot understand Helen's story without attempting to understand the techniques of myth or narrative; one cannot understand plot innovations in her story without chronicling their literary precursors. We cannot simply "grab" Helen as Faust attempts to do; in fact the next time we see Faust with Helen, he has gone back to ancient Greece.

Although I cover revisions of Helen's story across many centuries, I have chosen to organize this book thematically rather than chronologically. The same issues recur in each period (Was Helen guilty or not? What is the value of beauty?), and I wanted to avoid repetition. Some repetition is unavoidable, of course, but it is a question of what kind one tolerates; I have preferred to revisit texts rather than repeat arguments. Thus texts such as Homer's *Iliad* and Giraudoux's *Tiger at the Gates* recur in several chapters, but they illustrate different points.

Faust's journey in Goethe is episodic and fragmented. Mine shares some of these features (or faults). Although this book is wide in its coverage, it is not comprehensive. Generally I exclude material in foreign languages (Ronsard's Helen sonnets, for instance, or contemporary Greek poetry) and have little to say about American poetry (such as H. D.'s innovative psychoanalytical *Helen in Egypt*). At times the juxtapositions in chapters and arguments may seem large – moving from Aeschylus to Carol Ann Duffy in one paragraph, for instance – but my focus throughout is on continuity (or difference) in narrative treatment. This literary, specifically narratological, focus avoids (or tries to avoid) the eclecticism common to most studies of Helen to date which tend to mix archaeology, history, literature, and mythology without any sense that they are separate disciplines.

I have chosen to analyze representative texts in detail, rather than offer a breathless overview. My interest is in literary history and context, and this interest is best served through close reading and analysis. To take one obvious example: most readers know Marlowe's famous lines "Was this the face that launched a thousand ships / And burnt the topless towers of Ilium?" But were these lines original to Marlowe? Did the Renaissance see them as we do, as a pinnacle of poetry? (Apparently not.) What is the afterlife of these lines in quotation by other authors? And although we view them as a transparently awed reaction to beauty, is that how they work in context when addressed not to Helen of Troy but to a devil impersonating Helen of Troy?

The importance of context means that each chapter contains within it mini-chapters on related topics. In chapter 3 the subject of rape leads to an investigation of changing rape law in Elizabethan England and of the period's interest in the rape of another classical heroine, Lucrece; a

Victorian novel about Helen, discussed in chapter 6, leads to an attempt to identify its author; and so on. Helen's story is one of seduction and/or abduction; the structure of each chapter of this book literally demonstrates and embodies abduction (in writing we call it digression). Consequently the chapters are long but each is divided into multiple short sections. The topics of the subdivisions – the relation between beauty and nostalgia, for instance – are designed to translate into seminar topics for anyone who wishes to use this book in university teaching. I have quoted (and used) English translations of Greek and Latin texts since most readers first encounter Euripides or Ovid or medieval Latin poems in English versions. Translations are literary texts in their own right and are amenable to analysis independently. However, I have constantly compared my chosen English translations with the originals, and where there is significant discrepancy (i.e., poetic license) I have noted it: repetitions in the translation but not in the original, Christian vocabulary (e.g., "guilt") not in a pre-Christian text, expansion of an implication, and so on.

Goethe wrote, "We do not get to know works of nature and art as end-products; we must grasp them as they develop if we are to gain some understanding of them" (Goethe/Luke 1994: xix). This is true not just of revisions of a single author's work but of revisions of one story across centuries and cultures. I wanted to get to know Helen's story. However, this is not the same as getting to know Helen herself; indeed one of the arguments of this book is that Helen is strangely absent (emotionally, physically) from the story she has initiated. Although she is the narrative motor, she is an absent center, and literature deals with this absent center in various ways. This is a book about what is not there, what is not said, what defies representation, and what cannot be told.

It is appropriate that a book about absence should begin by thanking the institutions that have facilitated my absence, and the friends and colleagues who have tolerated it. My greatest debt is to the Leverhulme Trust for a Major Research Fellowship from 2006 to 2008, which relieved me of all teaching and administrative duties. The President and Fellows of Magdalen College and the English Faculty of the University of Oxford granted me permission to accept this award, and prefaced it with two terms of sabbatical leave and a term of unpaid leave in 2005–2006. Without such generosity from Leverhulme and Oxford it would have been impossible to engage on a project of this scope. At Magdalen I am grateful especially to Robert Douglas-Fairhurst, Simon Horobin, and Emma Rhatigan. In Oxford and Wytham the absence of social life has been tolerated with amazing understanding by Peter Friend, Miranda Stewart, and Martine Stewart.

Throughout this project I have incurred innumerable academic debts. To detail the generous contributions of my colleagues over many years would be a lengthy narrative in itself, so an alphabetical list must function, inadequately, as a statement of gratitude. For feedback, references, interrogation, objections, caveats, conversation, assistance, and unfailing stimulation I am grateful to Elizabeth Archibald, Jonathan Bate, David Bindman, Dympna Callaghan, Clara Calvo, Chris Cannon, David Carlson, Donald Childs, A. E. B. Coldiron, Karen Cunningham, Alex Davis, Frances Dolan, Tobias Döring, Laurence Dreyfus, Katherine Duncan-Jones, Elisabeth Dutton, Sos Eltis, Lukas Erne, Raphael Falco, Ewan Fernie, Larry Fink, Juliet Fleming, R. A. Foakes, Neil Forsyth, Elizabeth Fowler, Lowell Gallagher, Mark Haddon, Robert D. Hamner, Jonathan Gil Harris, Andrew Hobson, Barbara Hodgdon, Andreas Höfele, Lisa Hopkins, Katherine Hudson, Bettany Hughes, Chris Kyle, Matthew Leigh, Richard Linenthal, Kathryn Loveridge, Charles Martindale, Richard McCabe, Martin McLaughlin, Madhavi Menon, Kirsty Milne, Ben Morgan, Barbara Mowat, Lucy Munro, Randall Nakayama, Richard O'Brien, Stephen Orgel, Patricia Parker, Robert Parker, Richard Proudfoot, Maureen Quilligan, Neil Rhodes, Thomas Roebuck, Richard Rowland, Michael Rudd, Carolyn Sale, Elaine Scarry, Michael Schoenfeldt, John Scholar, Leah Scragg, Jim Shaw, Helen Small, Emma Smith, Tiffany Stern, David Sumners, Laura Swift, Oliver Taplin, Gary Taylor, Ayanna Thompson, Samuel Thompson, Margaret Tudeau-Clayton, Marion Turner, Derek Walcott, Michael Warren, Richard Waswo, Michael Winkelman, Gillian Woods, Blair Worden, Florence Yoon, and Antoinina Bevan Zlatar.

Several friends read draft chapters and offered invaluable feedback and discussion. I am indebted to all of them for their insights, their imaginative thinking, and the speed of their response. In alphabetical order they are Dympna Callaghan, Katherine Duncan-Jones, Elisabeth Dutton, Ben Morgan, Thomas Roebuck, John Scholar, Marion Turner, and Florence Yoon. Furthermore Katherine Duncan-Jones read five chapters (twice) and one three times, and offered valuable suggestions; I am more grateful to her than I can say for such generosity. All errors that remain are, of course, my responsibility. As John Lydgate wrote in his Troy Book, apologizing for his ignorance, "I beseech [readers] . . . to correct rather than disdain" (5.3477, 3482).

Invitations to speak at conferences and universities in America and Europe allowed me to send up trial balloons. I wish to thank audiences in Bochum, Bristol, Cambridge, Canterbury, Chicago, Geneva, Los Angeles, Murcia, New Orleans, Oxford, Philadelphia, San Diego, St Andrews, Stratford upon Avon, and Washington, DC.

I have received exemplary assistance from friendly, efficient, and generous librarians: Christine Ferdinand, Hilary Pattison, and Sally Speirs at Magdalen College, and from Sue Usher and her staff at the Oxford English Faculty Library. The staff of the Bodleian Library, the Bodleian Law Library, the Sackler Library, and the Taylorian Institute have also been unfailingly helpful and knowledgeable. In London my gratitude goes to librarians at the British Library, the Warburg Institute, the Cortauld Institute Library, and the University of London Senate House. In Stratford I am grateful to Helen Hargest and the staff of the Shakespeare Centre Library, and to Jim Shaw, formerly of the Shakespeare Institute Library. The entire staff of the English Faculty Office in Oxford have assisted in numerous ways from processing grant expenses to forwarding faxes; I wish in particular to thank Joan Arthur, Paul Burns, Charlotte Heavens, Jenny Houlsby, Katie McNulty, Hayley Morris, and Caroline Taylor.

Kathleen Dickson and Sonia Mullett at the British Film Institute were unfailingly hospitable during my visits to their archives, and Sonia valiantly helped with copyright difficulties. Mark Millidge of the script department at English National Opera was also helpful beyond the call of duty in locating material relevant to the company's 2006 production of *La Belle Hélène*. Sylviane Messerli at the Fondation Martin Bodmer in Cologny (Génève) not only responded to practical questions about manuscript access but generously shared her knowledge of medieval manuscripts and illustrations. At the Royal National Theatre Archives in London I received prompt and friendly assistance from Zoë Wilcox. Staff at the Dorset Records Office and the National Archives at Kew responded rapidly to queries as did Rachel Hassall at the Bristol Theatre Collection. I am also grateful to Jim Hahn at the Academy Film Archive in Los Angeles, Todd Wiener at UCLA Film and Television Archive, and Rosemary Hanes at the Moving Image Section of the Library of Congress in Washington, DC.

I have been fortunate throughout in my editor at Blackwell Publishing, Emma Bennett, whose support, encouragement, and imperturbability in the face of an increasing word count have been much appreciated. Heartfelt thanks are also due to the onscreen copy editor, Eldo Barkhuizen.

A project of this scope and length could not have been completed without the assistance of friends and family. Dympna Callaghan, Anne Coldiron, and Elisabeth Dutton, all formidably knowledgeable in so many areas of literature, drama, and theory, provided hours of stimulating conversation. I consider myself supremely fortunate to have had them for guidance and advice whenever I needed. The same applies to Ben Morgan and Thomas Roebuck, whose theoretical, classical, and historical coverage offered intellectual excitement at every encounter. Cho Cho Tin Ngwe kept the home fires burning; Anne Maguire dug the garden; and Peter Friend never complained. Sharing his life for so many years with the most beautiful woman in literature cannot have been easy. This book is for him: φαιδίμῳ ἀνδρὶ ὅς μοι μάλα πάντα τά τ' ἔλδεται θυμὸς ἐμεῖο (Quintus of Smyrna, *The War at Troy*).

Source Acknowledgments

I am grateful to the following individuals and institutions for permission to quote from copyright texts:

Carcanet Press for the extract "What's in a Name" from Andrew Waterman's *In the Planetarium* (Carcanet Press, 1990);

Curtis Brown for Lord Dunsany's "An Interview", which is reproduced with permission on behalf of the Estate of Lord Dunsany; copyright © Lord Dunsany 1938;

Nick Hern Books for quotations from Jo Clifford's *Faust* (Nick Hern Books, 2006);

Kit Hesketh-Harvey for quotations from his unpublished translation of *La Belle Hélène*, performed by the ENO at the London Coliseum in 2006;

Oxford University Press for permission to reproduce a version of material that appeared previously in my *Shakespeare's Names* (2007);

Sayle Screen Ltd and BBC radio for quotations from Mark Haddon's unpublished radio play, *A Thousand Ships* (broadcast BBC Radio 4, 28 January 2002);

A. P. Watt Ltd on behalf of Gráinne Yeats for permission to quote from W. B. Yeats's "No Second Troy" and "Leda and the Swan".

For permission to reproduce illustrations, I am grateful to the following:

Bridgeman Art Library: figure 1, *Helen on the Ramparts* by Gustave Moreau (Musée Gustave Moreau, Paris, France/Lauros/Giraudon/The Bridgeman Art Library), reproduced by kind permission;

Fondation Martin Bodmer, Cologny (Génève): figure 8, Guido delle Colonne, *Historia Destructionis Troiae*, MS CB 78, folio 25r, reproduced by kind permission;

Getty Images: figure 2, Sir Frederick Leighton, *Helen on the Ramparts*; figure 10, *The Private Life of Helen of Troy* (1927), both reproduced by kind permission;

Huntington Library, San Marino, California: figure 9, George Peele, *A Tale of Troy* (1589), sig. C3r, reproduced by kind permission;

Museum of Art, Chicago: figure 6, Canova, Bust of Paris, reproduced by kind permission;

National Theatre Archive and Simon Annand: figure 3, still from the 1995 production of *The Women of Troy* at the Royal National Theatre (© Simon Annand), reproduced by kind permission;

Royal Shakespeare Company: figure 4, Jennifer Coverdale in Marlowe's *Dr Faustus* at the Royal Shakespeare Company in 1946. Photo: Angus McBean; © Royal Shakespeare Company, reproduced by kind permission;

Royal Shakespeare Company/Shakespeare Birthplace Trust: figure 5, Maggie Wright in the 1968 *Dr Faustus* at the Royal Shakespeare Company, © Douglas H. Jeffery; every effort has been made to contact the copyright holder;

Victoria and Albert Museum, London: figure 7, Bust of Helen, School of Canova, reproduced by kind permission;

Derek Walcott and the University of New York at Albany, Museum of Art: figure 11, Derek Walcott, "Ideal head: Helen / *Omeros*" (1998), reproduced by kind permission.

Every effort has been made to trace copyright holders and to obtain their permission for the use of copyright material. The publisher apologizes for any errors or omissions in the above lists and would be grateful if notified of any corrections that should be incorporated in future reprints or editions of this book.

Conventions

I have Latinized the spelling of Greek names (e.g., Menelaus not Menelaos) except in quotations from sources that use Greek forms. I use both Greek and Roman forms of gods' names (Aphrodite and Venus) depending on the form used in the source under discussion.

In the interest of readability I have modernized the spelling and punctuation in quotations in texts from Caxton's *Recuyell* (c.1474) onwards. I have also modernized spelling in the titles of all texts. I have retained the original spelling in pre-Caxton texts because to modernize would, in most instances, amount to emendation and interfere with the meter; however, I have provided glosses in square brackets for particularly archaic vocabulary. Terminal punctuation has been added to all indented quotations.

The medieval Troy books are lengthy and most of them are divided, like epic, into multiple books. Some of these texts open a new numbering sequence within each book; others have through-line numbering. The former is more usual; in citations I represent it as 2.3456 (= book 2, line 3456). Where through-line numbering occurs I indicate it with the prefatory acronym TLN (e.g., TLN 12345). All other poems are cited with through-line numbering, but I use the acronym TLN only for medieval texts to distinguish them from other medieval poems that have a separate numbering sequence for each book.

Texts by Homer and Virgil are cited according to the conventions of the translation I have used. The *Iliad*, in Lattimore's poetic translation, gives book and line numbers with the lineation matching that of the Greek. The prose translations of the *Odyssey* and the *Aeneid* do not; for the *Aeneid* I follow the Harvard author–date system (as for critical works) but provide the relevant book number to assist readers who have a different translation to hand, and for the *Odyssey* I give the book number followed by the page number. I quote in English throughout (translations not attributed are mine).

Because of the large number of texts covered and the potential for confusion in their varied formats, I have tried to be as full and unambiguous as possible in references. Thus:

Goethe/Luke 1987: ix	refers to David Luke's introduction to his edition of Goethe's *1 Faust* (Goethe 1987)
1 Faust 8860	refers to the through-line number
Lindsay 1974: *57*	is the page number of a critical work
Iliad 4.790	is Lattimore's translation (Lattimore 1951) by book and line number
Odyssey book 11, p. 20	refers to Rieu's translation (Homer 1991) by book and page number

Expository texts in Greek are often divided into numbered paragraphs; I retain these paragraph numbers for the reader's ease of reference. Other elaborate subdivisions are retained for the same reason; for example, Pausanias vol. 1, 2.22 in 1918: 365–67. I distinguish the titles of individual works within an edition of a single author (e.g., *Catalogues of Women* in Hesiod 1977: 191). Similarly, when various anonymous works are collected in a volume that bears the name of a known author, my citation takes the form *Cypria* in Hesiod 1977: 499. When a Renaissance manuscript poem has been edited and published in a journal, I give the poet's name and that of the author of the article, as well as journal page number and poem line number (e.g., Trussell in Shaaber 1957: 425 [43]).

Introduction: *Ab ovo*

The "facts" of mythology are not fixed. (Malcolm Willcock, *A Companion to the Iliad*)

Where shall I begin, where end, my tale? (*Odyssey* book 9)

Beginnings

Homer's *Iliad* begins with the Trojan War in its tenth year. The American cable TV miniseries *Helen of Troy* (2003) begins approximately three decades earlier, with the birth of Paris (and the terrified premonitory scream of his sister, Cassandra: "Kill him!"). We could go back earlier, starting with the wedding of Peleus and Thetis, as does the anonymous medieval poem *Excidium Troiae*, which devotes the first quarter of its narrative to Achilles, beginning with the marriage that produced the Trojan War's hero. Herodotus, writing as an historian in the fifth century BCE, chooses to begin with the abduction of Io (then that of Europa, Medea, and Helen), explaining how East and West, Phoenicians and Greeks "came into conflict" (1965: 13). Dares Phrygius' account (first century CE) begins with the adventures of Jason and the Argonauts (Frazer 1966: 133–4); Dares' contemporary Dictys Cretensis mentions the abducted Europa *en passant*, then begins his central story in the third paragraph with Paris' abduction of Helen (Frazer 1966: 24).[1] Later medieval Troy books, even those that purport to be following or translating Dares or Dictys, take up to three thousand lines to reach the abduction of Helen, chronicling as narrative warm-up the founding of Troy.[2]

Paintings, on the other hand, regularly depict the "abduction of Helen," as if there is one decisive moment that causes war. In a sense there is: Helen's abduction is the last in a series of causes, the one that triggers war, the one that, as Giraudoux's Ulysses says (in a play written on the eve of World War II), gives "permission for war" (1955: 69). But the chain of events that precedes this moment of permission offers a complex sequence of causality.

In this chapter I chronicle the links in the causal chain. Although the Trojan War is one of the most famous stories of classical epic, and Helen of Troy its most (in)famous female, Helen's story is neither easily identifiable nor chronologically related in classical literature. Her narrative, like that of the ten-year war initiated by her flight (or abduction), exists only in disconnected episodes. (Indeed, as we shall see, it is not "her" story, although throughout this book I shall refer to "Helen narratives" as a convenient shorthand for texts in which she features, however marginally.) Here I gather events from various literary sources across many centuries, presenting them sequentially, beginning with the wedding of Peleus and Thetis.

Stories and Contexts

Thetis was a Nereid (a sea-goddess) on whom Zeus had amorous designs. After a thousand years of torture, Prometheus revealed details of a prophecy that Thetis would create a son more powerful than his father,[3] whereupon Zeus chose to marry off Thetis to the mortal Peleus. Because it was a semidivine wedding, and because it signaled the end of a thousand years of strife between Zeus and Prometheus, Olympia's gods and goddesses were invited to the nuptial feast, Eris (goddess of strife) excepted. Piqued at her exclusion, Eris disrupted the festivities by throwing onto the table a golden apple inscribed "for the most beautiful." Hera (the wife of Zeus), Pallas Athena (Zeus' daughter) and Aphrodite (for Homer, the daughter of Zeus and Dione[4]) competed for the accolade. Paris was selected to adjudicate the claims of the three goddesses.

Paris was an obvious choice for this task because he was exceptionally handsome (the logic being that the most beautiful of men would himself recognize beauty). George Peele's Venus, in *The Arraignment of Paris* (1584), accepts Juno's nomination of Paris because "it seemeth by his looks, some skill of love he can" (sig. B4r).[5] But a more compelling reason for choosing Paris was his reputation for impartiality. In a contest between Paris' favorite bull and another (the other being the god Mars in disguise), Paris had unhesitatingly awarded the victory to Mars.

However, Paris proves more partial in judging divine beauty than bovine strength. Each of the goddesses offers him a bribe appropriate to her realm. Hera, goddess of heaven, offers power over many kingdoms; Athena, a war goddess, offers Paris invincibility in war; Aphrodite, goddess of love, offers

Paris the most beautiful woman. Pulchritude wins out over power. Mark Haddon's Paris explains his choice in *A Thousand Ships* (2002):

> I was a farmer's son. I had never seen the border of our own kingdom let alone another. Foreign lands were names from poems. War was something that happened on the far side of the myths . . . but the most beautiful woman in the world . . . naturally I chose Aphrodite.

In the sixteenth century Peele's disappointed goddesses Hera and Athena demand a retrial and Paris is accused by Jove "of sentence partial and unjust" (sig. D3r) because he did not take merit into account (Pallas Athena e.g. had been confident in her *internal* beauty). Paris defends himself with the logic later adopted by Haddon's Paris. Wealth means nothing to a swain: running water, modest food, contentment count as wealth. Arms are irrelevant to a foeless herdsman. "And so [I] preferred beauty before them all" (sig. D4r).[6]

Helen's beauty is that of the "immortal goddesses" (*Iliad* 3.158) because she is herself half-divine. Her father was Zeus; her mother was the mortal Leda. In Homer, Helen says Castor and Pollux (the "Dioscuri") are her brothers (*Iliad* 3.238), and Leda is later mentioned as being their mother (*Odyssey* book 11, p. 168). Zeus, disguised as a swan, raped Leda; the product of this union was an egg, or two eggs, from which hatched Helen and a twin sibling. Euripides' *Helen* gives the earliest account of Leda and the Swan. In *Orestes* Euripides' reference to Helen's "swan winged beauty" is an allusion both to her swan-neck and to her origin (Euripides 1972: 349).

Helen's sibling might have been her sister Clytemnestra or her brother Pollux (Polydeuces). Pollux is more usually said to be the twin of Castor, in which case Leda had two sets of twins: the boys Castor and Pollux, and the girls Clytemnestra and Helen.[7] Joseph of Exeter's twelfth-century account of the Trojan War poignantly reveals that the only difference between the twin brothers is their different fears: "Castor feared the death of Pollux, Pollux of Castor" (Joseph/Bate 1986: 151). There are many variant accounts of the births of the Dioscuri. For the description of Helen's birth from an egg we are indebted to Sappho (fragment 166; 1955: 100), although for Sappho Leda simply nursed an egg she had discovered.[8] In Guido delle Colonne (1287), Helen, like her brothers, is the daughter of Zeus and Danäe (book 4, 8–15; delle Colonne / Meek 1974: 32). The *Cypria* tells us that Helen's mother was Nemesis (the goddess of measure or justice).[9]

Throughout Homer, Helen is called the daughter of Zeus or the child of Zeus. In the *Odyssey* Menelaus is told that, because he is the husband of Helen, he is "in the eyes of the gods, son-in-law to Zeus" (book 4, p. 61). Even so, Homer shies away from calling Helen a goddess. For that we have to wait until Euripides' *Orestes*, where Apollo appears at the end of the tragedy to explain why he "snatched her [Helen] up" and "saved her from [Orestes'] sword":

> From Zeus immortal born, immortal she must live,
> Reverenced as the goddess who saves seamen's lives,
> Enthroned beside her brothers in the folds of heaven.
> (Euripides 1972: 359)

In Euripides' *Women of Troy* an angry Andromache accuses Helen of having many (symbolic) fathers but denies that Zeus was one:

> You were never daughter of Zeus!
> You had many fathers; the Avenging Curse was one,
> Hate was the next, then Murder, Death, and every plague
> That this earth breeds. I'll swear Zeus never fathered you
> To fasten death on tens of thousands east and west!
> (Euripides 1973: 115)

In the early modern narrative poem *The First Rape of Fair Helen*, attributed to John Trussell, Helen first hears about her mother's rape by Zeus when Helen herself is raped by Theseus. Helen was in all versions pre-pubertal when Theseus raped her, although her precise age varies. Classical writers (Hellanicus of Lesbos, Diodorus Siculus, Plutarch, Pausanias, Hyginus) make her between seven and twelve years old. Later writers offer a range of nine to fourteen. In *Troia Britannica* (1609) Thomas Heywood says Helen was aged nine (canto 9, marginal note, sig. V4r); Goethe says she was ten years old (*2 Faust* 6530). John Trussell is the most specific: she is almost "eight score moneths" (160 months = thirteen and a third years).[10]

In most accounts Theseus' "rape" is an "abduction" and he gives Helen to his mother for safe keeping. Indeed the TV miniseries *Helen of Troy* makes much of the fact that Helen's nascent sexuality attracts her, with obvious frustration, to a man who refuses to touch her. Pausanias, who investigates the abduction as rape, further details its result: the birth of Iphigenia, immediately given to her aunt Clytemnestra for a shame-free upbringing.[11]

Helen is rescued from Theseus by her brothers and returns to Sparta where suitors from all over Greece (with one exception: Achilles) compete for her hand. The suitors take an oath to support the eventual winner.[12] Why Menelaus wins – given literature's consistent depiction of him as neither handsome nor clever – is unclear. In Hesiod's account he brings with him the greatest gifts (*Catalogues of Women* in Hesiod 1977: 199); in Bernard Drew's play (1924) he is the only one to declare his love for Helen; in Linda Cargill's novel (1991) Helen is attracted to Menelaus because he seems in-different to her.

There is no immediate cause-and-effect between the judgment of Paris and his arrival in Sparta. Paris, as a shepherd on Mount Ida, is enamored of the nymph Oenone (with whom, in some versions, he has a son, Corythus). There passes enough time for Paris to be identified as Priam's abandoned son, to return to Troy as a prince, to abandon Oenone (who gets a poem of her own in 1594: Thomas Heywood's *Oenone and Paris*) and then for him to visit Sparta. When Paris is later wounded in the Trojan War, he is brought to Mount Ida for cure by Oenone's herbal skill. She refuses. Distraught at his death she immolates herself on his funeral pyre.[13]

There are various accounts of the reason for Paris' visit to Sparta. According to some writers, Menelaus took him there. In Alcidamas (early fourth-century BCE), a version without the Judgment of Paris, Paris goes to Sparta because he has heard of Helen's beauty (Lindsay 1974: 157). In several medieval Troy books (which also omit the Judgment of Paris) Paris is motivated to visit Sparta because of the fame of Helen's beauty. In other texts, a *quid pro quo* abduction in retaliation for the Greek theft of Hesione is the aim of the expedition to Greece; in the medieval *Gest Hystoriale*, for instance, the Trojans plan to kill the Greeks, to plunder the land, and then seize some lady who may be exchanged for Hesione. Paris is hospitably entertained by Menelaus before his host has to leave (the *Cypria* tells us that Menelaus was called to attend a family funeral in Crete). Dictys stresses that Paris and Helen are related (both are descended from gods) and Menelaus is upset because his relative has wronged him (Frazer 1966: 27, 24).

In almost all texts the question of Helen's departure from Sparta with Paris – willing or forced – is addressed. In several medieval texts Paris and his men land at Cythera during a religious festival. This gives Paris the oppor-tunity to view Helen in the temple. Unprepared for her beauty, he falls instantly in love. Helen, curious to see what the Trojan visitor looks like, seizes the cover of worship to observe him. She flirts / falls in love. In Ovid's *Heroides* 16 and 17 (a letter from Paris to Helen and Helen's reply), we read of an oenological overture of love: Paris spills his wine on the table and writes in the liquid, "Helen I love you." The episode is later depicted in Spenser's *The Faerie Queene* 3.9.30.1–9 and in the Hollywood film *Troy* (2004).

Helen leaves with Paris; all texts stress that Paris took Helen and her valuables. Beginning with the *Iliad*, Helen's valuables are inseparable from

Helen herself. Homer uses the formula "Helen and all her possessions" (*Iliad* 3.70); similar formulae recur in Dictys and in the medieval Troy books. The wittily ironic Helen of John Erskine's novel *The Private Life of Helen of Troy* denies two allegations of theft: "Paris didn't steal me . . . I was quite willing. But if he had stolen me, I'd prefer to think he had no margin of interest left for the furniture" (1926: 49).

The *Cypria* (and later Herodotus) tells us that Paris took three days to return to Troy with Helen. Medieval texts present her progress into Troy, where she meets Priam and is married to Paris in a ceremony the following day.

In the *Iliad* Odysseus and Menelaus come on an embassy to Troy for Helen (3.205–8). In Dictys 25 envoys are sent to Troy; the Trojans are unwilling to return Helen because they will also have to relinquish the wealth that accompanied her (Frazer 1966: 26–7). They later suggest giving one of Priam's daughters – Cassandra or Polyxena – to Menelaus plus a dowry "to take Helen's place" (52). In 2002 Haddon's King Priam explains his dilemma (or rather the only possible solution, which therefore makes it *not* a dilemma) in a series of rhetorical questions: "What was I meant to do? Send her back? Rebuke my son and broadcast his humiliation to the world?" Giraudoux's Hector is determined to "giv[e] Helen back," but as Ulysses explains, "the insult to destiny can't be taken back" (1955: 70).

Preparations for war are made. In Dictys these preparations are itemized: the forging of weapons and preparing of horses takes two years; equipping the ships takes five years (Frazer 1966: 33). As in most accounts, the total preparations take ten years. In the ninth year of preparation the Greeks send a second envoy (Dictys in Frazer 1966: 42, 48). When Agamemnon gathers the troops of the pan-Hellenic alliance in the bay at Aulis, the favorable wind changes, and the men are forced to stay in Aulis for months; plague breaks out. The seer Calchas reveals that Artemis (Diana) is angry; in the *Cypria* her anger is because Agamemnon killed a stag sacred to her and "boasted that he surpassed even Artemis" (in Hesiod 1977: 493). Calchas counsels that Artemis' anger will be appeased by the sacrifice of Agamemnon's daughter Iphigenia. Consequently Agamemnon sends a letter to his wife, Clytemnestra, at Mycenae requesting that Iphigenia come to Aulis to be married to Achilles. The ruse works, Iphigenia arrives, and her throat is cut. In some versions Artemis snatches Iphigenia and substitutes a stag for her at the last moment, taking Iphigenia to the land of the Taurians on the shores of the Black Sea (*Cypria* in Hesiod 1977: 495; Dictys in Frazer 1966: 35).[14] The wind changes, and the Greeks sail for Troy.

The ten-year Trojan "war" is a siege. In Dictys no battles take place in winter; there are truces of weeks and months to bury the dead and perform funeral games; the Greeks even cultivate the soil, grow crops, and plunder the Phrygian settlements for supplies (Frazer 1966: 62). Given ten years of preparation and ten years of siege, Helen is middle-aged by the time Troy falls. In her final speech in the *Iliad* she says "now is the twentieth year upon me since I came / from the place where I was" (24.765–6).

Stesichorus reports that Aphrodite was angry with Tyndareus (Helen's father) because Tyndareus forgot to sacrifice to her, so she made his daughters "deserters of their husbands" (scholiast on Euripides' *Orestes*, 249, in Hesiod 1977: 191). That is the short version. A longer version concerns the house of Atreus. Atreus (father of Agamemnon) was the brother of Thyestes; both brothers competed over who should inherit the throne of Argos. Independently (but no doubt exacerbating the competition), Thyestes seduced Atreus' wife; Atreus (now King of Argos) banished him, only to recall him to a banquet prepared from the flesh of two of Thyestes' sons. Horrified, Thyestes cursed the house of Atreus. Atreus' sons were Agamemnon and Menelaus, each married to one of Tyndareus' daughters: Clytemnestra and Helen. Clytemnestra was unfaithful to Agamemnon (during the Trojan War) with Aegisthus (son of Thyestes) and both she and Aegisthus killed Agamemnon when he returned victorious from Troy – evidence of the family curse. (Homer knows of the death of Agamemnon but seems not to know about the legend of the house of Atreus.)

Helen spends ten years in Troy while war wages. Later tradition, inaugurated by Stesichorus in the sixth century BCE, says that the gods sent an *eidōlon* (a phantom) to Troy, and Helen spent the war in Egypt (the Trojan Helen is thus the original Stepford wife).[15] We do not possess Stesichorus' palinode, although we can access its contents indirectly from references in Plato's *Phaedrus* (§243a–b) and *The Republic* (§586c). In the *Phaedrus* Plato tells us that Stesichorus slandered Helen in an acidulous minor epic, for which he was struck blind. His recantatory palinode resulted in his regaining his sight:

> When he lost his sight for speaking ill of Helen, Stesichorus . . . was sagacious enough to understand the reason; he immediately composed the poem which begins: / False is this tale. You never / Went in a ship to sea, / Nor saw the towers of Troy. (§243; 1973: 44–5)

In the fifth century BCE Herodotus recorded an Egyptian variant without the *eidōlon* story:

> Within the enclosure there is a temple dedicated to Aphrodite the Stranger. I should guess, myself, that it was built in honour of Helen the daughter of

Tyndareüs, not only because I have heard it said that she passed some time at the court of Proteus, but also, and more particularly, because of the description of Aphrodite as "the stranger", a title never given to this goddess in any of her other temples. I questioned the priests about the story of Helen, and they told me in reply that Paris was on his way home from Sparta with his stolen bride, when somewhere in the Aegean Sea, he met foul weather, which drove his ship to Egypt, until at last, the gale continuing as bad as ever, he found himself on the coast, and managed to get ashore. (1965: 170–1)

Herodotus does not seem to have known of the *eidōlon* story, but he and Stesichorus agree that Helen spent the war in Egypt. This variant story is the basis of Euripides' play *Helen* (fifth century BCE), of H. D.'s long modernist poem *Helen in Egypt* (1952–4), and of Richard Strauss's 1928 opera *The Egyptian Helen*. Spenser adapts the Egyptian Helen story in his Florimell/Marinell sequence in *The Faerie Queene* (1590).[16]

In Aeschylus' *Agamemnon* Helen is called "polyandros": the wife of many husbands. If we put all the variant myths' husbands or would-be husbands together, the total is 11: Theseus, Menelaus, Paris, Deiphobus, Helenus (ousted by Deiphobus), and Achilles; Plutarch has Helen under threat from Enarsphorus, Idas and Lynceus; Corythus is a contender in Parthenius; and Euripides shows Helen outwitting Theoclymenus' attempts to marry her.[17] There are also variant accounts of the number of children Helen had. By Theseus she had Iphigenia. By Menelaus she had Hermione and Nicostratus (Hesiod is the authority for this latter, but other sources say Nicostratus was Menelaus' son by a slavewoman). The *Cypria* gives her three children with Menelaus and names one with Paris: Aganus. Other accounts give her three sons by Paris; Dictys, for instance, names Corythus,[18] Buonomus, and Idaeus. Names of other sons are offered by writers from Sophocles in the fifth century BCE to Johannes Tzetzes of Constantinople in the late twelfth century (Oswald 1905: 34n). In 1619 Thomas Gataker's treatise *On the Nature and Use of Lots* reveals that Paris and Helen had a daughter and "decided the controversy between them" about naming her (the controversy being whether she should be called Alexandra after her father[19] or Helen after her mother) by drawing lots (sig. L3v). She was named Helen.

Despite these multiple or variant children, the dominant and consistent impression in literature is that Helen has only one child: a daughter, Hermione. In book 4 of the *Odyssey* the household of Menelaus and Helen is preparing to celebrate two marriages: that of Hermione to Neoptolemus, and that of Menelaus' bastard son, Megapenthes. There is no suggestion that Helen and Menelaus – or Helen and someone else – have any other children. In Trojan War literature Helen is a curiously unfamilied creature: her brothers are absent from Troy (medieval writers say they died en route);

her mother hangs herself in anguish at Helen's infamy (*Helen* in Euripides 1973: 139); and, in a culture that values fertility, Helen has only one child.

Most accounts fail to tell us What Helen Did Next: what happened when Menelaus reclaimed her, whether she and her husband lived happily ever after. Euripides depicts the prevailing view: that Helen was to be given to Menelaus to be killed (a punishment Helen herself expects in the later Quintus) but Menelaus softens when he sees his wife.[20] Quintus of Smyra invents a touching and psychologically realistic reunion. The couple converses in bed about forgiveness and forgetfulness. Then: "tears of sweet lamentation poured from the eyes of them both. Gladly they lay beside each other, and their hearts recalled their marriage" (1968: 253). Later authors invent brutal punishments. In William Morris's *Scenes from the Fall of Troy* (c.1860–5) Menelaus kills Deiphobus (Helen's Trojan husband after the death of Paris) in bed, then forces Helen on the bloodied sheets. C. S. Lewis's Menelaus contemplates rape but decides against it (1959, published 1966). In the 2003 TV series *Helen of Troy* it is Agamemnon who rapes his sister-in-law against his brother's ineffectual protests.

In Maurice Hewlett's *The Ruinous Face* (1909) Helen commits suicide when Troy falls.[21] One classical tradition tells us that Helen was later hanged on a tree in Rhodes. Driven out of Sparta by Menelaus' bastard sons, Helen flees to a friend in Rhodes where the Rhodian ruler, a vengeful widow of the Trojan War, exacts vengeance by hanging her (Pausanias vol. 2, 3.19 in 1918: 123). But for most classical writers there is a blank between her repossession at the sack of Troy and her death. It is left to twentieth century poets to fill in the gap. Bernard Drew's *Helen of Troy: A Play* (1924) shows Menelaus and Helen living happily, lyrically, ever after. Rupert Brooke depicts the couple in old age, with a geriatric Menelaus tediously recounting his success at Troy and Helen dry-shanked and shrill-voiced. Henry Peterson's "Helen, After Troy" (1883: 49) presents a Helen who tolerates a dull, rich Menelaus because he is at least available ("Poor Paris, he is dead!").

Tradition has it that Helen married Achilles in the afterlife. Philostratus tells us that Poseidon made a new island for them. (Philostratus also has Achilles and Helen spend the entire war there; Wright 2005: 144.) The relationship of Helen and Achilles is treated by W. S. Landor, H. D., and Edward Bulwer Lytton, who writes of "Fame and Beauty wed together / In the isle of happy souls" (1866: 225).[22]

The period after the fall of Troy is the biggest gap in narratives about Helen. But it is not the only one. In this chapter I have sketched Helen's story in its chronological outline, trying to make as connected a narrative as possible. With this connected story in place, we can now look at the gaps in it. This is the subject of chapter 1.

1

Narrating Myth

When Paris came, I let him in. What happened afterwards we all know – at least, we know the events, but some of us are at a loss to interpret them (Helen in John Erskine, *The Private Life of Helen of Troy*)

To tell a story is to try to understand it (H. Porter Abbott, *Narrative*)

Stories never live alone. They are branches of a family that we have to trace back and forward (Roberto Calasso, *The Marriage of Cadmus and Harmony*)

Whose Story?

In her wide-ranging account of Helen of Troy as "goddess, princess, whore," Bettany Hughes writes that "Helen found in Homer the most brilliant of biographers," a sentiment expressed more specifically elsewhere when she describes the *Iliad* as "Homer's account of Helen" (2005: 343, xxxv). Hughes is but the most recent of many commentators who hold that the Trojan War is Helen's story and that the *Iliad* is "about" Helen (e.g., West 1975: 3; Pollard 1965: 22). In fact what is noticeable about the *Iliad* is how little it has to do with Helen, or rather how little it has to *say* about Helen, who is confined to three episodes in books 3, 6, and 24. In book 3 she appears on the battlements with Priam, identifying the Greek warriors for the Trojan king. In book 6 she criticizes Paris. In book 24 she is the third of the three female voices mourning Hector.[1] But in another sense Helen is everywhere in the *Iliad*, for without Helen there would be no war; no war, no story. In narratological terms Helen functions as a nucleus or kernel (the terms are those of Roland Barthes [1982: 295–6] and Seymour

Chatman [1978: 53–6] respectively). Take Helen away, untune that string, and hark what narrative discord follows.

And yet Homer did take Helen away. The *Iliad* announces its subject in line 1: "The anger of Peleus' son Achilleus." It is left to Helen to present her own narrative, becoming the rival poet to Homer. In her tapestry in book 3 we are reminded of her role in the events she depicts:

> she was weaving a great web,
> ... and working into it the numerous struggles
> of Trojans, breakers of horses, and bronze-armoured Achaians,
> struggles that they endured for her sake.
>
> (3.125–8)

To whom does the epexegetic phrase ("struggles that they endured for her sake") belong, Homer or Helen? There is competition here between Helen and Homer for choice and control of narrative subject. A character in a modern novel observes, "I'd always assumed that I was the central character in my own story but now it occurred to me that I might in fact be only a minor character in someone else's" (Hoban 1975: 186). Helen's tapestry shows her refusal to become a minor character in Achilles' story.[2] In book 3 she answers Priam's question about Agamemnon with a biography of her own life (3.166–80) "as if hers were the story most central to the warrior's life – which is in some sense the case" (Worman 1997: 160). Helen later assumes that she and Paris will take narrative centre stage, "made into things of song for the men of the future" (*Iliad* 6.358), and literary history proves her correct.[3]

The question then becomes What has Helen to do with the anger of Achilles? (Clader 1976: 6). How does one suggest the other? Critics have proposed several answers to these questions, of which the most convincing (in narratological terms) are based on the parallels between Helen's origins and attributes and those of Achilles. The hero and heroine of the Trojan War are each the offspring of a mortal and an immortal: the god Zeus and the human Leda created Helen; the mortal Peleus and the goddess Thetis created Achilles (Lindsay 1974: 92). The poem begins with the cause of Achilles' anger; it ends with the cause of the war, Helen herself (Clader 1976: 11). But more general thematic explanations for Helen's relevance to Achilles also have narrative logic: Helen and beauty make men act; Helen leads men to honor; the poem represents the birth of (oral) poetry and the immortality it confers, an immortality enjoyed by Achilles. Helen, in other words, enables Achilles' fame. Yet none of these answers is entirely satisfactory, for they concern Achilles' fighting, not his anger. His anger leads him to *withdraw* from fighting.[4]

The story of Helen is a story of withdrawal. The infant Paris is withdrawn from Troy to Mount Ida; Menelaus is withdrawn from Sparta to Crete; his absence enables Helen to be withdrawn from Sparta to Troy; Achilles withdraws from fighting; Aphrodite threatens to withdraw from Helen. In a narrative of absence and withdrawal, even passivity (absence of agency) becomes narratologically crucial: "the most important thing Menelaos ever did for epic was to lose Helen" (Clader 1976: 32). Thus this book, like the Trojan narratives that it explores, is a study of absence, lack, gaps, ambiguity, aporia, and the narrative impulse to completion and closure.

Absence

The *Iliad* is conspicuous for what it leaves out. Listeners and readers have long realized that the poem fails to present key events associated with the Trojan War, not least of which are the beauty contest on Mount Ida (the Judgment of Paris, in which Venus bribed Paris with the promise of a beautiful woman); the oath of Helen's suitors to support the successful suitor in the event of future trouble; the sacrifice of Agamemnon's daughter Iphigenia to secure a favorable wind for Troy and to alleviate plague; information about Achilles' heel, which makes him vulnerable; and the trick of the wooden horse, which enables the Greeks to infiltrate and destroy Troy.[5] Within a century of Homer's *Iliad* other epics arose to fill in the gaps.[6] Collectively, these works, known as the epic cycle, form an overarching narrative from the gods' decision to cause the Trojan War to Odysseus' death. The narrative sequence, including Homer's works, runs as follows: the *Cypria*; the *Iliad*; the *Aethiopis*; the *Little Iliad*; the *Sack of Troy*; the *Nostoi* (*Returns*); the *Odyssey*; the *Telegony*.[7] In the fourth century CE Quintus of Smyrna wrote a 14-book epic which begins with the death of Hector (Combellack 1968: 3). At every stage Quintus' text stresses its continuity from Homer. It picks up where the *Iliad* leaves off. The author's nomination of himself as "of Smyrna" links him with Homer's alleged birthplace.[8] And its title, the *Post-Homerica*, highlights its status as sequel, "the things after Homer."

One of the text's English translators, Frederick Combellack in 1968, offers a telling translation of the title: "What Homer Didn't Tell." Combellack's title foregrounds not Quintus' continuity but Homer's omissions. In so doing, it also highlights the paradox in Quintus' title where the very act of asserting completion reveals the threatening absence in the original. The *Iliad* closes with Achilles alive and Troy unsacked, but absence is pervasive from the beginning of the poem. Achilles is absent from the fighting in book 1; Helen notes the absence of her brothers, Castor and Pollux in book 3;

Aphrodite absents Paris from combat in book 3 and threatens to absent herself from Helen; even the poet absents himself from description of battle:
"it were too much toil for me, as if I were a god, to tell all this" (12.176).
Homer's next poem, the *Odyssey*, is an acephalous epic, a chronicle of the
problems that ensue when the patriarchal head is absent. And absence continues to be a feature of all Trojan War accounts, a stylistic quiddity and
a thematic principle rather than a structural failing. From the loss of Helen,
the absence of wind in the bay at Aulis, and the loss of Iphigenia, to the
consequences of war: absent kings and leaders, thrones unfilled, homes un-
fathered and emptied, widowed beds (*Agamemnon* in Aeschylus 1968: 52,
58, 65), what a twentieth-century musical hauntingly depicts as "empty chairs
and empty tables" (Claude-Michel Schönberg, *Les Misérables*). Absence,
like Helen, gets passed around the texts. Absence comes to stand for Helen;
she is both absent and absence itself.

Aeschylus' *Agamemnon* is centred on absence and loss. A grief-stricken
Menelaus (who is himself absent from the play) loses speech and loses his
appetite. Only his eyes are hungry: to see his missing wife. He is, the Chorus
tells us, haunted by present reminders of absence:

> O pillow softly printed
> Where her loved head had rested! . . .
> A ghost will rule the palace
> A home become a tomb!
> Her statue's sweet perfection
> Torments his desolation; . . .
> Visions of her beset him
> With false and fleeting pleasure.
> (Aeschylus 1968: 57)

Within a few lines comes war, and with it the cruellest manifestation of
absent presence: "ashes in an urn." Carol Ann Duffy's twenty-first-century
Menelaus is as tormented as Aeschylus':

> her side of the bed unslept in cold,
> the small coin of her wedding ring
> left on the bedside table like a tip,
> the wardrobe empty
> of the drama of her clothes.
> (Duffy 2002: 8)

Alongside these human and thematic vacuums are linguistic vacancies:
what one avoids saying, is reluctant to voice or cannot utter. The grieving

Penelope talks of "that city, evil Ilium, which I loathe to name" (*Odyssey* book 19, p. 303). Euripides' Menelaus comes to fetch "the Spartan woman, once my wife – even to speak / Her name I find distasteful" (*Women of Troy* in Euripides 1973: 118). In *Orestes* Pylades cannot bring himself to name Helen, calling her "that woman" (Euripides 1972: 340). In book 3 of the *Aeneid* Andromache talks of "Hermione, the granddaughter of Leda" (Virgil 1981: 85), bypassing Hermione's mother, Helen, altogether.

This is not an aversion confined to classical texts. C. S. Lewis's Menelaus thinks of his estranged wife as "the Woman" (1966: 129). In George Peele's *Tale of Troy* (1589, rev. ed. 1604) Helen enters the poem as a pronoun not a proper name: "She" (line 137). Shakespeare's Lucentio, neither a classical character nor one emotionally involved with Troy, also omits Helen's name: "fair Leda's daughter had a thousand wooers" (*Taming of the Shrew* 1.2.234).

Helen, the cause of war, is systematically linguistically suppressed from its literature. Although Caxton's *Recuyell* (c.1474), his prose account of the Trojan War, lacks a title page (because it is designed to look like a manuscript), it mentions Helen's "ravishing" in its prologue (1894, vol. 1: 7); by 1597 it has developed a title page but omits to mention Helen. Thomas Heywood's drama on the same subject, *2 The Iron Age* (1632) includes Helen on the title page but omits her from the list of dramatis personae. In Shakespeare's "Rape of Lucrece" Helen is referred to only as "the strumpet that began this stir" (1471); not only is she linguistically absent but Lucrece cannot find her in the painting. The most surprising suppression of Helen comes on the DVD cover of Wolfgang Petersen's film *Troy* (2004) where Diane Kruger's name does not appear at all. (The names of Brad Pitt, Eric Banna, and Orlando Bloom – Achilles, Hector, and Paris respectively – are the three advertised.) Although this makes sense in terms of film narrative – Kruger is little involved in the plot – it does not make sense in terms of PR where the search for Helen of Troy / Diane Kruger was publicized internationally, nor does it make sense in terms of film prominence where Kruger occupies large amounts of screen time.

If Helen narratives give us structural and linguistic absences, they also give us emotion caused by absence. The loss of Iphigenia haunts both Clytemnestra and Agamemnon in the USA TV series *Helen of Troy* (Clytemnestra takes revenge on Agamemnon for the loss of their daughter; Agamemnon, in a brutal concluding sequence, takes revenge on Helen). So important is the loss of Iphigenia in Troy narratives that legend emphasizes it through repetition. A variant tradition holds that Iphigenia was the daughter of Helen by Theseus; the illegitimate baby was given to Clytemnestra to be brought up as her own. Iphigenia is thus lost twice. It is this variant legend that structures Mark Haddon's radio play *A Thousand Ships* (2002), where Helen is haunted by the loss of her first daughter: at the birth of Hermione all she can feel is the absence of Iphigenia.

Narrative duplication is a feature of myth – we see it most overtly in the *eidōlon* (double) of Helen's story – but in Helen narratives it works as a constant reinforcer of (narrative) lack, an analogue for what is omitted. Narrative gaps must be filled, if only with substitutes. In the *Odyssey* Penelope's suitors remind us of the suitors for Helen; Odysseus' battle for his wife is a replay of Menelaus' battle for his. Whenever Clytemnestra is referred to as "Tyndareid" ("daughter of Tyndareus") in Aeschylus' *Agamemnon* or Euripides' *Electra*, we think of Helen to whom the description equally applies. By the Middle Ages, when the character of Criseyde is invented, a character whose situation parallels Helen's (she is half-Greek, half-Trojan in allegiance, transferred from one camp to another, sexually associated with men on both sides) Helen gains her most complex literary double. Shakespeare's decision in *Troilus and Cressida* to stage the moment at which Cressida is transferred to the enemy camp – a scene in which emotional loyalty conflicts with the pragmatic need for survival – depicts the female interiority omitted from most Troy narratives to date. Shakespeare stages Cressida's situation as a replay of Helen's. Helen thus haunts the texts from which she is excluded; she is both written out and written in, present by implication.[9]

Fragments and Narrative

To reception theorists from Hans Jauss to Wolfgang Iser, literature is a system of exclusion. It is about the relationship between what is present in the text and what is absent from it, a relationship that it is the responsibility of the reader to negotiate, providing continuity and connection (at the most basic level: of character), coordinating viewpoints, and bridging gaps. In a process of literary entelechy, tangents and diversions are transformed, fragments joined, blanks filled in.[10] This readerly activity of turning parts into wholes is even more applicable to classical epic, which is, by definition, a fragment. (I am using fragment as the generic term it became in the Romantic period, not as a label for something accidentally incomplete.) Epic is selective, episodic, unconcerned with chronology or completeness. The *Iliad* concerns only one episode in a decade-long siege (the implication being that this episode could happen only because Achilles had withdrawn from fighting). Homer begins the *Odyssey* with the traditional invocation to the muse: "tell us this story, goddess daughter of Zeus, *beginning at whatever point you will*" (book 1, p. 3, my italics). In book 8 of the *Odyssey* the bard, Demodocus, begins his story "at whatever point he chooses to begin" (p. 107). When King Alcinous asks Odysseus for a narrative of his adventures, Odysseus wonders "where shall I begin, where end, my tale?" (book 9, p. 124). As epics, classical Helen texts are inevitably fragments.

It is customary to view epic as the genre of completeness, a form striving for wholeness and panoptic vision. This is Michael O'Neill's view. He contrasts epic with fragment, which "celebrates incompleteness" and stresses "infinite possibility" (O'Neill 2005: 278). But fragment is embedded in epic and there seems to me a productive tension at the heart of Troy literature where episodic fragment plays against and with the host genre of epic. Fragments, as Sophie Thomas explains, "play explicitly on a dynamic of complete incompletion" (2005: 511). This is a topic I shall explore in chapter 2 in relation to Helen's beauty, but for now we may simply note the parallels between the fragment and the absolute nature of Helen's pulchritude: both complete in themselves, yet creating a longing for something more. The tension between fragment and completion, desire and satisfaction, part and whole, longing and cessation of longing is both a narrative and an erotic dynamic.

The function of the fragment-in-epic is thus analogous to the role of Helen-in-narrative. Narrative suspense and erotic longing are parallel; both seek conclusion/satisfaction yet can never attain it. Conclusion would redefine their essence, for, once satisfaction is gained, narrative tension or sexual desire cease to exist, at least *qua* tension and desire. Thus their permanent state is suspension, their ontology is paradoxically liminality (between two ontologies). Helen is their representative – pulled between Sparta and Troy, between husbands, between goddess and woman – in constant circulation. The story of Helen is the story of narrative itself.[11]

If there is tension between fragment and epic, there is also tension between fragment and story. Fragment "interrupts meaning" because it frustrates the boundaries of texts on which interpretation depends (Thomas 2005: 212). But if Trojan texts are stories ("tell us this story, goddess daughter of Zeus, beginning at whatever point you will"), they are not fragments. All stories have a beginning, a middle, and an end; they are not fragments except inasmuch as all literary forms are fragments, since "no story can ever be told in its entirety" (Iser 2006: 64). And if the poet does not provide this tripartite structure, readers will. This is the view of Iser on reading generally where "discontinuities of textual segments trigger synthesizing operations in the reader's mind" (Iser 2006: 66). And it is the view of Marjorie

Levinson on reading Romantic fragments where fragment invites inter-
active readerly involvement: "readers want an experience of resolution from
poetry, and where this is withheld . . . they will develop a closural effect
from the materials and principles at hand" (Levinson 1986: 25).

Attempts to close the gaps in classical epic begin early, as we saw above
in the case of the epic cycle, which fills in large narrative gaps. Other, later
versions tackle local details. In the sixth century CE Dares tells us that Castor
and Pollux were drowned en route to Troy (Frazer 1966: 142). This was
probably a detail invented by Dares to explain why the brothers were not
involved in the Trojan War. Their absence from Troy is striking given their
previous role as Helen's rescuers during her incarceration by Theseus, a
role one expects them to reprise given mythology's fondness for repetition.
Dares' invention clearly met with approval: it is reproduced in the later
Gest Hystoriale (anon c.1400).

In every century Helen's story, simply put, is an attempt to fill in gaps.
Was she abducted or did she go willingly? What did she feel in Sparta for
Menelaus and how did she feel in Troy among Trojans? What did the most
beautiful woman in the world look like? The most glaring gap relates to
her life in Sparta after the sack of Troy, what Rupert Brooke calls, dis-
paragingly, "the long connubial years" (1918: 93). This raises the question of narrative conclusions and thematic closure.

Closure

The *Iliad* ends with Hector dead, but Achilles lives, Troy is unsacked, and
Helen remains in Trojan hands. What is remarkable about Helen's story
is the way in which it consistently strives for but eludes closure. The simplest means of closure is death. In the fifth century BCE Helen's death is
the unspoken aim of the Trojan War: it is assumed that Menelaus will kill
his wife when he regains her.[12] In Euripides' *Women of Troy*, for instance,
Menelaus plans to kill Helen on the spot, relents, and says he will kill her
in Sparta. The gentleman doth protest too much, as Hecuba realizes: she
advises him against seeing Helen or traveling on the same ship, knowing
that desire will eclipse revenge. In Euripides' *Orestes* Orestes plots (unsuc-
cessfully) to remedy his uncle's omission. His attempt is thwarted by the
gods (who rescue Helen) just as Menelaus' attempt was thwarted by Helen
herself (who deployed her physical charm seductively). It is not until the
sixteenth century that a poet manages to kill off Helen: Thomas Proctor's
achievement in *The Triumph of Truth* (1580s) is rarely remarked. Twenty
years later in Thomas Heywood's *Troia Britannica* (1609), Helen commits

suicide (depressed by the loss of her youthful beauty). Heywood repeats this in his play 2 *The Iron Age* (1632).

When narrative fails to achieve closure, literary criticism steps into the breach. Interpretation provides one of the strongest forms of closure, turning blanks and discontinuities into connected meaning. Sometimes texts provide their own internal literary critics. We see this in Aeschylus' *Agamemnon* when the Herald offers a frustratingly vague piece of information: "Menelaus has vanished, ship and all!" The herald's announcement is literally un*satis*factory: it is not enough. It is no coincidence that his news is about absence. As we have seen, auditors and readers abhor narrative vacuums and are driven to occupy the space. Aeschylus' Chorus have already set themselves up as literary critics (Clytemnestra's "style eludes you. We interpret her") and now they supply three details omitted by the herald, in effect ventriloquizing him: "You mean, (1) he sailed with you from Troy, and then (2) a storm / Fell on the fleet and (3) parted his ship from the rest?" (*Agamemnon* in Aeschylus 1968: 64, my numerical insertions). They respond consistently to the herald's blank or incomplete answers ("I can't give it you"; "No one can tell, for no one knows"; 64) with demands for, and insertion of, detail: "You mean, I think, that . . ." (65). Literary interpretation, thus, like readerly response in general, completes the story. In their efforts to understand, critics provide closure; and reciprocally in attempting closure, they offer understanding.

But one can never know or understand Helen. This is partly because she exists only as a narrative device. Norman Austin notes that in the *Iliad* Helen "understands that her function is . . . to be first and foremost a story" (1994: 1). In Euripides' *Women of Troy* she reflects on "how the story goes" – the story of her role as originator of the Trojan War (1973: 120). In the same playwright's *Helen* she tells us about her birth, concluding "that is the story of my origin – if it is true" (1973: 136). Throughout the ancient world we are reminded of the value of story as expedient, appropriate, or fitting rather than as true. In *Agamemnon* Clytemnestra says, "I said, not long since, many things to match the time / All which, that time passed, without shame I here unsay" (Aeschylus 1968: 90). In the *Odyssey* Helen too has a fitting story – "just the one for the occasion" (book 4, p. 52).

Later in the *Odyssey* Odysseus recounts his adventures to King Alcinous, a lengthy narrative that takes up books 9–12. Book 13 begins "Odysseus' tale was finished" (p. 193); here "tale" is a synonym for truthful autobiography. Later in the same book Odysseus fabricates a self-protective identity to the goddess Pallas Athena, whom he has failed to recognize. He invents a story of murder and exile to account for his arrival in Ithaca. The narrative concluded, Homer says "that was Odysseus' story" (book 13, p. 201).

Here "story" means fiction.[13] How do we know when stories about Helen are self-serving fiction and when they are biography? We do not; we cannot.

We cannot know Helen because we experience her in the already-mediated form of story; we further lack knowledge of her because she is absent. One cannot become acquainted with what is not there. Helen is remote, self-contained, sealed in her beauty, the narrative equivalent of the Mona Lisa smile. Of Helen in the *Iliad*, Linda Lee Clader writes, "[Homer] never says that the war is being fought for a phantom, but his use of Helen in the drama suggests an image rather than a rounded personality" (1976: 17). Carol Rutter observes that the "tantalizing absence" of Helen in Shakespeare's *Troilus and Cressida* is the play's "in-joke, for Shakespeare, making Helen the entire matter of the play, keeps her entirely off-stage, out of sight; except for one, single scene" (2000: 231). Goethe's Helen narrates her experiences as if they had happened to someone else, "as though they were a literary construct" (Curran 2000: 171). Mark Haddon dramatizes this point from Helen's perspective in *A Thousand Ships*:

> The truth is that no-one cares who I am. You read the stories. You read the poems. You haven't got a clue. Nothing fits. Nothing makes sense. I have no character. You never get inside my head. I'm a sorceress, a victim, a whore, a wife. I'm the devil. I'm an angel. I'm every woman that ever lived. I'm nobody, a blank slate for you to write whatever you like on.

Here Helen accuses us of creating her blankness for our own interpretive convenience. Even characters within Helen-narratives comment on her emotional inaccessibility and unknowability. Paris feels distanced by Emily Putman's sardonic Helen in "Helen in Egypt" (1926), Lily Briscoe by Mrs Ramsay (a Helen figure, called "the happier Helen of these days") in Woolf's *To the Lighthouse* (1927). In this sense Lily Briscoe's comment on the deceased Mrs Ramsay / Helen – that without her their lives continue round a "centre of complete emptiness" (1992: 417) – applies to Helen whether she is alive or dead; she is always an empty center. Absence is her essence; there is no interior (or anterior) being.

What is absent cannot be contained, brought to closure. Despite this, narrative tries to know Helen, a process implicit in the act of turning her into narrative. Narrative is literally about knowledge. Its Sanskrit root *gnâ*, "know," leads to two separate Latin forms, the adjective *gnarus* (knowing) and the verb *narro* (I tell), a form of *gnaro* (elided from *gnarum facio*: "I make known").[14] To narrate is to make something known. Literature is literally know-and-tell (see Abbott 2002: 11; White 1987: 215n).

To know-and-tell Helen's story leads to danger. Knowledge has a long association with danger, which the Christian world best knows in the form of Eden's Tree of Knowledge. Helen's danger manifests itself textually in a series of shudders.

The Textual Shudder

In the *Iliad* Helen describes herself as "hateful" (3.404). The word she uses comes from the verb *stugeo* (fear, shrink from the sight of). Some English translations use the word "abhorrent," which conveys the word's literal effect: Helen is someone who makes men shudder (*horreo* in Latin, from which we derive "abhorrent," means "bristle" or "shudder").[15] A variant occurs at the end of the poem when Helen says people "shrank" when they saw her (from *phrisso*, "shiver with fear"; 24.775). Clader surveys this vocabulary (1976: 18–23): "in each of the three of Helen's appearances in the *Iliad* she is at some point described as a being to be abhorred – she makes people grow stiff or cold with fear . . . or makes them shiver with fear" (22). The shudder that Helen's presence causes in texts is related to her beauty: beauty disrupts narrative.

When Dante sees Beatrice, he shudders and trembles. When Belphoebe enters *The Faerie Queene*, it is the narrative itself that shudders: it pauses for ten stanzas of rapturous (descriptive) response. The only half-line in George Peele's poem *The Tale of Troy* occurs when Helen enters the text: her entrance causes a metrical shudder. In Tennyson her beauty effects a grammatical shudder. The phrase in which Helen's breasts appear in a dream to Lucretius, like the breasts themselves, is doubled, disembodied, and suspended: "Then, then, from utter gloom stood out the breasts, / The breasts of Helen" (Tennyson 1936: 808). The syntactical interruption signaled by the comma forces a pause at the end of the line after "breasts" – a pause for admiration, for a sharp intake of breath – before the sentence resumes, restating its subject and completing the interrupted possessive phrase. Many Helen texts stutter and come to a halt (William Morris's fragmentary "Scenes from the Fall of Troy," C. S. Lewis's abandoned story "After Ten Years") or are disrupted generically (Euripides' *Helen* and Shakespeare's *All's Well That Ends Well* push the generic boundaries of tragedy into comedy[16]) or have their narrative purpose diverted (in the *Odyssey* Odysseus reveals the Greeks' plan to Helen. Although "his mission into Troy was not to divulge but to gather information . . . men's purposes are easily swayed when Helen is in the room" (Austin 1994: 79). In Goethe's *2 Faust* Helen's first appearance inspires Faust to a spontaneous paean to beauty, a textual shudder corrected by Mephistopheles: "stick to your part" (6501).

From Homer onwards, shuddering is not just a reaction to beauty but is a consequence of knowledge. In the *Iliad* book 16 Hector slashes the top off the spear of Telamonian Ajax. This is, for Ajax, not a localized moment of dismay but a premonition of military disaster: "and Aias / knew in his blameless heart, and *shivered for knowing it*, how this / was gods' work" (16.118–21, my italics). In *Aeneid* 6 the gods reveal Aeneas' fate through a sibyl. On hearing her prophesy, "the Trojans felt an icy shudder run down their hard spines" (Virgil 1981: 148). When Adam and Eve eat from the tree of knowledge in Milton's *Paradise Lost*, "earth trembled from her entrails" (9.1000); this is surely the same physical reaction as the classical shudder. Yeats later associates sexual knowledge with historical knowledge. The sestet of "Leda and the Swan" begins:

> A shudder in the loins engenders there
> The broken wall, the burning roof and tower
> And Agamemnon dead.

Yeats concludes by wondering "Did she [Leda] put on his knowledge with his power / Before the indifferent beak could let her drop?" Yeats voices explicitly (albeit interrogatively) what is implicit in the earlier examples, that the beginning of a new historical sequence (exemplified for Yeats by the conception of a person, for Milton by the fall, for Virgil by a national future, and for Homer's Ajax by the threat of military loss) should be framed as a problem of knowledge.

In William Morris's *Scenes from the Fall of Troy* it is (unusually) Helen herself who shudders. Morris's Helen is given (again unusually for Helen narratives) considerable interiority and analytical foresight: she anticipates consequences (1915: 3), accepts the Greeks' desire for her death and imagines three possible ways of executing it (1915: 4), and realizes that Polyxena is younger and more beautiful than she (1915: 5). Her shudder is linked to knowledge: her awareness that the Greek soldiers live without domestic love, only with hatred of her (1915: 6–7).

We might expect the Greek language to make a distinction between shuddering with awe and shivering with abhorrence, yet the two are mutually intertwined. If Helen's beauty arrests people and freezes narrative, so too does the monstrous: the property of the Gorgon, for example, is to turn people to stone, to petrify them literally and emotionally. (Spenser understands and exploits this duality in *The Faerie Queene* in the adjective "astonyed.") Absolute beauty and the monstrous are kin: both are extremes.

Simply put, Helen, like the monstrous, should not exist. The Greek language subliminally realizes this, linking the shudders of awed admiration with those of horror (*stugeo, rigeo, phrisso*).[17]

In the fifth century BCE, Gorgias wrote that poetry causes "fearful shuddering and tearful pity and grievous longing" (Sprague 1972: 52). It is perhaps no coincidence that Gorgias' description of poetry comes from his defense of Helen. His phrasing describes poetry but these responses to poetry are identical to responses to beauty: the fearful shuddering of awe, emotional sympathy, and longing. We see these reactions to beauty in Plato (or Plato's Socrates): one who sees "a godlike face or bodily form that has captured Beauty well . . . shudders" (*Phaedrus* §251 in Plato 1997: 528). Poetry too is a bodily form that has captured Beauty well.

J. M. Coetzee illustrates this point in his novel *Elizabeth Costello* (2004).[18] Costello and another woman, a singer on a cruise ship, are discussing Emmanuel Egudu, a famous African oral poet with whom the singer is having an affair. Costello is trying to warn the younger woman against him:

> "*Aber kaum zu vertrauen*", she remarks to the woman . . . *Kaum zu vertrauen*, not to be trusted.
>
> The woman shrugs again. "*Die Zeit ist immer kurz. Man kann nicht alles haben*". There is a pause. The woman speaks again. "*Auch die Stimme. Sie macht dass man*" – she searches for the word – "*man schaudert*".
>
> *Schaudern*. Shudder. The voice makes one shudder . . .
>
> The voice. Her thoughts go back to Kuala Lumpur, when she was young, or nearly young, when she spent three nights in a row with Emmanuel Egudu, also young then. "The oral poet", she said to him teasingly. "Show me what an oral poet can do". And he laid her out, lay upon her, put his lips to her ears, opened them, breathed his breath into her, showed her. (2004: 57–8)

Here the shudder is a reaction to poetry, to oral poetry, to Egudu's voice.

Coetzee unites the beauty of poetry and physical beauty through contemplation of eternity and time. Despite the secular materiality of Elizabeth Costello's memory, the sexual episode is colored by the sacred. The poet is resonantly named (Emmanuel = God is with us); he sleeps with Elizabeth Costello for an archetypal "three nights in succession"; sex is seen as spiritual creation ("breathed his breath into her"); and the orifice of creation, as in New Testament narratives and Christian art, is the ear. Most important, Coetzee activates Costello's nostalgia in an oddly phrased time scheme ("near" implies moving towards something, not away from something. Technically one can never be "nearly" young). Here Coetzee, like epic, like poetry in general, refuses the linearity of time. The episode is not a sexual reminiscence, but a description of the effect of oral poetry.

Helen is regularly associated with epic oral poetry: in her weaving in the *Iliad*; in the effect of the pharmaceuticals she dispenses in the *Odyssey* that rewind time and make the recipients forget pain (Clader 1976: 33). But epic poetry as we have seen is full of blanks. It is the attempt to articulate this blank that leads to the textual shudder. As Barthes writes, "though incapable of being *spoken* there [in the text], bliss nonetheless transmits the shudder of its annihilation" (1975: 61; italics original). His vocabulary is both textual and sexual: the shudder is both a climax and dispersal of pleasure. Helen's beauty affects texts in the same way, simultaneously exciting and frustrating.

Myth and Repetition

It is true that there was a city called Troy, on the Dardanelles in Asia Minor (today's Turkey). It is true that Troy was destroyed and rebuilt on several occasions.[19] It is true that there was economic competition between Troy and ambitious thalassocratic Greek states. It is true that wars were fought over women. But that there was a woman called Helen, Queen of Sparta, that a pan-Achaian alliance was formed to regain her, and that Troy was destroyed in the process is not "true" in any factual sense. Helen's story, like that of Eve's to which it is surprisingly similar, is more explanatory myth than demonstrable fact. Both explore the origin of evil; in both a woman, a piece of fruit, and sex cause the downfall of civilization.

What is singular about Helen's story is that it is not singular. Elements we assume are exclusive to the Trojan War are often commonplaces of myth and folktale in the classical world and the ancient Near East. As Roberto Calasso writes in one of the epigraphs to this chapter, "Stories never live alone. They are branches of a family that we have to trace back and forward" (1994: 10). And Helen's family tree is extensive.

Paris' adjudication of the beauty of three goddesses seems to have been a development from the three gift-bearing nymphs who accompanied Hermes to which is added the Hellenic love of beauty contests (Lindsay 1974: 193). Competitions for women are also recurrent in myth: Atalanta, Jocasta, Hippodameia.

The decade of war, with Troy falling in the tenth year of the siege, derives from a mythical tradition of nine-plus-one. In the *Odyssey* Odysseus drifts for nine days before reaching land on the tenth (book 14, p. 216). In the

Iliad Niobe's deceased children lie in blood for nine days, "but on the tenth day the Uranian gods buried them" (24.612). Hesiod explains in the *Theogony* that when an immortal is punished by the Olympian gods, he is exiled for nine years and rejoins the immortals in the tenth (Hesiod 1988: 26). Troy may have suffered a long siege but it was not necessarily of ten years' duration.

The trick of the wooden horse is not unique to the Trojan War. When Pasiphäe (wife of the Cretan king Minos) fell in love with a bull, she was able to approach it concealed in a wooden cow (the offspring of this union, part bull, part human, was the Minotaur).

The phantom Helen, which Stesichorus introduces in the sixth century BCE, is not the only double made by the gods. Athena makes a phantom of Penelope's sister, Ipthina, and sends her to Ithaca to comfort her sibling (*Odyssey* book 4, pp. 68–9). In the *Iliad* Apollo makes a double of Aeneas (5.449–50); Juno does the same in the *Aeneid* (book 10), turning a fragment of cloud "into the shape of Aeneas . . . She gave to it words never real, sound without thought, and perfectly moulded the gait for its walking" (Virgil 1981: 270).

Helen as the (sexually) curious bad woman, breaking taboo, can be paralleled in Pandora, in the daughters of Cecrops, in Eve, and in the Blackfoot Native Americans' myth of the Feather Woman: unable to control themselves, each of these women unleashes disaster.[20] Their opposites – Penelope in the *Odyssey*, the virtuous wife of the Old Testament's book of Proverbs – provide a counterexample. In these examples, as so often, myth provides a memorable explanation of causes. Pandora, Eve, and the Feather Woman explain the origin of suffering; the transformation of Lot's wife into a pillar of salt explains salt formations in the Dead Sea; the odd consequence of Eve eating the forbidden fruit – awareness of nakedness – is perhaps an attempt to explain why animals have covering and humans do not (Norris 1998: 26). When the bard sings at the start of the *Aeneid*, "his song told why on each winter day the sun so hastens to dip in ocean, and told of the cause which then retards the nights and makes them slow" (Virgil 1981, book 1: 50).

The mythological detail that Helen went to Egypt is part of this interest in causal explanation. There are several variants of this sojourn: in the epic cycle, in Stesichorus, in Herodotus. M. L. West summarizes the variants:

> Some say she went there as well as going to Troy, others say she went there instead of going to Troy: everyone says she went there. Some say she went with Paris, some say she went with Menelaus, some say she went there by herself: everyone says she went. (1975: 5)

Disappearance (particularly seasonal disappearance: the absence of the sun, of leaves, of flowers) and recovery are a feature of myth. Paris is exposed on Mount Ida apparently dead to Troy, reborn as a Trojan prince. Oedipus too is abandoned and rescued. The unborn Dionysus is threatened with death when his mother, Semele, is consumed by lightning, but Zeus rescues his unborn child from the ashes and places him in his thigh until the time is right for his birth. Demeter rescues her daughter, Persephone, from the underworld but is tricked into returning her for six months of each year. Francis M. Cornford (1934) views this structure as a pagan personification of the seasons with a pattern of replacement or (sometimes repeated) disappearance and return.

Helen's name means "shining one" and associates her with the sun. One anthropological argument posits that Helen originated as a sun-goddess (West 1975: 7–13). Her sojourn in Egypt – the land of the sun – may be an attempt to explain not just *why* the sun disappears (as the *Aeneid*'s bard does, above) but *where* it goes. In this context it matters little whether Helen goes to Egypt before, during, or instead of the Trojan War. The important point is that it is from Egypt that she returns to Sparta (West 1975: 5). "How like a winter hath my absence been," says the poet metaphorically to his lover in Shakespeare's Sonnet 97; in mythology Helen's absence may literally have been a winter. The repeated abductions and husbands – Theseus, Menelaus, Paris, Deiphobus, Achilles (the five consistent names in totals of ten or more) accord with this logic. The sun vanishes and is recovered, again and again (Clader 1976: 82). Myth is thus an early form of the science of causation.

Myth is a repetitive form. It repeats situations and creates phantoms. It also often twins or doubles people: Menelaus and Agamemnon, Helen and Clytemnestra, the Dioscuri. The *Iliad*'s two Ajaxes were probably once one person, their variant attitudes and actions stemming from divergences in local legends. As narratives of their myth developed it became easier to accommodate the differences by turning them into two persons. Similarly the depiction of both Helen and Clytemnestra as Iphigenia's mother suggests "an original identification of the two" (Clader 1976: 52n).[21] Sometimes mythological stories offer inverted pairs. Penelope refuses her suitors, Clytemnestra accepts hers. Clytemnestra kills one man (Agamemnon), while thousands die for Helen. Odysseus slays the uninvited suitors in his house, while Agamemnon is slain by an uninvited suitor (Clader 1976: 28).[22]

In practical terms, repetitions, parallels, and pairs are ways of accommodating changes in myth or reapplying myth to new circumstances. In narratological terms they are ways of turning an episode into a pattern and a pattern into a symbol.[23] Myth provides a common vocabulary for structuring, rearranging, and developing stories. The stories convince because they are familiar; they continue to attract, to appear relevant, and to explain new circumstances because they are different. As the repetitions and parallels above suggest, Helen's story is no more "her" story than is any other myth of a hero or heroine, pagan or Christian. Nor is it any more "true."

Jean-Paul Sartre holds that there are no true stories (because all stories are mediated. They are representations; and representation can be mimetically verisimilar but it cannot be the real thing). But as H. Porter Abbott counters, Sartre's observation does not mean that stories are false (2002: 19). Helen's story is a true account of the forces that destroy cities and civilizations and unite communities and groups. Barbara Tuchman observes, "what it tells us about humanity is basic . . . It speaks to us of ourselves, not least when least rational" (2005: 43); and Michael Wood notes, "the story moves us so much that it must be true" (2005: 46). Arthur in *Tom Brown's Schooldays* illustrates Wood's point. Asked to construe a portion of the *Iliad*, Helen's lament over Hector's body, the schoolboy twice falters over the last two lines of her speech before bursting into tears (Hughes n.d.: 244–5). His tears are proof of how much "the story moves us" and his breakdown is accepted by both the schoolmaster and the narrator as an appropriate response to the lines in question. Arthur responds to Homer's human, rather than historical, truth: to grief, loss, death, fear, sorrow. His tears illustrate Armstrong's point that myth does not work by being factual; it works by being effective (Armstrong 2005: 10).

Origins

So where does Helen's story come from? Or, to put it another way, how does it begin? To answer these questions requires an excursus into the linked worlds of anthropology and etymology. A brief summary must here suffice.

Descriptions of Helen begin with – are embodied in – her name, which may have a religious history. *Helene* is the word used for a torch, and for a reed basket (both used in sacred cults; Clader 1976: 66–8; Lindsay 1974: 209–11). *Argein*, Argive Helen, also has a similar association. There is no logic to Helen being designated Helen of Argos since she is repeatedly said to live in Lacedemonia, in Sparta specifically (indeed in fifth century BCE drama she is often called the "Lacedemonian" or "Spartan" Helen).

Rather than referring to the place, *argein* can mean "bright," "shining" – attributes of and associations with a goddess (Clader 1976: 59–62).[24]

A reference to Helen's magical power at Therapnae (her ability to cure a baby girl of an ugliness so great that the parents forbade anyone to look at the infant)[25] and other references to her in the same place suggest she was a local goddess at Therapnae (Clader 1976: 69).[26] Shrines of *Helen dendritis*, a tree-goddess, are more widespread (found as far away as Rhodes, for instance).[27] Trees accord with other pastoral associations of Helen worship – rivers, dancing – and indicate that she was not just a goddess but a fertility-goddess. Dancing is mimetic of agricultural growth (stamping awakens the earth, leaping emulates tall crops); rivers and trees represent growth; the "shining" Helen, as we saw earlier, is associated with the sun. Agriculture, the result of nature's fertility, was seen as a sacred marriage of heaven and earth with the female soil receiving divine semen (seeds) and heavenly rain representing the sexual act, which leads to harvest (Armstrong 2005: 43). With the introduction of sacred prostitutes, the religious aspect assumed human form but the concept remained the same. Sex with one of these temple prostitutes ("prostitute" means, literally, a substitute: one who stands in [*stare*] for [*pro*] the goddess) was a symbol of sacred marriage.

Fertility-goddesses are permitted multiple partners and husbands, but as the relationship between myth and religion dwindles (leading to the "faded god" theory of epic, where the hybrid heroes (half-mortal, half-immortal) were once minor deities) the divine attributes are reapplied. Helen still has multiple partners but they are explained through a sequence of abductions and attempted seductions. Five is the usual number of partners assigned her but, as we saw in the previous chapter, others double the total.

If Helen as queen (rather than as goddess) is abducted and/or sexually besieged, she now has to be rescued. Helen's brothers, the Dioscuri, were possibly once her husbands: their role as rapists of their fiancées in the *Cypria* is perhaps a vestige of their earlier role as spouses to Helen. When Helen, the daughter of the sun, became the daughter of Zeus (who is also the Dioscuri's father), the Dioscuri could no longer be her husbands. Menelaus and Agamemnon, who in previous versions may have been husbands, twins, or one character, become a husband and a brother. (The Chorus in Aeschylus' *Agamemnon* calls them "twin monarchs of our warlike race, / Two leaders one in purpose"; Aescyhlus 1968: 45.) Helen's prepubertal association with Theseus fits this pattern. Theseus' dominant activity is abducting or raping (and occasionally marrying) women: Ariadne, Antiope (or Hippolyta), Persephone, Helen, Phaedra. But Theseus' connection with Helen and the Trojan War is tangential and it is likely that sometime in the sixth century BCE, with Athens enjoying prominence as the capital of the unified Attic communities, there was a desire to associate Athens and its most famous king (actually mythical but believed to be an early leader) with the Greeks' most famous international war.

The development and adaptation of myth does not have a recognizably linear progress. Although there is a logical connection between the abducted Helen and the fertility goddess, there is no plausible link between the tree-Helen and the Helen abducted by Paris. Helen's myth (in any of its variants) may have been a separate narrative that later became attached to the myth of the Trojan War. Furthermore all references to Helen-worship postdate Homer (Pollard 1965: 22), in which case we have to show how an epic heroine evolved into a religious figure; this is a more difficult development to explain than that of a goddess dwindling into a wife. My point here is simply to indicate the dynamic nature of myth, a dynamism that frustrates the precision of textual stemmatics.

Myth and Meaning

We are, as Karen Armstrong notes, meaning-seeking creatures (2005: 2) and the question Armstrong asks of myth – not "what happened" but "what an event meant" – is the question I ask in this book in literary redactions of the Trojan War. It is also the question asked by Beaumont and Fletcher in *The Maid's Tragedy* (1610–11), when one of the heroines, Aspatia, blatantly reinterprets the myth of Theseus to suit her own purposes.

Aspatia has just been jilted by her fiancé, and in act 2 converses with her waiting women, Antiphila and Olympias, about classical precedents in rejection: Oenone, Dido, Ariadne. She turns her attention to the tapestry Antiphila is weaving of Ariadne (whom Theseus abandoned). Aspatia identifies Theseus by his false looks and questions Antiphila about Theseus' violent end:

> Does not the story say his keel was split
> Or his masts spent, or some kind rock or other
> Met with his vessel?
>
> (2.2.46–8)

Antiphila's response is as we might expect: the cautiously diplomatic denial "not as I remember" (2.2.48).

Aspatia asks Antiphila to abandon the narrative she is currently stitching and to follow Aspatia's directions:

In this place work a quicksand,
And over it a shallow smiling water,
And his ship plowing it; and then a Fear:
Do that Fear to the life wench.

(2.2.54–7)

Antiphila objects, "'Twill wrong the story," but Aspatia counters, "'Twill make the story wrong'd by wanton poets, / Live long and be believ'd" (2.2.58–9).

This dialogue illustrates competing notions of story. For Antiphila a story is truthful (it is something that can be wronged). For Aspatia a story is untruthful – it has already been wronged – if it shirks moral closure: it fails to punish Theseus' perfidy. Aspatia wants to transfer the "false smile" she has observed on Theseus' face to the sea, with "a shallow smiling water" over a "quicksand." However, she does not say that this will "right" the story (although that is the implication) but that the new ending will make it last and "be believed." Aspatia gets to the heart of myth: it matters not whether it is true or not but whether you believe it to be true.

Yet this insight contradicts the implications of her previous description of Ariadne's/Theseus' story as something "wrong'd by wanton poets." If poets falsified the story, there was already something true to be misrepresented. That "something" may be emotional truth: she later criticizes Antiphila for not having made Ariadne sufficiently pale and sorrowful, instructing her "Do it by me; / Do it again by me . . . /And you shall find all true" (2.2.256–7). Aspatia sees her life as story, a story whose emotional intensity is transparently legible: "let all [i.e., everything] about me / Tell that I am forsaken" (2.2.70–1).

Aspatia wants to add emotion to Theseus' story. She not only wants the tapestry-Theseus to suffer death, she wants him to suffer emotional stress – fear – before he dies. She stresses it twice: "and then a Fear: / Do that Fear to the life." Fear is similarly personified in another play about epic, myth, and representation written a few years before *The Maid's Tragedy*, Shakespeare's *Antony and Cleopatra*. In 2.3 the soothsayer warns Antony that his guardian angel "becomes a fear as being o'erpowered in the presence of Caesar" (2.3.24).[28] There is something very *Antony and Cleopatra*-like in the scene between Aspatia and her women in *The Maid's Tragedy*. Aspatia recommends that her women, like Cleopatra,

take to [their] maiden bosoms
Two dead-cold aspics and of them make lovers;
. . . one kiss
Makes a long peace for all.

(2.2.23–6)

Antony and Cleopatra is also concerned with future and past revisions of myth. Anticipating his reunion with Cleopatra in Elysium, Antony says that Dido and Aeneas' entourage will follow Antony and Cleopatra as they wander through fields of asphodel (4.14.59–62). This is a blatant revision of mythology. Not only do Dido and Aeneas never meet in Elysium, but when Aeneas visits the underworld in the *Aeneid*, Dido explicitly rejects him (as he had previously rejected her in Carthage).

In act 5, *Antony and Cleopatra* shows its relation with epic in the form of Cleopatra's nostalgia. Reminiscing about Antony, Cleopatra calls up a larger-than-life hero: "his legs bestrid the ocean . . . Realms and islands were / As plates dropped from his pocket." Her 11 lines of hyperbolic description are followed by a question: "Think you there was or might be such a man / As this I dreamt of?" Dolabella has to disabuse her: "Gentle madam, no" (5.2.82–94). He brings her from wishful longing, the emotional nostalgia of epic, to the reality of Roman conquest.[29]

In Marlowe's *1 Tamburlaine*, characters expertly or ineptly revise myth for their purposes. Tamburlaine turns the myth of Icarus – a standard Renaissance trope of folly and failure – into an image of glory and daring (4.2.47–52); Mycetes, on the other hand, compares his attempts to conquer Tamburlaine to Paris' capture of "the Grecian dame" (1.1.66) – a bathetic and gender-inappropriate image. *1 Tamburlaine* shows that if you cannot apply myth appropriately (like Mycetes), you must simply remake it (as does Tamburlaine) – and as, later, do Antony and Aspatia. Myth is like the postman's definition of poetry in the film of *Il Postino*: not for the one who makes it but for the one who needs it. And need may necessitate alteration. The individual interprets, applies, and revises the story, (re)making its meaning.

Causes

Of the historical Troy ruled by King Priam, Michael Wood poses the question: Why would the Mycenaean Empire attack "such a small place?" (2005: 181). To answer this question we need to understand the pressures on Agamemnon as "high king" of Mycenae (the arch-king of all the other kings of mainland Greece). Mycenae was an expensive military fortress. Agamemnon

> needed to sustain his military following by generosity, that is, by gift-giving, food, hospitality and perhaps by grants of land. He had to feed his court and its officers, equip and reward his army . . . To do all this, and to keep his army loyal, his friends happy and his enemies subdued, he needed to take land, slaves, women, treasure and booty. (Wood 2005: 180)

Mycenaean war was essentially a piratical operation: skirmishes with theft as their aim. Women and slaves were important objectives and objects as slave labor fueled the domestic economy. Troy was famous for wool, yarn, textiles, horse-breeding, fish, and pottery (Wood 2005: 190). Economically Mycenae needed war; Troy was an obvious target. The medieval Troy book poems, with detailed realism, show how such a war could last ten years: fighting is punctuated not only by periods of rest, recovery, negotiation of terms for prisoners, and funeral rites, but by Greek excursions into Asia Minor to loot and plunder (cattle, crops, women). The Trojan War was more accurately a siege (as the title of the medieval poem *The Siege of Troy* indicates), with occasional battles.

That the war was precipitated or legitimized by the abduction of a queen may or may not have been true. If there was a theft, it was more likely to have been of a Palladium, the emblem of the goddess Athena, anthropomorphized subsequently as a divinely beautiful queen.[30] Most wars have complex prehistories, concentrated in one trivial apparent "cause" that functions as tinder. In this case, myth tells us that the tinder was literally Tyndar-eid.

In the afterlife Margaret Atwood's Penelope tells her cousin Helen that she never existed:

> "I understand the interpretation of the whole Trojan War episode has changed," I tell her, to take some of the wind out of her sails. "Now they think you were just a myth. It was all about trade routes. That's what the scholars are saying." (Atwood 2005: 187)

But Helen could have existed and the war still have been about trade. This is the plausible premise of all the film versions of Helen that show Agamemnon's imperial greed (and, in the 1955 Warner Brothers film, Helen's awareness of the danger he poses).[31] The most compelling literary treatment of Helen-as-excuse comes in Jean Giraudoux's antiwar play of 1935, *Tiger at the Gates*. This is the title of Christopher Fry's 1955 English translation. The French title is the wonderfully jussive *La Guerre de Troie n'aura pas lieu* (*The Trojan War Will Not Take Place*), which encapsulates the play's comic and preposterous logic. The fact that the most famous war in ancient history might not have happened, the fact that there is a moment, or sequence of moments, when it might have been averted, is something we rarely consider given its monolithic status in our mythological history.[32]

Giraudoux's Hector is committed to returning Helen to the Greeks. Like an earlier Hector – Shakespeare's in *Troilus and Cressida* – he does not want war. Whereas Shakespeare's play soberly shows how little you can prevent war by not wanting it (his Hector is resigned to acting against his ethical beliefs as early as act 2), Giraudoux's Hector continually attempts to return Helen until events escalate beyond his control in the last act.

The play begins with the extended metaphor that gives the play its English title. "Destiny, the tiger, is getting restive," says Cassandra. She juxtaposes the stages of the tiger/Destiny rousing itself with the innocent activities of Trojans:

> Hector has come home in triumph to the wife he adores. The tiger begins to rouse, and opens one eye. The incurables lie out on their benches in the sun and feel immortal. The tiger stretches himself. Today is the chance for peace to enthrone herself over all the world. The tiger licks his lips. And Andromache is going to have a son! And the horsemen have started leaning from their saddles to stroke tom-cats on the battlements! The tiger starts to prowl. (Giraudoux 1955: 3)

It is not just that the Trojan activities and attitudes are unconnected to war: they are determinedly pacific. Connubial love, sunbathing, pregnancy, soldiers stroking cats. The momentum towards war assumes a life of its own. A dozen lines before the end of the play Hector is still proclaiming, "The war is not going to happen," and although the stage manager clearly accepts this as a command (he starts to lower the curtain, interpreting Hector's declaration as a triumphant last line), the dying Demokos manages, in his last breath, mendaciously to blame the Greeks for his death, thereby guaranteeing, as Hector now says numbly, "the war will happen" (74).

War does not need reasons, it needs excuses.[33] As Ulysses tells Hector, "There's a kind of permission for war which can be given only by the world's mood and atmosphere, the feel of its pulse." He describes Troy's wealth, her agricultural abundance, her rich temples: "It isn't very wise to have such golden gods and vegetables." Hector realizes that "Greece has chosen Troy for her prey" (Giraudoux 1955: 69). But Greece needs a pretext for war. Like Hector, Ulysses does not want aggression but unlike Hector he is a realist: "I don't want [war]. But I'm less sure whether war may not want us" (67).

Ulysses explains that Helen is "one of the rare creatures destiny puts on the earth for its own personal use" (Giraudoux 1955: 70). Although Giraudoux's Helen is witty and ironic, coquettish and clever (and clever enough to act dumb), Giraudoux also presents her allegorically in two parallel scenes, one at the end of each act (Singerman 1976). At the end of act 1, the figure of Peace appears and converses with Helen, who is unable to see her clearly. Desperate to be visible, Peace reappears "outrageously painted." (As Cassandra observes laconically, "I think she means to make herself clearer"; Giraudoux 1955: 32.) In this confrontation Helen represents War; the audience is given a stage tableau of War versus Peace, and Hecuba will later compare Helen's face to the face of War (37), as will Demokos the poet (39); and the child Polyxene underlines the point of the comparison: "She [Helen? War?] is very pretty" (39). Peace, Cassandra tells us, "is always standing in her beggarly way on every threshold." But War treats the beggar-Peace as beggars are often treated: Peace is shunned, ignored, and War is unable to see her.[34]

Helen's lack of love for Paris is acknowledged pragmatically throughout the play by all the characters (except Paris). Cassandra explains, "They've become now a kind of symbol of love's devotion. They don't still have to love each other" (Giraudoux 1955: 23). Troilus' gauche adolescent approaches to Helen are presented as a fascination with War. Paris teases the teenager about his infatuation with Helen, offering him the option of becoming famous by kissing Helen in public. Troilus awkwardly refuses but later embraces the option (literally). At the end of act 2, as the descending theater curtain stops midway, the Gates of War swing open to reveal Troilus kissing Helen. The parallel with the end of act 1 is clear. Troilus is not kissing Helen as a woman: he is embracing War and the opportunity for fame. Hector cannot prevent war because people are in love with it.

(En)Closure

Myths are never discrete: as Calasso says "stories never live alone." I want to consider Menelaus' quest for his wife in Troy as a variant of Theseus' (incidental, accidental) bridequest in Crete. Theseus has to defeat the Minotaur, the creature at the center of the Cretan labyrinth – an impossible task, not least because of the difficulty of finding his way out of the labyrinth. Minos' daughter, Ariadne, who has fallen love with Theseus, gives him a thread to find his way back, "in recompense whereof he hath married her" (as Shakespeare's Fabian says; *Twelfth Night* 5.1.364). The links with Crete are more than thematic: the word "Troy" may be associated (aurally if not etymologically) with a word meaning "labyrinth." It appears on a seventh-century BCE wine pitcher as "a caption for a drawing of a labyrinth" (Habinek 2005: 18).

Place names are notoriously difficult to etymologize and the derivation of the word "Troy" is not clear. In the late-nineteenth and early-twentieth centuries, attempts were made to connect "Troy" with Latin words meaning enclosing or winding (*trua* and *truella*: a "ladle," "pan," "basin"). Jack Lindsay summarizes and develops these arguments (1974) and, although his efforts to connect "Troy" with both sexual and architectural windings and enclosure are not always etymologically convincing, his instincts are thematically interesting and probably correct: they have recently received independent support from Thomas Habinek (2005). Priam's city was, it seems, an enfilade construction of streets, gateways, corridors, and towers. The Trojan myth is a revised repetition of the Minotaur myth. The Etruscan *truia* (not cited by Lindsay) means labyrinth (see also Waswo 1988: 549). "Troy" may not "mean" these words but it is aurally associated with them.

Lindsay (1974) argues that the word "Troy" and its cognates mean not only to wind and circle, but to seal and close, for obviously if one winds and turns something sufficiently, one (en)closes it; the word thus comes to mean closure. (The related Latin *antrum* means a "cave" or the "hollow of a tree" in Ovid and Virgil.) Lindsay cites *redantruare*, "to repay a kindness" (and hence to "complete the circular arrangement and enclose both parties in a beneficent or uniting force"; 1974: 109). The verb is unusual but Habinek has found an occurrence in a description of a dance ritual: when the praesul is "given movements, the movements are in turn given back to him" (2005: 18, 265n). Lindsay's examples of the relationship between dancing and maze rituals from 1000 BCE (1974: 108–9) are also corroborated by Habinek (2005: 18–19).

Babylonian tablets c.1000 BCE studied by Lindsay and Habinek associate labyrinthine spirals with intestines and vice versa. The association with entrails becomes transferred to another interior body part: the vagina. The penetration of Troy to (re)gain a wife is an initiation rite, an entry into manhood. This is true not just of the triumphant Menelaus' sexual triumph but of the deaths of the many who assist him; war and sex are culturally equal rites of passage, twin arenas in which boys become men.

The acoustic nexus is thus of words meaning circle, wind, enclose; maze, labyrinth, sexual and architectural corridors and passages. The suggestion that "Troy" is related to (en)closure returns us to the start of this chapter and its discussion of attempts to close the narrative gap – in the epic cycle and in reading generally. To take Helen to Troy is to move her literally towards a site of closure. I have been arguing that attempts to relate Helen's story are always attempts at closure; but here it seems that her removal to Troy represents not closure of her story but of something else. The origin that needs to be contained predates abduction. That something else, I suggest, is beauty – the subject of chapter 2.

2

Beauty

HELEN: *It must be hard to be so ugly*
                             And have to live in so harsh a world.
MEPHISTOPHELES: *Not as hard as being beautiful.*
                             (Goethe/Clifford, *Faust: Part Two*)

You have to remember how ugly people were. Forget what you see on the vases. Club feet. Hair lips. Warts. Squints. Teeth like tree-stumps . . . beauty was gold dust. (Mark Haddon, *A Thousand Ships*)

She could not be called beautiful but Beauty itself. (Henry Rider Haggard and Andrew Lang, *The World's Desire*)

Excess and Deficiency

Consider the following statements about Helen's beauty from a sampling of nearly 25 centuries. Here is Guido delle Colonne writing in the thirteenth century: "Helen was famous for excessive loveliness" (book 8.136; delle Colonne / Meek 1974: 82).[1] Guido's phrasing is interesting: Helen is not the most beautiful woman in the world (a compliment: Helen as the absolute of womankind) but a woman with too much beauty (a hint of problem: that in this case surplus is deficiency).[2] Here is the Renaissance art historian Giovanni Petro Bellori arguing that Helen did not have enough beauty: "Helen was not as beautiful as they pretended, for she was found to have defects and shortcomings, so that it is believed that she never did sail for Troy, but that her statue was taken there in her stead" (Bellori 1968: 161). Here is Carol Rutter in 2000, who follows her analysis of the marketplace language of *Troilus and Cressida*, its verbs of buying, selling, stealing, disvaluing, and overpricing Helen, with a description of Helen's entrance in the 1990 RSC production: "the spectators' disappointment was audible . . . it wasn't that she wasn't beautiful. It was simply that she wasn't enough" (Rutter 2000: 233).[3] Four years later the *New York Times* film critic reacted similarly to Diane Kruger's portrayal of Helen in the Hollywood film *Troy*: "she isn't sufficiently fabulous-looking to be convincing as the face that launched a thousand ships" (McGrath). Finally, rewinding 2,400 years, consider the final Chorus in Euripides' *Helen* who accuse Helen of sin, of neglecting religious rites, and of boasting of her beauty.[4] The passage is garbled and may not be original. Its relevance here is that though this play's raison d'être is to exculpate Helen, the Chorus finds her blameworthy. Blameworthy for what? Norman Austin unravels the problem as follows: "someone, whether Euripides or some subsequent interpolator, knew that Helen was guilty of something . . . What was Helen's offence? Her beauty. Yes, that's it; she was too beautiful" (Austin 1994: 182).

Common to these statements is an economy of excess and deficiency, surplus and lack.[5] These binaries are attributed to beauty but are also properties of narrative, as John Pollard's phrasing in his account of Helen reveals: "there is on the one hand too much to say about Helen, and on the other not enough" (1965: 185). Effie Spentzou echoes Pollard when she writes, "there are at the same time too many and too few things said about Helen" (1996: 302). In this chapter I want to map the problem of Helen's beauty (and it is a problem, both for Helen and for the nations that war for her[6]) on to the problem of narrative. Plenitude and insufficiency, repletion and ascesis are common to both, and the result is the same: desire. In life we call it longing; in narrative it is called suspense.

Shakespeare's Enobarbus demonstrates the analogy between narrative and beauty when his attempt to describe ancient Egypt's most beautiful ruler has the same effect on the play's listeners as its subject, Cleopatra, has on her viewers: "she makes hungry / Where most she satisfies" (*Antony and Cleopatra* 2.2.237). Shakespeare's Tarquin experiences the perpetual longing caused by Lucrece's beauty: "having all, all could not satisfy; / . . . / . . . cloy'd with much, he pineth still for more" (*Rape of Lucrece* 96–8). In Dictys' fourth-century account of the Trojan War (a Latin version of a first-century Greek fragment) Panthus proposes returning Helen to the Greeks nine years after her abduction, because "Alexander, he said, had had time enough to satisfy whatever love he had had for Helen" (Frazer 1966: 52). Panthus here misunderstands the effect of beauty: it makes hungry where most it satisfies.

This is a chapter about representation: about representing Helen's beauty in narrative and in drama. Any attempt at literary representation of beauty invites detail (Was she blonde? Tall? What color were her eyes?) and all details about Helen prove (as we shall see) problematic, for reasons related to the binary economy sketched above: "detail . . . does not tell us enough and yet it tells us too much" (Stewart 2005: 27). What is true of Cleopatra is true of Helen and is true of narrative itself: detail makes hungry where most it satisfies. It is the literary equivalent of the dermatological itch, where one scratch of inflamed skin is too many and one hundred is never enough. In this sense the specific narrative problem of detail is a problem of closure for, in attempting to describe and to detail, narrative tries to pin down and to contain. Detail is really an attempt at closure (Stewart 2005: 26). As we saw in chapter 1, the history of Helen's story is a series of attempts to close that story, a closure Helen and her narrative consistently elude and frustrate. This chapter may illuminate why: closure is something that beauty (not just Helen's beauty) resists.

There are two reasons for this. The first I have indicated above: the common denominator of beauty and narrative in desire. Beauty, like its linguistic proxy, detail, paradoxically creates the one thing it tries to forestall: the longing for more. Of all other desires – a good meal, a new car, a bigger house – the fulfillment of the desire coincides with the termination of longing. When the object is acquired or the dream realized, desire ends; the longing is teleological (Scarry 2005: 50). Beauty, however, renews the longing. Philosophers frequently note this circularity. Simone Weil writes that beauty "offers us its own existence. We do not desire anything else, we possess it, and *yet we still desire something*" (1951: 166–7, my italics).

The second reason for beauty's resistance to narrative closure is its relationship with the divine, the transcendent, the infinite (Scarry 2000), which means that it is incompatible with the temporality of narrative. Description threatens infinity (Stewart 2005: 26); language tries, but fails to, kidnap eternity into time. Carol Ann Duffy articulates this in her poem "Beautiful" (2002), which juxtaposes Helen's beauty with that of Cleopatra. For Duffy both Helen and Cleopatra live outside of time. The section on Cleopatra begins, "she never aged." This follows immediately from the conclusion of the Helen section with the narrative silence of Helen's loyal maid:

> Her maid, who loved her most,
> refused to say one word
> to anyone at any time or place,
> would not describe
> one aspect of her face.
> (Duffy 2002: 10)

Refusal to describe and failure to age are one and the same phenomenon: an avoidance of time, of entropy, of closure.

Ageing and agelessness are features of many Helen narratives as we shall see later in this chapter. But to be ageless – beyond the reach of time – is to be beyond the reach of narrative. No wonder that representing an eternally beautiful Helen is so difficult.

*

Beauty, says the eponymous protagonist in Marlowe's *1 Tamburlaine*, is the "mother to the Muses" (5.1.144) a statement borne out by every anthology of English verse. This apparently uncontroversial observation proves problematic, however, as we see in Tamburlaine's anaphoric conditional conclusion. "If all the pens that ever poets held," inspired by beauty; "if all the quintessence" poets try to turn into poetry; if these resulted in just one poem about beauty – yet, Tamburlaine concludes ruefully, beauty would remain something "which into words no virtue can digest" (5.1.161, 165, 173). Poetry cannot represent beauty; beauty cannot be contained in language.

The Chorus in Aeschylus' *Agamemnon* anticipates empirically Tamburlaine's observation. They remember Helen's arrival in Troy in lines that have a terminative emphasis: "there came / One in whose presence shone / *Beauty no thought can name*" (my italics). But they fight against the silence that their declaration of linguistic inability demands, with four consecutive, inadequate attempts to "name" this "beauty":

> (1) A still enchantment of sweet summer calm;
> (2) A rarity for wealth to dote upon;
> (3) Glances whose gentle fire
> Bestowed both wound and balm;
> (4) A flower to melt man's heart with wonder and desire.
> (Aeschylus 1968: 68, my numerals)

Aeschylus' Chorus enacts in literary terms the experience of all those (from ancient warriors to contemporary authors) who encounter Helen: irresistibly drawn to her and brought low by her. The Chorus chooses to spend time with Helen (five lines of imagery about her beauty) against their better judgment (one line acknowledging the narrative impossibility of describing her beauty).[7] The lure of Helen is here, as elsewhere, specifically a linguistic lure. It is not paralleled in art history where paintings of Helen are few. Artists paint the judgment of Paris; it is poets who paint (or try to paint) Helen.

Narrating the Absolute

In this section I want to consider the difficulty narrative, and specifically Troy narrative, has in depicting absolutes. Seeing how accounts of the Trojan War deal with perfection and nadirs will provide a useful touchstone when we come to consider how they represent the beauty of Helen.

One of literature's recurrent tactics when faced with extremes is omission. Authors simply abdicate narrative responsibility, refusing to (or declaring themselves unable to) describe. Thus Guido delle Colonne in the *Historia Destructionis Troiae* (1287) says it is "useless" to describe Polyxena's beauty "since she surpassed . . . all other women" (1974: 86). The author of the *Laud Troy Book* (c.1400) also gives up on narrating Polyxena's beauty: "Ther is no man that is on lyve / Hir fairnesse that might discryve" (TLN 12007–8).[8]

Sometimes writers give justifications for their omissions. In *Troia Britannica* (1609) Heywood declines to describe Helen's beauty because it would require "a world of paper and an age to write" (canto 10.32, sig. Z2v). In his *Troy Book* (1414–20) John Lydgate couples his failure to describe extreme emotions with an excuse, but here the excuse is not that of impossibility. On the contrary, the task has already been accomplished only too well by Chaucer (3.4192–8). Lydgate is a devotee of Chaucer, whose poetry he praises at every opportunity, but referring the reader to other sources is a rhetorical tactic throughout his *Troy Book*. When he declines to describe Helen of Troy, it is (he says) because he has no rhetorical skill, so he refers the reader to Guido's description of Helen:

> I . . . you remitte to Guydo for to se
> How he discriveth bi ordre hir bewte;
> To take on me it were presumpcioun.
> (2.3689–91)

When authors do attempt description, they describe not the object of contemplation, but another object, sometimes in a simple comparison, sometimes in a process of displacement whereby only the alternative is described. Lydgate employs this latter tactic in depicting Medea. Medea is the most beautiful of women just as the rose is the most beautiful of flowers. He then gives us an extended description of one half of the equation: the rose (1.2599–623).[9]

Other comparative tactics involve a change of media to the art world. In *Agamemnon*, Iphigenia's beauty "surpassed / A painter's vision" (Aeschylus 1968: 50). Seven centuries later, in *Erehwon* (1872) Samuel Butler specifies which "painter's vision" when he refers a beautiful scene to neoclassical landscape painters: it "made a picture worthy of a Salvator Rosa or a Nicolas Poussin" (1970: 50).[10] In Henry Fielding's *Tom Jones* (1729) Fielding declines to describe Bridget Allworthy because her beauty has recently been represented: "The lady . . . is remarkable for beauty. I would attempt to draw her picture, but that is done already by a more able master, Mr Hogarth himself, to whom she sat many years ago" (1978: 79). Elsewhere comparisons work by accumulation or exaggeration. In his *Troy Book* Lydgate reinforces his statement that no one was more grief-stricken than Helen with a list of the no ones: Cleopatra, Thisbe, Orestilla, Julia, Portia, Artemisia (4.3654–84). In *The Siege of Troy* (fifteenth century?) the anonymous poet is similarly rhetorical: Helen of Troy was so beautiful that "myght no man tellyn her fayrnesse," not even Virgil, Aristotle, or Neptanebus (TLN 535–46).

I reserve narrative's most innovative tactic for last: the blank space of nonrepresentation. Helen of Troy enters Laurence Sterne's novel *Tristram Shandy* (1759–67) by association: the Widow Wadman is a sexually predatory female character who is associated with Helen of Troy from early in the novel (Telotte 1989: 121). When he comes to describe the beautiful widow, Sterne gives us a blank page, and enjoins the reader, "Call for pen and ink – here's paper ready to your hand. – Sit down, Sir, paint her to your own mind – as like your mistress as you can – as unlike your wife as your conscience will let you –" (Sterne 2003: 422–3).[11] He uses this tactic earlier in the novel when he presents a black page for Yorick's death (2003: 31–2). Ostensibly a tribute, a textual representation of mourning, his black page, like the later blank page, is actually a failure of language (and an implicit acknowledgment of that failure). What can one say when a Yorick dies? It has already been said, in *Hamlet*.

A sixteenth-century chronicler anticipated Sterne in using blank space to stand in for the unrepresentable. In the manuscript *Vita Henrici VII* from his *Historia Regis Henrici Septimi* (c.1500–2) Bernard Andreas confesses himself unable to represent the epic battle of Bosworth, and gives us one-and-a-half blank pages instead: "inalbo relinquo" (1858: 32). Andreas was blind, possibly from infancy, and often draws attention to his inability to describe fully events he had not seen; but nowhere else does he offer a paragraph of apology ("Auctoris excusatio") and leave blank pages.

The art world also often responds to the concept of the absolute with a blank page or canvas. Botticelli's illustrations of Dante's *Divine Comedy* draw a blank, literally, in the last canto when called upon to depict Dante's beatific vision.[12] In Gustave Moreau's paintings of a shimmering Helen on the walls (1880s) Helen's face is expressionless: blank (figure 1). So too is

Figure 1 Gustave Moreau, *Helen on the Ramparts* (oil on canvas) (1826–98).
In this painting Helen's face is inscrutable. Musée Gustave Moreau, Paris,
France / Lauros / Giraudon / The Bridgeman Art Library. Reproduced by kind
permission of the Bridgeman Art Library.

Figure 2   Sir Frederick Leighton, *Helen on the Ramparts*. Leighton's Helen also has a blank expression – or is this the look of an anguished and exhausted woman? Reproduced by kind permission of Getty Images.

the Helen of Sir Frederick Leighton (figure 2). Painting Helen in the late fifth century BCE, Zeuxis is said to have assembled the five most beautiful maidens from the city of Croton so that he could combine the best features of each. But when François-André Vincent in the eighteenth century depicted Zeuxis painting Helen, he left a blank canvas at the centre of his picture.[13] Lily Briscoe in Virginia Woolf's *To the Lighthouse* does the same: her portrait of the Helen figure, Mrs Ramsay ("the happier Helen of our days") is a triangle of color, the color purple.[14] In chapter 1 we saw how metaphorical blanks typify Helen narratives. Faced with her beauty, the blank becomes textually a blank space.

Staging the Absolute

Shakespeare's characters, in traditional literary fashion, abandon the attempt to describe exceptional beauty. Cassio says Desdemona is

> a maid
> That paragons description and wild fame;
> One that excels the quirks of blazoning pens,
> And in th'essential vesture of creation
> Does tire the ingener.
> (*Othello* 2.1.61–5)

In *Antony and Cleopatra* Enobarbus is able to describe everything around Cleopatra, and influenced by her, in sumptuous and erotic detail. The winds that fan her are lovesick; the water on which she floats is amorous; but for the fact that nature abhors a vacuum, the air would have gone to gaze on Cleopatra. But Enobarbus is unable to describe Cleopatra's actual person: "For her own person, / It beggared all description" (2.2.197–8). Shakespeare is being ingenuous, of course. For Homer before him, as for Sterne after him, not to describe is not to represent. But drama cannot *not* represent. Drama is representation. And what cannot be described – Desdemona, Cleopatra, Helen – still has to be represented.

Of the several plays that feature a Helen character, I want to mention four that have a documentable stage tradition: Euripides' *The Women of Troy*, Marlowe's *Dr Faustus*, Shakespeare's *Troilus and Cressida*, and Giraudoux's *The Trojan War Will Not Take Place* (written in 1935, translated into English as *Tiger at the Gates*). Kenneth Tynan reviewed the first London production of *Tiger at the Gates* in 1955: Diane Cilento [Helen of Troy] was "fetchingly got up in what I can best describe as a Freudian

Figure 3   Helen (Janie Dee) as a Marilyn Monroe look-alike in the 1995 production of *The Women of Troy* at the Royal National Theatre. © Simon Annand. Reproduced by kind permission of National Theatre Archive and Simon Annand.

slip" (1984: 156). Helen's sexuality was also to the fore in a production of *The Women of Troy* at the National Theatre in 1995, directed by Annie Castledine. In this modern-dress production Helen was a Marilyn Monroe look-alike (figure 3); the stage's hot-air system recreated the famous New York subway-grating pose.

Three RSC productions of *Troilus and Cressida* provide striking images. Lindsay Duncan's Helen of Troy, in 1985, with her alabaster skin and regal deportment, looked every inch a serene princess, in contrast to the anguished vulnerability of Juliet Stevenson's more impulsively kinetic Cressida; in 1968, by contrast, Helen and Cressida were visually indistinguishable blondes, an important casting decision which underlined the play's debate about value as subjective and relative. In 1990 Sally Dexter's voluptuous Helen entered borne aloft on an enormous cushion, wrapped in shining gold fabric, reminding us of her reification as a valuable "prize." Paris slowly circled her and unwrapped her in a sequence "half ritual, half strip tease" (Rutter 2000: 233).

Reviews of twentieth-century productions of *Dr Faustus* seldom mention Helen of Troy, probably because productions rarely attempt verisimilitude. Helen of Troy is recognizably a devil in disguise, like the whore-wife of act 1, and often the devil who represented the wife at the beginning represents Helen of Troy at the end. At the other extreme is the classical beauty of Jennifer Coverdale (1946): she merits a photograph in the Shakespeare Centre archives (Stratford on Avon) but still no mention in reviews (figure 4).

The sole Helen to attract attention was the 24-year-old Maggie Wright in 1968, but she was singled out, not for her acting, or for her part in Faustus' damnation, but for her costume: she did not wear one. Stratford's first naked actress had a long blonde ponytail, a tiara, and a Max Factor fake tan (figure 5). Not only was this Helen mentioned in all the reviews but she was a front-page news item in most national and local papers. The director, Clifford Williams, explained that nudity "was the best way to portray an image of physical beauty" (quoted in an anonymous review in *Reading Evening Post*, June 28, 1968).[15] If language is the dress of thought, a naked Helen is a Helen who cannot be described.[16]

Detailing Helen

In this section I want to try to compile Helen's appearance from classical references. The subject will lead us to Helen's hair, her height, her movement, her clothes, and her breasts.

Figure 4   Jennifer Coverdale's classically poised Helen of Troy in Marlowe's *Dr Faustus* at the Royal Shakespeare Company in 1946. Photo: Angus McBean; © Royal Shakespeare Company. Reproduced by kind permission of the Royal Shakespeare Company.

Figure 5 Stratford's first naked actress (Maggie Wright) in the 1968 *Dr Faustus* at the Royal Shakespeare Company. Image courtesy of Royal Shakespeare Company / Shakespeare Birthplace Trust. © Douglas H. Jeffery. (Every attempt has been made to contact the copyright holder.)

The "shining" hair of Helen is possibly a poetic way of saying that she was blonde.[17] This is a feature Helen shares with gods and goddesses: Homer's Artemis has the formulaic epithet "of the beautiful hair" (*Odyssey* book 20, p. 306) and she has golden hair in Euripides' *Hippolytus* (Euripides 1973: 20, line 130). Helen's hair not only shines; it also curls. In Johannis Malalas' *Chronographia* Helen has curly golden hair (1831, book 5: 91) as she does later in Virgil.[18] Later poetry consistently depicts Helen with hyacinthine curls, and the art world shows her with Pre-Raphaelite ringlets.[19]

Aristotle says that height is a necessary component of beauty (cited by Irwin 1990: 210 n23). This is also one of the features of the classical gods and goddesses. Eleanor Irwin notes that "on the Parthenon frieze seated gods and goddesses occupy the same vertical space as standing human beings" (1990: 210 n23). When the Sybil in book 6 of the *Aeneid* becomes inhabited by celestial power, "she appeared taller and spoke in no mortal tones" (Virgil

1981: 148). Odysseus rejects King Alcinous' identification of him as immortal on the grounds that he has "neither the looks nor the stature of the immortal gods" (*Odyssey* book 7, p. 101). Stature can refer to stance and posture but it can also depict height (in a standing position). The gods consider height a gift of beauty worth bestowing on mortals. When Hera, Artemis, and Athena protect the orphaned daughters of Pandareus, Hera makes them beautiful, Athena gives them skills to create beautiful objects, and Artemis makes them tall (*Odyssey* book 20, p. 306). Comparisons in height (between mortals and goddesses or between goddesses themselves) are frequent. The princess Nausicaa is "tall and beautiful as a goddess" (*Odyssey* book 6, p. 85). In book 1 of the *Aeneid*, Virgil tells us that Diana is "taller than all other goddesses" (1981: 43).

If gods and goddesses are taller, they also move differently. Aeneas recognizes his mother, Venus, in book 1 of the *Aeneid* because "her gait alone proved her a goddess" (Virgil 1981: 40).[20] When Cupid in the same book imitates Achanes, he "copied [his] way of walking" (Virgil 1981: 48).[21] In *Aeneid* book 5 the goddess Iris assumes human form but the nurse is not deceived: "Observe those marks of divine beauty, those burning eyes; her commanding mien, her countenance, *her walk*, her voice's tone" (Virgil 1981: 139, my italics).

The medieval Troy books note Helen's eurhythmic movement. In Joseph of Exeter's *Iliad of Dares*, for example, Helen "lightly skimmed the ground as she went her carefree way: her swift and graceful limbs lent an elegant poise to her body" (Joseph/Roberts 1970: 44). In his *Memoirs* Yeats notes the stature and movement of Maud Gonne (whom he repeatedly cast as Helen):

> a stature so great that she seemed of a divine race. Her movements were worthy of her form, and I understood at last why the poet of antiquity, where we would but speak of face and form, sings, loving some lady, that she paces like a goddess. (1972: 40)[22]

The kinds of gowns Helen wears are detailed in book 1 of the *Aeneid*, where items rescued from the fall of Troy include clothing from Helen's wardrobe, gifts to her from her mother Leda: "a figured gown stiff with gold lace, and a mantle hemmed with a yellow thistle-pattern" (Virgil 1981: 47).[23] This is an unusual amount of detail. When goddesses wear such garments, they usually accessorize them with gold jewellery: Calypso has a golden belt in the *Odyssey* (book 5, p. 76), for example. In *Aeneid* book 4 (Virgil 1981: 101) Dido (like Helen) has a mantle with an embroidered hem and (like Calypso) gold jewellery: a clasp in her hair and a brooch at her neck. Helen wears gold sandals in Euripides' *Orestes* (1972: 351). In the *Odyssey* we are told that Helen makes her own clothes and that they are "elaborately woven" (book 15, p. 226).[24]

Collectively the above details, interesting though they are, tell us little visually about Helen. In fact many of the details are formulaic, shared not only with other characters but with the immortals. The aim may be thus not to pinpoint Helen's appearance but to associate her with the gods.

What is consistent in descriptions of Helen of Troy, from Homer to the twenty-first century, is absence of detail. Homer describes Helen as having "the face of immortal goddesses"; she wears "shimmering garments" and has glistening hair. In Virgil she wears silver robes and has hyacinthine curls. The lack of specificity makes sense: if Helen is indisputably the most beautiful woman in the world, as soon as you provide details you make her beauty disputable. The reaction to Diane Kruger's Helen of Troy, quoted at the start of this chapter, illustrates this problem. So too does the reaction of Giorgio Melchiori to Yeats's discussion of Helen's beauty. Yeats wrote several poems to Helen (and the Helen figure in his life, Maud Gonne) but made the mistake of musing on the "kind of beauty appropriate to Helen" (Melchiori 1960: 129). Rejecting Botticelli's and Rossetti's beauties (Botticelli's have "too much curiosity," Rossetti's "too much passion") he settles on Burne-Jones' women (Yeats 1925: 68; 1937: 133). This choice would not have been Melchiori's, who talks of "the *disappointment* of an identification of Helen's beauty with the lifeless grace of Burne-Jones' figures" (Melchiori 1960: 129, my italics).

To depict Helen's beauty, then, one has to depict the Helen effect, and working back from that effect we may call its source "beauty." That is the subject of the next section.

The Beauty Effect

In book 3 of the *Iliad* seven elders of the people sit by the Skaian gates. When they see Helen, they happily accept a war on her behalf: "Surely there is no blame on Trojans and strong-greaved Achaians / if for long time they suffer hardship for a woman like this one" (3.156–7). Although they change their mind immediately ("Still, though she be such, let her go away in the ships") for one moment beauty has had the power to overturn their views.

This is in keeping with Homer's depiction of that other form of absolute: divinity. In Homer, characters know when a god has been with them (or someone else) because of the change in them: "He felt the change and was overcome with awe, for he realized a god had been with him"; "It is obvious that the gods are teaching you this bold and haughty way of speaking" (*Odyssey* book 1, pp. 12, 14).[25]

It is not just Trojans who respond to Helen in this way. In Quintus of Smyrna's account of the end of the war, Helen, blushing with shame and "fearful and trembling" lest the Greeks abuse her, veils her head and accompanies the captive Trojan women to the ships. The Greek soldiers who had reviled her just moments before "looked with amazement on the splendor and lovely beauty of the faultless woman. Not a man ventured to assail her with insults, either secretly or openly. They found pleasure in looking at her, as though looking at a goddess" (1968: 250–1).[26]

This tradition of presenting beautiful women in terms of their effect on others is surprisingly constant in literature. In Marlowe's *Hero and Leander* (published 1598) Hero affects not just men ("He whom she favours lives, the other dies"; 124) but gods (Apollo sees her hair and offers her his throne as a dowry, and Cupid becomes blind by looking in her face) and the world of nature: her breath is so beautiful that bees mistake it for honey, the winds delight in playing upon her hands because they cannot keep away from her beauty, and Nature herself weeps because Hero has bankrupted her of beauty. (Leander, by contrast, is presented in terms of his physical beauty: his neck surpassed "The white of Pelops' shoulder. I could tell ye / How smooth his breast was and how white his belly"; 65–6.) John Ogle's narrative poem *The Lamentation of Troy* (1594) extravagantly represents the causes of dark and light as Helen-dependent: when Helen closes her eyes, the earth becomes dark; when she opens them, the world is flooded with daylight (sig. D3r). In William Poel's production of *Dr Faustus* (1898) the audience saw Helen only from behind. It was Faustus' reaction that defined Helen's beauty (Tydeman 1984: 77).

Aeschylus is the only dramatist of the fifth century BCE to describe the emotional effect on Menelaus of Helen's absence. Unable to eat or speak, he stares at Helen's statue and is tormented by dreams of her.

> There lies her husband fasting
> Dumb in his stricken room . . .
> Visions of her beset him
> With false and fleeting pleasure.
> (*Agamemnon* in Aeschylus 1968: 57)

Menelaus here anticipates his emotionally erethistic descendants in the medieval Troy books where Menelaus swoons, takes to his bedchamber for an extended period, laments at length and nearly dies when he discovers Helen's abduction.[27]

Beauty leads to another negatively tangible effect, an effect visited on the body of the beautiful person herself/himself: rape. This is the fate of Ganymede, of Cleitus, and of countless other Greek mortals and semimortals (Ganymede's beauty prompted Zeus, in the form of an eagle, to carry him away; for Cleitus see *Odyssey* book 15, p. 230). Beauty is the excuse given by Renaissance literary rapists, like Pyrocles in Sidney's *The Old Arcadia* who blames Philoclea's beauty for his sexual violence towards her: "I offered force to her; love offered more force to me" (cited by Catty 1999: 46). Rape is the event feared by Rosalind in *As You Like It* when she and Celia flee to the forest. Rosalind views sexual attack as stemming directly from female beauty:

> Alas, what danger will it be to us,
> Maids as we are, to travel forth so far!
> Beauty provoketh thieves sooner than gold.
> (1.3.108–10)

Her disguise name, Ganymede, is a reminder of the kind of theft beauty provokes.

Helen's beauty is defined by another effect: the war conducted in her name. By a process of back projection, the effect is made "a quality of its cause" (Richards 1925: 21) In P. F.'s English Faustbook Helen is deemed "more than commonly fair, because that when she was stolen away from her husband, there was for her recovery so great bloodshed" (ch. 45; TLN 2348–50 in Jones 1994). Shakespeare's Troilus voices this view with bitter irony: "Helen must needs be fair when with your blood you daily paint her thus" (*Troilus and Cressida* 1.1.80–1). Goethe's Faust offers to have the negligent watchman killed in *2 Faust*, not as punishment for his lack of vigilance but as testament to the power of Helen's beauty (a power that Helen does not wish to have) (9246–57). Lord Dunsany's Helen takes the opposite view to Goethe's, enumerating the effects of her beauty with pride:

> "And were you pleased?" they asked of Helen in Hell.
> "Pleased?" answered she, "when all Troy's towers fell;
> And dead were Priam's sons, and lost his throne?
> And such a war was fought as none had known;
> And even the gods took part; and all because
> Of me alone! Pleased? I should say I was!"
> (1938: 61)

I shall return to definitions of beauty as an effect rather than a quality at the end of this chapter. I want now to look at the effect of one (or two) specific part(s) of Helen's beauty: her breasts.

Helen's Breasts

If the effect of Helen's beauty at the start of the war is to unite Greece in fighting for her, the effect of that beauty ten years later is to prevent the Greeks killing her. This effect is usually concentrated in one dramatic moment, the moment when Menelaus first sees his wife at the sack of Troy. Menelaus, it seems, intended (or was expected) to kill Helen when he reclaimed her at Troy.[28] Ibycus tells us that when Menelaus saw Helen, he dropped his sword. Isocrates offers a variant: the Greeks went to stone Helen but "the moment they saw her face, they let the stones fall from their hands." This anecdote comes from the scholiast on Euripides' *Orestes* 1287, where Electra waiting and listening at the door for sounds of Helen's murder ("sacrifice") wonders, "are their swords blunted at the sight of beauty?" (Euripides 1972: 345). It is the *Little Iliad* and Aristophanes who relocate the site of Helen's affecting beauty from her face to her breasts. The former says, "Menelaus . . . when he caught a glimpse somehow of the breasts of Helen unclad, cast away his sword" (in Hesiod 1977: 519). In *Lysistrata* Lampito asks the women "din ye mind how Menelaus threw away his sword when he saw but a glimpse of Helen's breasties?" (Aristophanes 1973: 185).[29]

Peleus (Achilles' father) scorns Menelaus in Euripides' *Andromache*:

> You did not kill the woman.
> She only had to bare her breast, and you threw down
> Your sword, you let her kiss you, gave the treacherous bitch
> Loving caresses – you contemptible, amorous
> Weakling!
>
> (Euripides 1972: 166)

For Peleus, Menelaus' reaction represents uxorious emasculation (the detumescent significance of the dropped sword is obvious.) Menelaus rebuts this accusation. It was not erotic fervor that made him refrain from killing Helen, but its opposite: "self-control" (Euripides 1972: 167). Quintus of Smyrna offers an extended account of the husband–wife reunion. Menelaus was

> planning to kill her . . . but lovely Aphrodite restrained his strength, knocked the sword from his hand, and checked his attack. She removed his black jealousy from him and roused sweet desire in his heart and eyes. An unexpected amazement came upon him, and when he saw Helen's conspicuous beauty, he could no longer bring himself to strike her neck with his sword. (Quintus 1968: 244)

Given the mention of Aphrodite's intervention (often a euphemistic deo-morphization of "desire") it is easy to imagine the precise location of Helen's "conspicuous beauty."

The *Little Iliad*, quoted above, notes but does not speculate on how Helen's breast "somehow" became "unclad." Euripides' Peleus assumes that the display was not a textile accident. In his phrasing, Helen controls the maneuver – "she only had to bare her breast" – and literature repeatedly sides with Peleus. Margaret Atwood's *Penelopiad* even echoes Peleus' phrasing when an aggrieved Penelope complains that "all [Helen] had to do was bare one of her peerless breasts, and he was down on his knees . . . begging to take her back" (2005: 21). Given that Paris also sees Helen's breasts when her robe falls open in Ovid's *Heroides* (1990: 156) Helen is either careless with clothing or tactical in self-exposure. The latter is more prob-able; Aphrodite bears her bosom to Paris in Colluthus' account of the judg-ment of Paris.

In the medieval *Iliad of Dares* by Joseph of Exeter, Venus displays her face and her breasts to Paris. Removing her hood to reveal her face, she implores, "Do not reject a face as beautiful as yours" (2: 606/7; Joseph/ Bate 1986: 115). Then she removes her cloak to expose her body: "Her body was naked, her bared breasts glistened in total beauty" (2: 608/7; Joseph/Bate 1986: 117).[30] Later, however, Helen resists the same impulse: "she would like to show her face and her naked breasts [presumably, like Aphrodite, her face and her breasts are her greatest marks of beauty] but her sense of decency reproves her and represses these full-blown excesses!" (3.237–9; Joseph/Bate 1986: 135). Edward Dowden's Helena (1873) con-fesses, "thus I draw the robe aside / And bare the breasts of Helen," where the change from first to third person shows her replacing personhood with self-objectification, an act that (she knows?) will save her life (1914: 34).[31]

In Stephen Vincent Benét's version (1920) Itys falls in love with the young Helen, whose breast seems accidentally bare:

> Itys stood at gaze;
> Seeing in all things one miraculous face,
> And how her tunic left one bright breast bare.
>   (1920: 6)

(Note it is the tunic, not Helen, that exposes the breast.) In 1911 Sara Teasdale's Helen ponders how to save her life as she contemplates Menelaus' punitive uxoricide:

> And yet he shall not slay me. I shall stand
> With lifted head and look into his eyes,

> Baring my breast to him and to the sun.
> He shall not have the power to stain with blood
> That whiteness – for the thirsty sword shall fall
> And he shall cry and catch me in his arms.
>
> (1937: 11)

Her decision is to do with more than mere self-preservation, or self-preservation as an end in itself. She wants to live so that she can make Greece love her again, rehabilitate if not her reputation, her ability to cause a pan-Hellenic reaction: "I shall go back to Sparta on his breast. / I shall live on to conquer Greece again!" (1937: 11). The breast changes from Helen's mammary to Menelaus' pectorals. But the image is odd: how does one return on one's spouse's breast rather than the expected – if clichéd – arm? Perhaps the phrase is an (awkward) externalization of "in his heart."

In Tennyson's *Lucretius* (1868) Helen's peerless breasts receive their most memorable treatment in literature, where they function not just as a firework display but as flame-throwers – designed to extinguish the heat they have aroused:

> Then, then, from utter gloom stood out the breasts,
> The breasts of Helen, and hoveringly a sword
> Now over and now under, now direct,
> Pointed itself to pierce, but sank down shamed
> At all that beauty; and as I stared, a fire,
> The fire that left a roofless Ilion,
> Shot out of them, and scorch'd me that I woke.
>
> (1936: 808)

From being the *face* that launched a thousand ships, Helen's beauty is now concentrated in one part of her anatomy (the anthropomorphized sword refuses to pierce her breasts, "shamed at *all that beauty*"; my italics) and that anatomical part is disconcertingly disembodied. It is not Helen who appears to Lucretius, but her breasts.[32]

Lucretius' neglected wife has administered an overpotent love philtre to correct her husband's intellectual preoccupation. His life's imbalance is now simply redirected, not rebalanced: he is "fancy-borne" not by three hundred hexameter scrolls but by lightning storms and erotic dreams. The vocabulary of antithesis throughout the poem illustrates Lucretius' tendency to see in nature only a propensity to "clash" – yesterday's "dusty-dry" becomes today's "riotous confluence of water courses" – rather than to reconcile (Danzig 1967: 579–82). The antimeric and the symbiotic have no place in his rigid philosophy: "Twy-natured is no nature," he believes.

Appropriately (although he cannot recognize such duality) Lucretius' overheated dream is extinguished by fire; the very source of his arousal is also the means of its extinction. Helen's pyrotechnic breasts are cause and cure. Just as nature has "all-generating" light and heat, it has the same power, destructively, in lightning; so too Helen's breasts "capable of nourishing" may also destroy (Danzig 1967: 579).[33]

This double symbolism of breasts – as fertility objects and as secular erotic objects – has a complex history. Helen's breasts were not always erotic. Tradition has it that she consecrated a cup on Lindos on Rhodes, designed in the shape of her breast. Here her breast is sacred not secular, an object of veneration.[34]

Helen was probably a fertility goddess before she became anthropomorphized as a Spartan queen (although it is possible that the influence is in the reverse direction: the Spartan queen developed into a fertility goddess). Many aspects of her story – for instance, the multiple abductions (discussed in chapter 1) – find a logical explanation in the multiple consorts enjoyed by fertility goddesses. Breasts featured frequently in ancient fertility icons. They nursed and nurtured (the religious and agricultural metaphors are obvious), they multiplied (the polymaste Artemis of Ephesus) and they metamorphosed: breasts were sometimes represented as, or supplemented by, dates, figs, acorns, flowers, or sacks of honey (indicating goddesses' and women's fertility associations with the plant kingdom). When classical phallocentric deities such as Zeus ousted the maternal mother earth goddess Gaia, the fertility imagery was simply transferred. Marilyn Yalom cites an example of a seventeenth-century BCE wood carving in which Zeus extends Hera's breast as a goddess would do herself. The later Marian nursing icon is possibly an attempt to make the new religion of Christianity familiar by linking it to earlier matriarchal religions. Images of the goddess Isis nursing her son Horus are a likely prototype for medieval *madonne del'latte* (Yalom 1997: 11).

The breast Helen exposed was likely to have been small. According to Marilyn Yalom, large breasts were not an erotic desideratum (or not represented in art as such) until the work of Rubens in the seventeenth century (Yalom 1997: 102). Homer is silent on Helen's cup size, but the compliment given to breasts in the drama of classical Athens is "apple-like." In Aristophanes' *Assemblywomen* a young girl boasts "rounded like apples are our breasts" (Aristophanes 1978: 253).[35] In the line from *Lysistrata* quoted above, the translator's phrase "Helen's breasties" is literally "the apples of Helen." Attic culture valued small breasts, just as it valued small penises, viewing large sexual organs as animal-like; but "apple-like" breasts indicates firmness and roundness as much as size and therefore functions as a shorthand for Helen's youth.

Helen may also have an epicene beauty, which is not how we normally think of literature's most beautiful woman, where the stress is on *woman*. In "Beautiful" Carol Ann Duffy links Helen with icons such as Cleopatra, Marilyn Monroe, and Princess Diana.[36] In this context let us take a look at Antonio Canova's bust of Helen and the tradition of androgyny in Western art.

Androgyny

I first came across an image of Canova's Helen on the website of an eminent university (figure 6). But I had a choice of many websites (and some books) from which to copy or download the image, all of which agreed in identifying it as Helen. The face is indeed feminine, demure, beautiful, framed by hyacinthine curls. The only oddity is the headgear – a Phrygian cap – not worn by women or non-Trojans. In fact this image turns out not to be of Helen at all; it is a bust of Canova's Paris.

What, then, does Canova's Helen look like? There are fewer reproductions of his Helen, perhaps because the sculpture (in its most famous form) is not on public view, residing still in the Venetian Palazzo Albrizzi for whose original owner (Isabella Albrizzi) Canova had completed the commission in 1812. The paucity of images may have led to the misidentification of the Canova Paris as the Canova Helen. But although paucity of access may perpetuate misidentification, it is not in itself sufficient to create it. If we compare Canova's Helen with his Paris, there are few distinctive differences between the two. Helen's curls are longer, forming ringlets reaching her shoulder, whereas Paris' climb abundantly up his cap. Both characters have full soft lips and round chins; both have classical noses although Helen's is longer and more aquiline, starting high up between her eyes whereas Paris' has more of a ski-slope curve (in this respect, Paris' profile is more "feminine" in today's terms). Both have blank eyes gazing into the distance. Helen wears a skull-cap, Paris a Phrygian cap. Were it not for the headgear, would one easily or reliably be able to distinguish between the two? Had we only one sculpture could we confidently identify it? That gender is prosthetic is not news. But is beauty also?[37]

The confusion of male and female, and the depiction of one as the other, has a long and respectable tradition in western art. Androgyny was a Greek sculptural desideratum, embodied in sculptures of beautiful boys from

Figure 6 Bust of Paris by Canova, in the Museum of Art, Chicago. This bust of Paris is very similar to the bust of Helen below.

Figure 7 Bust of Helen by school of Canova, © V&A Images/Victoria and Albert Museum, London.

adolescents to ephebes. One might argue that there is a difference between feminine boys and boyish females. Not so, says Camille Paglia. "Hellenistic sex is in such free flow that the gender of shattered statues can be doubtful. Misidentifications have been common" (1991: 124).

Art does not need to be classically Greek to represent males and females androgynously. In the Italian Renaissance, Donatello's David is feminine, in his shoulder-length hair, his coquettishly angled hat, his physique and his proleptically Mona Lisa-ish smile (Paglia 1991: 146–7). Michelangelo's *Giuliano de Medici* has a "sinuous, swan-like and feminine" neck (Paglia 1991: 163). The angel in Leonardo's *Madonna of the Rocks* is so feminine that "students seeing the picture for the first time insist he is a woman" (Paglia 1991: 156). The fluidity continues in later periods. Elizabeth Siddal's face, which was for Dante Gabriel Rossetti the face of Helen, became for Burne-Jones the face of male beauty (Paglia 1991: 122).

"This is a boy, sir. Not a girl. If you're baffled by the difference it might be as well to approach both with caution," warns the policeman as he unravels the ending of Joe Orton's *What the Butler Saw*. In fact from classical literature to early modern, being unable to tell the difference between male and female indicates that you are in the presence of great, even divine, beauty. Philip Vellacott tells us that Euripides' Dionysus has a "youthful, almost feminine beauty" (*The Bacchae* in Euripides 1973: 191). In Ovid's *Metamorphoses* 8 Atalanta has "features which in a boy would have been called girlish but in a girl they were like a boy's" (1955: 187).[38] Dares' beautiful Helen looks like her beautiful twin brothers (Frazer 1966: 142). Throughout Shakespeare's sonnets, the beautiful young man looks like a woman. In Sonnet 53 the poet tries to depict the young man's beauty: "On Helen's cheek all art of beauty set, / And you in Grecian tires are painted new." The young man is as beautiful as a male Helen, he is a male Helen.[39] Marlowe's Ovidian epyllion *Hero and Leander* offers this information about Leander: "some swore he was a maid in man's attire / For in his looks were all that men desire" (84–5). As Dympna Callaghan explains, androgynous or hermaphroditic beauty was the ideal: "Such fused gender identities were understood, from an aesthetic point of view, to be manifestations of beauty that transcended gender distinction by incorporating the best features of both sexes" (2007: 35). In looking at an androgynous Helen we are not looking at a voluptuous *femme fatale* but at what Kitt Hesketh-Harvey punningly dubs a "Troy boy."[40]

This androgynous tradition of beauty colors Heywood's Epithalamion to the Elector Palatine and the Princess Elizabeth (*A Marriage Triumph*) (1613). In a paean to the Elector Palatine's beauty, Heywood hymns:

> He for his years
> And beauty, such a general name hath won,
> They take him all, for Venus, or her son.
> A mixed grace he in his visage wore,
> And, *but his habit showed what sex he bore*,
> The quickest sighted eye might have mistook
> Having female beauty in a manly look.
>
> (sig. B3r, my italics)

As in the misidentification of Canova's Paris/Helen, it is costume – Paris' Phrygian hat, the count Palatine's "habit" – that decides gender.[41]

In Marlowe and Shakespeare, Helen is compared not just to masculine ideals but to male gods. In *Doctor Faustus* Helen is not more beautiful than Semele or Arethusa but more beautiful than *Jove* when he appeared to Semele or wantoned with Arethusa:

> Brighter art thou than flaming Jupiter
> When he appeared to hapless Semele,
> More lovely than the monarch of the sky
> In wanton Arethusa's azured [B-text: azure] arms.
>
> (5.1.106–9)

In *Troilus and Cressida* Shakespeare also compares Helen to a god, to Apollo: in exchange for Hesione the Trojans have gained someone "whose youth and freshness / Wrinkles Apollo's" (2.2.78–9).

Unorthodox though it may initially sound, comparing Helen to a male, or to male paradigms of beauty, makes perfect sense. Helen sets the standard of female beauty; to compare her to another female is a meaningless comparison because Helen constitutes the category against which other women are judged. To describe Helen, then, one has to go outside the category. Androgyny is an entirely independent category because it is not dependent on an Other (whereas masculinity is defined in opposition to the feminine and vice versa).

I want now to consider the subject of Helen as the absolute of beauty via an odd physiognomic detail that enters Helen narratives in 1578, a detail so unusual and unexpected that its function, sources, and afterlife demand attention: the scar on her face.

Helen's Scar

At the opening of Lyly's *Euphues* (1578) the narrator tells us that Helen had a scar on her chin. He uses this as an example of the way in which beauty is enhanced by imperfection:

> the sweetest rose hath his prickle, the finest velvet his brack, the fairest flour his bran . . . and true it is . . . that in all perfect shapes, a blemish bringeth rather a liking every way to the eyes than a loathing any way to the mind. Venus had her mole in her cheek, which made her more amiable, Helen her scar on her chin which Paris called *cos amoris*, the whetstone of love, Aristippus his wart, Lycurgus his wen [wart]. (sig. B1r)

This may be a detail Lyly made up; there are also no known references to Aristippus' wart or Lycurgus' wen, which seem therefore to be Lyly's invention.[42] But unlike the men's warts, the women's marks enter narrative tradition; all other references to Helen's scar postdate *Euphues* and occur in phrases or contexts which make it clear that their source is *Euphues*. In the second part of *Wit's Commonwealth* (1634) Francis Meres quotes the passage acknowledging his source in Lyly (sig. F7v–F8r). Robert Parry's *Moderatus* (1595) quotes Lyly almost verbatim (without acknowledgment) and transfers Lyly's general aphorism to a specific situation. Priscus sees "his handsome Pastora sitting by a fair spring," where her pastoral dishabille makes her

> beautiful visage . . . far more amiable: for a blemish in all perfect shapes, bringeth rather a liking to the eyes, than a loathing to the mind: else had not Paris called the scar which Helen had in her chin, and Mars the mole which Venus had in her cheek, *Cos amoris*. (sig. S3r)

In *Nature's Embassy* (1621) Richard Brathwaite paraphrases the sentiment, but the sequence from Venus' mole to Helen's scar strongly suggests the influence of Lyly: "it is not Venus' mole nor Hellen's scar, / adds fuel to affection" (sig. H1v).

In Greene's *Mourning Garment* (1590) the second sister discourses:

> The fairest rose hath his canker, the bravest branch his caterpillars, the brightest sun his cloud, and the greatest beauty his blemish. Helena had a scar, Leda a wen, Lais a spot in her brow, and none so fair but there is some fault: but grant all these be graces as Paris called Helen's scar *Cos amoris*. (sig. E2r)

The passage begins and ends with Lyly's influence. but in the middle Greene adds examples of his own, transfers Lycurgus' wen to Helen's mother, Leda, and Aristippus' mark to his mistress, Lais of Corinth.

In *Ciceronis Amor* (1589) Greene interprets or redefines the scar as a dimple: "Lentulus casting his eye upon his love, seeing a dimple in her cheek which was to him *cos amoris*" (sig. C2r). This is also Thomas Heywood's interpretation in *The Fair Maid of the Exchange* (1625), where Frank offers an anatomical blazon of his love Phyllis (the fair maid of the title) working his way from her forehead and hair to her cheeks (where, like Venus, she has a mole) as he tries to deny Phyllis' attractions:

> Venus' mole was not more natural; but what of that, I am Adonis, and will not love . . . Let us descend: her chin, O Helen, Helen, where's your dimple, Helen? it was your dimple that bewitched Paris, and without your dimple I will not love you Helen. (sig. C3v)

The absence of references to Helen's scar before Lyly's *Euphues* leads one to conclude that the detail was Lyly's invention, although Heywood was both a good classicist and an avid reader of medieval versions of the Troy narrative (his poem *Troia Britannica or Great Britain's Troy* (1609) is indebted to the medieval Troy books). We therefore need to consider the traditions Lyly inherited.

Dares Phrygius' account of the Trojan War, allegedly an eyewitness account written by a Trojan warrior but actually a fiction,[43] exists in a sixth-century Latin manuscript. Dares' account was enormously influential throughout the Middle Ages, along with the eyewitness account of his contemporary the Greek Dictys. (Dictys' was also a fiction though presented as the narrative of someone who fought at Troy.) Dares' account includes a series of portraits of Greek and Trojan warriors and their ladies. Dares tells us, "Helen was beautiful, sincere, charming. She had the best legs and mouth. Between her two eyebrows she had a distinguishing mark [*notam*]" (Dares 1873: 14, §12, my trans.). What was this distinguishing mark? R. M. Frazer translates it as "a beauty-mark," which it might well be (1966: 142). But for the moment, let us leave it as a general distinguishing mark.

We might note that Dares frequently focuses on eyebrows. Briseis has eyebrows "joined above her lovely eyes" (Frazer 1966: 144). We might also note that Polyxena is described in terms we might have expected to apply to Helen: "surpassing all the others in beauty" (Frazer 1966: 143). But there is a bit of an overlap between all the women. Whereas Helen's *legs* are the best, Polyxena's *feet* are the best ("cruribus optimis"; "pedibus optimis"; Dares 1873: 14, 16). Both Polyxena and Briseis are described, like Helen as ingenuous or sincere ("simplicis"; Dares 1873: 14, 16, 17). Briseis, like Helen, is charming ("blandam"; Dares 1873: 14, 17). Thus a number of stock adjectives are being repositioned. These portraits are not in Dictys, and they were probably not in the original (lost) Dares.

The sixth-century Dares manuscript shows the influence of a sixth-century Syrian monk called Johannis Malalas, writing in Greek, whose work

(*Chronographia*) also contains portraits. His Helen has curly golden hair, beautiful breasts, beautiful eyebrows and the best face; Briseis' eyebrows are joined together. Polyxena has beautiful everything, small feet, and big eyes (1831: 91, 101, 106). These narrative portraits in Malalas and Dares were extremely popular, so much so that manuscript extracts of the portraits circulated separately.

Joseph of Exeter, writing in the 1180s, describes Helen at length. Joseph notes that Helen's chin protruded slightly, she skimmed the ground as she walked, and that a single spot splashed boldly between her eyebrows, dividing them into two slender arches (Joseph/Roberts 1970: 44). This single spot is actually given a double description: it is first a *labes* (mark, spot) and then four words later it is a *macula* (mark, blemish; 4.191–2). Briseis again has linked eyebrows and Polyxena is the most beautiful woman in Troy (Joseph/Roberts 1970: 43, 42). The men, here as elsewhere in the manuscript tradition, have flaws: Nestor has a beaky nose, Pyrrhus stutters, Hector has a lisp and a squint (Joseph/Roberts: 43, 41).[44]

In Benoît's *Roman de Troie* (1184 CE) Helen has a mark in the middle of her eyebrows, "which suited her greatly" (TLN 5133–6; Benoît 1904: 265–6). So from a neutral statement in Dares and Joseph (who tell us simply that she had a mark between her eyebrows) this now becomes a compliment, the mark an asset. (This presumably is why some translators of the two earlier works translate it as a beauty spot.) In Benoît Briseis' eyebrows are joined together but this *does not* suit her (TLN 5279–80; Benoît 1904: 265–6); again, a neutral statement is changed into a value judgment, here a negative one.[45] (As an additional piece of information in Benoît, we are told that both Polyxena and Helen have nice eyebrows.)

With Guido delle Colonne's *Destructionis Troiae* (c.1287) things get more specific. Helen now has *two* marks: a dimple in the middle of her chin and a scar between her eyebrows: "a small and delicate scar which became her in marvelous fashion" (delle Colonne / Meek 1974: 82; "modicam et tenuem cicatricem que miro modo decebat eandem" in delle Colonne / Griffin 1936: 83). This latter mark – and remark – is attributed to Dares. But in fact it is Guido who turns Dares' generalized *nota* (notable mark) into an unambiguous *cicatrix*. Here we see what is probably a mole in Dares, Joseph, and Benoît become a scar (figure 8).[46]

When we reach Chaucer, we encounter Criseyde's famous monobrow, a decided blemish in her beauty according to the poet: "And save hire browes, joyneden yfeere / Ther nas no lak, in aught I kan espien" (5.813–14).[47] Earlier she has been compared to both Helen and Polyxena: Criseyde "fairer was to sene, / Than ever were Eleyne or Polixene" (1.454–5). The comparison makes sense in the context of the medieval tradition in which

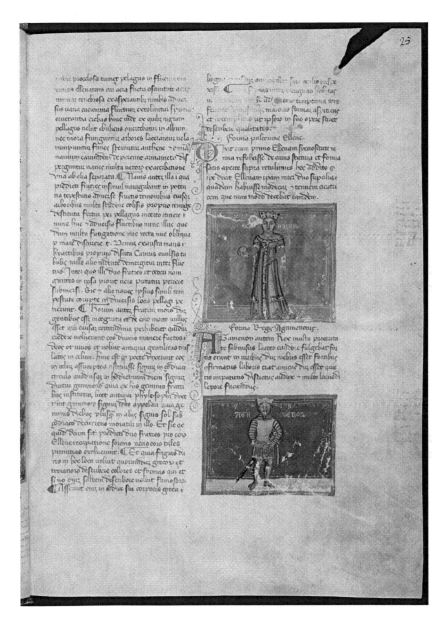

Figure 8   Guido delle Colonne, *Historia Destructionis Troiae*, MS CB 78, folio 25r. Guido mentions a dimple on Helen's chin and a scar between her eyebrows but the illustrator has not included these details. Reproduced by kind permission of the Fondation Martin Bodmer, Cologny (Génève).

Polyxena's outstanding beauty is always stressed. Polyxena is to Troy what Helen is to Greece: the most beautiful woman. And Criseyde, says Chaucer, is more beautiful than either. The triangle of women here also contains within it the end of the poem: the men who love these icons of beauty will be killed (Benson 1980: 137).

The anonymous *Gest Hystoriale* (of unknown date, perhaps 1400?) reproduces Helen's dimpled chin from Guido but omits the scar: "Hir chyn full choice was the chekys benethe, / With a dympull full derne [small], dainte to se" (TLN 3059–60).

We come lastly to a curious detail in Lydgate's *Troy Book*. Lydgate gives a series of portraits of Greeks and Trojans, drawn he tells us, from Dares:

> Al to discrive Dares dide his cure,
> In Grekysche tong, be-gynnyng at Eleyne,
> Liche as to-forn ye han herde me seyne,
> Of hir beute and hir semlynes
> How ceryously Guydo doth expresse
> (Saue he seide, in a litel space,
> *A strype ther was endelonge hir face,*
> Whiche, as he writ, be-cam hir wonder wel,
> Embelyssching hir beute everydel
> Like as Dares maketh discripcioun).
>   (2.4522–31, my italics)

What is a stripe along one's face? The *Middle English Dictionary* glosses this as "scar" or "weal." Lydgate's use is the first citation; the meaning is perhaps established by Guido's *cicatrix*, although Guido places it between Helen's eyebrows. (It will be over 20 years before the noun appears in Middle English literature again, meaning a weal.) "Along her face" sounds like a substantial mark; and if *endelonge* refers to latitudinal direction rather than longitudinal, it is perhaps likely to be on the chin.

I think it is possible to see a process of conflation going on in the above texts. The mark between the eyebrows becomes a mole; the mole becomes a scar; the scar becomes conflated with the dimple, and so it drops down to the chin.

It is important to note that there is fluidity in the portraits between the various redactions: Lydgate's Cassandra and his King of Persia have acquired the warts of other writers' Agamemnon;[48] in the anonymous *Gest Hystoriale* Cassandra has acquired the squint that belongs to Hector in Joseph of Exeter. The portraits work as a photokit with a number of details open to rearrangement. But the sequence of moles and scars do not seem willful rearrangements so much as progressive misunderstandings or mis-translations Lyly may have inherited.[49]

I advance this as a stochastic suggestion rather than as a confirmed conviction. But whether Lyly inherited or invented the scar, he adopted it for a reason. That reason will become clear in the next section.

Relativizing the Absolute

The story of Helen is the story of beauty; and the story of Helen's beauty is the story of language. In Neil Forsyth's encapsulation, "[la] beauté . . . des femmes . . . [est] aussi [la beauté] des mots" (Forsyth 1987: 11). I want to think here about one particular aspect of language: poetic or metaphoric language.

Metaphor is, in a sense, about violent coupling.[50] Poetic (metaphoric) language asserts that two different things are actually the same and brings them together in a momentary, violent union. To compare two like things would result in tautology or linguistic redundancy, a problem illustrated by Spenser (a poet fascinated by beauty, language, unity, and doubleness) in book 1 of *The Faerie Queene* when he compares Morpheus, the god of sleep, to someone who is asleep. Archimago has sent a spirit to Hades to fetch a false dream from Morpheus with which to delude the Red Cross Knight. When the spirit arrives, Morpheus is asleep: "as one then in a dreame" (I.1.42.7). But Morpheus cannot be *like* someone who is asleep because he *is* the god of sleep. Morpheus is therefore the standard of "asleepness"; he is the absolute of dormancy.[51] As such he is beyond language, which relies on the relative, on there being two positions, on a momentary fix between two separate things (whether in poetic metaphor or in structuralist theory). Like Spenser's Morpheus, Milton's God is beyond language: God simply *is*; he is transparent; and so Milton's God speaks without metaphor (which may be theologically and philosophically responsible but is poetically disastrous, as generations of readers of *Paradise Lost* have registered). And like Morpheus or God, Helen too is beyond language and for the same reason: as the paradigm of beauty she is absolute.[52]

Lucian had introduced the problem of absolute beauty in the second century CE: "Now we looking not simply for beauty but for the great beauty . . . ; we are in search of a definite thing, the supreme beauty, which must necessarily be *one*" (*Hermotimus* in Lucian 1905, vol. 2: 67). Absolute beauty is singular – "one" – but language is not: language is plural. We recall Lydgate's problem when faced with the beauty of Helen:

> And certeynly, yif I schal reherse
> Hir schap, hir forme, and feturis by & by,
> As Guydo doth by ordre ceryously,
> From hed to foot, clerly to devise,
> I han non englysche that ther-to may suffyse;
> It wil nat be, oure tonge is not lyke.
> (2.3674–9)

In other words, "I can't describe all her features as Guido does; English is not up to it." Lydgate implies that the problem is with the English language (Latin can manage it). In fact Latin cannot: Guido may have an extended description but his details tell us little more about Helen than does Lydgate. The problem lies not with a particular language; the problem lies with language generally. Extremes of any kind are one, absolute, fixed; language is plural and relative.

To talk about Helen, the absolute of beauty, one has to force her into a relative position (as Ben Morgan points out, personal communication). Mythological and literary narrative has numerous ways of doing this. It can double her (the *eidōlon* of Greek tradition, the calque of Shakespeare's Cressida[53]). It can sexualize her and abduct her, thereby forcing her body into a system of physical relations, moving her from the absolute to the real. Throughout the Middle Ages, the many versions of the Troy story present Helen's abduction as a narrative foreplay: it is always outwith the main body of the text. The *Laud* Troy book makes this explicit: over 3,000 lines into the book, having described Helen's abduction, the poet says, "Herkenes now, both grete and smale! / For now begynnes al this tale" (TLN 3293–4). The tale *begins*? What does he think he has been doing for 3,000 lines? But he realizes that only with abduction can Helen be narrated.

Thus literature can double her or abduct her. Or it can damage her: this, I think, is what lies behind the otherwise inexplicable innovation of making Helen physically flawed by giving her a scar on her chin. Marring her beauty in this way forces it into a relative position, one that can then be iterated. No classical authority mentions Helen as scarred, nor is there any need to: the *eidōlon* tradition serves the same purpose, providing something against which to measure Helen. And this, perhaps, as Elisabeth Dutton observes (personal communication), is why drama has less trouble in representing Helen: drama is already a form of doubling, as we are aware of the actor representing the character.

The absolute is a term (and a concept) beloved of Thomas Heywood. When Edward IV sees and falls in love with Jane Shore, he says "I never did behold / A woman every way so absolute" (*1 Edward 4*, sig. D4r). In *A Challenge for Beauty* (1636) the vain and arrogant Queen Isabella believes that for beauty she is a *non pareille*. The honest courtier Lord Bonavida disputes this on the grounds that nature does not deal in absolutes:

> Nature hath yielded none so absolute,
> To whom she made no fellow. First for beauty,
> If Greece afforded a fair Helen, Troy
> Her paralleled with a Polyxena.
>
> (sig. B1v)[54]

He unwisely concludes:

> Madam though I must confess you rare, . . .
> Yet not so choice a piece, but the wide world
> May yield you a competitor.
>
> (sig. B1v)

Queen Isabella consequently issues the challenge for beauty of the play's title, a challenge to Bonavida's theory of aesthetic relativity.

*

Helen's story is a story of containment and disruption, of movement from outside to inside, of invasion. This is visible at every stage of the Trojan War narrative. It begins with Paris expelled only to return. (Hecuba had dreamed that she would give birth to a firebrand that would destroy Troy; when Paris was born, he was abandoned on a hillside. Rescued and raised by shepherds, he is later identified and welcomed back into the Trojan royal family.) The Spartan Helen is captured, and brought from Greece to Troy. In defense of her, the Greeks enter the Trojan horse; the Trojan horse enters Troy. This movement from outside to inside is recapitulated repeatedly in the narrative, which becomes a parable of containment and excess, of controlled space and disruption of that space.

At the center of that narrative is Helen who, as an absolute of beauty, is linguistically disruptive: she halts the narrative. This is true of all literature's indescribably beautiful females, from the divinely lit Britomart to the ruttishly luscious Cleopatra. Faced with the absolute, the narrative pauses and indulges in rapt reaction. In Dares' account of the first meeting of Helen and Paris, they "spent some time just staring, struck by each other's beauty" (Frazer 1966: 141). In Joseph of Exeter's version of Dares, Paris walks on the beach, trying to attract Helen's attention. When he sees her, he "stops, forgetting to continue his stride" (Joseph/Bate 1986: 135). In Spenser's *The Faerie Queene*, narrative stops for ten stanzas of description when Belphoebe enters the poem. "It is a privileged moment of hieratic stillness and silence, as if a frame of film were frozen before us" (Paglia 1991: 178). Paglia's analogy with film is pertinent. When Menelaus (James Callis) sees Helen (Sienna Guillory) on the battlements during the fighting in the TV series *Helen of Troy* (2003), the action freezes for 40 seconds while Menelaus gazes and adores. Here we see the reason for the narrative disruption whenever Helen enters the scene, which we observed in chapter 1. The narrative stutter, the filmic freeze, the linguistic repetition, the metrical disruption: these are not just an effect of beauty but a defining property of beauty; it is not simply that beauty halts narrative but that beauty is itself "a moment of arrest, poise" (Kirwan 1999: 67).[55] The fabric of the play/poem/plot/film comes momentarily apart at the seams because to be an absolute is to be outside time – detached, separate, independent.

"Absolute" derives from the Latin verb *absolvere* (to loosen). Since *solvere* on its own means "to loosen," the "ab" in *absolvere* functions as an intensifier, emphasizing the irreversibility of the separation (and giving rise to the *Oxford English Dictionary* meaning [II.2] of absolute as "complete, entire"). When Milton's Adam sees Eve, he comments,

> yet when I approach
> Her loveliness, so absolute she seems
> And in herself complete.
> (*Paradise Lost* 8.546–58)

Absolvere is emphatic about the completeness of the action it denotes, an irreversibility that can be viewed as a refusal to belong to a sequence of actions. *Absolvere* is premised on the possibility of an action that can conclude sequence altogether and begin time afresh. ("Absolution" has the same root; absolution separates the sinner from his/her previous actions and from the past narrative sequence in which they occurred.)

These two senses of absolute come together in Giraudoux's *Tiger at the Gates*. The pacifist Hector, determined that the Trojan War shall not take place, asks, "what . . . [Helen] has given to us, worth a quarrel with the Greeks" (1955: 16). The mathematician replies that Helen has provided a new standard for mathematical measurements:

> There are no more feet and inches, ounces, pounds, milligrams or leagues. There is only the weight of Helen's footfall, the length of Helen's arm, the range of Helen's look or voice; and the movement of the air as she goes past is the measure of the winds.

He does not use the word "absolute," in English or in French, but that is what he is describing. Priam then offers his opinion:

> You have only to look at this crowd, and you will understand what Helen is. She is a kind of absolution. To each one of these old men . . . to all the old failures, she has shown they always had a secret longing to rediscover the beauty they had lost. If throughout their lives beauty had always been as close at hand as Helen is today, they would never have tricked their friends, or sold their daughters, or drunk away their inheritance. Helen is like a pardon to them: a new beginning for them, their whole future. (Giraudoux 1955: 17)

It is easy, prima facie, to fall into the trap of seeing Priam's response as an alternative or corrective to that of the mathematician. But etymologically his argument is identical: the absolute is "a kind of absolution."

I have been arguing that the absolute needs to be relative before it can be represented and that Helen's scar serves this purpose. But there is another way of phrasing this: that it is because it is flawed, and because that flaw does not matter, that we know we are in the presence of perfection.[56] This is Lyly's view: "a blemish bringeth rather a liking everyway to the eyes than a loathing anyway to the mind" (his examples are of roses, flour, and linen). This is also Francis Meres' view, using a different trio of examples which are also derived from Lyly: "as the fairest leopard hath his spots, the finest cloth his list, & the smoothest shoo his last: so the most blazing beauty hath some blemish" (1634: sig. P8v).[57] And it is Enobarbus' view of Cleopatra: "she doth make defect perfection." If Helen is the absolute of beauty, what makes her absolute is not that she is perfect but that she is not, and that paradoxically the flaw seems perfect.[58] Furthermore the scar individualizes what might otherwise be a stereotype of extreme beauty.

Whether flawlessly perfect or defectively so, the absolute is unique, singular, one. And if Helen is outside time, she cannot age – which causes problems when the war on her behalf is located specifically in time, ten years. Most writers about Helen realize that the question of her aging (or not) has to be addressed at some stage. Let us look at some of these works before returning to the question of language and the absolute.

Helen and Old Age

Ibycus informs us that Idomeneus still loved Helen even when her hair had turned grey (Pollard 1965: 34). The grey hair functions here as the scar does in Lyly, a relative marker reinforcing beauty. Less happily, Helen in

Ovid's *Metamorphoses* laments the loss of her youth: she weeps "when she sees herself in the glass, wrinkled with age, and asks herself why she was twice carried off" (1955: 340–1). This is part of Ovid's focus on mutability. His example, popularized by Arthur Golding's translation of the *Metamorphoses* in 1567, impressed itself on early modern writers: it is cited several times (by Austin Saker in *Narbonus* [1580], by Thomas Adams in *The Black Devil* [1615], by Thomas Heywood in *2 The Iron Age* [1632], by Francis Meres in *Wit's Commonwealth* [1634]), usually in *ubi sunt* contexts. Francis Meres, for example, uses Helen elegiacally: Helen "in her new glass viewing her old face, with smiling countenance, cried *Beauty where is thy* blaze?" (sig. P9r). George Peele simply calls Helen a "wither'd flower" (*Tale of Troy*, l. 479) a position Edward Grant expands at length in *A Precedent for Parents* (1571):

> Helena (that flower of fairness, and the chiefest jewel that ever beauty had), in her age [i.e., old age] suffered the like deformity. For whom (being in the flower of her green years) the Grecians and Trojans were turmoiled in their ten years war; but when she was old and well struck in years, neither shepherds nor swineherds, muleteers nor horsekeepers would take up hostility to enjoy her.[59] (sig. C7r)

Thomas Heywood's Helen in *2 The Iron Age* (1632), like his earlier Helen in *Troia Britannica* (1609) is so despondent at the ravages of age that she commits suicide. William Morris's Helen three times expresses concern about the deleterious effect of advancing years on her famed beauty (1915: 44, 45, 46). In Margaret George's novel *Helen of Troy* (2006) Helen welcomes old age as "deliverance from the bondage of my beauty" (596). The title of Edgar Fawcett's poem "Helen, Old" (1903) is clearly meant to catch our attention, perhaps even as an oxymoron. In it Helen asks Venus to reendow her beauty: "Then, if thy mood wills, dash me dead!" Dying young and beautiful is preferable to seeing her aged reflection in the mirror. R. C. Trevelyan offers a Hardy-esque moment of fatality in "Helen" (1934) when Helen plucks out her first white hair; Paris enters and gallantly says that Troy will perish before Helen's hair turns silver: that is, "Never." Whereupon

> Helen opened
> Her small palm and sighed: "Already,
> See, it is fallen."
>
> (1934: 16)

In Eva Salzman's poem "Helen's Sister" (2004), Clytemnestra wryly observes, "Any woman would slay a thousand soldiers / not to get older."

In the teen novel *Eric* (1990) a comic-satiric version of the Faust legend, Eric finally receives his wish to see the most beautiful woman in the world. His disappointment is extreme on finding a plump woman with "the beginnings of a moustache," encumbered by seven children.

> "But it said her face launched a thousand ships – ." "That's what you call metaphor," said Rincewind . . . "Anyway, you shouldn't believe everything you read in the Classics . . . They never check their facts. They're just out to sell legends" (Pratchett 2000: 93, 95).

At the other extreme, three writers stress Helen's agelessness. In Quintus of Smyrna's *War at Troy* the abandoned Oenone questions Paris about his new love: "people say she is ageless" (1968: 198). In John Erskine's novel *The Private Life of Helen of Troy* Menelaus confesses that he does not understand how Helen's looks last so well, and later concludes that she is outside of time, like music or the sea (1926: 273, 280). Ben Jonson's comic charlatan Volpone, in disguise as a mountebank, tries to sell an age-defying cosmetic as used by Aphrodite and Helen of Troy:

> It is the powder that made Venus a goddess, given her by Apollo, that kept her perpetually young, cleared her wrinkles, firmed her gums, filled her skin, coloured her hair; from her derived to Helen, and at the sack of Troy, unfortunately, lost: till now, in this our age, it was as happily recovered by a studious antiquary. (*Volpone* 2.2.236–41)

The comic irony here, as in most cosmetic advertising, is of course the falsity of its claim: that anyone could be "perpetually young."[60]

The above writers use the topic of Helen's relationship to time sentimentally or satirically. It is noted, accepted, dismissed, moralized, elegized, or parodied. In the twentieth century two writers – Rupert Brooke and C. S. Lewis – engage with the subject more extensively.

Rupert Brooke's poem of paired sonnets "Menelaus and Helen" contrasts the beautiful Helen for whom the honorable Menelaus went to war ("the perfect Knight before the perfect Queen") with the aged couple many years later (Menelaus deaf, garrulous, reminiscing about Troy; Helen a shrill scold, "gummy-eyed"). The first sonnet, full of kinetic verbs and chivalric terms, stresses beauty and knighthood, glorious and divine protagonists, and war for honor. Sonnet 2 exposes this as a poetic fiction with the opening sentence undercutting the first sonnet: "So far the poet." The subject of the second sonnet is not the stuff of poetry; Brooke underlines what the poet "does not tell you." And what is absent from the poetic renderings, from all Troy narratives, is the anticlimactic sequel: the "long connubial years," children, nagging, deafness, interminable repeated anecdotes. Menelaus "wonders why on earth he went / Troyward": the romantic "Troyward" is the only relic of the earlier honorable quest, a poetic form that seems as out of place in this second sonnet as the chivalric fiction it indicates. But what initially reads like a bitter antiwar poem (was this worth fighting for?) concludes with an eirenic vision of Paris paradoxically the gainer through death because spared the pathos of age: "so Menelaus nagged; and Helen cried; / And Paris slept on by Scamander side."[61]

In 1959 C. S. Lewis began a story/novella about Helen and Menelaus at the end of the Trojan War, "After Ten Years." The story is told from Menelaus' point of view. It begins with Menelaus' thoughts of revenge on Helen as he is incarcerated in the belly of the wooden horse, and ends with – in fact it does not end. Lewis was unable to complete the story, which simply breaks off, without even a punctuation mark. The 19-page fragment (in five chapters) survives along with comments by Roger Lancelyn Green and Alistair Fowler with whom Lewis had corresponded and talked about his difficulties in executing the story. Their conversations had centered on plot; I think it is beauty that lies at the heart of Lewis's narrative difficulties.[62]

Lewis's Menelaus, like most Menelauses, is not clever, but this one knows it, and his attempts to analyze war, torture, revenge, his marriage, politics, and Agamemnon grant him narrative sympathy. His indeterminate plans for revenge on Helen are aposiopestically Learlike: "he would do such things to her . . ." (Lewis 1966: 128). He plans to rape her; to give her to the slaves to rape; to sacrifice her ("no rape, no punishments; just solemn, stately, mournful, almost regretful killing, like a sacrifice"; 128); to save her ("destroy a trophy like that?"; 131). At times he cannot name her except as "the woman" (129).

When in the second section of the story Menelaus reaches the innermost rooms in the palace, he recognizes Helen only by her voice:

> he had never dreamed she would be like this; never dreamed that her flesh would have gathered in her chin, that the face could be so plump and yet so drawn, that there would be grey hair at her temples and wrinkles at the corners of her eyes. Even her height was less than he remembered. (Lewis 1966: 134)

Pity for his estranged wife is quickly superseded by shame: "he had dreamed of living in stories as the man who won back the most beautiful woman in the world, had he?" (134). Agamemnon's reaction to the aged Helen is both pragmatic and political. He fears that the army will not believe that the captured queen is Helen. "They'll think you have a beautiful Helen

– the Helen of their dreams – safely hidden away." So he arranges for Menelaus and Helen to embark quickly and quietly, leaving him to handle the situation (perhaps by "pass[ing] some other prisoner off as Helen. There are some remarkably pretty girls"; 141).

In chapter 5 of the story Helen and Menelaus land in Egypt, where their Egyptian host maintains that Menelaus' companion is not Helen. The story turns – or was to turn – on the reversal of the *eidōlon* myth. As Roger Lancelyn Green reveals, Lewis's premise was that Helen's phantom was in Egypt and the real Helen in Troy. (In Stesichorus' version the gods had sent a phantom to Troy while the real Helen rusticated in Egypt.) The story breaks off at the moment when the Egyptian who has looked after Helen for ten years presents his charge. Music plays; candles glow. " 'Daughter of Leda, come forth', said the old man. And at once it came. Out of the darkness of the doorway." It is, I think, no coincidence that the story is abandoned at the moment when Lewis has to describe Helen – an eternally beautiful Helen. As Green explains, out of the doorway was to come

> the beautiful Helen whom Menelaus had originally married – Helen so beautiful that she must have been the daughter of Zeus – the dream beauty whose image Menelaus had built up during the ten years of the siege of Troy and which had been so cruelly shattered when he found Helen in Chapter II. (Lewis 1966: 147)

But Lewis had boxed himself into a corner. He might be able to describe an aged Helen; but he is unable to describe an eternal one. Once again, beauty's temporal transcendence throws its narrative spanner in the works. Here it halts the narrative, not for ten stanzas (as in *The Faerie Queen*) or for 50 lines (as in *Antony and Cleopatra*) or for 40 seconds (as in the 2003 TV series of *Helen of Troy*), but permanently. Helen's beauty can have no greater tribute. Lewis's failure is his subject's success.

We need to return here to the question of the absolute, in particular, the problem of the absolute incarnated in the real. If Christianity is paradoxically the most material of religions (because it posits the incarnation of a transcendent deity in a physical body), Helen's story similarly locates the incarnate in the real (and by "the real" one can understand both Helen's body and the narrative in which that body is chronicled). The problem of representing Helen thus has an anterior problem: ontology.

That Helen's beauty is not a problem of representation but a problem of ontology is becoming increasingly clear, for, despite the examples given throughout this chapter, narrative does not have representational problems with beauty. The young man in Shakespeare's sonnets is given lyric space. Beautiful goddesses – Aphrodite, Hera, Athena – are described. So is Lucrece. And since for many centuries female beauty was often equated with female artifice, literature can depict the former via the latter. When Hera prepares to distract Zeus by seducing him in the *Iliad*, she beautifies herself cosmetically: with a bath, moisturizer ("sweet olive oil"), perfume, ambrosia, hair dressing, a designer dress ("that Athene / had made her"), jewellery (brooch, belt, earrings, clothes, and glorious shoes). The description is not of her essential beauty, but of her beauty as prosthetic: "she . . . clothed her body in all this loveliness" (14.172, 178–9, 187). In a military epic this is a scene of *female* arming (Willcock 1976: 159). Women's armor is beauty; beauty is something one can put on.

Beauty can therefore be represented, even divine beauty. Helen's beauty is not a problem of appearance but of being.

But if Helen's beauty is a problem of being (half-mortal, half-divine) and of morality (the ethical status of beauty) it is also a political problem in a way that Lucrece's beauty, despite its political effects, is not. Lucrece's story is not "about" her beauty but about her chastity, in narratological terms. (In Livy, as in Shakespeare, it is her virtue that inflames Tarquin.) But Helen's beauty is inserted consistently in politics, as the Trojan Council debate in Shakespeare's *Troilus and Cressida* makes clear, where the central question is not "What is Helen's beauty worth?" but "How does one value a king?"

We can consider this issue through its apparent opposite, ugliness. I say "apparent" opposite because for some theorists of aesthetics, the opposite of beauty is not ugliness but the dissociation of being and value (Kirwan 1999: 50). This provides a helpful definition of beauty – the union of being and value – which is a hallmark of Shakespeare's Helen debate in *Troilus and Cressida* (2.1). Beauty's relationship to value, to the polarities of time and transcendence, is paralleled in its relationship to another binary dyad: subjectivity and objectivity.

Beauty: Subjectivity and Objectivity

No one would question the assertion that a rose is beautiful. The statement that neoclassical architecture is beautiful is also unlikely to cause a disturbance, form and proportion being agreed constituents of the beautiful from Pythagoras, Plato, Polycleitus, Galen, and Augustine. The beautiful has identifiable, objective qualities.

This is not true of beauty, which is entirely subjective, as clichés like "beauty is in the eye of the beholder" indicate. Shakespeare's Theseus puts it more specifically (and more poetically): "the lover . . . / Sees Helen's beauty in a brow of Egypt" (*Midsummer Night's Dream* 5.1.10–11). In other words, a tawny complexion will seem as beautiful as that of Helen of Troy to a biased lover. Since Theseus' speech is about imagination, it is clear that beauty is not objective form but is a mental event.

Yet we continue to talk about beauty as if it were objective, as Lysander, in the same play, illustrates. He justifies his change of emotional allegiance from Hermia to Helena on the grounds of objective appreciation of beauty:

> Not Hermia but Helena I love.
> Who will not change a raven for a dove?
> The will of man is by his reason sway'd;
> And reason says you are the worthier maid.
>   (2.2.113–16)

Helen is "worthier" because she is more beautiful (or milder-tempered), "a dove" in comparison to "a raven." It is in the nature of post-Enlightenment subjects to invoke logic to explain actions and emotions, but Shakespeare's pre-Cartesian characters also think in this way.

Immanuel Kant begins his *Critique of Judgment* (1790) as follows:

> In order to distinguish whether anything is beautiful or not we refer the representation, not by the understanding to the object for cognition, but by the imagination . . . to the subject and its feeling of pleasure or pain. (1964: 280–1)

The relationship between beauty and imagination (subjectivity) and its related opposite, beauty and judgment (objectivity), underpins the work. For example: "beautiful objects are to be distinguished from beautiful views of objects."

Lysander's fusion of imagination with reason, or rather the sleight-of-hand that disguises the former as the latter, exposes the unease we feel when gripped by what Shakespeare calls the imagination, what Kant calls the "singular judgment," and what we call subjectivity. Here is Kant:

> I describe by a judgment of taste the rose that I see as beautiful. But the judgment which results from the comparison of several singular judgments, "roses, in general, are beautiful," is no longer described simply as aesthetical, but as a logical judgment based on an aesthetical one. (1964: 289)

In changing "I find a rose beautiful" (a personal reaction) to "roses are beautiful" (an objective statement) we perform the same act of syntagmatic ratiocination as Lysander when he justifies his change of affection as being the logical rejection of a raven (obviously black) for a dove (obviously white). In act 3 he again justifies his treatment of Hermia in the same terms, telling Helena "I had no judgment when to her [Hermia] I swore," to which Helena replies curtly, "nor none, in my mind, now you give her o'er" (3.1.134–5). Like Lysander we consistently use objective language for a subjective event. Like Lysander we *know* when someone is beautiful. (Or we do *not* know: Helena's complaint is that Lysander "will not know what all but he do know.")

Alexander Pope combines subjectivity and objectivity in a neat aphorism:

> 'Tis with our Judgments as our Watches, none
> Go just alike, yet each believes his own.
> (*Essay on Criticism*, 9–10 in Pope 1963)

What is unique about the case of Helen's beauty is that all judgments go just alike. Her beauty might be subjective but it is felt as an objectivity perceived by all. No one in classical or medieval literature disputes that her beauty is worth fighting for.

This brings us back to the representation of beauty by its effect on others, an issue with which we began this chapter. Philosophers of aesthetics have had many attempts to define beauty, but the most helpful, to my mind, comes from a philosopher best known for his literary criticism. In *Principles of Literary Criticism*, I. A. Richards writes, "We continually talk as though [beautiful] things possess qualities, when what we ought to say is that they cause effects in us of one kind or another" (1925: 21). This landmark text was published in 1924. Richards's view is paralleled in the work of John Erskine, professor of English at Columbia University. The two English dons separated by an ocean had much in common. Both had an interest in philosophy (Richards read Moral Sciences at Cambridge) and both were committed to humanist aspects of literature (Erskine being dedicated to the introduction of foundation courses in liberal humanities in English departments in the United States). Erskine was also a novelist, and in 1925 published *The Private Life of Helen of Troy*.

Discussing his mother-in-law's beauty with his newly-wed wife, Erskine's Orestes says:

> Beauty is simply an effect – the effect of extreme approval ... When we are wiser we shall say that such women are beautiful, not that they have beauty, or better still, we'll say they make the favourable impression called beauty. (1926: 293)[63]

Thirty years before Erskine's novel, Henry Rider Haggard and Andrew Lang had negotiated this problem successfully in an otherwise unsuccessful novel, *The World's Desire* (published serially in 1890, but in book form in 1894).[64] They present Helen not just as beautiful but as the absolute of beauty – "Beauty itself"[65] – and they do so by combining subjectivity and objectivity. When Helen appears, the crowd goes wild with adoration. They are united in their reaction, yet each man sees her differently. To some she has blue eyes, to others brown; to some she is blonde, others brunette:

> when they looked upon her, none could tell the semblance of her beauty, for to one she seemed dark and the other fair, and to each man of them she showed a diverse loveliness . . . so that it seemed to each man that she only was his Heart's Desire. (Haggard and Lang 1894: 98)[66]

It is more helpful to think of beauty not as a quality but as an effect. There are expressions of this conclusion over the centuries in Petrarch, in Firenzuola, Giordano Bruno, Sir Thomas Browne, Spinoza, Addison, Schiller, Pascal, and Hume. The word itself in Greek continually reminds us of this: *kalos/kallis* (beautiful), which Ficino links with *kaleō*, which he defines as "I provoke." His etymology is spurious: wordplay rather than legitimate derivation. Nonetheless there is a link between *kaleō* (I call, summon) and Plato's argument that beauty is a summons from another world, a call to the soul from God (Ficino 1985: 86, 5.2). The pseudo-Dionysius (late fifth century) recognizes as much when he writes that "beauty . . . call[s] (*kaloun*) all things to Itself (whence also it is called Beauty)" (1897: IV, §7). For him, as later for Ficino, beauty is synonymous with provocation: it is something that has an effect.

But if beauty is an effect, it is an effect created by us, as Yeats realized when he described his own Helen of Troy, Maud Gonne. Her beauty moved crowds; but symbiotically that beauty was "in *some way the crowd's creation*, as the entrance of the Pope into Saint Peter's is the crowd's creation" (Yeats 1955: 364, my italics). Yeats extends his description of Maud Gonne in this passage. He describes what we would expect – her stature,[67] her inscrutable face, the associations of her beauty ("joy and freedom"). But he adds:

> Besides, there was an element in her beauty that moved minds full of old Gaelic stories and poems, for she looked as though she lived in an ancient civilization where all superiorities whether of the mind or the body were part of a public ceremonial. (1955: 364)

This association of great beauty with the past is something he observes elsewhere in *Memoirs*: "I had never thought to see in a living woman so great beauty. It belonged to famous pictures, to poetry, to some legendary past" (1972: 40). Throughout Yeats's poetry Helen's beauty epitomizes the contrast between a "noble past" and a "mediocre present" (Melchiori 1978: 120). If we recall this chapter's introduction to beauty as something that, like narrative, arouses great longing, the association of Helen's beauty with nostalgia begins to fall into place. For Yeats is not alone in his reaction to beauty as something that summons up memories of, or creates longings for, a (national) past.

Beauty and Nostalgia

Poe's first "To Helen" poem (1849) opens with a comparison of Helen's beauty to Odysseus' homecoming:

> Helen thy beauty is to me
> Like those Nicean barks of yore
> That gently, o'er a perfumed sea
> The weary, wayborne wanderer bore
> To his own native shore.

In the second stanza Helen's "hyacinth hair" and her "classic face" bring the poet "home / To the glory that was Greece / And the grandeur that was Rome." This is not Helen as destructive beauty but as safe bark, and in the third stanza the poem relates Odysseus' physical search for home to the poet's spiritual search for literary origins, as the Helen figure merges into Psyche (and psyche). Greece was for Poe what Ireland was for Yeats, but the country matters less than the emotion of longing and the motif of *nostoi*. (Nor is this a motif confined to recent writers on Helen.)

Epic is, of course, the genre of nostalgia. Homer repeatedly contrasts the physical ability of his heroes with the lesser strength of "such as men are now" (*Iliad* 5.303–4; 12.383; 20.287). In Homer, in Quintus of Smyrna's *War at Troy*, and in the medieval Troy books, Helen variously longs for her husband, her home, her daughter, her brothers, her country. Of most interest in this context is the moment in Quintus of Smyrna when Helen herself is equated with Greece as the object of homesick men's longings. Troy has been sacked and the Greek soldiers finally set eyes on Helen as she walks to their ships alongside the captured Trojan women:

She stood visible before them, a sight they had all longed to see, just as when men have been roaming through the restless sea, and after a long time their native country comes in sight in answer to their prayers, and, escaped from the sea and from death, they stretch out their hands to their native lands, with infinite joy in their hearts. (1968: 250–1)

Isocrates makes the same point: when Helen is abducted, the Greeks feel the loss "as if the whole of their country had been plundered"; similarly the Trojans feel pride in their conquest of Helen "as if they had conquered [Greece]" (§49; 1894: 302). Quintus and Isocrates here understand what later philosophers of beauty articulate, that beauty is an emotion and an association (or set of associations) rather than an object. A so-called beautiful place (for example) is rather a memory of "a point in time" (Kirwan 1999: 10). This explains why seemingly beautiful objects or events – a musical symphony or view – do not always retain their beauty under different circumstance. Hardy's Tess of the D'Urbervilles meditates on the life she has had in two very different agricultural terrains and the loves and sorrows she has experienced in each, prompting her narrator to observe that "beauty to her, as to all who have felt, lay not in the thing but in what the thing symbolised" (Hardy 1978: 373). And what Helen's beauty symbolizes, as Quintus realizes, is Greece.[68]

Nostalgia (literally pain for home) is, despite the finitude expressed in its etymon, an exact parallel to beauty: neither is a longing for an object but a longing associated with the object, in fact the emotion of longing itself. As Susan Stewart explains, "nostalgia is a sadness without an object . . . : the past it seeks has never existed except as narrative." At the center of nostalgia is an absence, and the feeling of nostalgia is the present feeling of what is past, "a felt lack" (Stewart 2005: 23). The only paradise, as Proust said, is that which is lost.

Vladimir Jankélévitch compares nostalgia to love (1974: 288), but it might more accurately be compared to beauty. Petrarch's praise of beauty in Sonnet 77, in which he talks about Simone Martini's portrait of the beautiful Laura, values the painting precisely because of its ability "to excite longing in the beholder's breast; fulfilling that desire is not part of its business" (Schwyzer 2004: 69). Philip Schwyzer analyzes this sonnet in his discussion of early modern nationalism and memory. In this period, he notes, the impossibility of fulfilling desire was an important constituent of poetry and painting alike. To note the absence of speech in painting and sculpture was not to observe lack (a criticism) but to feel longing (a desideratum). "For Donatello and his audience, frustrated longing for the irrecoverable was another name for beauty" (Schwyzer 2004: 69).

Schwyzer traces the origin of this early modern nexus of nationalism and beauty, and their common denominator in longing, to John Bale's attempt to find a new object of aesthetic admiration after the dissolution of England's Roman Catholic beauties: abbeys, icons.

> Bale's principal debt to Petrarch lies in a simple realization. The gaze that fixes on a beautiful and lifelike piece of art and the gaze that bores into the ancient past are one and the same. Both produce aesthetic gratification out of a longing for the irrecoverable. (Schwyzer 2004: 71)

Schwyzer's comment has not just localized value in describing the early modern but can be applied as a theory to classical texts. Helen's beauty is inseparable from her loss, or threatened loss, because it is in absence that one experiences longing. This partly explains her multiple abductions, for only by being in constant circulation can she be an object of nostalgia. She moves from Tyndareus to Theseus, to Menelaus, to Paris, to Deiphobus, to Achilles . . . This constant circulation anticipates Marx's view of value where, in capitalism, goods achieve value simply by never coming to rest. Beauty, as we saw above, is ontologically linked to value – and is inseparable from it in the classical world, where, before the invention of money, men traded beautiful objects.

What happens when Helen is recovered by Menelaus? If beauty is defined by longing, does she now cease to be beautiful? Perhaps she does: the absence of a Helen narrative after the sack of Troy is notable; there is no longer a story to tell. But Homer's *Odyssey* book 4 presents Helen after she has come to rest in Sparta; in this book she is no less beautiful in Telemachus' eyes (or in the eyes of the poet). This may mean that she is still under threat of abduction. What has been stolen once may be stolen again (and again), and Menelaus' confidence in his wife's fidelity seems fragile as we see in the conflicting narratives of husband and wife where each tells Telemachus a story about his father in Troy. Helen relates an episode in which she recognizes the disguised Odysseus in Troy, gives him access to information, and keeps his secret. This is a story about Helen as loyal to Greece – a woman who suffers from, and is motivated by, nostalgia:

> I was already longing to go home again. I had suffered a change of heart, repenting the blindness which Aphrodite sent me when she brought me to Troy from my own dear country and made me forsake my daughter, my bridal chamber and a husband who lacked nothing in intelligence and looks. (book 4, p. 52)

This is nostalgia in its extremest form, for nowhere else in the literature is Menelaus presented as intelligent or good looking.[69] Menelaus now tells a story about his and Odysseus' experiences inside the Trojan horse. In his account, Helen imitates the voices of the Greek warriors' wives. She tempts the men to "come out or give an instant answer from within" (book 4, p. 53). This is a story about Helen as traitor to Greece – a woman who manipulates nostalgia, the longing of the Greeks for their wives and their homelands, a longing so strong that it encourages them to believe the impossible: that their wives are in Troy or that the wooden horse is in Greece.[70] The two stories and their contradictory views of Helen have long troubled commentators. But we do wrong to focus on their difference at the expense of what they have in common. And what they have in common is an examination of nostalgia.[71]

If nostalgia is longing, just as beauty is, both require absence.[72] This returns us to the absence at the heart of Helen narratives, which is an offshoot of the absence at the heart of beauty: the inscrutability or unknowability of the person behind the beautiful face. The most famous example of this is the smile of Leonardo's Mona Lisa, but Camille Paglia locates her smile in a tradition of sculpture and painting: Donatello's David, from there to Michelangelo's Victory, thence to Verrochio, on to Leonardo's Mona Lisa and finally to "Bernini's androgynous angel impishly piercing St Teresa" (Paglia 1991: 149). It is no coincidence that these examples are also Paglia's examples of androgyny, cited above. The sexual fluidity in these sculptures and paintings, Paglia asserts, has less to do with ambiguous physiology than with the ambiguity of the smile. The smile connotes – or conceals – a blankness she also finds in the remote, dreamy, self-sufficient literary heroines of Laura and Beatrice and in the Rossetti paintings of Elizabeth Sidall: "What is Mona Lisa thinking? *Nothing*, of course. Her blankness is her menace and our fear. She is Zeus, Leda, and egg rolled into one, another hermaphrodite deity pleasuring herself in *mere being*" (Paglia 1991: 154, my italics).[73]

In paintings of Helen she typically looks into the distance, abstractly, distantly. Even Evelyn de Morgan's Helen, apparently gazing narcissistically into her hand mirror, is not actually looking at her reflection. Her eyes do not align with the mirror. There is a pragmatic reason for this – gods and goddesses cannot gaze upon themselves – but it is also part of the representational tradition of Helen in art and literature that this chapter, and the previous one, have examined: the blank. The absent space of description; the nocturnal blank of oral storytelling; the stillness of Helen-as-object on the battlements in *Iliad* 3; the 1597 title-page of Caxton's *Recuyell*, which makes no reference to Helen; the omission of Helen's name from the dramatis personae of Heywood's *2 The Iron Age*; the blank page of Sterne's *Tristram Shandy*; the blank canvas at the center of François-André Vincent's painting; Maggie Wright's naked Helen; C. S. Lewis's abandoned short story and William Morris's unfinished *Scenes*; the purple triangle of Woolf's Mrs Ramsay; the silence of Helen's maid in Carol Ann Duffy's poem; the missing name on Petersen's DVD cover of *Troy*. This is the blankness of unknowability. Unknowability occupies all characters' relationships with Helen in fiction, and all authors' attempts to depict Helen as they try to fill in the blank, turning an ontological problem ("mere being") into a representational problem. We cannot know Helen, but we can try to depict her. And we can pretend that the latter equates to the former.

3

Abducting Helen

It is obvious that no young woman allows herself to be abducted if she does not wish to be (Herodotus, *The Histories*)

PENELOPE: *They were raped without permission.*
JUDGE (chuckles): *Excuse me, Madam, but isn't that what rape is? Without permission?*

Margaret Atwood, *The Penelopiad*

Missing Moments

If Helen's story is the story of beauty, it is also the story of rape. As Linda Lee Clader writes, "what Helen is best known for is rape, and secondarily . . . marriage" (1976: 71). Like beauty, but for different reasons, rape is a topic that cannot easily be represented. Celia Daileader's study *Eroticism on the Renaissance Stage* began, she explains, with a gap in the text. Reading Middleton's *Women beware Women*, Daileader was troubled by the sequence in which a "lustful male and a resistant female meet onstage, grapple a moment, exit from stage, and return some three minutes and one ejaculation later, leaving unspoken either the word 'rape' or the word 'seduction'" (1998: 1). This absence characterizes all literary rape narratives before the twentieth century. In the texts covered in this chapter, rape takes place off-stage, or in the blank space between stanzas, or in ambiguous phrases, or is represented via a substitute person or scene. In *Titus Andronicus*, for instance, Shakespeare cannot present the rape of Lavinia but he can give us a proxy: the suggestive landscape in which the murder of Bassianus is staged, with its dark hole or pit, guarded by a bush, streaked (after the violent act) with blood. Given that absence is already a feature of Helen narratives – absence of agency, interiority, aesthetic detail

– to have her fame (or infamy) associated with an act that cannot be depicted makes her story doubly difficult to tell.

In legal history, rape narratives are narratives of gaps, omissions, displacement, of what is not told. In the early modern period – which will be the focus of most of this chapter – rapes were rarely reported. In Sussex in Elizabeth's reign Nazife Bashar notes only 14 rape prosecutions but over 1,000 cases of larceny, 150 burglaries and 100 homicides (1983: 33); Miranda Chaytor notes "five accusations a decade" in northern England in the second half of the seventeenth century (1995: 378). Garthine Walker writes that in terms of victim testimony, rape is "a non-history, a history of absence" (1998: 1); because early modern women lacked access to the language of violence ("the language of true self-defence was male"; 8), they cannot present themselves as fighting back even when it is obvious that they did so. Women also lack legal vocabulary and Latin phrases; when depositions switch to legal euphemisms such as "carnal knowledge," Walker speculates that we are hearing the language of the male clerk, not the female victim. Victims often go into descriptive detail about environment, about domestic furnishings or activities in which they were engaged at the time of the attack, but their accounts of the attack itself are short and unspecific. A further problem is that in medieval and early modern literature it is not always clear what "rape" means since the noun in both its layman's and legal (Latin) use (rape or *raptus*) covers abduction and forced coition: both nouns derive from Latin *rapere*, to seize. (Throughout this chapter, unless otherwise specified, I use "rape" in its ambiguous sense, covering both crimes.)

Rape thus instantiates the general narratological predicament of Helen narratives – absence and ambiguity – in a specific form. This chapter will explore specific rape-related absences – absence of consent and absence of agency – and the ambiguity of language, of statutes, and poetic structures as they attempt to represent or conceal these absences. All of these concerns are articulated in Helen texts (just as Helen is used as an example in legal texts) but they are often displaced from Helen on to other women (Briseis, Criseyde). Thus this chapter performs its own act of abduction, leading away from the rape of Helen as an initiating act in the Trojan War to look at adjacent and contextual rapes and women, metonymic substitution, and the relation between literature and the law.

Homer, the *Iliad*

The abduction of Helen appears nowhere in the *Iliad*, which begins with the Greek warrior Achilles "sorrowing in his heart for the sake of the

fair-girdled woman whom they were taking by force against his will"
(1.429–30). Achilles has as his concubine a spoil of war, the beautiful
Briseis ("fair-cheeked Briseis"; 1.184).[1] Agamemnon also has a concubine,
Chryseis, daughter of the Trojan priest of Apollo, Chryses.[2] When Chryses
asks that the Greeks return his daughter, Agamemnon refuses; Chryses' petitions to Apollo result in the god's inflicting a plague on the Greek camp.
The Greek army persuades Agamemnon to return Chryseis; Agamemnon
then demands reparation for his loss – Achilles' concubine, Briseis.

Like Agamemnon, Achilles initially refuses. When he is prevailed upon
to relent, he too takes something else in return: he takes back his military
service.[3] Thus, returning one woman does not solve any problems; it starts
a chain reaction by angering someone else.

The vocabulary in which the *Iliad* presents this episode is worth paus-
ing over: Achilles sorrows for the woman "whom they were taking by
force against his will" (1.430). In English the line is tautological. "By force"
implies "against his will." Briseis is not being kidnapped or stolen as Helen
was (or was alleged to have been) from Menelaus – that is, without the
male's knowledge. Achilles agrees but does not want to agree. Thus Briseis
goes "against his will." What, then, does "by force" mean? In this context
"force" cannot mean physical violence (one of the English word's connotations), but compulsion: en*force*ment. The tautology also appears in
Greek (where it is less of a problem, given epic's fondness for pleonasm).
The line literally reads, "whom they were taking by force [*bia*] from him-
unwilling" [*aekōntos*].[4]

The *Iliad* thus opens with several of the topics of this chapter: absence,
ambiguity, substitution. It begins with the abduction of a woman but that
woman is not Helen. It introduces the concept of conflicted agency: the
vocabulary of rape is here applied to Achilles who is passive, enforced, unwilling even as he is cooperative. And it substitutes Briseis for Chryseis, using
a narrative technique that will become standard in later literary rape narratives of Helen: displacement.

The historian Herodotus (born in the late fifth century BCE in Asia Minor)
unites these topics in his introduction to his *Histories* but also expands them,
providing a contextual history of rape. For him, the abduction of Helen
that leads to the Trojan War is the culmination of a series of abductions.
Visit any art gallery today and the chances are high that you will find a group
scene titled "The Rape of Helen." But Helen's seizure is only one in a sequence
of related abductions, although it happens to be the best known one. Herodotus chronicles these related abductions and their pre-Trojan context – a
context which reveals that the crime against Helen/Sparta, as in many wars,
was not an independent causal event but a final straw, the trigger (or excuse)

following a history of prior hostilities. But what is interesting in this case is that the prior hostilities, although plural, are all the same: rape.

Herodotus, the *Histories*

Herodotus sets out his narrative aim in the first paragraph of his *Histories*, dividing his general aim ("inquiries into history") into two more specific sub aims: to record the achievements "both of our own and of the Asiatic peoples"; and second, "to show how the two races came into conflict" (1965: 13). In the ensuing pages he chronicles a series of *quid pro quo* attacks.

It began with the Phoenicians,[5] a maritime culture who explored the Mediterranean, established settlements, and traded by sea. When they came to Argos, the King's daughter, Io, and other women (presumably her waiting-women) came to shop for Phoenician goods. "Suddenly the Phoenician sailors passed the word along and made a rush at them. The greater number got away; but Io and some others were caught and bundled aboard the ship" and taken to Egypt. Thus East attacks West. This, says Herodotus, was the first in a "series of provocative acts" (1965: 13). Later, inevitably, the Greeks retaliate, abducting the Phoenician princess Europa, "thus giving them [the Phoenicians] tit for tat" (14).

There the matter should have ended with a goal scored on each side, the Greek abduction of an Asian princess repaying or canceling the Asian abduction of a Greek. But a third outrage follows, initiated not (as one might expect) by the Phoenicians but by the Greeks. Armed Greek merchant sailors abduct Medea, the daughter of the king of Colchis. When the king demands "reparations and his daughter's return," he is told unequivocally that "the Greeks had no intention of offering reparation, having received none themselves for the abduction of Io from Argos" (1965: 14). The Greeks' impeccable rhetorical balancing here – Medea for Io – conceals their sophistical reasoning: their lack of reparation for Io is irrelevant since the Greeks in effect helped themselves to reparations by abducting Europa.

And so this third abduction gives rise to a fourth.

> Some forty or fifty years afterwards Paris, the son of Priam, was inspired by these stories to steal a wife for himself out of Greece, being confident that he would not have to pay for the venture any more than the Greeks had done. And that was how he came to carry off Helen. (1965: 14)

History again repeats itself. The Greeks' demand for return and reparations is rebuffed with a reference to precedent: "the seizure of Medea and the injustice of expecting satisfaction from people to whom they themselves had refused it, not to mention the fact that they had kept the girl" (14).

Herodotus is sanguine about these international diplomatic incidents: "thus far there had been nothing worse than woman-stealing on both sides" (14). His benign attitude implies a four-way equivalence: Europa equals Io; Helen equals Medea. But as Timothy Long points out (1987: 48), Europa, Io, and Medea are all unmarried virgin princesses; Helen is a wife and a queen. The equation becomes unbalanced when Paris steals Helen.

Technically the terms of the equation are equal because all women are the property of a male, whether their father or husband, although Helen's situation is complicated by her morganatic status: without her as queen of Sparta, Menelaus would not be king. Yet the value of Helen (and hence the imbalance of the equation) is a recurrent theme in Helen stories. As Shakespeare's Troilus puts it:

> for an old aunt whom the Greeks held captive,
> He brought a Grecian queen, whose youth and freshness
> Wrinkles Apollo's and makes stale the morning.
> (*Troilus and Cressida* 2.2.79–81)

The "old aunt," Priam's sister, Hesione, is not a feature of Herodotus' account, although she features prominently in medieval and early modern narratives, where the abduction of Helen is the Trojans' revenge for the Greeks' capture of Hesione, and where the value of an aged Hesione versus a young Helen is much debated.[6]

Herodotus does not interrogate the logic of his *quid pro quo* abductions. Instead of questioning the Trojans, he shows the Persians taking the Greeks to task for their folly in defending Helen. "Abducting young women . . . is not, indeed, a lawful act; but it is stupid after the event to make a fuss about it" (14). Their reason for this view is given in the first epigraph to this chapter, a shortsightedly straightforward belief that a woman cannot be forced against her will.[7] They stress the slightness of the international insult ("merely on account of a girl from Sparta") as the cause of pan-Achaian mobilization and the enmity of Greece and Asia.

Herodotus' is a story of origins. It is also a story of stories. Paris' abduction is "inspired by these stories" of Io and Europa. He is also inspired by the fact that these stories have no end, no consequence (moral or literary): he is "confident that he would not have to pay for the venture any more than the Greeks had done." Herodotus' account presents both the Persian and Phoenician stories. In the Persians' account of the enmity between Greece and Asia, Io was abducted. But the Phoenicians have a different story, one that denies the rape narrative. "On the contrary, the girl [Io] while she was still in Argos went to bed with the ship's captain, found herself pregnant, and, ashamed to face her parents, sailed away voluntarily to escape exposure" (1965: 15). In these few brisk paragraphs Herodotus encapsulates three recurring topics in Helen narratives. This is a story of rape. The rape may have been willing or unwilling. And Helen's is not the only rape.

Wherever one begins (or ends) the narrative it is a story of rape. The *Cypria* tells of the rape of Nemesis by Zeus (in Hesiod 1977: 499) that leads to the birth of Helen; other accounts offer the rape of Leda by swan-Zeus as the origin of Helen. Helen is then abducted by Theseus. The seizure of the Trojan Hesione by the Greek Telamon is a focus of all medieval Troy books. This motivates the Trojans' retaliatory rape of Helen. The *Iliad* begins with Agamemnon's seizure of Achilles' girl-captive Briseis. Nor does the Trojan War halt the sequence. In Euripides' *Women of Troy* Helen says that after the death of Paris, his brother Deiphobus, "*defying the whole city's wish*, took me by force / And kept me as his wife" (Euripides 1973: 121).[8] Dictys Cretensis repeats this information (Frazer 1966: 101). And the abductions continue. In his *Historia Destructionis Troiae* Guido delle Colonne tells us that after the Trojan War, Pyhrrus "abducted Hermione [the daughter of Helen and Menelaus] by stealth from Orestes [her husband]" (delle Colonne / Meek 1974: 257). That gives us a total of seven rapes before one factors in Herodotus' additional three.

Any account of rape is also a story of agency (as today, where a key question in rape trials is: Did the woman consent?). I want to emphasize one point in Herodotus: his stress on female agency in alleged abduction. He switches to the present tense to tell us that women cannot be abducted against their will. He tells us that, in the Phoenicians' view, at least one woman (Io) "voluntarily" left Greece to cover up the fact that she had illicitly enjoyed sex. The Phoenicians also grant agency to Io's women who engage in consumer pastimes at the Phoenician market, "buying what they fancied" (1965: 13). These women "deal for what they want" (Long 1987: 46). But what kinds of goods are we talking about? Agency here is interpreted as agency elsewhere.

The issue of female consent, and how it functions in Helen stories with plural rapes, is the focus of the rest of this chapter.

Chaucer and Narrative Gaps

The text that best illustrates the ambiguity of consent is Chaucer's *Troilus and Criseyde*.[9] Helen has little to do in this Trojan narrative, which is, as its title indicates, a love story (or a story of illicit sex) between the Trojan prince Troilus and the Trojan daughter of Calchas (Homer's Chryses), the priest of Apollo who has defected to the Greeks. Troilus pines and starves in traditional medieval fashion for love of Cressida. Troilus' friend, Pandar, uncle to Cressida, manipulates his niece into situations of professed innocence that enable Troilus to view Cressida, maneuver her into visiting him on his sickbed, gain her pity, secretly invade her bedchamber, win her love, and eventually spend nights with her.

One such situation occurs at a dinner party at the house of Prince Deiphobus, Troilus' favorite brother (and, later, Helen's husband after Paris' death). The ostensible reason for the dinner is that Criseyde, as a guest, may approach her host Deiphobus and ask for his protection in a law-suit brought against her. (As a widow, Criseyde is wealthy; this law-suit against her land holdings clearly has a prior existence but its current threat is a fabrication of Pandar.) The real reason for the dinner is to create an opportunity for Troilus to meet Criseyde alone. Suffering from fever, Troilus absents himself from the meal and goes to bed. His family visits him but because "the chaumbre is but lite [little]" (2.1646) Pandar excludes his niece. He then despatches Deiphobus and Helen to the garden to read a business letter on which Hector needs advice; and he prevails upon Criseyde to visit and comfort the sick Troilus after the family visit has concluded.

Throughout the preceding dinner Helen is a model of grace and compassion. This is Helen domesticated: a hostess, initiating conversation (2.1605, 1625–7), holding Criseyde's hand (2.1604), comforting Troilus (2.1672–3), exuding sympathy (2.1576–7). But there is an undercurrent of sexual tension, apparent to any reader who knows of her subsequent marriage to Deiphobus. When Deiphobus suggests the dinner in support of Criseyde, his first thought is to invite Helen because she has influence with Paris. But as Baswell and Taylor wonder, "why not just invite Paris himself?" (1988: 307).

At the dinner Helen and Deiphobus function as a couple. When they retire to the garden to peruse "a tretys and a lettre" (2.1697), they spend an hour in "an herber greene" [a green arbor], which is "not the usual spot for legal discussions" (Baswell and Taylor 1988: 307). This Helen is "Chaucer's creation": McKay Sundwall reminds us that although she "appears briefly in *Il Filostrato* she speaks no words" (1975: 152). Chaucer does not present Helen as unequivocally overstepping the boundaries of brother–sister friendship, but he allows the possibility. The frequency with which he stresses her title "Queene," a homonym for "quean" [= harlot] (Baswell and Taylor 1988: 306), and the stress on the terms "brother" and "sister," which are not just familial but a "halfway house on the road to courtly love" (Sundwall 1975: 153), coupled with Pandarus' confidence that Deiphobus and Helen will be absent for an hour, leads Sundwall to conclude that the episode is "a double tryst": Deiphobus and Helen are as eager for privacy as is Troilus (Sundwall 1975: 155).

Criseyde is (probably) innocent, her tryst a set-up by Pandarus and Troilus. But the depiction of Criseyde struggling with and succumbing to temptation is a slow-motion gloss on Helen's earlier situation. Classical literature is silent about the moment of Helen's transfer from Sparta to Troy; Helen has no interiority. The medieval Troy books chronicle the transfer at length: Helen's curiosity to see Paris' renowned beauty, her techniques of flirtation, her willingness (or reluctance or ambivalence), her later regrets and nostalgia for Sparta. Joseph of Exeter (1180s) who has most interest in pseudo-psychological matters, presents *raptus* from two points of view, that of the willing and unwilling woman. His Helen is willing, "ready to touch hands if asked and yet wanting to be forced"; "Trojan Paris snatches Helen as she holds out her hands, encouraging him with her happy expression" (Joseph/Bate 1986: 137, 139). Hesione, the Trojan princess abducted by Telamon, is unwilling. Joseph dwells on the emotions of the abducted woman as she endures her own wedding celebration:

> Only Hesione upsets the festivities with her unsmiling face. She scorns the applause and hates the well-wishers, unmoved by her new position or marvellous dowry and unimpressed by her new life-style. She thinks of herself as abducted [*sibi rapta videri*]. She complains sadly, and . . . fears for herself as a captive, not trusting in her freedom, but going into a forced marriage afraid and under duress [*sed iussa in thalamos timide ventura coactos*]. (83)

Antenor perceptively questions whether a captive can "find pleasure from her captor," but Telamon, "snatching unwelcome kisses from the weeping Hesione," replies, "I earned by my sword the right to enjoy her embraces" (85).

In *Troilus and Criseyde* book 3, Chaucer offers a related moment of sexual tension and enforcement: not between Troilus and Criseyde but between Criseyde and her uncle. Unlike Joseph's text, Chaucer's is characterized by ambiguity and omission; and it is what he does not say that interests me here. Let us look at how Chaucer leads up to the episode.

Chaucer's Pandarus is both uncle to Criseyde and bosom friend to Troilus; he is himself an unrequited lover, experiencing the same despair as Troilus. Long before he manipulates his niece, however, his morals are shown to be wanting. In book 1 he makes a casual suggestion of incest: he would not block Troilus' unknown love even if it were love for his sister-in-law, Helen (1.676–8). Book 2 opens with Pandarus half asleep until the noise of the swallow wakens him fully. The swallow, Procne, sings of the incestuous rape of her sister Philomel (turned into a nightingale after she was raped by her brother-in-law). The fact that Pandar is "*half* in slomberynge" (my italics) is suggestive: is it his conscious or unconscious thoughts that are attuned to Philomel's story? He sets out to see Criseyde and talk to her of love. Is he still thinking of incest here, as later in the same book when he enables Deiphobus' and Helen's privacy?[10]

In book 3 he himself seems to engage in incestuous dalliance or activity with his niece Criseyde. Chaucer does not say what happened between uncle and niece in bed any more than he tells us what happened between Deiphobus and Helen in the arbor. But he draws our attention to what he is not saying ("I passe al that which chargeth nought to seye"; 3.1576), to what cannot be said.

The episode begins with Pandarus visiting Criseyde in her bedroom in his house after Troilus has left, the young couple having spent their first night together. Criseyde blushes in embarrassment and covers her face with the sheets, whereupon "Pandarus gan under for to prie" (3.1571). Then, "his arm al sodeynly he thriste / Under hire nekke, and at the laste hire kyste" (suddenly he thrust his arm under her neck and finally kissed her; 3.1574–5). Is there an interlude (and if so, how long?) before the "at the laste"? Whatever happens after this kiss happens in the blank space between the stanzas and is over (or continues) when the poet resumes narration:

> I passe al that which chargeth nought to seye.
> What! God foryaf his deth, and she al so
> Foryaf, and with here uncle gan to pleye,
> For other cause was ther noon than so.
> But of this thing right to the effect to go:
> Whan tyme was, home til here house she wente,
> And Pandarus hath fully his intente.
>
> (3.1576–82)

This stanza begins and ends by excising the female point of view. The poet passes over the unimportant ("which chargeth nought to seye"). But unimportant to whom? Not, presumably, to the surprised and compromised Criseyde. It ends with the smugly triumphant acknowledgment that Pandarus got what he wanted. Sandwiched between is Criseyde whose act of apparent agency ("*gan* to pleye") is seen as reactive, defensive, coerced: "other cause was ther noon than so" [there was nothing else she could do but respond to him].[11] And as is typical of narratives of *raptus*, whether legal or literary, the narrative omits the emotional event and proceeds to the aftermath: "right to the effect to go."

Marion Turner points out (personal communication) that if Chaucer draws our attention to narrative lack, so too, in a different way, does the Riverside commentator, Stephen A. Barney, who protests:

> The now widespread view that Pandarus here seduces or rapes Criseyde, or that Chaucer hints at such an action, is baseless and absurd. The statement, for example, published in 1979, that "criticism has widely ignored or failed to appreciate the suggestiveness of this scene" is incorrect; all too much has been written about its "suggestiveness." (Chaucer 1987: 1043, note to *Troilus and Criseyde* 3.1555–82)

So vehement is Barney in his protestation, so insistent that there is nothing there, that he fails to include a citation for the 1979 view to which he is objecting. The combination of editorial presence (blustering tone) and academic absence (lack of reference) indicates not just denial but editorial breakdown (Turner, personal communication).

Criseyde (later called Cressid or Cressida in the early modern period) is relevant to any exploration of Helen of Troy's *raptus* because she is regularly associated with the name and behavior of Helen of Troy. In fact in the early modern period "Cressida" and "Helen" were interchangeable onomastic shorthand for the type of the sexually wanton woman. In George Pettie's *A Petite Palace of Petty's Pleasure* (1576), the married Procris repels an unwelcome suitor, challenging his assumption that she is sexually available: "you are conversant with no Cressid, you have no Helen in hand" (sig. Y2v). Like Petty, contemporary academics, whether writing about Chaucer or Shakespeare, view Cressida and Helen as parallel or related characters. For Sundwall, Chaucer's Helen is "a foil for Criseyde" (1975: 155); for Baswell and Taylor she is a "mirror" and a "model" for Criseyde (1988: 310); for Rutter she is Cressida's "distorted twin" (2000: 229). In Shakespeare's *All's Well That Ends Well* the clown associates the heroine Helen with her namesake, singing a popular ballad (" 'Was this fair face the cause,' quoth she, 'Why the Grecians sacked Troy' "; 1.3.70–1), but the courtier Lafew associates her with Cressida (leaving her with the King, he comments "I am Cressid's uncle, / That dare leave two together" (2.1.97–8). Helen and Cressida are consistently linked.

With the exception of medieval Troy books, which present the meeting of Helen and Paris in Sparta (or Cythera) in considerable detail, most Helen narratives place her in Troy. That is where her story begins in Chaucer, it is where stories of *raptus* begin in law: "that is, *after* the act" (Cannon

2001: 78). The law is not interested in motivation, emotion, persuasion, seduction, vacillation, conflicted personal allegiances, reluctance, fear, regret, happiness (at whatever cost), consent or the conditions under which it might have been granted or coerced. Shakespeare, however, is. Like many literary works from Homer onwards, his play about the Trojan War, *Troilus and Cressida*, does not depict origins; it "leaps o'er the vaunt and firstlings of those broils, / Beginning in the middle" (Prologue 27–8). But that does not mean that Shakespeare neglects those origins. Through the figure of Cressida, he investigates the position of Helen, writing a scene in which a woman is removed from one man in her home town (Troilus in Troy) and handed over to another (Diomedes in the Greek camp). He offers an action replay of the circumstances in which Helen might have changed allegiance in the other direction, from Greece to Troy.

Helen and Cressida

From the outset Shakespeare's Helen and Cressida are equated: Pandarus says Cressida is "as fair a' Friday as Helen is on Sunday" [i.e., Helen in her Sunday best is as beautiful as Cressida is daily] (1.1.76). When Paris' servant describes Helen in 3.1, Pandarus assumes from the description that he is referring to Cressida:

SERVANT: . . . the mortal Venus, the heart-blood of beauty, love's invisible soul.
PANDARUS: Who? My cousin Cressida?
SERVANT: No, sir, Helen. Could not you find out that by her attributes?
PANDARUS: It should seem, fellow, thou hast not seen the lady Cressid.
(3.1.32–8)

Troilus refers to both women as a "pearl." In the RSC production of 1968, the women were visually indistinguishable, making a mockery of a war fought over one of them, and illustrating the play's premise that value is subjective.

The situations and seductions of Helen and Cressida are parallel. Both women have a dual identity: Helen is a Greek, living in Troy; Cressida is a Trojan, summoned to her father in Greek territory. Both women are loved by a Greek and a Trojan. As Baswell and Taylor observe of Chaucer's *Troilus and Criseyde*, men put Cressida in a position where "she must betray someone": to cleave to Troilus is to betray her father; to go to the Greeks means betraying Troilus. Her options mean "she must be Helen either way" (1988: 310).

Nowhere is this clearer than in the scene in which Shakespeare's Cressida is delivered to the Greek camp. Cressida's situation replays Helen's: a beautiful woman is forced to leave one man (Menelaus/Troilus) and is carried away by a foreigner (Paris/Diomedes). Although Helen's complicity in her abduction was by no means certain, by the early modern period her guilt was a foregone conclusion: one school test of pupils' debating skill required students to argue *pro et contra* Helen (cf. Colie 1966: 8–9). In Marlowe's *Edward 2* Lancaster compares Gaveston to "the Greekish strumpet" who "trained to arms / And bloody wars so many valiant knights" (2.5.15–17). Emilia Lanyer chastises Helen with lack of virtue in *Salve Deus Rex Judaeorum* (lines 190–2). Shakespeare's Lucrece inveighs against Helen as "the strumpet that began this stir" (*Rape of Lucrece* 1471). Shakespeare is not as judgmental as his Roman heroine, however. In *Troilus and Cressida* he writes the scene that all other early modern Helen narratives leave out: the scene of transition between home and abroad. Medieval Troy books present Helen's temptations and ambivalence at length, but Shakespeare replaces their slightly cartoonish emotional tug of war with Cressida's complex conflict.

Troilus has apparently abandoned Cressida emotionally: he talks about the relationship in terminative terms, passively accepts her removal (contrast her passionate refusals to leave), and leaves her with so many comminatory assumptions of her infidelity that she, not unreasonably, concludes, "oh heavens, you love me not" (4.4.82). On arrival in the Greek camp she is exposed to further trauma – the verbal and osculatory equivalents of gang rape, with a group of soldiers making bawdy jokes and taking turns at kissing her: "our general doth salute you with a kiss. / . . . 'Twere better she were kiss'd in general" (4.5.19–21). As Laura Johnstone points out (personal communication), the silence of this normally vocally assertive woman for a full 20 to 30 lines after her entrance into the scene is striking. She eventually finds her emotional feet, and her tongue, retaliating wittily, "In kissing do you render or receive? . . . I'll make my match to live, / The kiss you take is better than you give" (4.5.36–8). This defensive self-assertiveness, occasioned by the situation in which she finds herself, is interpreted by Ulysses as coquetry:

> There's language in her eye, her cheek, her lip,
> Nay, her foot speaks; her wanton spirits look out
> At every joint and motive of her body.
>
> (4.6.55–7)[12]

Cressida turns to her guardian in the Greek camp, Diomedes, but he abuses his position. He pressurizes Cressida to give him the love token from her

Trojan lover, a sign of her transfer of love from Troilus to Diomedes. He ignores Cressida's evident reluctance, pain, and ambivalence, using a simple tactic – anger – thus making the episode one of male coercion rather than female agreement. Cressida's instinct is to halt his anger at all costs. "Nay, but you part in anger," says Cressida to Diomedes (5.2.44), and Troilus (eavesdropping on the scene) asks, aside, "Doth that grieve thee?" His interpretation could not be more wrong. It does not grieve Cressida; it frightens her. The dialogue between Diomedes and Cressida repeats one pattern throughout the scene: she asserts herself in making a request, he breaks off in evident anger, and she capitulates. Diomedes is on the point of exit several times in the scene, but Cressida cannot let him part in anger. He gets what he wants, even though it is clear that this is not what she wants. Her "No" goes unheard. (I omit all asides from the three eavesdroppers and add stage directions.)

> CRESSIDA: Tempt me no more to folly . . .
> DIOMEDES: Nay then – [*he offers to exit*]
> CRESSIDA: I'll tell you what –
>
> (5.1.18–21)

*

> CRESSIDA: I prithee do not hold me to mine oath,
> Bid me do anything but that, sweet Greek.
> DIOMEDES: Good night . . . [*he offers to exit*]
> CRESSIDA Diomed –
> DIOMEDES: No, no, good night; I'll be your fool no more. [*he offers to exit*]
> CRESSIDA: Hark, a word in your ear . . .
>
> (5.1.26–34)

*

> DIOMEDES: And so, good night. [*he offers to exit*]
> CRESSIDA: Nay, but you part in anger.
>
> (5.1.44–5)

Cressida then gives Diomedes Troilus' pledge but instantly regrets the gift and recalls it. Diomedes insists on having it, and aggressively questions Cressida about its original owner. It is clear from the conversation between Diomedes and Troilus in 4.4 that Diomedes can be in no doubt about the identity of his rival, but his insistent "Whose was it?" (repeated four times at 71, 87, 88, 90) indicates his need to have Cressida surrender fully. Cressida bravely defies Diomedes – "I will not keep my word" – but Diomedes' angry threat of exit, his fifth (at line 98), is more than she can cope with: "You shall not go. One cannot speak a word / But it straight starts you" (5.1.100–1). She accurately identifies his behavioral pattern (i.e., "I can't say anything without you reacting with anger and withdrawal"). He ignores her diagnosis *cum* plea, uttering only a terse (and, in the BBC film, extremely menacing) response: "I do not like this fooling" (5.1.101).[13]

As Clifford Lyons points out (1964: 115), the storyline of Shakespeare's Cressida–Diomedes plot is simple: Diomedes will leave her if she will not submit. And Cressida needs Diomedes' protection (she twice calls him "guardian"; he refers to her as his "charge") at any cost. As Chris Cannon observes of the equivalent scene in Chaucer, Cressida's submission to Diomedes takes place under such "conditions of 'force' and 'fear' that it is hard to distinguish between rape and betrayal" (2001: 87). Shakespeare critics note that Cressida, like Helen, emerges as the victim of a world that condemns her for behaving in the very way it has forced her to behave to survive. Out of such self-protection is reputation lost – and legend born. The myth of Helen, Shakespeare suggests, may originate in circumstances more complex than words like "consent" or "abduction" or "rape" suggest.

In contrast to the scenes between Cressida and her lovers, the scene between Helen and Paris in *Troilus and Cressida* is remarkable in the play for its emotional reciprocity and conversational health. The couple *converse*. Paris shares a joke with Helen (3.1.52–3); they assess Pandarus' mood (3.1.127–30); Helen volunteers information in response to Paris' general question about Troilus (3.1.137–40); Helen compliments Paris (3.1.99–100), and he compliments her (3.1.150–4). Paris' mode of address to Helen is permissive and petitionary rather than peremptory: "*Let us* to Priam's hall . . . / Sweet Helen, *I must woo you* / To help unarm our Hector" (3.1.148, 149–50, my italics). Given his position in Troy as Helen's lord, he might put his requests more into command than entreaty – as do Hector, Troilus, and Diomedes to Andromache and Cressida. Instead, we have a scene of conversational give and take remarkable in the play for its straightforward honesty. The manipulative anger of Diomedes, which forces Cressida's betrayal in act 5, scene 2, contrasts with Paris' treatment of Helen and her evident acquiescence in her sojourn in Troy.

But to infer Helen's attitude at the point of seduction/abduction from her subsequent behavior in Troy is impossible. Baswell and Taylor point out all the logical reasons why Helen must "enjoy" herself in Troy: she is personally vulnerable if she does not. And together these scenes raise the question of what consent means in the play and in the early modern world.

The topic of sexual consent interested Shakespeare throughout his career.[14] It is also a topic that English law was debating in the 1590s. Law and literature were in constant dialogue in the early modern period, if not mutually constitutive; plays, like rhetoric, science, and the law, were fascinated with proof, demonstration, suspicion, and adjudication.[15] For details of rape law we can read the statutes but statutes, by their nature, do not read between the lines: they pronounce; they do not comment. For commentary we need to turn to T. E.'s *The Law's Resolution of Women's Rights* (1632), a 400-page book whose subtitle explains its contents and purpose: *The Law's Provision for Women. A Methodical Collection of Such Statutes and Customs, with the Cases, Opinions, Arguments and Points of Hearing in the Law as Do Properly Concern Women.* Although published in 1632, T. E.'s illuminating compendium discusses material from medieval legal authorities onward, for little had changed between the first statute of Westminster in 1275 and 39 Elizabeth in 1597. T. E. offers personal opinions on the subject of consent and introduces a term and a distinction – willful versus unwilled *raptus* – which appears in relation to Helen of Troy in Shakespeare. First let us turn to *The Law's Resolution*.

The Law's Resolution of Women's Rights (1632)

Although a lawyer or law student, T. E. himself is not (he says) the author of this book. He explains that he found the work so useful that he decided to publish it with his own corrections and additions (of reasons, opinions, cases, and resolutions of cases). The book claims to be useful for women but the legal detail, as well as the frequency of sentences and paragraphs in Latin, suggest that its primary audience was lawyers. But this is not a law handbook; it is a reflective personal interpretation of the law as it relates to women, written by a man with a compassionate attitude to women and the injustices to which they were vulnerable.

T. E. abhors rape and sexual violence of any kind. "What was it that made the law so meek in Edward I's time," he asks, "that the first statute against rape speaketh of it so mildly as if it had been . . . a very small trespass" (1632: 380). He is amazed at the ineffectiveness of Westminster 2: "a man would have thought that this statute should have repressed for ever all violence towards the persons of women" (381). And he acknowledges male pressure: "if the rampier [rampart] of laws were not betwixt women and their harms, I verily think none of them, being above twelve years of age and under an hundred, being either fair or rich, should be able to escape ravishing" (377).

T. E. explains that the word ravishment covers "two kinds of rape." The first kind is "when a woman is enforced violently to sustain the fury of brutish concupiscence" and is "left in the place where this crime occurred" such as her own house or bed. An example of this type of victim is Lucrece. The second kind of rape – what T. E. calls "right ravishment" – is abduction. His examples here are Helen, abducted by Paris, and the Sabine Women, abducted by the Romans. But the clear-cut distinction between forced coitus and abduction is complicated by a Latin parenthesis that describes abduction itself as of two types: the woman may be *volente vel nolente rapta* (willingly or unwillingly seized).

T. E. twice notes the problematic conditions in which female consent to coition can hardly be consensual: fear of death, duress, force (1632: 396, 400). "Assent must be voluntary," he writes, otherwise "it is a rape against her will" (396). He cites a woman who submitted yet accused her violator of rape; she explained that "her flesh consented to him but her soul and conscience did ever abhor him" (400). T. E. is consistently interested in distinctions of this kind, and devotes one section to "a question what is meant by ravishment with force."

To us today the phrase is tautological, as Margaret Atwood's judge jocularly points out in the second epigraph to this chapter. The legal authority William Lambarde (1536–1601) thought the phrase "but declaratory [i.e., only emphatic]," T. E. says. T. E. concludes that the statute "must needs intend two kinds of ravishments," that it views one as "more odious than the other," and observes that it decrees death "to him which ravisheth with force." Rape with force, says T. E is "of all other most hateful" (1632: 397).

Like his distinction between consent of the flesh and consent of the mind, T. E.'s discussion of rape with and without force raises problems. As Barbara Baines explains:

> when unwilled (involuntary) carnal pleasure is defined by such phrases as "consent of the body" or "the will of the body," then the phrase "consent of the mind" becomes necessary to represent what the word "consent" alone should signify. "Consent of the mind" is, however, as redundant as "forcible rape" or "rape with force." (1998: 91)[16]

Literary characters often distinguish between two kinds of rape. When Marston's Sophonisba declares "thou maist enforce my body but not me" (sig. D2v) she is granting consent of the body and withholding consent of the mind. A similar distinction is raised in relation to Helen of Troy through the character of Nell Quickly in Shakespeare's *Henry 4* and *Henry 5* plays.

In the early modern period "Nell" was a standard abbreviation for "Helen" – and for Helen of Troy. Helen of Troy is called "Nell" by Middleton and Rowley in *The Old Law*, by Fletcher in *The Tamer Tamed*, and by Shakespeare in *Troilus and Cressida*. Shakespeare critics have long viewed this last example as pejorative or ironic, the reduction of an icon to a homely diminutive, but the frequency with which early modern writers call Helen of Troy "Nell" militates against any negative association. It is simply a variant form like Mary and Moll. Literary Nells therefore demand inclusion in a study of Helen of Troy in literature. And Shakespeare's Nell Quickly in the *Henry 4* and *Henry 5* plays is parallel to her Trojan namesake.

Nell Quickly is fought over by two suitors, Nym and Pistol; like Helen, she engages in needlework, living (suggestively) by the prick of her lodgers' needles (*Henry 5* 2.1.32–4); when she and Doll Tearsheet face arrest we are told, in an ambiguity of personal pronoun that could apply to either woman, "there hath been a man or two kill'd about her" (*2 Henry 4* 5.4.6). Of particular interest then is the Hostess's unusual collocation in *Henry 5* 2.1 when Nym and Pistol, her rival suitors draw: "if he be not hewn now, we shall see willful adultery and murther [murder] committed" (2.1.36–8). The Riverside gloss suggests that the Hostess intends "*assaultery*, her own version of *assault and battery*" (2.1.37n). This gloss is based on the assumption that "willful adultery" (= consenting adultery) is both a malapropism and a tautology. The first it may be, but the second is valid in contemporary terms only where we take for granted that the *Oxford English Dictionary* definition of adultery – "violation of the marriage bed" (1a) – refers to voluntary violation. Involuntary violation goes by another name: rape. But in the early modern period, the question of consent is irrelevant legally, if not emotionally. *Raptus* was a crime against the male owner of the woman (her husband or her father). Thus in *The Law's Resolution* T. E. devotes a section to adultery with and without consent, yet classifies both as rape (1632: 390; Catty 1999: 13).

Like rape and abduction, the concepts of rape and adultery were inextricably intertwined in the early modern period: what the law has joined together critics cannot put asunder. But early modern women, like Nell Quickly, can. For women the two categories – willful and unwilled adultery – are inevitably distinct. Mistress Quickly is legally aware (in *1 Henry 4* she challenges Falstaff with his debts [3.3.65ff]; in *2 Henry 4* she brings a lawsuit against him [2.1.1–131]); and in *Henry 5*, in the linguistically feminized space of the tavern, she appropriates for herself the Adamic power of naming, making a distinction where the law does not. Mistress Quickly names as a separate category – willful adultery – what the law calls rape.

Like Marston's Sophonisba she sees the difficulty in subsuming under one heading a spectrum of sexual activity or crime.

Distinguishing adultery from rape is a problem throughout Helen narratives, usually phrased in the blunt binary interrogative Was she willing or was she abducted? Given that legal history uses one term, *raptus*, for a variety of acts (adultery, abduction, forced coition) answering that question proves difficult.

Statute Change in 1597

The penalty for *raptus* was severe: capital punishment. Marriage to the victim was a way of avoiding this penalty. (In fact the law itself could enforce marriage to the victim; thus abduction – or the penalty for abduction – could be a way for lovers to elope and marry without parental consent.) Malefactors could also plead "benefit of clergy." By claiming membership of an educated class (formerly the clergy, a claim proven by one's ability to read; subsequently the test of privilege became itself the ground of privilege), an abductor could save his life.

In 1597 a statute addressed "*the taking away of women against their will unlawfully.*" The point of the statute change was to remove benefit of clergy from male abductors who hoped to avoid capital punishment. Statute change does not come from nowhere, and we might wonder what prompted this change in law.[17] The act begins with a gesture to context:

> *whereas of late times diverse women, as well maidens as widows and wives, having substance, some in goods moveable and some in lands and tenements, and some being heirs apparent to their ancestors, for the lucre of such substance have been oftentimes taken by misdoers contrary to their will and afterward married to such misdoers, or to others by their assent, or defiled . . .*

Recently, then ("*of late*"), the abduction of propertied women has increased.

But a specific abduction case was associated with this tightening of the law. Hayward Townshend's journal for this parliament reads:

> It was thought the cause of this motion was by reason one Mr Donnington had stolen a great heir in Devonshire or that ways but yet with her consent which she constantly stood unto, the said Donnington being arraigned here at Newgate for the same and acquitted before this parliament. (Hartley 1995, vol. 3: 232)

In fact the "great heir" came not from Devonshire but from Dorset as we find in the Acts of the Privy Council for June 14. Her name was Alice Stoite, she had been taken away "by violence," she had been in the custody of the Sheriff of London, and was now to be returned to Dorset to give evidence at the Assizes against her abductor (Dasent 1903: 201–2). Five months later Alice Stoite's case came to parliamentary debate: the bill passed as 39 Elizabeth cap. 9 was read in the Commons and Lords in early November.[18]

As it happens, Alice's father, Henry, had made his will in January of that year, so we have an exact reckoning of his wealth, and Alice's inheritance, as it stood a few months before her elopement/abduction, as well as the environment in which she lived.[19] Stoite has a son (with whom he jointly holds a lease on a farm) and three daughters, Elizabeth, Christiane and Alice, of whom the last (his youngest) is unmarried. Alice is young (she is to receive her bequeathed items when she reaches 16 or on her marriage day) and she is clearly a concern: money is left to a neighbor "to the intent he should be a guide unto my youngest daughter Alice, in the government and usage of such cattle as by this my will shall be bequeathed unto her." All three daughters are well provided for. Elizabeth receives 6 cows, 100 sheep, and Stoite's best silver salter. Christiane receives 30 cows, a bull, 2 mares with their colts under a year old, 30 sheep, and "half a dozen of my best silver spoons" as well as the remaining lease of years on parkland in a neighboring parish. The bulk of Stoite's goods go to Alice: the leases of years yet to come on 2 pieces of land; 22 cows, a bull, and all his hog sheep; his half part of the lease on the farm and its chattels held jointly with his son; £300 in cash; "my best bedstead and best cupboard, two pairs of sheets, two pairs of blankets, two coverlets and my best feather bed and bolster, and also my spayed mare with her late mother's saddle and furniture, and also half a dozen of my best silver spoons."

Given the large number of livestock bequeathed to others beside his children, and the bequests of money to friends, relatives, and the poor, Stoite was relatively affluent. To earn the £10 given to each of two friends' daughters on their marriage day, a playwright would have to write five plays at the standard rate of £2 a play (contracted playwrights such as Shakespeare generally wrote two to three plays a year). Alice's £300 of "current money of England" is a substantial amount, plus land, livestock, furniture, and silver. Townshend's description of her as a "great heir" seems justified.[20]

Nazife Bashar writes that because the statute of 1597 "treated abduction separately from rape . . . [it] had the indirect effect of establishing rape and abduction as separate offences" (1983: 41). This is the statute with which T. E. in 1632 concludes his section on rape. But he has little to say about it beyond repeating its terms, and certainly does not pick up on its implications as articulated by Bashar above. This may be because he has already established rape and abduction as separate offences in his own discussion. The further implication noted by legal historians also goes unremarked: that the separation of rape from abduction indirectly introduces a concept if not a word that characterizes all rape trials today – consent (because abduction may have the woman's consent but rape (in the modern sense) never does; hence from 1597 lack of consent became an offense against the woman herself, not against her male "owner"). Once again, T. E. has previously had much to say on the subject of consent, so does not discuss it here.

Although Alice Stoite's name is associated with the parliamentary debate and statute change of 1597, hers was a convenient case on which to base a debate rather than a *cause célèbre* that prompted outrage and change. The same bill had been broached in Parliament in 1593 but had not passed. It is therefore too much to claim that Alice Stoite's case in 1597 and the consequent statue change would have made the distinction between rape and abduction, or the concept of consent, a widespread contemporary debate and topical issue. T. E.'s work in 1632 illustrates how one can be interested in this distinction independently of any legal topicality. But Parliament's two debates on the topic in 1593 and 1597 coincide with Shakespeare's most intense exploration of female consent in Helen-related situations. And, as Marion Wynne-Davies notes, the very fact of new rape legislation "after a century's inactivity reveals a peak of interest in, and concern about, sexual assault" (1991: 131). Let us move from the late to the early 1590s.

The Rape of Lucrece (1594)

Rape provides not just a sexual trauma but an ontological impasse for the early modern woman: if a woman struggles to resist her assailant, kicks, screams, calls for help, she violates the decorum of her sex and class; and a woman who is deemed vocally and physically active in this context is deemed active in other contexts. As Elizabethan and Jacobean drama shows, a woman who opens one orifice (her mouth) will open another (Paster 1987) just as Herodotus indicates that a woman who bargains in one sphere can bargain in another.

Shakespeare's Lucrece is verbally vociferous in her resistance of Tarquin:

> She conjures him by high almighty Jove,
> By knighthood, gentry, and sweet friendship's oath,

By her untimely tears, her husband's love,
By holy human law and common troth,
By heaven and earth, and all the power of both,
That to his borrowed bed he make retire
And stoop to honor, not to foul desire.

(568–74)

We witness her eloquence when, in line 575, the poem switches to direct speech and Lucrece's voice is heard appealing to Tarquin with emotive and logical arguments for 91 lines. Nor does she show any sign of stopping; her flow is cut off midline by Tarquin, "'No more,' quoth he. 'By heaven I will not hear thee'" (667).

When Lucrece relates her experience to Collatine, Brutus, and her father, however, she edits out this part of the story. Instead, she presents herself as one who began to "start and cry" and who was speechless: "My bloody judge forbod my tongue to speak, / No rightful plea might plead for justice there" (1648–9). She presents herself as the conventional Renaissance female: passive not active, a victim not a protester, for if the paradigm of chaste womanhood is passivity, a passive woman is one who is seen to consent to rape.

Despite Lucrece's lengthy verbal appeals to her assailant, the poem problematizes the question of her consent or resistance. The physical impediments to Tarquin's progress both resist and yield – "each unwilling portal yields him way" (309) – and, like other rapists of the 1590s (and beyond) Tarquin "consters [construes] their denial" as foreplay: "Like little frosts that sometime threat the spring / To add a more rejoicing to the prime" (331–2). Later, the lamenting Lucrece chastises her hand for "yielding" (because her hand failed to deflect Tarquin by scratching him.) The series of obstacles – doors, bolts – which obligingly "yield" to Tarquin as he makes his symbolic journey from outside to inside, from Ardea to Rome, from guest bedroom to Lucrece's chamber, not only enact rape but raise the troublingly ambiguous question of Lucrece's consent (Fineman 1985: *passim*). This was an issue that had occupied commentators from St Augustine on. If Lucrece was innocent, why did she commit suicide? So morally ambiguous was Lucrece's story that, like Helen's, it became a topic for formal disputation (Donaldson 1982: 40).

But what does it mean to consent when the alternative is death and infamy (the alternative that Tarquin offers Lucrece when he threatens to kill both Lucrece and a slave, placing them in each other's arms, thereby bringing shame on Lucrece, Collatine, and Collatine's family)? In one sense Lucrece "consents" to being raped – a hybrid category for which we have no vocabulary.[21]

However, at the moment of Tarquin's penetration of Lucrece, there is no ambiguity. Whereas Ovid and Painter (Shakespeare's sources) depict Lucrece as yielding (succumbing to the threat of shame), Shakespeare's Lucrece is gagged with her own nightgown while Tarquin cools "his hot face in the chastest tears / That ever modest eyes with sorrow shed'" (682–3; Catty 1999: 66). There can be no ambiguity here: Lucrece is raped (in our modern sense).

It is ironic, then, that the victim of one rape should fail to sympathize with the victim of another. Seeking distraction for the agonizing hours until Collatine can return to Rome, Lucrece contemplates a painting of the fall of Troy, addressing it directly: "Show me the strumpet that began this stir" (1471). Fineman views the painting's theme as "ill chosen since, for Shakespeare, if not for Homer, it is the rape of 'strumpet' Helen . . . that occasions the siege, rather than, as happens with the chaste Lucrece, the other way round" (1985: 201). But for Shakespeare, Helen is not a strumpet. Furthermore Lucrece is victim of a rape to which many forces have contributed: her husband's boasts about her superlative beauty, her obligation to provide hospitality to a guest, the rapist's threats, her decision that rape is a lesser shame than that of adultery with a slave. Helen's case may be as complex; certainly, of the factors I have just listed in Lucrece's case, the first two are carbon copies of Helen's situation. Nonetheless Lucrece assumes as she looks at the painting that Helen's case must be unequivocal. She is an unsympathetic biased reader. Shakespeare's implied question (in both *Rape of Lucrece* and *Troilus and Cressida*) is: Are we guilty of the same misreading of Helen?

Helen (of Troy)

For many early moderns, Helen's name was a shorthand for infidelity (a topic explored in the next chapter). It is precisely this condemnatory association from which Shakespeare wishes to rescue his Helen characters when he places Helen or her proxies in plays in which sexual submission or betrayal comes under sympathetic interrogation (Maguire 2007: 74–119). But there is another part to her name: the toponymous addition "of Troy." And that epithet is relevant to the topic of rape.

There is a tense moment in the Hollywood film *Troy* (2004) when Paris presents his Spartan bride to his royal father. "Father, this is Helen," says the prince. "Helen?" inquires Peter O'Toole's Priam sonorously. "Helen of Sparta?" His son corrects him: "Helen of Troy." The film stages a key linguistic transition in Helen narratives, collapsing it into one moment, the moment in which the woman we know as "Helen of Troy" was named. The 1955 film *Helen of Troy* presents the same onomastic issue more leisurely when Helen wonders if she will ever be a Trojan, a proleptically ironic reflection since, for us, Helen is associated only with Troy; her first name is inseparable from her toponym.

It was not always thus. In classical writing she is Helen, Spartan Helen, Helen the Tyndarid (daughter of Tyndareus), Spartan Tyndarid, the Lacedemonian (from Lacedemon, the area in the southeast Peloponnese of which Sparta was the capital),[22] Argive Helen, Leda's Helen. Throughout Ovid's *Metamorphoses*, as throughout most early modern writing, she is simply "Helen." In Thackeray's *Vanity Fair* (1847–8) Helen's name still had currency as a noun without geographical identification: John Jones, intercepted on the point of offering his hand to "the brilliant and exclusive Mrs Rawdon Crawley" [Becky Sharp] at a dinner party, laments that "the young patrician . . . whisked my Helen off without so much as a word of apology" (1977: 570). But for Walter Pater, just 22 years later, Helen had become "Helen of Troy": "Leda was the mother of Helen of Troy, and . . . St Anne the mother of Mary" (1986: 80).[23] Paralleled syntactically with Mary ("the mother of Helen of Troy" / "the mother of Mary"), Helen's name is no longer Helen but "Helen of Troy." By the 1960s "Helen" had lost all cultural currency without her identifying epithet "of Troy." In *One Flew Over the Cuckoo's Nest* (1962) Harding and McMurphy have a conversation about the sexual effects of Nurse Ratched. Harding asks his fellow inmate, "could you get it up over her even if she . . . was young and had the beauty of Helen?" The classical reference is lost on his companion: "I don't know Helen, but . . . I couldn't get it up over old frozen face in there even if she had the beauty of Marilyn Monroe" (1977: 69). Clearly by this date, for McMurphy at least, an identifying tag – "of Troy" – had become necessary.

The moment at which Spartan Helen became Helen of Troy cannot be identified with any precision, but a dialogue in Middleton and Rowley's *The Old Law* (1619) debates the toponymic transition. In a tavern the clown, Gnotho, is enmeshed in a conversation, subsequently a wager, with the cook as to whether the name of a seductive "fair Greek" was Siren or Hiren. The tailor intervenes to caution the clown about his confidence in betting so much money given the tautology of his claim ("Siren's name was Siren, for five drachmas"), and the conversation shifts from Siren to Helen:

CLOWN: Do not I know our own countrywomen Siren and Nell of Greece, two of the fairest Greeks that ever were?
COOK: That Nell was Helen of Greece too.

CLOWN: As long as she tarried with her husband she was Ellen, but after
she came to Troy she was Nell of Troy, or bonny Nell, whether
you will or no.

(4.1.60–5)

Nell, as mentioned earlier, was a standard early modern diminutive of Helen.
In fact the clown views Helen's name as Nell rather than Helen, and it is
the cook who volunteers the full form Helen. The clown insists that she
was Helen (Ellen and Helen were interchangeable variants) only when she
lived in Greece ("as long as she tarried with her husband she was Ellen");
on removal to Troy her name changed ("after she came to Troy she was
Nell of Troy"). The debate is thus about a double name change: "Helen"
becomes "Nell," and "of Greece" becomes "of Troy." The clown has been
interested in names, language, and puns throughout, as are many early modern clowns, albeit less self-consciously, but is his insistence on "Nell of Troy"
reinforcement of an onomastic novelty or reinforcement of a known fact?

Occurrences of "Helen of Troy" are infrequent in the early modern period
compared with occurrences of "Helen of Greece" but both are unusual. I
know of only two sixteenth-century texts that refer to "Helen of Troy":
John Grange's *Golden Aphroditis* of 1577 and Leonard Wright's 1589
Summons for Sleepers. It is the mid-seventeenth century before the epithet
appears again, in Henry Peacham's *Valley of Variety* (1638) and then in
1680 in Charles Blount's translation of Philostratus. Middleton's clown seems
to have identified a mild swell before it became a sea change.

In the same period references to "Helen of Greece" are more numerous.
Lyly's *Euphues* (1578) three times refers to Helen in this way.[24] Thomas
Watson also refers to "Helen of Greece" three times in his *Hekatompathia*
(1582).[25] This is the formula used by the students in Marlowe's *Dr Faustus*
(c.1589) when they determine "that Helen of Greece was the admirablest
lady that ever lived" (5.1.11–12).[26] In 1595 Thomas Churchyard talks of
"faire Helen of Greece" in *A Musical Consort of Heavenly Harmony* (sig.
C1r). John Ford refers to "Helen of Greece" in *Honor Triumphant* (1606)
(sig. D2v) as does Richard Brathwaite in *Nature's Embassy* in 1621 (sig.
G7v). A 1623 translation of Mateo Alemán's *The Rogue* offers "Grecian
Helen" (sig. Tt5r); so too does Philaretes' *Work for Chimney Sweepers* (1602;
sig. A3r). In *The Taming of a Shrew* (1594) she is "Grecian Helena" (sig.
B2r); in Pikering's *Horestes* (1567) she is "the Grecian dame" (line 579).

In the early modern period the phrase "of"-plus-place-name indicates one's
place of origin: John of Bordeaux, Godfrey of Boulogne, Guy of Warwick,
John of Gaunt, Edmund of York, old Sly's son of Burton-heath (*Taming
of the Shrew* Induction 2.18), "Marian Hackett, the fat ale-wife of

Wincot" (*Taming of the Shrew* Induction 2. 21–2), the witch of Edmonton, "my maid's aunt of Brainford [= Brentford]" (*Merry Wives of Windsor* 4.2.170–1). By this logic, Helen can only ever be "of Sparta." But if we recall two observations from the start of this chapter – Chris Cannon's observation that legal rape narratives begin "*after* the act" and Linda Clader's statement that "what Helen is best known for is rape" – the phrase "Helen of Troy" makes sense. Helen of Troy is, by definition, Helen *rapta*: raped or abducted.

With very few exceptions Helen's story is a story after the act of abduction, after the moment of transfer (of spouses, allegiance, country), after the moments of decision or indecision or regret or resignation. Middleton's and Rowley's clown articulates this precisely: "after she came to Troy she was Nell of Troy." Helen is so identified with the story of rape (Clader's "what Helen is best known for is rape") that we have telescoped her story into a genitive phrase: Helen of Troy. In narrative terms these three words probably provide the shortest rape story ever.

Rape as Revenge

Earlier in this book I noted that rape does not end with the death of Paris or with the fall of Troy: Deiphobus seizes Helen as wife, Neoptolemus later seizes her daughter, Hermione, whom Orestes in turn reclaims. But the most chilling of the many rapes occurs at the end of the American TV film *Helen of Troy* (2003).

This accomplished film covers not just the Helen–Paris love affair but their entire mythological history, beginning with Cassandra's prophecy at the birth of Paris and the infant's immediate exile. Sienna Guillory's gazelle-like and tomboyish Helen is shown in childhood where she has the chastest of abductions by Theseus. Theseus is protective and paternal towards her, a teacher rather than a rapist, and refuses to touch her despite her growing adolescent feelings towards him. When the Dioscuri arrive to rescue Helen, they misunderstand the situation – there is nothing from which to rescue her – and despite Helen's desperate preventive attempts, Theseus is killed.

In this first half, the film is *Taming of the Shrew* meets *Titanic*: a girl who does not fit in in Sparta, and who has no interest in men, finds a new life and would rather die with Theseus than return to royal restrictions. When Helen is compelled to return, she is displayed naked to her suitors, to the evident dismay of the sensitive Menelaus and the distanced appreciative observation of Rufus Sewell's saturnine Agamemnon. Agamemnon is aware of Helen's beauty at this and other moments in the film, an awareness conveyed through cruel and objectifying flickers in his eyes.

Although laconic and tyrannical, to his wife as well as his army, this Agamemnon has one weak spot: love of his daughter Iphigenia. This Iphigenia is no teenage bridal candidate but a six-year-old who plays hopscotch and hide-and-seek with her parents and whose tinkling laugh haunts the film (and her father) as a voice-over after Agamemnon sacrifices her at Aulis. The sacrifice is an excruciating decision for Sewell's Agamemnon and leads to one of the film's concluding sequences: revenge not by Menelaus for the loss of his wife but by Agamemnon for the loss of his daughter.

Up to this point the film has had nothing to do with rape. Theseus is an adoptive father; Paris and Helen are soul mates whose destined meeting (they first "see" each other in youthful visions) is presented as divine decree rather than as abduction or adultery. It comes as a shock, then, when Agamemnon seeks Helen at the sack of Troy and his vengeful sexual purpose becomes clear.

Soldiers fling Helen on the ground. Agamemnon grabs her hair, hurls her backwards on a table, and brutally rapes her. The act is unflinchingly repetitive and Helen's screams mingle with Menelaus' frantic powerless shouts, "Leave her!"; the sequence turns to slow motion as Agamemnon's thrusting and Helen's screams continue. This is a Troy story that *ends* with rape.[27] Even in a version that has nothing to do with causal rape, rape continues.

When we next see Helen she is silent, numbed, shocked. Cassandra is aghast at the change in her sister: "What has he done?" Helen is unable to answer the question. Justice is meted out to Agamemnon when Clytemnestra kills him in his bath: not because of her desire to be with her lover, Aegisthus (who is absent from this version) but because of her husband's murder of their daughter. This is not a story of female infidelity.

Before the sack of Troy, Guillory's Helen had gone in secret to the Greek camp to offer herself in exchange for Hector's dead body. Agamemnon had responded with steely scorn. "And you think that's enough? You think my daughter's death was for nothing? . . . There is no trade. I want you." He reminds Helen of this conversation when she is hurled to the floor before him in Troy: "As I said: no trade." These five monosyllables are the only words he addresses to her. His vocabulary takes us back to Herodotus' at the start of this chapter, where Io and her women were presented as agents in commerce. In this film Helen is not allowed to deal. Sienna Guillory's Helen ran away willingly but the punishment for sexually erring females is itself sexual. Helen will be made a sexual creature either as cause or as punishment.

This duality makes it difficult to acquit her of blame. Attempts to blame or defend her are the topic of chapter 4.

4

Blame

*So many stories have been told. How am I meant to tell the differ-
ence between what I did and what they said I did?* (Helen, in Mark
Haddon, *A Thousand Ships*)

*The Greek poets were never certain about Helen: she could stand for
human innocence or for human guilt* (Kenneth J. Reckford, "Helen
in *Aeneid* 2 and 6")

What could she have done being what she is? (W. B. Yeats, "No Second
Troy")

Accounts

Helen's story is, in every period, one in which authors hold her accountable for the Trojan War or try to reduce her accountability. In effect, this
reduces her story to one of two narratives: a story of elopement or a story
of abduction. In the first, Helen is an adulteress, guilty, someone to be blamed;
in the second, she is a victim, innocent, someone to be defended.

Yet this starkly moral black-and-white admits intermediate grey. For a
start, issues of blame are very different in pagan and Christian literature.
In the former, writers are able to separate responsibility and guilt. Thus in
the *Iliad* no one is in any doubt that Helen is the *cause* of the war, but
few hold her to *blame*. When the epic cycle introduces revenge, it also introduces the notion of Helen's personal culpability; and once we encounter
Christian writers, words like "guilt" and "forgiveness" regularly make their
appearance. In the anonymous *Gest Hystoriale* Menelaus promises, "All
[Helen's] gilt to forgiff, and to grace take" (TLN 11581).

The narrative techniques for presenting moral greyness are varied: authors
depict Helen's emotional conflict (as happens in the medieval Troy books

that present her genuine vacillation[1]); they introduce beauty as a compensation for or cancellation of blame (Quintus of Smyrna) or political confeder-
ation as a benefit of the war caused by Helen's departure (Herodotus,
Isocrates); they allow Helen herself to have a voice (Euripides); or they
evaluate her action not by any independently ethical criteria but by its
effect on others. In this last case, attempts to adjudicate Helen's morality
parallel attempts to understand her beauty: we concentrate on the effect,
working backwards from it.[2]

Casting Blame: Helen, Paris, and the Gods

Many texts blame Helen by stressing her volition in going to Troy. The
Chorus in Aeschylus' *Agamemnon* makes Helen's agency clear:

> Lightly she crossed the threshold
> And left her palace, fearless
> Of what should wake her fears.
> (1968: 57)

This Helen is an active participant in her own abduction: there are no emotional impediments (she is "fearless") or physical obstacles ("lightly she
crossed the threshold").

In Euripides' *Women of Troy* Cassandra says Helen "was not plundered
from [Menelaus], but went willingly" (Euripides 1973: 102). Dares' more
diplomatic (or emphatic) litotes says Helen "was not unwilling" (Frazer
1966: 141). As a Phrygian, Dares is particularly anti-Greek of course,
but the Cretan Dictys makes the same point. Helen attends the public
assembly which debates her fate, and states her position unambiguously:
"she had not sailed, she said, unwillingly, for her marriage to Menelaus
did not suit her" (Frazer 1966: 28–9).

In the anonymous *Excidium Troiae*,[3] Helen tells Paris she is willing to
be abducted, either a contradiction in terms – or a definition of elopement,
not abduction (Anon / Atwood and Whitaker 1944: 8, and cf. 62n). Paris
has given as his reason for visiting Greece Venus' promise that he "should
take from here a wife." Helen, already in love with Paris, volunteers, "I
am willing, if indeed you wish it too, for you to take me from here as your
wife." Paris offers the technical objection that she is already married but
Helen brushes this aside: "if you will not take me for your wife, I shall die
from love of you" (8). Paris now anticipates practical problems in Helen
exiting the royal palace, but she outlines escape plans, telling Paris what
he must do in the way of nautical preparations. Unsurprisingly he submits.
Throughout this dialogue it is clear who is leading and who is following.[4]

Texts that defend Helen tend to do so by blaming someone else. It is clearly difficult to defend Helen's action and its consequences per se (ambitious or ludic rhetoricians like Gorgias, Isocrates, and Ovid excepted); simpler to view Helen as a pawn of the gods or a victim of Paris' lust. In the *Iliad* Priam blames the gods (3.164) and Hector twice blames Paris (3.39–42; 6.281–5). In the *Aeneid* Venus intercepts Aeneas' violent anger at Helen as he prepares to kill her at the sack of Troy. Despite his anger, Aeneas is clear about what he hopes to achieve: "I shall have some credit for having stamped dead a mortal sin, and punished a wrong which cries out for justice; and it will be joy to have glutted my desire for the vengeance of the fire" (Virgil 1981, book 2: 68). He speaks the language of morality and justice (vengeance is an afterthought) but Venus explains that he has misidentified the culprit: "You must not blame the hated beauty of the Spartan Tyndarid, or even Paris. It was the gods who showed no mercy; it is they who are casting Troy down" (69).

There is considerable irony in her words because Venus herself is one of the culprit gods: she is blamed in the *Cypria* (in Hesiod 1977: 491). Although Joseph of Exeter identifies Paris' lust as the cause, it is Venus who both supports his erotic drive and facilitates his access to Helen (Joseph/Bate 1986: 139). In Quintus of Smyrna's *War at Troy* Agamemnon restrains Menelaus' anger, explaining that "Helen is not to blame, as you think, but Paris, who forgot Zeus, the god of guest and host, and forgot what he owed your table" (1968: 244). Paris' crime against hospitality is frequently stressed in texts, even indirectly: in book 4 of the *Odyssey*, Eteoneus' reluctance to grant Telemachus access to Menelaus' palace in Sparta after the war is clearly a caution borne of experience.

With his tongue firmly planted in his cheek in *Ars Amatoria*, Ovid offers a new candidate for blame: "stupid Menelaus" who encouraged his wife's adultery:

> . . . Were you crazy, Menelaus?
>   Why go off leaving your wife
> With a stranger in the house? Do you trust doves to falcons,
>   Full sheepfolds to mountain wolves?
> Here Helen's not at fault, the adulterer's blameless –
>   He did no more than you, or any man else,
> Would do yourself. By providing place and occasion
>   *You* precipitated the act. What else did she do
> But act on your clear advice? . . .
> Oh, Helen wins my acquittal, the blame's her husband's.
>   (Ovid 1982: 202)

Needless to say, this is also opportunist Paris' view in Ovid's *Heroides*.[5]

Between these polarized positions – Helen or someone else to blame – is the concept of joint culpability, as in the *Odyssey* when Helen says that Aphrodite "brought me to Troy . . . and made me forsake my daughter, my bridal chamber, and a husband who lacked nothing" (book 4, p. 52). Helen is both active and passive; she does the forsaking but is passively "made" to and "brought."

Later writers – Euripides, Herodotus, and Isocrates – introduce another concept, what a Christian writer in the fourth century CE, St. Augustine, would call a *felix culpa*. For Herodotus and Isocrates there was a positive gain to the decade of destruction: a unified Greece, a strengthening of civic and nautical might. But the most extraordinary articulation of this position comes from Menelaus himself in Euripides' *Andromache*:

> . . . Helen's trouble
> Came by divine volition, not from her own choice;
> And through it she conferred great benefits on Hellas.
> Weapons and fighting formerly were unknown to them;
> The war brought out their manly qualities, and, further,
> Brought different kinds of Greeks together – contact is
> A great teacher.
>
> (Euripides 1972: 167)

Helen's unwilling adultery created not only military alliance and technical developments but social and cultural unity. Menelaus is possibly the only cuckold in literature to view his personal humiliation in such politically positive terms. This extreme defense balances the extreme accusations of the play's opening, where Andromache, as one would expect from antiquity's ideal wife, abhors Helen. Helen killed Achilles, she says. Achilles' father adds to Andromache's accusations. Helen is a whore; indeed how could she be otherwise given the immodest upbringing of Spartan girls (who wear short clothes and engage in athletic competitions with young men)? If Menelaus invokes national unity as direct benefit, Peleus invokes regional custom as indirect cause (Euripides 1972: 153, 165).

And then there is beauty. Whereas Christian writers later bifurcated female transgression and compensation (Eve's sin is cancelled by Mary's immaculacy), Trojan narratives locate the crime and the compensation in Helen. Her sexuality caused a war; her beauty made it worth it. This is the view of the old men at the Skaian gate in *Iliad* 3 who briefly allow their negative judgment to be affected by the sight of Helen, and it is the view of Quintus of Smyrna whose Greek soldiers forgive Helen when they see her, view her as "faultless" and immediately forget "their painful labors or fighting" (Quintus 1968: 250–1).[6] Quintus' Menelaus, far from decapitating his wife as he had intended to do (244) suggests that he and she forget everything that has happened and all painful emotions: "Think of these things no more now, but check the sorrows in your heart. I hope the black hall of forgetfulness may shut all this somewhere deep within. It is not proper to remember evil things any longer" (253). Helen's beauty here achieves what her pharmaceuticals do in the *Odyssey*: amnesia and oblivion; the lengthy husband–wife reunion is the most poetically tender part of Quintus' epic.

Sidestepping Blame: Sympathy in the *Iliad*

In the *Iliad* the person who is harshest to Helen is Helen herself. In book 3 she calls herself a "slut" for forsaking her husband (3.180); in book 6 she calls herself "a nasty bitch evil-intriguing" (6.344). In Greek, "slut" and "bitch" are the same insults, meaning literally "dog-faced" (*kyōn*). In origin the insult had a specific logic: as Linda Lee Clader explains (1976: 18), dogs are an obstacle in the "hero's path to an honorable death" (because heroes do not want to be eaten before burial).

A few lines after chastising herself in book 6, Helen moves the blame by implication on to Paris: "I wish I had been the wife of a better man than this" (6.350). This is not the attitude of one who views the world well lost for love. Indeed throughout the *Iliad* Helen speaks of Paris, and to him, with contempt. In book 3 she derides his martial ability (3.428–36), tells him "I wish you had died there [in the duel]" (3.428), and refuses to go to bed with him. This is a stronger act of resistance than my phrasing makes it sound, because Helen has to stand up to Aphrodite. (Even allowing for the possibility that Aphrodite is here a metaphor for passion, and the dialogue is a psychomachic struggle between Helen's head and her passions, the resistance requires reserves of strength.) Aphrodite has rescued Paris from combat with Menelaus and placed him in his chamber, waiting for Helen. Aphrodite describes Paris' attractions and the attractions of the nuptial bed (3.391–4). Helen self-assertively not only refuses to cooperate ("not I. I am not going to him . . . I will not serve his bed"; 3.410–11), but implies critically that she has been a substitute for Aphrodite:

> Go *yourself* and sit beside him, . . .
> stay with him forever and suffer for him, look after him
> until he makes *you* his wedded wife, or makes you his slave girl.
> (3.406–9, my italics; cf. Meagher 1995: 26)

Aphrodite responds with anger and with a threat, telling Helen, in effect: watch out in case I make life difficult for you and kill you (my paraphrase of 3.413–17). Helen yields from fear: "Helen daughter of Zeus was frightened" (3.418).

A woman who yields to bedroom activity because of threat, anger, and her subsequent fear is a familiar theme from chapter 3. But Homer prefaces the sexual interlude with gentle words from Paris (3.438–46) nor does he elsewhere present Helen as a victim. Although Paris says he "carried [her] away" (3.444) and Hector accuses him of taking Menelaus' wife (3.53) (both of which could imply abduction) and although Helen laments and longs to escape (2.356; 2.589–90) and is homesick for Menelaus (3.139–42), she elsewhere implies that she came to Troy voluntarily: "I came hither / following your son" (3.174–5; cf. 24.765–6). Her current feelings may be the result of a change of attitude: "my heart even now is confused with sorrows" (3.412). In presenting Helen ambiguously Homer makes it clear that he is interested less in blame than in emotional predicament.

Given Colin Burrow's argument that the *Iliad* is an exercise in sympathy, we need to pay attention not to accusations or defenses but to images of Helen. She weaves; she averts her eyes from Aphrodite; she is domestic with Hector, trying (along with Andromache) to persuade him to relax. She has two moments of extreme pathos, in books 3 and 24. In book 3, when she is unable to see her brothers from her position on the Trojan battlements, we sense her isolation, not only bereft of relatives but bereft of tried-and-tested protectors (the Dioscuri had rescued her from her abduction by Theseus). This latter point is underlined by the name of the attendant who accompanies Helen on the battlement: Aethra, Pittheus' daughter. Aethra is the mother of Theseus, given to Helen by Theseus as an attendant.[7] The effect here, as elsewhere in the poem, is to stress Helen's vulnerability.

In this context it is worth revisiting the episode with Aphrodite in book 3, after the scene on the battlements. If the *teichoskopia* restages the bride-contest for Helen, the dialogue in which Aphrodite calls Helen to join Paris in bed restages the moment of abduction. As Paolo Vivante puts it, "when Aphrodite bids Helen leave the ramparts and go to Paris, she echoes a fateful summons given long ago in Sparta" (Vivante 1991: 103). Helen accuses Aphrodite of leading her on, quite literally: "will you carry me further yet somewhere among cities / fairly settled? In Phrygia or in lovely Maionia" (3.400–1).[8]

For Vivante the introduction of these two geographical names is "not casual": it "portends new destinations in the ways of love, ever recurring ventures under the spell of Aphrodite" (Vivante 1991: 103). Vivante sees this as a moment when myth meets personal experience. Without disagreeing with this, I want, instead, to relate it to the ambivalence of Helen, and of her poets, as regards the question of Helen's agency or passivity. The answer is here staring us (or Helen) in the face: Aphrodite. "Passion" has the same root as "passive" (Latin *passivus*, from the verb *pati*: to "undergo patiently," "suffer," "tolerate," "bear"). One suffers passion, one is subject to passion, acted upon by an external agency; yet paradoxically this emotion injects one with such energy that one becomes active, enthusiastic, willing. Passivity becomes agency; polar opposite nouns become the same. As James Kirwan observes, passion is an emotion that is only "nominally volitive . . . Venus impels!" (Kirwan 1999: 72). Homer stages this paradox, showing us the volition and helplessness of passion, Aphrodite's prospects of "new destinations" and "ever recurring ventures" even as he depicts Aphrodite's past compulsion. Volition and compulsion are one and the same. Helen is willing and passive, to blame and not to blame.

In this epic Homer is ever human. In book 12 he interrupts an epic simile about weighing and balancing wool to depict the emotional and economic needs of the wool-carding widow who is "working to win a pitiful wage for her children" (12.435). In book 13 he focuses on a father's bereavement (13.658).[9] Moments like these recur in later centuries when Helen's story is used in antiwar literature. But Homer's poem is not antiwar so much as pro-human. Homer is as able to feel pity for Helen, who causes death, as for those whose deaths she causes. Sympathy sidesteps blame.

Competing Narratives: the *Odyssey*

The theme of women's sexual unreliability is introduced at the start of the *Odyssey* when Telemachus says, "my mother certainly says I am Odysseus' son but for myself I cannot tell. No man can be certain of his parentage" (book 1, p. 9). The poem may extol the virtue of Penelope but it here impugns her, just as it introduces the untrustworthiness of Helen, the murderous deception of her sister Clytemnestra, and the machinations of the several female figures Odysseus encounters on his travels (Calypso, Circe, the Sirens) as well as the disloyalty in Ithaca of 12 female servants who become lovers of the suitors. Like Hector in the *Iliad*, who wishes Paris dead, Eumaeus, Odysseus' swine-herd, wishes the same for Helen. His master "is dead and gone. And I wish I could say the same of Helen and all her breed, for she has been the death of many a good man" (book 14, p. 209). But unlike Hector, Eumaeus expands his disapproval from one woman to the entire sex: "Helen and *all her breed*." Blaming or hating Helen, like blaming Pandora or Eve, often turns into a condemnation of the entire female sex. As Creusa says in Euripides' *Ion*, "life is harder for women than for men: they judge us, good and bad together, and hate us" (Euripides 1973: 54). At the end of the *Odyssey* Agamemnon contrasts Penelope with Clytemnestra, describing how the latter has shamed all women, even the good ones: "she has destroyed the reputation of her own sex, virtuous women and all" (book 24, p. 360). Odysseus performs the same misogynist metonymy as Eumaeus when he castigates Zeus as "a relentless foe to the House of Atreus from the beginning," but notes that Zeus "work[s] his will through women's crooked ways" (book 11, p. 172; literally: "female plans"). Who is to blame here? One god or all of womankind?

In book 4 Menelaus and Helen offer competing anecdotes about Helen's behavior in Troy. In chapter 2 I considered both stories in relation to nostalgia. Here I want simply to underline the obvious: the simple fact of there being *two* stories. Conflicting stories epitomize in miniature the narrative predicament in judging Helen: there are always two stories. The frustration experienced by Mark Haddon's Helen in the first epigraph to this chapter is also the experience of the reader: how are we meant to tell the difference between what she did and what they said she did?[10]

In Euripides' *Electra* Clytemnestra says:

> when people judge someone, they ought
> To learn the facts, and then hate, if they've reason to
> And if they find no reason, then they should not hate.
> (Euripides 1973: 140)

But as we saw in chapter 1, the facts of mythology are not fixed. Judgment is consequently firmly prejudiced or frustratingly open-ended.

"Twisting Eulogy / And Censure Both Together"

Euripides' *Electra* presents angry accusations against Helen. The chorus opines that Helen "by her guilt has brought / Grief without measure on Hellas and [Electra's] family' (Euripides 1963: 111).[11] Electra accuses her absent aunt of lasciviousness, continuing, "they talk of Helen's 'rape' – / She embraced her own corruption!" (141). Electra's rage against Helen stems from the loss of her father in the aftermath of the war Helen caused. Clytemnestra's similar emotional outburst stems from the loss of her younger daughter. She describes how Helen's abduction led to the sacrifice of Iphigenia:

> He [Agamemnon] took my child
> To Aulis, where the fleet lay bound; lured her from home
> With lies about Achilles; held her high above
> The altar; then her father cut her soft white throat –
> My Iphigenia. If he had done it to avert
> The capture of his city, or to exalt his house;
> Or if, to save his other children, he had taken
> One life for many, he could be forgiven. But no:
> Helen was a whore, her husband didn't know how to handle
> A randy wife; and *that* was Agamemnon's reason
> For murdering my daughter.
>
> (1963: 140)

The abduction of Helen was, to Clytemnestra, insufficient justification for the loss of a daughter. Nonetheless, she continues, Iphigenia's death itself would not have made her kill her husband. The final straw was Agamemnon's return from Troy with "a second wife, / A fellow-lodger – two kept women in one house" (140). Her murder of her husband was not a retaliation for filicide but a response to sexual humiliation.

She then hypothesizes about how she would have behaved if the positions had been reversed:

> Suppose Menelaus had been abducted secretly,
> Would I have had to kill Orestes, to get back
> My sister's husband Menelaus? Would your father
> Have stood for that? No: he'd have killed me if I'd touched
> His son; he killed my daughter – why should he not die?
>
> (1963: 141)

The Chorus acknowledges the justice of Clytemnestra's example, but questions the right of a wife to agency. Socially conservative, they are unable to enter into evaluative debate on this subject if a wife refuses to accept her husband's judgment.

The Chorus fails to comment, however, on an anomaly in the parallel Clytemnestra sets up. Her opening supposition – that "Menelaus had been abducted secretly" – is not parallel to the Helen example she offered immediately before this: "Helen was a whore, her husband didn't know how to handle / A randy wife." Clytemnestra's language inadvertently presents Helen as both innocent and guilty. She cannot have it both ways. This is not an example of plural blame (as in Aeschylus' *Agamemnon*) but of blatant contradiction, a text at war with itself (indeed, the authenticity of this passage is questionable and most editors bracket it) – what Euripides elsewhere calls "ambiguous speech . . . twisting eulogy / And censure both together" (*Orestes* in Euripides 1972: 332).

Texts which explore Helen's innocence or culpability often behave in this bifurcated way. Perhaps the most blatant example is John Pollard's 1965 book on Helen in which his attempts to defend his subject are repeatedly undermined by his systemically low opinion of the sex to which she belongs. "The tragedy of love is that its victims, and in particular women, find it irresistible, and rarely stop to count the cost, no matter how high it may be" (Pollard 1965: 89). Comparing Helen with Eve and Pandora as pawns of the gods, Pollard writes, "all that Eve was guilty of was giving way, under powerful persuasion, to the inborn human trait of woman's curiosity, which differs from that of men in its overmastering immediacy and refusal to be denied" (165).[12] Of beautiful women Pollard tells us "their own degree of responsibility for any particular tragedy is . . . often hard to assess, and so it was with [Helen]" (20). In sections like these, ostensibly dedicated to Helen's defense, Pollard's readers come away with contradictory impressions.

A similar, if localized, tension occurs in Guido delle Colonne's *Historia Destructionis Troiae* (1287).[13] Priam has offered advice to Paris, advice that is agreeable to the prince: that the Trojans retain Helen. Delle Colonne writes, "Paris . . . heard the king's word, approved the king's advice . . . because Helen, his wife, was not to be returned to her husband" (delle Colonne/Meek 1974: 179). The personal pronouns here are confusing: Helen is Paris' ("his") wife, but she has a different ("her") husband. This confusion exists only in the English translation. But there is still a battle for language in Latin, fought out in nouns rather than pronouns: we have one husband (*marito*), one wife (*consors sua*), but three characters. Texts dedicated to blaming or defending Helen often pull in two directions; here the tension is grammatical.

Voicing Helen: Euripides

In Euripides tension is presented as dialogue – dialogue in which Helen herself is given a voice.

Euripides put Helen on stage three times. In *Orestes* (as we shall see later in this chapter) Euripides deifies Helen. In *The Women of Troy* he allows her to defend herself; in most critics' view she condemns herself in the process. She blames Hecuba for giving birth to Paris, and Priam for not killing him; she accuses the goddesses, Paris, and Menelaus – in short, she blames *everyone* except herself. This speech is, for Norman Austin, "nothing more than the cheapest courtroom pleading" (1994: 139). Philip Vellacott offers a more sympathetic response, interpreting Helen's self-defense as Euripides' ironic exposé of the human need to find causes and assign blame. Vellacott paraphrases Helen's argument as follows: "you are trying to fix the blame for all this suffering – on me. You made the war, I was the cause of your action; Paris was the cause of my action; his parents were the cause of Paris – where are we to stop?" (Euripides 1973: 19–20). For Vellacott Helen is not serious in blaming Priam for not killing his son; parents do not kill their children. She is showing the absurdity of trying to identify cause and assign blame.

In *Helen* Euripides makes the most extensive exculpatory move of any ancient writer: he totally rewrites her story, thus mounting a full-scale defense of Helen. Helen has spent the ten years of the Trojan War, plus a further seven years, at the court of Proteus in Egypt. With Proteus' death she is now vulnerable because Proteus' son Theoclymenus wishes to marry her. A shipwrecked Menelaus (still attempting to reach Sparta after the war) is washed ashore in rags. He is astonished to see Helen, or what looks like Helen, since he is, he believes, traveling with his wife, whom he has secured in a cave on the Egyptian seashore. (His traveling companion is an *eidōlon*, a phantom created by the gods; it is the phantom who has spent the war in Troy with Paris.)[14]

When Helen asserts her identity, and husband and wife are reunited, Menelaus' slave arrives with the news that the (phantom) Helen in the cave has "vanished into the air! She just went up and disappeared! Now she's out of sight, in the sky!" (Euripides 1973: 154). Before Menelaus can plot their escape from Egypt, the priestess Theonoe discovers them and has to be persuaded not to tell her brother Theoclymenus of Menelaus' arrival.

A plot is hatched: Menelaus will masquerade as a messenger reporting Menelaus' death and Helen will ask Theoclymenus for ships to hold a memorial service at sea according to Greek custom. With these ships she and Menelaus will escape. Euripides rescripts the Helen story with the husband as legitimate abductor (Segal 1971: 606). The ruse is successful and Theoclymenus, outraged at being "so miserably outwitted by a woman" (Euripides 1973: 187) tries to take revenge by killing his sister. Tragedy is averted by *fratres ex machina*, the Dioscuri, raised by Zeus to godhead, who convert Theoclymenus to clemency and the play to comedy. Even as this play rescues Helen's reputation, it shows the difficulty of doing so: to render Helen blameless Euripides has to rewrite her story totally. The substitute whose appearance is so attractively and convincingly beguiling is not the phantom Helen but mythological narrative itself (Wright 2006: 142–57).

Furthermore revising Helen's story in this way makes it not her story. As Aristophanes phrased it, in what later became something of a catchphrase, this is the "new-style Helen" (Wright 2005: 50, 116). Or, as Norman Austin writes, offering not a new but a negated ontology, this is "not-Helen of Troy" (1994: 11) for, as we saw in chapter 3, to be Helen of Troy means to be someone who transgresses sexually. Euripides' Helen both is and is not Helen. Bifurcation and doubles simply haunt her story in a new form.

Helen Among the Sophists

In Gorgias of Leontini in Sicily (c.483–c.385 BCE) and his pupil Isocrates (436–338 BCE) we find two defenders of Helen. Gorgias' *Encomium of Helen* was composed in the second half of the fifth century BCE. It may predate Euripides' *Women of Troy*, which was produced in 415 BCE and whose debate between Hecuba and Helen seems indebted to Gorgias' sophistic forensic rhetoric. Isocrates' *Encomium of Helen* was written about 370 BCE. With Gorgias and Isocrates the issue of Helen's culpability becomes less a debate about ethics than an opportunity for rhetorical display. As Matthew Wright points out, Euripides' *Helen* exonerates Helen by offering an alternative myth; in the same period Gorgias exonerates Helen "not by denying her elopement but by justifying her acts" (2005: 277).

Both Gorgias and Isocrates are orators; both approach their subject analytically; both take into account the importance of the gods, beauty, and politics. But there is one crucial difference; whereas Isocrates takes his defense of Helen seriously, Gorgias is having fun. As he says in his last line, "I wished to write the speech as an encomium of Helen and as an amusement for myself" (§21, Gorgias 1982: 31). The amusement comes from attempting the impossible: a defense of someone who cannot be defended.[15] The personal and professional challenge is clearly irresistible (Gorgias was a teacher of rhetoric). But this ludic piece also has a serious aim – even though that aim is not the one its title advertises. Gorgias shows what words and ingenuity are capable of. Rhetorical ability was considered an essential skill for a politician. To defend Helen was essentially to argue that black was white. In a period of continued warfare and threats (the Peloponnesian War lasted from 431 to 404 BCE) perhaps politicians could similarly argue war into peace?

Gorgias' *Encomium of Helen* begins with rhetoric's ethical imperative: justice. One should not just praise or blame those who merit tribute or censure, but also rescue those who have been unfairly praised or wrongly vilified. Helen belongs to the latter category. He proposes to "free the slandered woman from her accusation" (§1, Gorgias 1982: 21).

Gorgias first establishes Helen's preeminence. She is the daughter of a god, divinely beautiful, and her beauty united Greece's rulers in love for her. This introduction is not part of Gorgias' intended defense for he concludes this paragraph by saying that he will now "proceed to the beginning of my intended speech" (§3, Gorgias 1982: 23). As we saw in chapter 2, beauty halts narrative; here it stops the narrative at its very beginning.

Gorgias offers four possible reasons for Helen's "departure" to Troy: (1) divine necessity; (2) force; (3) rhetorical persuasion; (4) love. He disposes of the first two swiftly. Helen could not have resisted the gods; if they are responsible, Helen is not to blame. If she was seized by force, it is her abductor who deserves accusation and punishment. In this case, not only is Helen not to blame; she is a victim, someone who "suffered" (the translator uses the word twice; there are two separate forms in the Greek: §§7–8, Gorgias 1982: 22, 23). She therefore deserves pity (a conclusion Helen herself draws in Euripides' *Women of Troy*).

These two possible causes of Helen's action occupy one paragraph apiece. The third possible cause, speech, takes up the bulk of the treatise: this is not an encomium of Helen but of speech. Speech is superhuman in its ability to create powerful effects (it removes fear and sorrow, creates joy, increases pity). Gorgias considers different kinds of speech: poetry, incantation, false speech, persuasion. He compares speech to drugs: "some speeches cause sorrow, some cause pleasure, some cause fear, some give the hearers confidence, some drug and bewitch the mind with an evil persuasion" (§10, Gorgias 1982: 27). The applicability to Helen is tucked away in the middle of this: it is the persuader, Paris, who is guilty, not the persuaded, Helen, because she is compelled, acted upon as if by a drug.

In offering his fourth cause, love, Gorgias also expounds at length. He defines love as the action of sight upon the brain. Thus, in being attracted to Paris, Helen suffered "a human malady and incapacity of mind," which "should not be blamed as an impropriety but considered as an adversity" (§19, Gorgias 1982: 29). In not one of his four examples, he concludes, can one "consider the blame of Helen just."

Gorgias' defense is rhetorically manipulative in several ways. He limits the case to four scenarios, and in disposing of them encourages us to believe that all scenarios have been disposed of. He imposes definitions upon us, such as that of love, and therefore conducts the argument on his own narrow terms. (His gift is to make this narrowness seem inclusive.) Above all, however, he shows how style can distract from (lack of) substance. The syntactical balancing with antithetical and parallel phrases, conveyed by D. M. MacDowell's translation in an elegant Augustan English, is a linguistic equivalent of his subject. One can forgive him anything, overlook anything, because of his beauty. What is true of a Sicilian sophist is true of a Spartan queen.

Isocrates writes with greater purposefulness than his master. He criticizes Gorgias' debating techniques and points out that his *Encomium* is a defense, not a praise. He makes his own encomiastic genre clear: "it is fitting . . . to praise those who excel in any noble quality" (1894, vol. 1, §15: 294). Nonetheless Isocrates' *Encomium* begins and ends only with Helen, offering an intermediate lengthy digression on Theseus.

Isocrates begins, like Gorgias, by stressing the high status of Helen. She was the only woman fathered by Zeus; Zeus granted her beauty, an attribute greater than Hercules' strength (because beauty "is destined to bring even strength into subjection to it"; vol. 1, §16: 295). The Trojan War is viewed by Isocrates in a positive light. Since renown comes as a result of battle, being endowed with the beauty that causes battle is a (female) form of the renown that military heroes achieve in war (vol. 1, §17: 295).

As we saw in the introduction, Helen's story is linked to the Theseus story. Isocrates introduces Theseus as an important component of his promotion of Helen. Despite all his glories Theseus "did not consider life worth living" without Helen (vol. 1, §18: 295). Isocrates is aware that, had Theseus been "an ordinary man instead of one of the most distinguished, it would not yet be clear whether my discourse is an encomium or an accusation of Theseus" (vol. 1, §21: 296). But his point is to show "that those who loved and admired [Helen] were themselves more worthy of admiration than the rest of mankind" (vol. 1, §22: 296). This gives him license to detail Theseus' exploits and achievements for a further 16 paragraphs, confessing that having begun to praise Theseus, "I do not like to stop halfway," yet aware that "I am travelling beyond the proper limits of my subject" (vol. 1, §29: 298). He concludes that "we shall never be able to produce a more trustworthy witness or a more convincing authority upon the good qualities of Helen than the judgment of Theseus," and then resumes his Helen narrative "that I may not seem to dwell too long upon the same topic from lack of ideas" (vol. 1, §38: 300).

He begins anew with the oath of the suitors, alleging that through this Helen unified Greece. Here Euripides' and Herodotus' argument about alliance is (p)redated; no longer a consequence of Helen's abduction it is an effect of Helen's beauty. He praises Paris' choice of Venus (and his acceptance of Helen) as selfless (Athena's and Hera's gifts "would not endure beyond the terms of his life," whereas marriage to the daughter of Zeus is a heritage he can give his children, vol. 1, §44: 301). Furthermore beauty is clearly a valuable attribute if the goddesses are rivals in a beauty contest. Helen's unifying power is extolled again, this time in the expected way as the cause by which the Greek states "sunk their differences." And as we saw in chapter 2 Helen becomes a synecdoche for nation and national pride: at her abduction "the Hellenes were as indignant as if the whole of their country had been plundered, while the barbarians were as proud as if they had conquered us all" (vol. 1, §49: 302).[16]

Isocrates extols Helen because of her power to unify. In the next paragraph he extols her because of her power to divide. When engaged in conflict, the Olympians had previously been unified (as in e.g. their war against the Giants), but "for Helen they fought against one another" (vol. 1, §53: 303).

Isocrates now turns to beauty – its "influence," its "superiority," its effect upon us. These paragraphs function less as debate than as praise. They do not move the argument forward (nor should this surprise us: beauty does not advance narrative; it impedes it). Isocrates considers beauty in terms of *telos*, the gods' love of beauty (vol. 1, §§59, 60: 304–5), and, in a movement that happens subtly and without any signposting, Helen's deification. We are told that "she not only won immortality herself, but . . . obtained power equal to that of the gods [i.e., she was deified] . . ." (vol. 1, §61: 305). She uses this power to turn her brothers and subsequently Menelaus into gods. Paragraph 63 concludes with the corroborating historical tourism of Herodotus: "even at the present day, at Therapnae, in Laconia, they offer up holy sacrifices according to the custom of their ancestors in honour of both of them; as *unto gods*, and not as unto heroes" (vol. 1, §63: 305, my italics).

Isocrates is now proceeding by a process of discursive accretion rather than precise terms of debate. He continues in this way, chronicling Helen's divine power (to blind Stesichorus and restore eyesight; to commission the *Iliad* from Homer). The implication is that because Helen has the power to punish and reward, it behoves us to honor her. Honor can take the form of worship of, and offerings to her, as "a divinity." Those less wealthy – philosophers – must honor her by endeavoring 'to speak of her in terms worthy of the material at hand'" (vol. 1, §66: 306). And that material is the material covered by Isocrates: mythological-historical (the judgment of Paris), mythical-biographical (Helen's abduction by Theseus), cultural (Helen's shrine at Therapnae), aesthetic (the importance of beauty), and political (Greek unity and subsequent expansion).

Isocrates' is a wide-ranging defense although he does not consider that he has had the last word: there is still "ample opportunity of praising Helen more than I have done in this discourse" (vol. 1, §69: 306). Certainly Isocrates has introduced areas of debate. But he has also made blame of Helen impossible by closing down one area of debate in a tactic he does not even comment upon. That tactic is the deification of Helen.

Two other writers deify Helen – Euripides in *Orestes*, and the Elizabethan poet John Ogle in *The Lamentation of Troy* (1594); I will return to their work (and the tactic of deification) later in this chapter. First let us move to the Middle Ages and writers who blame or defend Helen by granting (or denying) her agency.

Agency (1): Joseph of Exeter

A tactic used in both defenses and accusations of Helen is the granting of sexual agency. Depicting Helen as sexually willing, even (as we shall see) as the initiator of romance with Paris, is a way of rescuing her from victimhood. Whether it rescues her from blame depends on the interaction between her actions and her emotions. Of all Helen narratives it is the medieval Troy books that devote the most extensive narrative space to the meeting of Paris and Helen.

Joseph of Exeter translated Dares Phrygius' *Iliad* in the 1180s.[17] Like most translations before the nineteenth century, Joseph's is creative and adaptive. He offers a lengthy account of the judgment of Paris, for instance (Joseph/Bate 1986: 87–117), about which Dares has little to say (7). He draws on Dictys to supplement Dares (plus Ovid, Lucan, Statius; 7) and although interested in Christian morality, he novelistically provides pseudo-psychological accounts of character interiority (cf. 9). Thus his is the first version to portray Helen's thoughts at length. His is also the first – and only – version to offer a sex scene between Helen and Paris.

The sex scene in book 3 is not the first intrusion of the physical in the text. Greece's first navy is described in an extended metaphor of deflowering, a metaphor made all the more visible by the pun on *pinus* (= pine = boat) with penis (Joseph/Bate 1986: 157). The anthropomorphized boat hesitates, then is launched: "the sea now deflowered took on all comers, exposing her lap to any traveller" (41). A momentary moral qualm about foreign conquest as a form of rape is quickly justified by imperialism: "if it were not for the use of oars, Memphis would not have known Rome, nor India Spain, nor Scythia Athens, nor our Britain France" (45). Joseph is repeatedly interested in sex, willing and unwilling. His account of the abduction of Hesione, discussed in chapter 3, negotiates the discrepancy between Hesione's perspective, "going into a forced marriage afraid and under duress" (83) and that of Telamon as conqueror: "I earned by my sword the right to enjoy her embraces" (85).

But his is no prurient interest. Joseph is a novelist *manqué*. In book 1 we are treated to crisp, fast narrative (Joseph/Bate 1986: 45ff) with *en passant* observations about anger (55), rumor (53), mythology (55–7). Joseph is a master of description as of dialogue. Book 2 provides a beautiful description of Hesione's wedding banquet (77–83). This is an invented scene, a "medieval wedding feast in classical dress" (168).[18] In the Judgment of Paris, Joseph is in his element with descriptions of divine beauty, of Venus' strategic self-exposure, and of satirical Billingsgate bickering among the goddesses (101). This is the detailed, realistic narrative environment in which Paris meets Helen.

Joseph's Paris is both arrogant and ingenuous. Having heard of Helen's beauty he leaves his fleet to try to see her, confident "in his beauty and aware of his handsome features." He walks up and down the beach with a self-conscious casualness, practicing his pace, stopping, then, "fearing to be thought acting suspiciously, he quickly transfers his gaze to other things as if amazed at all he sees" (Joseph/Bate 1986: 135). This is an *ingénu* wooer, not a romantic hero.

Helen, Joseph tells us, shows "more self-control." She manages to view Paris discreetly (she "steals sidelong glances at him") and deliberately does not smile. But Joseph lets us know what she is feeling: she would like to "show her face and her naked breasts," but restrains herself (Joseph/Bate 1986: 135). Again he shares Helen's psyche with the reader: she is "ready to touch hands if asked and yet wanting to be forced" (137). Paris interprets the situation correctly: seeing Helen's "seducing eye" and "unspoken desire," he realizes that he has "an easy prey" at hand (135–7).

Joseph now addresses Paris, telling him that he need not worry about seductive rhetoric because his wealth is sufficient temptation. Furthermore the circumstances are favorable for abduction: the city is empty, the wind in the right direction. Above all, Helen is "complaisant" (Joseph/Bate 1986: 137). But when Paris decides to abduct Helen, Joseph reproves him for violating Menelaus' hospitality, his marriage, and general morality. The narrator has both encouraged and repressed his protagonist, like Helen herself.

The moment of abduction is emotionally reciprocal, however. "So Trojan Paris snatches Helen as she holds out her hands, encouraging him with her happy expression – or rather Paris is snatched by her" (*rapit ergo Lacenam / tendentemque manus et leta fronte vocantem / Dardanus aut rapitur potius*; Joseph/Bate 1986: 138, 139). Helen is not merely willing; she is doing the snatching. Joseph's condemnation of her, and his revision of her narrative's conventional terminology ("abduction") is clear: "you are running away, never abducted!" The Latin's expression of this statement in three stressed words is even more rhetorically scornful: *nunquam rapta fugis* (138, 139).

Joseph's view of Helen as an agent who snatches gives him license to invent a scene in which Helen also takes the sexual initiative. "Helen now not only kisses him first but does not hold back if kissed first. Lying on him with her whole body, she opens her legs, presses him with her mouth and robs him of his semen" (Joseph/Bate 1986: 143). She initiates physical action ("kisses him first"; "presses him with her mouth"); she is uninhibited ("does not hold back"); she positions herself on top ("lying on him with her whole body"). Just as Helen had seized Paris in the temple ("Paris is snatched by her"), she here steals his sperm ("robs him of his semen"). This may be a further illustration of her agency or it may be a coy reference to the prematurely ejaculated liquid, subsequently depicted on the purple bed linen that "bears witness to his unseen dew" (143). Premature ejaculation is considered the punishment for the medieval sin of women on top.[19] Or is it Joseph's sexual depiction of the textual shudder? Helen's beauty, as we saw in chapter 2, repeatedly interrupts the text, where the shudder, as Barthes writes, "signals the bliss of its own annihilation." In Joseph, Paris stops walking when he sees Helen ("stops, forgetting to continue his stride"; 135); in bed with Helen he also stops prematurely.

Agency (2): Middle English Troy Books

Other medieval writers continue to grant Helen sexual agency though never as explicitly as does Joseph. Using the same source as Joseph of Exeter, the poet of the *Siege of Troy* composes poetic romance. This is Middle English, not medieval Latin; and when Helen and Paris meet, we are given the beautiful four strong-stress line "Ether beholdeth oder lovely" (TLN 577).[20]

In the anonymous *Gest Hystoriale*[21] Helen hears of Paris' beauty and "was lappit in longyng that lovely to se[e]" (TLN 2909). She has "wilfull desyre," she longs "with lust" to go to the temple to see him, and Menelaus' absence enables her to do so (TLN 2910–14). The poet chastises her (and through her the shamelessness of women; TLN 2920ff) for not restraining herself, for not staying at home,[22] and for hypocrisy (because under pretense of worship she contrived to see Paris; TLN 2971–5). In the *Laud* Troy book Helen similarly goes to the temple of Venus because she wants to see Paris' famed beauty. When he sees her, his heart is set on her; when she sees him, "she wolde wel fayn hane ben his wife." They are locked in looking and lust: "Sche loked on him, and he on hir; / Eyther other now desir" (TLN 2801–2). They speak together and are of one mind.

For John Lydgate in his *Troy Book* literature is a truth-telling art: without writers, knowledge would have died (Prologue 159–67). Nonetheless Lydgate regularly blames his sources (Statius, Ovid, Guido, and Chaucer) for material and attitudes that originate in Lydgate's own adaptation and expansion. Thus 20 lines of invective about bad women (1.2072–96) are based on one sentence in the source. Elsewhere Guido's misogynist opinions are detailed at length, only for Lydgate to protest against them. "Guydo seith" (3.4303), "seith Guydo" (3.4329), "and eke he seith" (3.4331), "thus techeth Guydo, God wot, & not I! – . . . ful evel mote he thrive" (3.4343, 4355). Lydgate advises the reader to skip over Guido about women (3.4413–17), but Lydgate himself does not.

This accuse-and-apologize tactic is visible in the first meeting of Paris and Helen. As in the other Middle English versions above, Helen rushes to the temple to view Paris' beauty. All women will go where men are, says Lydgate (and Guido):

> Thus Guydo ay, of cursid fals delit,
> To speke hem [them] harme hath kaught an appetit,
> Thorugh-oute his boke of wommen to seyn ille,
> That to translate it is ageyn my wille.
> . . .
> I am sory that I mote reherse [must repeat]
> The felle [cruel] wordis in his boke y-founde.
> (2.3555–61)

Paris subsequently meets Helen: "In whom he fonde no maner resistence; / It sat hir nat, sche was so womanly, / For to Paris she yalde [yielded] hir outterly" (2.3834–6). Her yielding, in fact, has already taken place before Paris' overture: "Hir hert in hap was yolde or sche cam there, / Therfor to yelde hir sche had lasse fer" (2.3832–7). The three occurrences of "yield" in three lines could not make her compliance more clear.

At the end of his *Troy Book* Lydgate asks his readers to "voide & adde where hem semeth nede" (5.3539). The second of these readerly invitations is, as we have seen, a central activity of reading and it is an activity crucial to reading Helen narratives. As Lydgate reveals at the beginning, books tell the truth about men after their deaths. Lydgate's recurrent criticism of Guido's misogyny implies that books might not tell the truth about women after their deaths. Nonetheless that is an omission that Lydgate's book does not rectify. As we see throughout this chapter, his praise-and-blame duality is not unusual.

Lydgate's successor in Trojan War narrative, William Caxton, translated and printed Raoul Lefèvre's French version as *The Recuyell of the*

Histories of Troy. (*Recuyell*, a French word imported into English, means "a collection.") Caxton's collection is comprehensive, beginning with the genealogy of Saturn. This large volume, the first book printed in English by an Englishman (although not in England) had its first edition c.1474 in Bruges. The second edition was printed in London in 1503. New editions appeared at regular intervals thereafter, showing its popularity well into the eighteenth century.

Caxton's Helen is formed, it seems, to be the recipient of the Gaze. Paris notes that she is so beautiful that "it seemed properly to them that saw her that nature had made her to be beholden and be seen" (Le Fèvre 1894, vol. 2: 531). The tautology ("be beholden and be seen") implies that Helen has to be looked at twice, the medieval equivalent of "worth a second glance." In the next line, viewing is doubled in a different way as both Paris and Helen gaze at each other: "and as he beheld her, in likewise Helen beheld him also, many times and oft." Helen now takes the initiative: she makes "a token or sign to Paris that he approached to her" (532). When Paris leaves the temple where these visual overtures are taking place, "Helen sent after him her eyes also far as she might" (532). Gazing frames the episode, with Helen's viewing of Paris mirroring his viewing of her at the beginning. In both instances gazing is a deliberate and physical action by the viewer: Paris "*began strongly* to behold her" (531, my italics); "Helen *sent after him* her eyes also far as she might" (532, my italics). Their optical agency is equal.

This equality changes on board ship when Helen, like other Troy book Helens, weeps. When Paris promises she shall be his wife, not his prisoner, Helen responds to his declaration with resignation: "I have no puissance to resist it" (Le Fèvre 1894, vol. 2: 536). The puissance she lacks is ambiguous. Is it literal power she lacks (as a weak woman she is unable to overcome her current physical conditions)? Or is it emotional power (her heart cannot resist)? When Lydgate comments, "Thus was Helen recomforted a little," it is unclear whether the adverb "thus" refers to her resignation or Paris' promises. The next sentence offers little help: "And Paris did do please her with all his power &" (536). Paris has the power she lacks – a masculine Anglo-Saxon power against her feminine French puissance – and the delicately gesturing ampersand hints at the nature of that power.

Ten years later, in an unusual sequence for Troy narratives, Caxton's Priam agrees to return Helen to the Greeks. The Greeks promise (feignedly) to "do her no wrong" despite the "great evils and hurts that were fallen from her" (Le Fèvre 1894, vol. 2: 665; cf. 666, 668). The Greek punishment of stoning is here updated to the medieval punishment of burning at the stake (a punishment reserved for witches and heretics, for women who committed murder, arson, robbery, or petty treason). It is only the fluency of Ulysses that prevents this punishment.

Caxton concludes his account by drawing attention to the ways in which Troy narratives differ: "for diverse men have made diverse books which in all points accord not" (Le Fèvre 1894, vol. 2: 701). His observation is particularly true of the ways in which texts assign, reassign, or remove blame. In none of the texts examined in this chapter is the question of blame or innocence clear-cut. The blame–praise dyad in texts is parallel to narrative's desire for Helen and its simultaneous recoil from her; both beauty and blame form part of the pattern of doubles and twins that haunt Helen's story. Praise turns into blame and vice versa.

George Peele, *The Tale of Troy* (1589)

In the sixteenth century George Peele has a different approach to the competing claims of agency and culpability. In his narrative poem *The Tale of Troy* he foregrounds not plurality or contradiction but alternatives, offering two scenarios for what may or may not have happened when Helen left Sparta. In the process his ending completely undoes the confident tone in which the body of the poem blames Helen.

Peele had a long and palimpsestic relationship with this work. He probably wrote it while an undergraduate at Oxford between 1572 and 1579 (see Peele 1952: 37). The poem was first published in 1589 but its composition predates its publication by several years, for in the dedicatory epistle Peele refers to it as "an old poem of mine own" (sig. A2r).

Peele subsequently revised the poem. The revision probably occurred around 1596 when Peele sent the poem as a gift (which is to say, a literary begging letter) to Lord Burghley, the Lord Chancellor. A secretary filed Peele's poem and accompanying letter "with others from cranks and crackpots" (Peele 1952: 108). Peele died later that year but in 1604 a revised version of the poem was published (presumably the revisions for the 1596 Burghley refurbishment) in a tiny (one and a half inches high) presentation volume of which only one copy is extant, now in private hands.[23] Lines from the poem also appear in Peele's earlier court pastoral, *The Arraignment of Paris* (1584). Thus, if the *Tale of Troy* was written when he was at college, Peele recycled lines from the poem into the play.[24]

Until the final lines the poem consistently stresses Helen's love of Paris. She gazes on him, studies his face, is inflamed with love. Although she is torn between right and wrong (Peele 1952: 169), love "will not be over-ruled,"[25] and so she "arms her boldly to this great amiss" (176). The couple are "lovers"; Helen's willing flight constitutes marital "treason."

But the final paragraph offers an alternative reading of Helen's departure for Troy and a bathetically tentative ending. I quote from the 1589 edition, noting 1604 revisions in brackets:

> *My author says, to honor Helen's name* [1604: in favor of her name],
> *That through the world hath been belied by Fame:*
> *How when the king her pheer* [husband] *was absent thence,*
> *A tale that well may lessen her offence,*
> *Sir Paris took the town by arms and skill,*
> *And carried her to Troy* [1604: And carried Helen thence] *against her will.*
> *Whom whether afterward she lov'd or no,*
> *I cannot tell, but may imagine so.*
>
> (sig. C3r)[26]

The coda is extraordinary for three interpretive moments. One is the alternative beginning to Helen's story in which Paris "carried Helen thence against her will" (Peele 1952: 493). Another is the introduction of moral commentary in the form of hesitant exculpation – "*a tale that* well may lessen *her offence*" (my emphasis). The third is the attempt at emotional imagining – did Helen love her abductor? – accompanied by a recognition that we cannot answer that question ("*I cannot tell*"), followed by an inability to accept that inconclusiveness as an answer: for, despite the terminative feel of the two iambs which begin the final pentameter ("*I cannot tell*"), the line trails off into the vague and conjectural "*but may imagine so.*" Why may he imagine so (given that he proffers no evidence)? Could he not equally imagine the opposite? Why voice the possibility of abduction now when, earlier in the poem, extended passages made Helen's love clear, called it a "revolt" against Menelaus, and smoothed it over with the jaunty couplet "and for her heart was from her body hent [snatched], / To Troy this Helen with her lover went" (177–8). Even as Peele concludes his poem, he opens it out again, admitting the possibility of an alternative scenario, and ending with an after story that is pure conjecture. He – and we – no more know the details of events than we know the feelings of its principal subject. The alternative narrative coda "well may lessen her offense" but there is no authorial conviction as to whether it does or does not. It is up to us to decide.

Bullen's edition misrepresents the poem, or its compositor, in a crucial way. In Bullen the last eight lines follow on as a continuous part of the poem. In the 1589 edition they are distinguished typographically (italic to the poem's roman), they are separated by four lines of white space, and begin with a large woodcut majuscule M that forces the indentation of the second line – as happens at the beginning of the poem with the factotum initial (figure 9). The Elizabethan compositor has intentionally differentiated the lines – and their content invites such typographical treatment. Peele has left Helen's narrative behind and taken us on to Aeneas and Italy; the return to Helen's story is abrupt, unexpected, and unmotivated. The poem, like Helen's story within it, has no defined ending.

Deifying Helen: John Ogle, *The Lamentation of Troy* (1594)

If one wants to defend Helen, the simplest and quickest way to do it is to present her as a god. Not the "daughter" of a god; writers from Homer onwards do that without it being a defense of Helen. Children of gods in Greek mythology, like the gods themselves, indulge in morally dubious episodes, often those including sexuality. (Isocrates defends divine infidelity on the grounds of the irresistible pull of beauty; §60. Infidelity is excused by beauty, not by divinity.) There is a paradox here. Gods can be blamed; but when humans are deified, they are beyond blame.[27]

Certainly those texts that deify Helen view it as a gesture of rescue (of body and of reputation). We see this most obviously in Euripides' *Orestes*, where Orestes has hold of Helen, ready to plunge his sword into her throat, when suddenly "Helen was gone! / Vanished from the room, from the whole house!" (Euripides 1972: 352). Apollo later appears from above to explain that "from Zeus immortal born, immortal she must live, / Reverenced as the goddess who saves seamen's lives" (359). He repeats his pronouncement in the play's penultimate speech:

> Helen I will conduct to the mansion of Zeus;
> There men shall adore her, a goddess enthroned
> Beside Hera and Hebe and great Heracles.
> There she, with her brothers, Tyndareos' sons,
> Shall be worshipped for ever with wine outpoured.
>
> (360–1)

This is the first explicit reference in literature to Helen as a goddess. It recasts Orestes' plot to kill Helen not as the misguided justice with which he views it but as dangerous blasphemy. It is he, not Helen, who has a narrow escape.

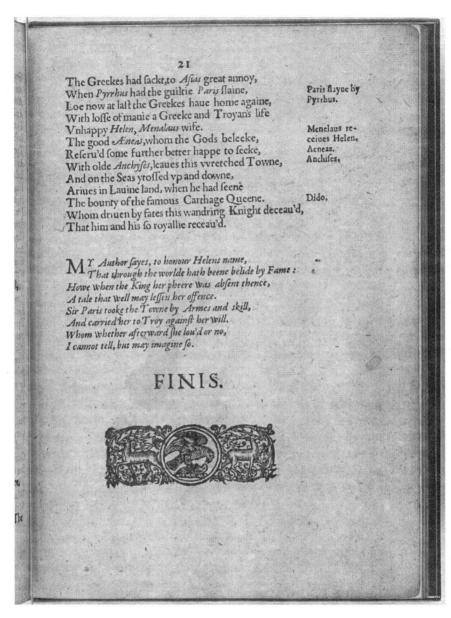

21

The Greekes had fackt,to *Asia* great annoy,
When *Pyrrhus* had the guiltie *Paris* flaine,   Paris flayne by
Loe now at laft the Greekes haue home againe,   Pyrrhus.
With loffe of manie a Greeke and Troyans life
Vnhappy *Helen, Menalaus* wife.   Menelaus re-
The good *Æneas*,whom the Gods beleeke,   ceiues Helen.
Referu'd fome further better happe to feeke,   Aeneas.
With olde *Anchyfes*,leaues this vvretched Towne,   Anchifes.
And on the Seas ytoffed vp and downe,
Ariues in Lauine land, when he had feene
The bounty of the famous Carthage Queene.   Dido.
Whom driuen by fates this wandring Knight deceau'd,
That him and his fo royallie receau'd.

M Y *Author fayes, to honour Helens name,*
    That through the worlde hath beene belide by Fame :
Howe when the King her pheere was abfent thence,
A tale that well may leffen her offence.
Sir Paris tooke the Towne by Armes and skill,
And carried her to Troy againft her will.
Whom whether afterward fhe lou'd or no,
I cannot tell, but may imagine fo.

FINIS.

Figure 9 George Peele, *A Tale of Troy* (1589), sig. C3r. The compositor presents the alternative ending of Peele's poem as a coda: he distinguishes it by italics, separates it with white space, and opens it with a large initial letter. Reproduced by kind permission of the Huntington Library, San Marino, California.

Other texts less dramatically, and with varying degrees of implicitness and explicitness, present Helen as a goddess. (In the *Aeneid*, e.g., Menelaus' immortality is due to his spouse's divine status; in Isocrates' *Encomium*, as we saw above, Helen obtains "power equal to that of the gods.") But perhaps the most extraordinary sequence of rhetorical maneuvers comes at the end of John Ogle's *Lamentation of Troy* (1594).

In comparison to most Renaissance literature, which usually condemns her, Ogle's narrative poem is an unusually sympathetic account of Helen. It is a dream vision in which the city of Troy laments her own destruction. She / the poem presents a series of laments by the Trojan royal family for Hector. As in the *Iliad*, Helen's lament is last; consequently it lingers. And as in the *Iliad* Helen appears vulnerable in the absence of her protector: "Now Hector's dead, who shall for Helen fight?" (sig. D4r).

Before Helen speaks, Paris gives his account of the war. He explains the need to view the Helen episode in the context of the long history of Greek/Trojan enmity: "'Twixt Greeks and us there was an ancient jar, / Which every man did with revenge inflame" (sig. C4r). The immediate occasion for this outbreak of hostilities was the abduction of a woman: Priam's sister, Hesione. Paris denies personal sexual interest in the Trojan expedition to Greece, correcting the narrative: "I did not go to please / Lascivious will as some unjustly fain" (sig. C3v). The expedition is purely political: he eight times says it was for revenge.[28] Venus' involvement is an afterthought: "Venus *besides* said to me: 'Paris go'" (sig. D1v, my italics). The personal and political become entwined when Paris and Deiphobus, the two Trojan princes who later marry Helen, head the Phrygian fleet.

Helen's lament follows Paris' narrative. She mourns over the body of Hector in 12 stanzas of lamentation that culminate in a *Lear*-like moment in which Helen mistakenly believes Hector to revive (sig. D3v). She then offers a logical defense of her presence in Troy, blaming Juno for her determination to destroy the city. Like Paris, she sees Venus' intervention as an *arrière pensée*: "Venus *besides* commanded me to come" (my italics). She protests that she is "unjustly . . . blamed" and concludes that since it was the gods' will, "Helen is no whore" (sig. E2v).

If Helen has argumentative logic on her side, the poet has a more powerfully persuasive tool: Christian metaphor. He had introduced Christian images earlier when, describing Helen's tears falling into her bosom, he comments "who couched was there, might think that he was blessed" (sig. D2v). Now he tells us that Helen speaks with an "angel's voice" (sig. D3v). Within two verses the gap between speaking like an angel and actually being an angel is collapsed when he asks the fates "why do you not restore his eyes to light, / now that the voice of such an angel prays."

Helen petitions with "an heavenly grace" (sig. D3v). She kisses Paris and when he inhales her breath, it makes his lungs "blessed" and offers him "bliss." When Helen later takes a seat beside Andromache, she is described as a "saint."

Ogle has earlier associated pagan poetry with Christian imagery – Homer writes with an "angel's tongue" (sig. B1r). Poetic and angelic voices are later linked when we are told that no one, not even "angel's tongues" can describe Troy's grief. But the Helen images are different from this kind of fleeting hyperbole. They are consistent, repeated, and incremental. We move from Helen as angel to dispenser of bliss and blessedness to saint.

Pagan literature can deify Helen. Monotheistic Christian literature cannot; but it can sanctify her. The difference is one of theology, but the exculpatory tactic is the same.

Mimetic Desire, the Scapegoat, and Blasphemy

Since in this book I am concerned with gaps in Helen's story, I want now to turn to the first moments in which we lose sight of Helen – at the oath of the suitors and at the onset of war. Let us consider the second first. The structure of the Trojan War epitomizes René Girard's theory of mimetic rivalry (2000 and 2005). For Girard desire is mimetic. Girard distinguishes between appetite and desire: human appetite is biological but desire is learned. Because humans learn by imitating others, and because we do not know what we desire, we "imitate the desires of others" (Kirwan 2005: 19): we want what they want and we want what they have. Children provide vivid examples of mimetic rivalry in action; so too does capitalism, which formalizes and institutionalizes acquisitive mimesis in the form of advertising. But whereas objects can be multiplied and mass produced, humans cannot. Hence mimetic desire leads to rivalry and often conflict.

The Trojan War is mimetic rivalry sustained over a decade. The Trojans want Hesione because the Greeks have her; the Greeks want Helen back because the Trojans have her; the Trojans want to keep her because the Greeks want her back; Agamemnon wants Briseis because Achilles has her; Neoptolemus wants Hermione because Orestes has her; and so on. And as the rivalries continue and escalate, the woman is lost sight of – at least *qua* woman. As Shakespeare's *Troilus and Cressida* makes clear, Helen is a "*theme of honor*" (2.2.199). With competitive desire, the object of desire becomes less and less relevant. One can apply the same logic to the oath of the suitors, where mimetic rivalry is increased from two to one hundred. The Greek princes and kings desire Helen because she is desired by Greek princes and kings.

When mimetic desire remains at the level of rivalry and does not proceed to outright conflict, it can be healthy: it has a unifying effect, binding people together in shared goals. We see this in the oath of the suitors. And, as we saw above, several texts also invoke this benefit postconflict in an attempt to justify Helen's loss and the war to regain her.

Where the Trojan War narrative differs from Girardian theory is in its handling of the scapegoat. For Girard when mimetic rivalry leads to conflict, the social disorder must be cured by the expulsion or sacrifice of a designated victim: the scapegoat. The chosen victims are usually the cause of the crisis; their sacrifice cures the chaos they instigated. Thus the attitude to scapegoats after their death/expulsion is a complex mix of good and bad, praise and blame.

As we saw in chapter 1, narrative needs Helen dead. Helen's death is the only satisfactory closure in narrative terms. But Helen is the scapegoat who refuses to die. She is to be stoned, decapitated, burned – it matters little which version we read – in all, she is to be punished by death. But death is something she evades whether by beauty (just "being"), by sexual manipulation (revealing her breasts), by pleading (*The Women of Troy*), or by proxy (Ulysses' eloquence in Caxton).[29] Ethics are not relevant to Helen's ontology. Sacrifice works by taking something from this world and giving it up to another world. But, as we saw in chapter 2, Helen is already not of this world. She is slippage: woman and goddess, the beautiful and the monstrous, absence and presence. She cannot be killed, because she was never alive in any normal way. Helen is an ontological problem the scapegoat tries to resolve through an ethical problem. It is this clash of systems – being accountable versus mere being – that hovers behind the bifurcated texts discussed in this chapter for reasons that will now become clear.

The verb "to blame" embodies the conflicts embodied in Helen herself, that between a mortal and a (semi)goddess. It shares its root with "blaspheme," arriving in English from Greek and Latin (*blasphēmos, blasphemus*) via old French: *blâme, blasmer*. The root means evil speaking. Hence to blame means to speak evilly of a person; to blaspheme means to speak evilly of a deity. But both meanings were for a long time present in just one verb, *blame*, as we see in Peele's *Arraignment of Paris*: "Ah Venus, but for reverence unto thy sacred name, / To steal a silly maiden's love, I might account it blame" (sig. C2v). Here "blame" means "blasphemy." English later developed two separate verbs, one limited to the secular, one to the sacred.

The congruence of meaning etymologically is helpful to bear in mind when considering texts about Helen. In their bipolar linguistic behavior, their accusatory and exculpatory pull, their competing tensions, it is as if they are aware that to blame Helen is an act of blasphemy. Removing her from the action as does Euripides when his *deus ex machina* rescues her from Orestes' murderous sword, or removing her from secular language as does Ogle with Christian vocabulary of saints, blessing, and angels reminds us that Helen's essence is absence. Essence, absence, ex-sense: "outside the senses, beyond understanding" (Taylor 2001: 30). There is something almost theological about the textual and physical lacunae, and the representational difficulty, in Helen narratives. And the texts in this chapter that negotiate Helen's blame show inevitable confusion between an ethical and an ontological problem.

Yeats encapsulates this predicament – and simultaneously answers it – in the rhetorical question that concludes, "No Second Troy": "What could she have done, being what she is?" The first half of the line concerns action, ethics, behavior, blame, responsibility; the second is about ontology. The latter determines the former: being ("what she is") leads to doing ("have done"). Blame is thus an irrelevant concept, one attached to decisions and agency (as he acknowledges in the poem's opening line: "Why should I blame her?"). Helen, "being what she is," lacks agency; there was no other course for her to follow ("what could she have done?").

Yeats's Helen, as we saw in chapter 2, is not Homer's beauty but Ireland's: Maud Gonne, the source of Yeats's "misery." Yeats had fallen in love with Maud at first sight in 1889 and she was to be his muse for more than 80 poems in which he characterized her as both Celtic and classical heroines and goddesses. By 1908, when he wrote "No Second Troy," Maud had had three children (of whom two survived), a long-term French lover, an Irish husband followed by a legal separation (in 1906), a spiritual marriage to Yeats in 1898, and an affair with him from June 1908 to May 1909 (consummated in Dec. 1908). In 1902 she played Cathleen ni Houlihan in Yeats's play of that name; her beauty and her political (nationalist) activism identifies her in Yeats's work with the twin ideals of beauty and of Ireland.

"No Second Troy" marks Yeats's return to Hellenism after two decades of Celtic subjects and two decades of troubled relations with Maud (McKinsey 2002: 174). The poem is both a meditation on Maud and on the current state of Ireland. Maud's aristocratic beauty and classical poise contrast with the violence she engenders (through her fervent grass-roots activism and political teaching). "No Second Troy" works through contrasts: the ideal and the reality; timeless beauty and local politics; then and now; Petrarchan subjectivity (the plangent "I") in a classically French sonnet form (a *douzaine* rather than the Italian or English 14-line form);[30] Greece and Ireland. This last contrast informs the entire poem. The implicit answer to the poem's concluding rhetorical question – "Was there another Troy for her to burn?" – is "No" (modern Ireland is not the heroic ancient world). These (the title and the question) are the only references to Troy, and they are negative: the heroic military past is not being reenacted in Ireland's contentious present.

Although the poem is rooted in contemporary politics and the poet's personal life, it illustrates several of the features of Helen narratives. Its protagonist is absent: Maud-Helen is only named as a pronoun, as "she." Her beauty is conveyed by its (and her) effect on others: it/she engenders violence. Furthermore Maud, like Helen, is given a passive agency: in the last line ("Was there another Troy for her to burn?"), as McKinsey observes, it is "as if she had wielded the torch herself" (2002: 187n).

And, most relevant to this chapter: although the poem aims to exculpate Maud-Helen, it succeeds in blaming her. The opening "Why should I blame her that she filled my days / With misery" offers the grounds of blame that are being forgiven, grounds that are then expounded and expanded over ten lines. The poem's blame is "retracted but nevertheless persist[s] under erasure" (McKinsey 2002: 181). This ghostly presence, typical of all Helen narratives, enters the poem even before its first line: the title invokes Priam's city only to assert its extinction.

In a poem dedicated to absolution, Yeats offers two ways of exculpating Maud-Helen. The first is by blaming not her but the times ("an age like this"). The second is by arguing that Maud-Helen cannot be blamed for events caused by her being: "What could she have done, being what she is?" This is a question of ontology, not of morality; of being, not blame. Ethical categories and ontological categories cannot overlap – you cannot blame someone for being who they are. Yeats makes explicit what the texts in this chapter acknowledge only implicitly – that as the embodiment of Beauty and as the epitome of Desire, Helen cannot be personally responsible for the acts and effects of desire. This is the category problem we encountered in chapter 2: to be the category is simultaneously to be outside that category.

Yeats's last line leaves open (or unstated) what Maud-Helen "is." Or rather, his grammatical structure hints that she simply *is*. That is a transcendental structure, a theological structure, and hence a categorical problem. In chapters 2 and 3 we saw attempts to define "what" Helen "is": Helen is Beauty, Helen is Wanton Sexuality. In both cases Helen *is* the category, the paradigm of beauty or illicit sexual behavior. And if to "be" Helen means to be the beautiful wife of Menelaus, who goes to Troy with Paris, that is beyond the realm of blame.[31] As Robert Meagher explains in relation to Aphrodite's commands to Helen in book 3 of the *Iliad*, "Helen has no choice. Like Aphrodite, she *is* desire. Helen can no more resist the power that defines her than others can resist her" (1995: 27).

This point is illustrated in the early modern period in the use of Helen's name as a byword for blameworthy sexual behavior. When the early modern uses Helen's name as a common noun, we have the most cogent illustration of the way in which Helen is outside normal categories, becoming her own category.

Naming and Shaming

As we have seen, the usual name in Renaissance England for the woman we know as Helen of Troy is simply "Helen." Shakespeare's Theseus talks of the infatuated lover who sees "Helen's beauty in a brow of Egypt" (i.e., imagines a dark-skinned complexion, not valued by the Elizabethans, to be as beautiful as Helen of Troy). Shakespeare's Sonnet 53 compares the young man to Helen: "On Helen's cheek all art of beauty set, / And you in Grecian tires are painted new" (lines 5–8). In *Pierce Penilesse* (1592) Thomas Nashe lists sexual wantons: "Lais, Cleopatra, Helen"; *Romeo and Juliet* invokes love heroines: "Laura . . . Dido . . . Cleopatra . . . Helen . . . Hero" (2.3.30–2); *As You Like It* lists famous women: "Helen . . . Cleopatra . . . Atalanta . . . Lucretia" (3.2.145–8). On no occasion does the reference to Helen require explanatory expansion. "Helen" in the early modern period had only one referent: Helen of Troy.[32] This is why the additional epithet "of Troy" is unnecessary. To invoke "Helen" is to invoke Helen of Sparta/Troy. There was a one-to-one correspondence between signifier and signified.

Although the sign is secure, the meaning of that sign is debatable. Today Helen of Troy automatically signifies great beauty; it has no negative associations (otherwise the cosmetic accessory company in Texas, producer of hair dryers, shower caps and rain hats, would not have named its business "Helen of Troy"). When the student in Andrew Waterman's poem "What's in a Name?" (1990) reflects on the beauty of his English literature teacher, he muses on the appropriateness of her first name, Helen:

> Chosen by parents hot on myth
> called Paris. So you see,
> her moniker's no drab hieroglyph:
> it tells her what to be.

What she has to "be" is beautiful, like Helen of Troy. He contemplates the risk her parents took in naming her:

> But how, at first, could her crowd know
> she'd not grow up flat-chest-
> ed, spotty, bum immense, wits slow
> that name a cruel jest?

This is a profoundly Renaissance concern, the relation between name and identity. Renaissance dictionaries included proper names (place names, biblical names, mythological names) viewing them as words that had a meaning. Was the meaning of Helen "beauty" as in Waterman's twentieth-century poem? Was it wantonness, infidelity, disaster? Or was it both, an immoral interior covered in external beauty?

For many early modern writers "Helen" clearly meant beauty. The adjective that most often prefaces her name (redundantly) is "fair." In *Anatomy of Melancholy* (1621) Robert Burton discusses Theseus' infatuation at first sight with Helen's beautiful face. Robert Allott's section "Of beauty" in *Wit's Theatre* three times refers to the power of Helen's beauty. For Robert Greene, Thomas Lodge, Thomas Fenne, and Robert Parry the primary association for the word "Helen" is beauty.[33] In texts that refer to an aged or wrinkled Helen, such as Francis Meres' *Wit's Commonwealth* (1634), Austin Saker's *Narbonus* (1580), Thomas Adam's *The Black Devil* (1615), John William's sermon on patience, *Perseverantia Sanctorum* (1628), and Arthur Golding's translation of Ovid's *Metamorphoses* (1567), the contrast, specified or implied, is between faded beauty and famed beauty.

But for many writers, there was an additional meaning: irresponsible sexuality. In de la Marche's *Travelled Pilgrim* (1569) the poet considers the number of beautiful women who do not succumb to sinful flight with a lover: "a thousand Helens now doth reign in pulchritude and shape / yet very few that minds to leave that sin for to escape" (D3v). In *The Poet's Willow* (1614) Richard Brathwaite talks of ruin by "a Helen." In fact Brathwaite conveniently explains his noun: it means lust. Lust is "the bane of flourishing empires," is epitomized by "a Helen," and "may be thus defined: she is respectless of the means so she may attain the end: her aim is to satisfy her own exorbitant affection, which to gain she is secure of her own ruin, country's desolation" (sig. F1v).

In all the above examples the referent for Helen is the woman whose sexuality led to the destruction of Troy. In William Camden's *Remains* (1605), however, Camden identifies Helen with the mother of the emperor Constantine. That this is *not* the primary "meaning" of Helen is surprising, given both the significance of St Helen in Christian history and her unavoidable presence in London's cultural, architectural, and ecclesiastical landscape. The church of St Helen in Bishopsgate, a thirteenth-century Benedictine foundation, was Shakespeare's parish church when he lived in the district in his early years in London. It survived both the Great Fire of London and the Blitz (although it suffered from two IRA bombs in the 1990s) and can be found tucked away in Great St Helen's, just off Bishopsgate Street.[34] Yet, despite this cultural and physical reminder, the

Christian Helen never replaced the pagan as the "meaning" of Helen. When "Helen" is used to denote the mother of the emperor Constantine, the name *always* receives appositive explanation. Thus in *1 Henry 6* we read, "Helen, the mother of great Constantine" (1.2.142).[35] The appositive definition is constantly required because "Helen" on its own clearly means something other than "mother to Constantine."

This is made clear in *The Second Part of the Mirror for Magistrates* (1578) by Thomas Blenerhasset. In a paean of praise to Constantine's mother, Blenerhasset wonders if there is "any Goddess . . . which may compare with Queen Helena?" Realizing the trap he has set himself, he hastily explains, "not she of Greece, which brought final destruction unto the flourishing Troy, but she of Britain, who redeemed her decaying country from foreign tyranny" (sig. C1v). In early modern England, then, to be Helen means to be Menelaus' queen, Paris' queen, not Constantine's mother.

So fixed was the equation of "Helen" with "Helen of Troy" that the name developed currency as a common noun, denoting the beauty or the behavior of Helen of Troy. In the anonymous *Death of Robert Earl of Huntington* (1601) the Queen scorns Matilda's beauty: "Is this the Helen, this the paragon?" (sig. G3r). Lyly's Euphues praises Lucilla, "for beauty she was the Helen of Greece" (*Euphues*, sig. R4r), and in 1602, in a presciently modern warning, Philaretes describes tobacco as "a Grecian Helen" (something that seems lovely but is pernicious; sig. A3r). In Jonson's *Poetaster*, Tucca asks Crispinus to identify "thy Helen" (4.3.26). Marlowe's Dido fears for her sexual reputation: "all the world [will] call me a second Helen / For being entangled by a stranger's looks" (5.1.141–5). She reiterates her shame just three lines later: "And I be call'd a second Helena!" (5.1.148). Lamilia in Robert Greene's *Groatsworth of Wit* is less hesitant in inhabiting the Helen image than Dido. "Lamilia herself, like a second Helen, courtlike begins to salute Roberto yet did her wandering eye glance often at Luciano" (sig. C2v).[36] George Pettie's Procris rejects a suitor, correcting his misperception of her availability: "you have no Helen in hand" (1576: sig. Y2v). Margaret, the fair maid of Fressingfield in Greene's *Friar Bacon and Friar Bungay* worries lest she become a Helen not just in beauty but in sexual history: "Shall I be Helen in my froward fates, / As I am Helen in my matchless hue, / And set rich Suffolk with my face afire?" (x.93–5). Renaissance authors are not quite sure if Helen's name "means" beauty or something more blameworthy. As a noun, her name (like the texts explored in this chapter) has two interpretations. This duality continued for centuries. F. W. Bourdillon's Helen articulates her divided identity in 1893:

I am Helen, and my name
Is a glory and a shame
For my beauty was earth's crown
And my sin shook cities down.

(19)

What is significant, however, is that her name sets the standard for a category, simply by being turned into a common noun. Franz Rosenzweig writes that

> with the proper name, the rigid wall of objectness has been breached. That which has a name of its own can no longer be a thing . . . It is incapable of utter absorption into the category for there can be no category for it to belong to; it is its own category. (Quoted in Natanson 1979: 533)

In every chapter of this book so far we have seen that Helen is "incapable of utter absorption into the category." She "is" Beauty; she "is" the seized woman. And when her name is used as a noun indicating lust or blame it supports Yeats's point about her being blameless. As a common noun she is outside the category that bears her name and so cannot be guilty of what she embodies, of what "she is."

*

By the Victorian period, beauty had become the primary association of the name Helen. When Henry Rider Haggard and Andrew Lang use Helen's name as a common noun (the heroine is not Helen but "the Helen") in their novel *The World's Desire* (1890), the generic name is not a standard of shame but the paradigm of beauty. How did a name and noun representing sin and shame come to be a name/noun meaning beauty? The transition from blame to beauty, like the transition from Helen of Greece to Helen of Troy, is first visible in Renaissance drama. Shakespeare treats the name Helen sympathetically (see Maguire 2007: 74–119) and it is Helen's beauty rather than Helen's shame that his Theseus imagines in a female brow. Marlowe's Faustus immortalizes the *face* that launched a thousand ships, and Faustus' students decide that Helen of Greece was the most beautiful lady, not the most reprehensible, who ever lived.

Faustus' paean is the most famous response to Helen's beauty. I want now to examine its contexts: the Faust legend that Marlowe inherited and the authors who adapted the legend after him. That is the subject of chapter 5.

5

Helen and the Faust Tradition

But Satan-sweethearts, though quite charming in their way,
Can't pass for Homer's heroines even today.

Goethe/Luke, *2 Faust*

MEPHISTOPHELES: *I thought you wanted to explore the limits of*
human experience.

FAUST: *Well yes. But within limits.*

Goethe/Clifford, *Faust: Part One*

In the sixteenth-century Helen of Troy becomes the bedfellow to Dr
Faustus, the man who sold his soul to the devil, and she gives birth to a
baby boy. This story, published in Germany in 1587 and translated into
English the next year or early 1589, provided Christopher Marlowe with
the plot of his play *Dr Faustus* (probably written c.1589 although not published until 1604, then reprinted in a revised text in 1616).

In the eighteenth century the Faust story returned to Germany, where
Goethe spent more than 60 years preparing *Faust*, a massive two-part drama
that is more or less unperformable (although it has been performed).
Goethe first planned it in the 1770s but wrote it in phases, sometimes putting
it aside for decades. Nonetheless he carried Helen around with him
throughout his life, he said, like an inner fable ("inneres Märchen";
Goethe/Luke 1994: xx), and in 1827 he published *Helen: An Intermezzo*
(*Zwischenspiel*) *for Faust*. This separate publication of what is essentially
act 3 of *2 Faust* (the complete play was not published until Dec. 1832)
allows Goethe's Helen to be considered not in isolation from the rest of
the unwieldy work to which she belongs but in some measure independently
of it. In 2006 the Scottish playwright Jo Clifford adapted Goethe's *Faust*,
making the work theatrically viable, abbreviating it, and transposing it to
twenty-first-century Scotland.

The above material divides itself neatly into two pairings: Marlowe's *Dr Faustus* and the Faust book prose source from which he worked (an English translation of the German original); Clifford's *Faust* and Goethe's German original. Throughout this book I generally exclude Helen material in foreign languages (unlike Faustus I am aware of the need to adhere to limits). In this chapter, however, I include German material because of the difficulty of considering Marlowe or Clifford without their sources. Clifford's plays overhaul Goethe's: they are radically different from, and yet clearly indebted to, their Romantic predecessors. Similarly Marlowe uses only the general framework of P. F.'s English translation of the German Faust book.[1] But, in keeping with the flexibility of early modern concepts of translation, P. F. has already adapted and expanded the German original. And what he adds, Marlowe tends to omit. Both P. F. and Marlowe are interested in women and devils but in very different ways.

This, then, is a chapter about Faust book traditions and variants, but it is also a chapter about translation. If Helen is frequently abducted, she is as often translated. That statement is tautological, for translation is a form of abduction: the word comes from the Latin *translatio* (carrying across); translation is a process of carrying across languages, cultures, and eras. We tend to think of translation as a process of simple equivalence, the turning of one language into another, when in fact translation is interpretation and adaptation. The Elizabethans were unselfconsciously aware of this. Thomas Drant prefaced his translation of Horace, *A Medicinable Moral, that is, the two books of Horace's Satires* (1566) with the following explanation:

> I have interfarced [inserted] (to remove his obscurity, and sometimes to better his matter) much of mine own devising. I have pieced [expanded] his reason, eked and mended his similitudes, mollified his hardness, prolonged his curtal kind of speeches, changed & much altered his words, but not his sentence: or at least (I dare say) not his purpose. (sig. aiiir–v)

What the Restoration later called "adaptation," and what we call "(re)appropriation," Drant called "translation." And for Drant, as for his age, translation was a creative act, a dialogue between the past and the present, a cultural linking, an intertextual moment (see Bate 1993: 31). When P. F. translates German into English and Marlowe translates prose into drama and Goethe translates puppet traditions into symbolist poetry and Clifford translates Romanticism into contemporary sexual politics, we have a complex sequence of carryings across and carryings on (in both senses).

Form and Appearance in the English Faust Book

The Faust legend is generally known for one of two things: it is the story of a man who sells his soul to the devil;[2] and the story of a man who commits gross moral turpitude with Helen of Troy. There was a real-life Dr Faustus, flourishing in Germany from the early sixteenth century until his death in c.1539, but the Faust book legends of devils and Helen of Troy are fictional accretions. Johann or Georg or Jörg ("George") Faust was an astrologer, natural philosopher, necromancer, and physician who died in dramatic circumstances, probably while performing a chemistry experiment (Jones 1994: 3–4; Marlowe/Trussler 1989: x). His story became conflated with tales about other magicians (e.g., their raising of spirits), and when Luther described Faust's death as the "devil's reward" (Jones 1994: 4) a back-story inevitably developed: a diabolic end must be preceded by a diabolic pact. The story grew and grew until it was published in German in 1587. The book was a publishing sensation, the print run exhausted within a few weeks, and "three more editions and two new recensions, each with additional chapters of anecdotes, appeared during the same year" (Jones 1994: 9). An English translation followed within 12 months: *The History of the Damnable Life and Deserved Death of Doctor John Faustus.*[3]

The English Faust book (EFB), as it is known, is an excitingly eclectic work. It contains science and pseudoscience; magic and tricks, fireworks and performances; chorographic description; misogynist aphorism ("hell, the woman's belly and the earth are never satisfied"; Jones 1994: 645–6, ch. 15[4]), conversationally realistic dialogue and a chatty narrative style ("Well, let us come again to his conjuration where we left him at his fiery globe"; 112–13, ch. 2[5]); terrifying descriptions of hell; domestic ambience (the happy *ménage à trois* of Faust, Wagner, and Mephistopheles); comic impatience (Faust is vexed at the devil's delay in ch. 2,[6] Mephistopheles at Faust's insatiable curiosity in ch. 16: "I am loth to reason with thee any further, for thou art never satisfied in thy mind but always bringest me a new"; 1715–16); beautiful women and sex.

Form is very important in the EFB, cuing us to the topic of beauty long before the appearance of Helen of Troy. The EFB regularly describes Mephistopheles' appearance – nay, appearances, for he is characterized by an ability to metamorphose. He first appears as a dragon, then as a flame that becomes a burning globe, then as a man-height burning devil, becomes a fiery man[7] and finally a greyfriar. The friar's costume in EFB has nothing to do with Faust's request (as it later does in Marlowe) although, having seen the devil in this human disguise, Faust stipulates that Mephistopheles should "always come to him like a friar, after the order of St Francis, with a bell in his hand like St Anthony" (Jones 1994: 213–14, ch. 5). (The devil's appearance is irrelevant to everyone else, for only Faust can see him.)

If Faust is pragmatically preoccupied with appearance in the EFB, he is also intellectually concerned with it, and many of his conversations with the devil deal with outward form. He asks Mephistopheles what Lucifer looked like before he fell (479–80, ch. 13). Mephistopheles encourages Faust to learn how to run through walls, to slither like a snake, swim like a fish, and fly like a bird (810–12, ch. 18).[8] Faust questions Lucifer about the "ugly, odious" animal appearance of the devils (916, 928–9, ch. 19); experiments with transforming himself into a hog, a worm, a dragon (944–5, ch. 19);[9] and is given explicit descriptions of hell (descriptions conspicuously absent from the 1604 text of Marlowe's play and delayed until act 5 of the 1616 text when the Bad Angel gives a 12-line description of what Faustus sees on the stage direction "Hell is discovered").

From practical concerns about costume and metaphysical conversations about form we move to physical involvement: Faust in the EFB has several encounters with beautiful women. In chapter 9 he asks the devil for a wife. Mephistopheles loses his temper, threatening Faust with torture and death for this blatant repudiation of their contract, for, as he explains, echoing the Book of Common Prayer, "wedlock is a chief institution ordained of God" (357, ch. 9). As if this were not reason enough to deny Faust's request, Mephistopheles throws in a casual piece of early modern marital misogyny: "think with what unquiet life, anger, strife and debate thou shalt live in when thou takest a wife" (364–5, ch. 9). Faust is terrified to mention matrimony again lest the devil dismember him, but two hours later he renews his request,[10] which Mephistopheles grants via sleight of hand: the appearance of "an ugly devil, so fearful and monstrous to behold that Faustus durst not look on him" (386–7, ch. 9). In additional lines of dialogue by P. F., Mephistopheles exults in his triumph: "How likest thou thy wedding?" (388, ch. 9). There is no sense here (as there is in Marlowe's version of the episode, where both the A-text and B-text stage directions are explicit) that the devil is in disguise as a bride-wife.[11] Whereas the EFB's Faustus "durst not look on *him*," Marlowe's Faustus exclaims, "A plague on *her* for a hot whore" (A-text 2.1.153, my italics). Here, as so often, Marlowe's play is gender-conflated, referring to a man as a woman.

Having made his antisacramental point, the EFB Mephistopheles promises Faust "what woman soever thou wilt, be she alive or dead," which indulgence Faustus "practised and persevered in a long time" (395–6, 400, ch. 9). Whenever Faustus is tempted by spiritually Christian thoughts, the devil distracts him with a sexual temptation: "straightways the devil would thrust him a fair lady into his chamber, which fell to kissing and dalliance with him" (705–6, ch. 15). Mephistopheles promises to teach Faustus how to cuckold royalty, "to have [his] pleasure of their fair ladies, wives and concubines" (808–9, ch. 18).[12] During his world tour, Faustus encounters the Turkish emperor and is displeased by his harem: "this liked not Faustus, that one man might have so many wives as he would" (1606–7, ch. 22). As we might by now expect from my many notes and parentheses on the subject, this comment about Faustus' reaction is P. F.'s interpolation.

The addition is more than usually conspicuous, for, on this occasion, P. F. has failed to integrate it in his prose: it interrupts, without any narrative motivation, a description of the architecture of Constantinople. I italicize the insertion:

> This city was surnamed by Constantine the founder thereof, being builded of very fair stone. In the same the Great Turk hath three fair palaces, the walls are strong, the pinnacles are very huge and the streets large: *but this liked not Faustus, that one man might have so many wives as he would.* The sea runneth hard by the city, the wall hath eleven gates. (1603–8, ch. 22)

P. F.'s additions continue in this paragraph and subsequent pages; indeed this is one of his most heavily reworked chapters.

The lengthy sexual narrative begins with Faust's envy of the emperor's splendor ("for his pomp he thought was more fit for himself") and Faust's indulgence in a "little apish play" (fire and illusions; 1614–16, ch. 22). He then visits the harem, where P. F. continues the material of his earlier interpolation with Faustus' imperial envy becoming sexual envy. He plans to extend the experience of the wives and concubines (the italicized material below is P. F.'s addition):

> *Then Faustus took the fairest by the hand and led her into a chamber, where after his manner he fell to dalliance, and thus he continued a whole day and night: and when he had delighted himself sufficiently with her, he put her away and made his spirit bring him another, so likewise he kept with her 24 hours play, causing his spirit to fetch him most dainty fare.* And so he passed away six days, having each day his pleasure of a sundry lady, and that of the fairest. (1643–50, ch. 22)

After this unusual week, which reads like a parodic creation (for six days Faustus labored and on the seventh he rested), the six ladies praise the sexual ability of their visitor (whom they call "the God Mahomet") in terms that might furnish advertising copy for Viagra. Once again, P. F. adds to the account, this time by giving one of the women a subtle sexual compliment to the emperor. The emperor asks if "actual copulation" took place.

> "Yea my Lord," quoth one, "*as if you had been there yourself, you could not have mended it* [improved upon it], for he lay with us stark naked, kissed and colled us, and so delighted me that for my part, I would he came two or three times a week to serve me in such sort again." (1669–73, ch. 22; the italics represent P. F.'s addition)

When in the EFB Faustus later conjures up Alexander the Great and his paramour, the translation preserves the physical aesthetics of the German original. It lingers appreciatively on the woman's clothing, her complexion, her figure, and her beauty: "she was clothed in blue velvet, wrought and embroidered with pearls and gold, she was also excellent fair like milk and blood mixed,[13] tall and slender, with a face round as an apple" (1893–5, ch. 29). P. F. follows this with an additional descriptive phrase about her movement: "and thus she passed certain times up and down the house." The episode is relevant to the later Helen episode in one important way. Faustus conjures up Alexander and his nameless paramour at the specific request of the Holy Roman Emperor (Charles V), but offers a prefatory disclaimer:

> Your Majesty shall know that their dead bodies are not able substantially [i.e., in substance] to be brought before you, but such spirits as have seen Alexander and his paramour alive, shall appear unto you in manner and form as they both lived in their most flourishing time. (1873–6, ch. 29)

Magic here has the same limitations as the medical profession that so disappoints Marlowe's Faustus: it cannot make men live again. The Faust book stresses that these are simulacra. Nonetheless the Emperor is so impressed by the representation that he disbelieves Faust's explanation: " 'Sure it cannot otherwise be,' said he to himself, 'but that the spirits have changed themselves into these forms and have not deceived me' " (1898–1900, ch. 29). If Faustus' deception by the devil works in tandem with self-deception, his fault has an imperial parallel.

Having sampled the text's interest in form and beauty, we are now ready to meet Helen of Troy.

Helen in the English Faust Book

Helen of Troy occupies two separate chapters in the EFB: chapter 45 when Faustus conjures her up for the students, and chapter 55 when he makes her "his common concubine and bedfellow" (2665). Helen first appears at the request of the students.[14] One Sunday evening the students are debating female beauty, with everyone (in another of P. F.'s additions) comparing what they have seen of beauty with what they have heard on the topic. Accordingly (in both German and English) one student expresses a wish to see Helen of Greece: she must be exceptionally beautiful, he says, if one judges by her effect (she caused "so great bloodshed"; 2349–50, ch. 45).

Faustus responds as he has done to the emperor Charles V. He will bring Helen as she was in her prime, dressed in her customary attire, and the students must remain silent. Helen's appearance is notable for being the only extensive description of Helen of Troy in early modern literature. She is tall and slender, and wears purple velvet, richly embroidered. She has thigh-length blonde hair; her eyes are black, her face round, her lips and cheeks red, her mouth small and her neck swan-white. (This last is perhaps, as elsewhere, an allusion to her paternity.) She is also deliberately and flauntingly sexy: with "amorous" eyes and a "wanton countenance," she looks around "with a rolling hawk's eye" (2367, 2371–2, 2371, ch. 45) and the students are later unable to sleep for thinking about her. Unlike the Emperor, however, they make an effort to remind themselves that Helen is a spirit.

Nonetheless they ask Faustus if they can see Helen again, in the company of a painter who will take her portrait. Faustus denies their request – he cannot summon up Helen on demand, he says – but gives them a portrait which he says will be "as good to you as if yourselves should see the drawing thereof" (2380–1, ch. 45). This is an odd statement about art and verisimilitude: why should the students only believe the counterfeit if they have watched it being drawn, given that they have already seen the original (albeit an original counterfeit) against which to measure the painting? Furthermore the emphasis accorded this discussion of painting is bathetically undermined when, having received Helen's portrait from Faustus, we are told the students "soon lost it" (2382). (Beauty, it seems, resides in anticipation rather than reality.)

It is five years and ten chapters before Faustus makes Helen his paramour. (He is already sleeping with seven of the world's most beautiful women; is Helen an addition or a replacement?) The syntax is perplexing: "he had a great desire to lie with fair Helena of Greece, *especially her* whom he had seen and showed unto the students of Wittenberg" (2660–2, ch. 55, my italics). The implication is that there are multiple Helens; in context it probably means that he desires sex with the spirit representing Helen he saw in chapter 45, happy to have this substitute. Faust not only has sex but falls in love with her and cannot be parted from her for one hour (not, adds P. F., "if he should therefore have suffered death, she had so stolen away his heart"; 2666–8, ch. 55). Helen becomes pregnant and gives birth to a baby boy. In the course of a year this infant prodigy not only acquires language and political knowledge but sees into the future; in a father–son bonding he imparts his knowledge to Faustus.[15] When Faustus dies the following year, however, both Helen and her son vanish.

Faustus in the EFB is much concerned physically with female beauty (and beautiful females) and this is paralleled by his intellectual interest in diabolic morphology. But he is also a domestic creature and the chapter of (implied) domesticity with Helen and their son is not the first such chapter in the book. In chapter 7 Faustus completes his contract with the devil, and P. F. concludes with an ironic addition: "Thus the spirit and Faustus were agreed and dwelt together: no doubt there was a virtuous housekeeping" (311–12). But the chapter begins with an addition which stresses Faustus' domestic isolation – Faustus "having but one only boy with him" (273) – and in chapter 8 we are told (in both German and English) that "Faustus loved the boy well" (324). This sentiment is made more explicit in chapter 56: "This Wagner was so well beloved with Faustus that he used him as his son: for do what he would his master was always therewith well content" (2680–2). In his will Faustus leaves Wagner his house, garden, 1,600 guilders, a farm, a gold chain, and "much plate and other household stuff" (2685–7, ch. 56).

In chapter 8 P. F. expands the statement of the German Faust book that "Faustus loved the boy well" with the additional clause "and he was fellow with Mephostophiles" (326). This clause makes Wagner and Mephistopheles coevals (indeed coevils). To motivate this additional clause, P. F. omits a sentence from the German Faust book which continues the father–son relationship of Faustus–Wagner (I italicize the omitted material): "Faustus loved the boy well; *and like all youngsters he was more prone to wickedness than piety.*" The tone in the German is one of parental frustration with mischief as much as narratorial disapproval of evil. This is a "youngster," Faustus' "boy," his pupil. When Mephistopheles joins the household, it is not that Wagner acquires a mischievous brother but that Faustus acquires a dutiful wife. The German and English Faust books continue: Mephistopheles "ever was diligent at Faustus' command, going about the house, clothed like a friar, with a little bell in his hand, seen of none but Faustus" (328–9, ch. 8). Silent, invisible, obedient to command: Mephistopheles is the ideal early modern wife. Indeed when Marlowe's Mephistopheles tells the doctor to ignore marriage – "If thou lovest me, think no more of it" (A-text 2.1.155; B-text 2.1.151) – he is perhaps implying more than that devils don't deal in sacraments; when one male says this to another, the nuance is inevitably more complex. Marlowe's Faustus is a lonely character (one who, as Kay Stockholder shows

[1988], has banished women as well as parental figures from his life) and his conversations with Mephistopheles reveal a poignant need for companionship. In the English Faust book, when Mephistopheles exits angered at Faustus' temerity in asking about God, and threatening to dismember him, Faustus weeps and howls "not for his sins towards God, but for that the devil was parted him so suddenly and in such a rage" (867–9, ch. 19). Again this entire (lengthy) sequence occurs only in the EFB.

Thus P. F. has underlined or expanded his German original in thematically consistent ways. He is interested in bodies (their appearance, shape, transformation, and function);[16] he is interested in women; and he is interested in the household. (Other of his concerns – travel, science, magic – also receive expansion but are not germane to this chapter.)

And what P. F. takes such care to add, Marlowe omits. His play lacks women;[17] Faustus' interest in shape is uncerebral; Wagner is a student rather than a substitute son; and Helen is an off-stage moment rather than a household fixture. P. F.'s concerns are not Marlowe's concerns. P. F.'s EFB is an inquiry into form, transformation, and deformation. He is as interested in devil shapes as in female shapes or the mental transformation from a dutiful to a transgressive scholar. Marlowe is interested in limits.

The Faust story, in whatever century or form, from German puppet play to early modern tragedy, from Berlioz's *Damnation of Faust* (1846) to Broadway's *Damn Yankees* (1955), is inescapably a tale of limits and boundaries. A man who makes a pact with a devil is a man who wants to transcend human limitation. This is made explicit at the start of Marlowe's *Dr Faustus*, where, in a soliloquy assessing his achievements in the university quadrivium, Faustus rejects all academic subjects because he has already reached their limits, attained their "end." Furthermore these limits are themselves limited: medicine cannot resurrect the dead; law's practitioners aim only at "external trash" (A-text 1.1.35). Outside the university, similar limitations obtain: power politics have geographical, jurisdictional boundaries: "Emperors and kings / Are but obeyed in their several provinces" (1.1.59–60). The attraction of magic is that it "stretcheth as far as doth the mind of man" (1.1.63): that is to say, it is potentially without limits. For Marlowe, Helen becomes a story about a specific kind of limit: the limits of language.

Dr Faustus and Language

Two related episodes in *Dr Faustus* and *Tamburlaine* cement the link between Helen of Troy and language. The first is the unexpected moment at the end of *1 Tamburlaine* when Tamburlaine, a physical character if ever there was one, pauses during the battle for Damascus to deliver a lengthy metaphysical meditation on beauty. "What is beauty, saith my sufferings, then?" is the opening of Tamburlaine's 14-line attempt to put beauty into words. Contrast this with the physical reaction of Faustus, a metaphysical scholar, to beauty: he asks Mephistopheles to give him "unto my paramour / That heavenly Helen which I saw of late" (5.1.84–5). There is nothing untoward about academics desiring sex: Shakespeare's Berowne defends his divagation from study as empirically educative (women's eyes are "the books, the academes"; *Love's Labour's Lost* 4.3.299), and if the aim of study is, as the King of Navarre asserts, "that to know which else we should not know" (1.1.56), then sex is the original forbidden knowledge.[18] However, if we put Faustus' reaction next to Tamburlaine's, the common denominator is not the forbidden but the unattainable.

Tamburlaine begins with the specific beauty of Zenocrate ("ah, fair Zenocrate, divine Zenocrate! / Fair is too foul an epithet for thee"), contemplates the relation between beauty and creative artistry ("beauty, mother to the muses"), then equates beauty with suffering, the suffering of the writer as he realizes that beauty cannot be digested into words (5.1.160ff). Alexander Leggatt points out that Tamburlaine's frustrations with beauty parallel his frustrations with world conquest: the inability to conquer it with a pen (Leggatt 1973: 29). Faustus' difficulty is similarly one of limits, whether of the university quadrivium or of political power.[19] In the EFB Faustus simply wants to be a spirit; in Marlowe he wants to be a god: a "mighty god" in the A-text (1.1.64) or a "demigod" in the B-text (1.1.61). Faustus wants "the whole extent," "all that is possible." These are the *Oxford English Dictionary* definitions of "all," an adjective recurrent in Faustus' vocabulary (my italics):

> *All* things that move between the quiet poles
> Shall be at my command.
>
> (1.1.58–9)

> Resolve me of *all* ambiguities.
>
> (1.1.82)

> [S]earch *all* corners of the new-found world.
>
> (1.1.86)

> [T]ell the secrets of *all* foreign kings.
>
> (1.1.89)

> I'll have them wall *all* Germany with brass.
> (1.1.90)

> [R]eign sole king of *all* our provinces.
> (1.1.96)[20]

Collapsing limits was, in many respects, a humanist project: the bringing of the past into the present, resurrecting the classics through translation. Faustus is a humanist scholar but he is, in all respects, a bad humanist scholar (Bevington and Rasmussen 1993: 17). He translates Helen of Troy into the present not for the purpose of study but for sex.

When Faustus rejects theology for necromancy, the rejection is not just spiritual but linguistic, for in a postlapsarian world, where language and meaning have lost their one-to-one correspondence, necromancy enables the magician to regain Adamic power:

> *ipse nunc* . . .
> I see there's virtue in my heavenly words . . .
> Such is the force of magic and my spells.
> (1.3.22–3, 28, 32)

Magic's power to do what language cannot do, to "abolish the gap between sign and referent" (Forsyth 1987: 13) is dramatically exemplified in a seventeenth-century story of the extra devil who appeared on stage at a performance of Marlowe's *Dr Faustus* (Marlowe / Bevington and Rasmussen 1993: 50). The play ceased to be a representation, becoming itself a spell.

It is not magic that is dangerous, but language, and Helen becomes a metaphor for language. "Be silent then, for danger is in words" (5.1.25), Faustus warns the scholars just before he brings in Helen of Troy. The geminatory structure of the scene, in which everything to do with Helen is doubled (she appears twice, between two cupids [in the B-text], and is herself a double, a devil impersonating Helen; Forsyth 1987: 12), illustrates the danger Marlowe has in mind: the duplicity of language. Marlowe exploits the *eidōlon* tradition and does so in a way that emphasizes Helen's role as an emblem for a sign system in which you do not get what you seek but a substitute for it. Faustus' encounter with Helen replays his first encounter with women in the play (he asks for a wife and is given "a hot whore") in which he does not get what he asked for. The Young Vic production of the play in 2002, starring Jude Law as Faustus, underlined this point by staging Helen as an optical illusion, created by lights and mirrors.[21]

The Faust story is particularly suited to an investigation of boundaries, even today. As Tydeman points out, in the twentieth century the diabolic pact seemed less important than Faustus' "pathetic need to transcend his own limitations" (Tydeman 1984: 21). But the play also invites us to consider other boundaries: theatrical, textual, sexual.

Dr Faustus and Boundaries

Endings have always been problematic in Helen narratives, and become even more so in *Dr Faustus*. The word "end," invoked so frequently, slips between meanings: purpose, utmost limit, termination. The play's conclusion, a motto about endings, is deemed untranslatable: "Terminat hora diem; terminat author opus." Thomas Healy invites us to consider the difficulty of deciding where *Dr Faustus* begins and ends. Is it with the prologue and epilogue, or with the inset drama's opening and conclusion? Is it with the A-text act 5, which concludes with the devils claiming Faustus, or with the B-text's last scene, which depicts the morning after when the three scholars find Faustus' severed limbs? Or is it with the actors' acceptance of applause when the cast revive, ready for another play (Healy 2004: 188)? Faustus and Mephistopheles both have the same job: putting on theatrical spectacles for paying audiences (Faust stages Alexander and his Paramour for the Emperor, Mephistopheles the Seven Deadly Sins for Faust); the Emperor pays with patronage, Faustus with his soul. The play enacts the porous boundaries of theater and life, pushing the limits of the stage.

As Healy points out (2004: 188), what Helen stimulates in Faustus is a desire for theatrical role play: he will be Paris, he will be a medieval knight, a classical female (Semele) to Helen's classical male (Jupiter). And when, as in the last example, gender boundaries are crossed, the result is either self-annihilation (Semele was dazzled to death by Jupiter's glory; Healey 2004: 188) or dizzying sexual experimentation: since Helen is played on stage by a boy, Faustus is, as David Wootton points out, having "three kinds of sex at once: with a woman [Helen], a man [the male actor], and a demon [the devil enacting Helen]" (Marlowe/Wootton 2005: xviii).

Another of the blurred boundaries in this story is the overlap between author and protagonist. Just as Marlowe was quickly identified with his first dramatic creation for the public stage, *Tamburlaine*,[22] so posterity has identified Marlowe with Faustus. The Baines note provides the specifics that fuel such congruence, accusing Marlowe of atheism, tobacco, pederasty/paedophilia: these unorthodox attitudes and behaviors are stepping-stones to the ultimate in transgression: Faustus' pact with the devil. But the identification of author with protagonist or play need not be negative. Goethe's overreaching ambition in writing his two-part *Faust* (which runs to nearly 17,000 lines, the length of over five Shakespeare plays) encourages us to see parallels between the titular hero and his writer.[23] So too, more poignantly and more explicitly, does Jo Clifford's adaptation of Goethe's *Faust*. Clifford's commission to translate Goethe was interrupted by the sudden death of his wife from cancer. Mephistopheles' identification of himself with purposeless destruction ("I am the spirit of perpetual negation"; *1 Faust* 1987: 1338) made him a far-from-imaginary being to Clifford. Faust's search for joyful moments, and the transformation of the Poet in Clifford's *Part Two* from male to female (as Clifford assumed both parental personalities in his new life) offer personal parallels throughout. This is not to say the play is veiled autobiography; rather it is Clifford's personal experiences that provide the contemporary contexts for his twenty-first-century translation of Goethe.

To these two Faustus texts I now turn.[24]

Goethe (1749–1832)

Faust was a favorite subject for the German puppet theaters (and something of Marlowe's play may even have made its way back to Germany via the *Puppenspiel* as well as through the English players who toured Germany in the sixteenth and seventeenth centuries).[25] It was as puppet drama that Goethe first encountered the Faust story, a story that never left him; he finished it (if it possible to talk of such an episodic and accretive structure as "finished") in his eighties. The drama was not originally conceived as two parts nor was it written sequentially. Act 2 of *2 Faust* was written after act 3 (the Helen act) as a rationale to this *opus supererogationis* (the term is Goethe's; Goethe/Luke 1994: xxviii).

Faust is not really a "drama" if by drama we mean something written for performance. Although Goethe was director of the Weimar Theater from 1791 to 1817, translated Euripides' *Iphigenia among the Taurians* and Shakespeare's *Romeo and Juliet*, and wrote plays of his own, *Faust* is what Hart Wegner calls "imaginary theater" (Wegner 1987: 87).[26] David Luke talks of Goethe's "literary irresponsibility" in writing the *Walpurgis Night's Dream* scene in *1 Faust*, which is but an "irrelevant collection of epigraphs,"[27] and academics even invite students to skip this episode (Schweitzer 1987: 71). In all these respects – episodic scenes, a stand-alone act, unintegrated material – the work is typical of Romanticism for which the fragment is the quintessential art form.[28] As the Director in Goethe's

1 Faust (Scene 2: Prelude on the Stage) metatextually observes, "Why offer them a whole? They'll just fragment / It anyway" (102–3).

The Faust story, with its diabolic pact and conjuring up of Helen of Troy, was inevitably attractive to the Romantic mind. Romanticism was drawn to myth, folklore, ballad, the past; to darkness, alchemy, the occult, the satanic; to human genius and aspiration, and to nature and innocence as complements, contrasts, or conduits to human desire for experience beyond the quotidian (Haberhern 1987: 102). Goethe's disillusioned Faust desires not knowledge but experience – a moment when he may say "beautiful moment, do not pass away!" (*1 Faust* 1700) – and although he eventually utters this phrase at the end of *2 Faust*, the devil, sidetracked erotically by angels, loses the opportunity to capture Faust's soul.[29] Thus the self-proclaimed "tragedy" ends happily.

Goethe and Representation

Goethe's play begins as a tragedy of translation. In *1 Faust* scene 6 Faust tries to translate the opening of St John's Gospel. His frustration is intense as he considers the respective merits of "Word," "Mind," "Force" to express *logos*, settling finally on "Deed." The relation between Word and Deed will be explored throughout the play. Indeed they have already been introduced by the Director in scene 2: "Come, that's enough of words! What I / Want now is deeds" (*1 Faust* 214–15; cf. his similar statement at 89). When we first meet Faust at his desk in scene 4, he vows to "stop peddling in words that mean nothing to me" (*1 Faust* 385). But the irony is, as Neil Flax points out, that in fleeing the world of words Faust takes with him a book (*1 Faust* 419–20). As in Marlowe, Faust's adoption of magic "far from liberating him from the constraints of 'empty' language, only thrusts him deeper and deeper into the discontents of the semiotic condition . . . Faustus reinforces the linguistic limits he hoped to escape" (Flax 1983: 185). He never encounters unmediated experience. The world(s) he experiences are constructed along semiotic lines: representations, analogies, pictorial equivalents, duplications, citations (Shakespearean, biblical, classical, artistic), reflections.

Helen of Troy will be part of this lesson. She is not recognizably a spirit as she is in Marlowe (or, if she is, we are not encouraged to dwell on the fact), but her first appearance with Paris is nonetheless a simulacrum. Neil Flax explains that the couple appear to the audience in emulation of a painting of another mythological couple, Luna and Endymion (*2 Faust* 6509; Flax 1983: 193–5). Helen is, whether spirit as in Marlowe or artwork as in Goethe, a copy, a representation. Goethe's Faust goes to the Mothers to find an archetype, that is, an origin: the Helen scenes, like the rest of the play, demonstrate the futility of this quest.

The Helen of Troy scenes are thus, on one level, ironic. But they are also part of Faust's serious quest for experience – for wholeness (union with Helen), for classical order, harmony, and beauty (Romantic desiderata). Faust first sees Helen at the court of the Holy Roman Emperor in *2 Faust*, where, in a variant of the Faust book, he is asked to conjure up not Alexander and his paramour but Helen and Paris (*2 Faust* 6183–7). Mephistopheles is unhappy at the command – "pagans are not my period" (6209)[30] – but in scene 7 he enables cloud formations to assume the shapes of Paris and Helen. Mephistopheles is the first to react to Helen, in a critical deflation that, on stage, must do much to prevent the potential anticlimax of staging Helen: "Pretty, but not what I'd call / Exciting; she's just not my type at all" (*2 Faust* 6479–80). This clears the way for the Astrologer to react with poetic awe:

> Though I had tongues of fire, here there would be
> No more for me to do than say: Behold,
> Now beauty comes! As poets sang of old,
> The sight of beauty maddens; to possess
> It is good luck in dangerous excess.
>
> (*2 Faust* 6482–6)[31]

Faust's reaction is equally rapturous, concluding with his pledging himself to Helen. Mephistopheles intervenes, "Compose yourself, keep calm, stick to your part" (*2 Faust* 6501). Faust's interruption is a form of textual shudder: he fails to adhere to his role as a distanced observer watching clouds imitate characters. The textual shudder develops into an on-stage physical explosion. When Paris tries to carry Helen off, Faustus seizes her, despite Mephistopheles' reminder that this is not reality ("it's all in your mind, the mad spooky scene"; 6546), and in the tumult Faust is knocked unconscious and the cloud-characters vanish.

In act 3 (scene 11: In Front of The Palace of Menelaus in Sparta) we meet Helen. She and a Chorus of captured Trojan women have returned from Troy, and are following Menelaus' instructions to prepare for sacrifice. When the aged housekeeper Phorcyas (Mephistopheles in disguise) reveals that Helen is to be the sacrifice, she/he arranges for Helen's rescue: hence we move to scene 12 and a medieval-style castle owned by a chivalric knight (Faust), in which Helen can take shelter from Menelaus.[32] Faust and Helen fall in love, and in scene 13 (Arcadia) we meet them with their son

Euphorion, who is now old enough to run, leap, skip, and disobey his parents. When he falls to his death, Helen too vanishes, leaving Faust holding her empty dress and veil.

The entire Helen sequence, which occupies all of act 3, is the length of a typical Greek tragedy: 1550 lines. It was published separately by Goethe in 1827 as "Helena: A Classical-Romantic Phantasmagoria Intermezzo for *Faust.*" It is a *tour de force* of poetic form(s), whether in German or in David Luke's masterful English translation. Covering three thousand years of history from the fall of Troy to the death of Byron, the act begins with the six-stress unrhymed trimeter verse and style of Athenian tragedy, the ode form of the Greek Chorus, and stichomythic dialogue between Helen and Phorcyas, before moving through medieval rhymed couplets into early modern iambic pentameter. That Helen is extratemporal (see chapter 2) could not be better illustrated: to read or hear scene 11 is to read/hear the rhythms and phrases of Greek tragedy in the 1820s. Goethe has done what Mephistopheles cannot: he has made Helen come alive, at least acoustically.

Critics debate whether Helen in this scene is allegorical. In favor of verisimilitude, John R. Williams observes that, unlike his encounter with her in act 1, Faust is now "not only allowed to touch Helen but to become her protector, her lover, and the father of her son" (Williams 1983: 29). Against this, however, he notes a Helen who is torn between past myth and present identity, who is protected by a Frankish crusader, who inhabits an Arcadian grotto, who speaks in rhyme, whose son grows up instantly, and who retires to Hades when her child dies. Arguing for realism, Alexander Gillies notes that Helen returns from Troy independently of Mephistopheles, suffers seasickness, and resists the Chorus's depiction of her as ideal beauty to present herself instead as an individual. Even so Gillies acknowledges that "the farther away she gets from Sparta, the less real she grows" (Gillies 1957: 163).

But "less real" does not mean "allegorical." Helen is never given an explicit statement of the kind the characters in the Carnival masque have: "we're allegorical" (2 *Faust* 5531; "Wir sind Allegorien"). Instead she seems aware of her identity as a literary construct. Like Euripides' Helen in his *Helen* play, she laments the way she has been turned into story ("legend . . . report"; 8515).[33] Phorcyas presses this vulnerable point, accusing her of literal duplicity (the phantom, the double appearance in Egypt and Troy). Helen is distressed and questions her identity: "which of them am I? Even now I do not know" (2 *Faust* 8875). Phorcyas then strikes the cruelest blow to Helen's reality, reminding her of her (postmortem) union with Achilles. Helen painfully acknowledges, "A phantom to a phantom, thus I joined with him. / . . . / I vanish, I become a phantom even to myself" (2 *Faust* 8879, 8881). This last line also indicates the stage action: she faints, supported by the Chorus. Alexander Gillies astutely observes that "it is as if she is brought to realize by the reference to Achilles that she is a myth" (Gillies 1957: 152).

Indeed this is the ontological struggle Helen has faced since Euripides' *Helen*, the struggle between her personal self and the self that myth and narrative have constructed for her. The contrast in *Faust* is not between an allegorical classical Helen and a real eighteenth-century peasant, Gretchen (Faust's sweetheart in *1 Faust*), but between an individual Helen and a Helen imprisoned in representation. In this sense there is no difference between the art-world Helen of scene 7, conjured up as Luna to Paris' Endymion,[34] and the legendary Helen of Mephistopheles/Phorcyas' biased narrative in scene 11. Both are representations.

Goethe and the Beauty of Language

In scene 12 Goethe illustrates the way in which beauty arrests dramatic action. Lynceus the watchman is sentenced to death for dereliction of duty. Instead of announcing Helen's arrival he does nothing, transfixed with admiration. Helen insists that the man's life be spared (since she is the cause of his negligence) and he offers her, in gratitude (and in rhyme), his treasure hoard. The offer is refused but Lynceus' rhymes have caught Helen's attention:

> tell me why the speech of that good man
> Had something strange about it, strange and friendly:
> Each sound seems to accommodate the next,
> And when one word has settled in the ear
> Another follows to caress the first.
>
> (9367–71)

She wishes to learn this way of speaking. (As critics wryly note, the more difficult feat she has already accomplished, that of speaking German, goes unremarked.) With Faust as her partner-in-rhyme she instantly starts to share end rhymes and half-lines. Within 36 lines Helen has mastered internal rhyme: "I feel so far away, and yet so near; / How willingly I say: Look, I am here!" (9411–12).[35]

Phorcyas interrupts this "amorous alphabetic fiddling" with news of Menelaus' arrival. Menelaus is quickly vanquished and Faust proposes that he and Helen move to Arcadia to begin married life. The Arcadian scene 13 with Euphorion is manifestly unlike its brief precursor in the German Faust book, where Faust's voluptuousness, rather than love, is stressed and Helen is without personality. The work of the devil is clear in the German Faust book; in Goethe, on the other hand, human marriage and parenthood are celebrated lyrically. Of her son, Helen says:

> Love uniting man and woman
> Shapes a joy of two made one;
> Two, with rapture more than human,
> Are made three; this love has done.
> (2 *Faust* 9699–702)

The first two lines of her description of love here are remarkably analogous to her earlier description of rhyme: both shape "a joy of two made one."[36]

Faust's union with Helen is a union of literatures, of eighteenth-century Europe and classical Greece, allegorized, as David Luke writes, as a "magic love-story." As we saw in Marlowe's *Dr Faustus*, magic and poetry have a common denominator: both achieve the impossible (cf. Reinhardt 1968: 105). Helen vanishes; her clothes are left behind. But she is no mere blank. To any lover of the classics, her lines are the most memorable in Goethe's drama. Helen vanishes but the poetry she creates (whether in rhyme or in symbolic offspring) survives.[37]

Such a reading complements rather than tugs against the play's exposé of sign systems. *2 Faust* is a lesson in semiotic substitution and Helen is a mosaic of quotation. She is "compounded out of citational materials that were her prefiguration" (Flax 1983: 195). When Faust has a dream of her, he pictures not Helen herself but Caravaggio's Leda and the Swan; even the dream world is metonymic. "Any appearance of Helena is necessarily embedded in a vast, encoded, literary-iconographic system" (Flax 1983: 194). The impossibility of reaching an "original" Helen or Helen's origins is a familiar topic from previous chapters; but it is new to Faustus. Helen's varied linguistic forms – Greek, medieval, early modern (and a son equated with Romantic poetry) – dramatize the irreducibly literary nature of her existence.

But if her origins are poetic, not biological, that is, if she derives from poetry, she also gives birth to poetry. And the poetry to which Helen gives birth is embodied in one line: Marlowe's "Was this the face that launched a thousand ships?" Before returning to Faust and the subject of sources and adaptations, let us explore the origins and afterlife of Marlowe's famous line.

The Face That Launched a Thousand Ships

It is, it seems, impossible to write about Helen of Troy without invoking Marlowe's lines "Was this the face that launched a thousand ships? / And burnt the topless towers of Ilium?" These lines are regularly quoted out of context as if they are a transparently awed reaction to beauty (which they may be). But productions frequently remind us of the visual and dramatic context that anthologies of florilegia omit: the lines are addressed not to Helen of Troy but to a devil impersonating Helen, and Faustus is responding to, at best, a clever illusion, at worst, a cheap trick; that is, he is deceived or self-deceiving. (Neil Forsyth [1987] has even suggested that the lines register disappointment, not admiration.) Nonetheless Marlowe's/Faust's lines have become the paradigmatic poetic description of Helen, such that Andrew Lang, writing in 1882 had to preface his quotation with self-defensive justification, a combination of praise for Marlowe's lines and apology for citing them: "the speech of Faust is almost too hackneyed to be quoted, and altogether too beautiful to be omitted" (1882: 203).

Other writers negotiate this dilemma with less self-consciousness. Not one page into his book *Helen of Troy* (1965) John Pollard quotes Marlowe. "A thousand ships" is also the title of his first chapter, just as "the face that launched a thousand ships" is a section heading in Bettany Hughes's *Helen of Troy*. Introducing the Faust legend David Luke explains (irrelevantly):

> The Helen motif was made memorable by the famous passage in Marlowe's dramatized version in which Faustus, seeing the apparition of Helen, exclaims: "Was this the face that launched a thousand ships / And burnt the topless towers of Ilium?" etc. (Goethe/Luke 1994: 251 nxii).

It is the "etc." that arouses interest here: a reader who needs an introduction to the importance of Marlowe's lines is nonetheless expected to know how these lines continue.

Writing about Helen of Troy in art, Margaret Scherer was obviously determined to include Marlowe at whatever cost. She manages to achieve this in the last lines of her article in an awkward, illogical, and grammatically anacoluthic construction: "The story of Helen has indeed no true ending. As the daughter of Zeus she was immortal, and her story shared her immortality: the legend of 'the face that launched a thousand ships / And burnt the topless towers of Ilium'" (Scherer 1967: 383). Perhaps the most extreme example of dislocated Marlowe is the bibliographical entry on a university website reading list for a classics course. Here Marlowe's single line from Faustus has attained the status of an independent work. The entry reads, "Marlowe, Christopher. 'Was this the Face that Launched a Thousand Ships?' ca. 1588–92."[38] The entry keeps company with complete titles such as H. D.'s *Helen in Egypt* and Oscar Wilde's "The New Helen." The phenomenon of fragmentation and incompletion that we explored in chapter 1 is here demonstrated *in extremis*.

The popularity of Marlowe's line means that creative writers encounter a monolithic Bloomian anxiety of influence. However, they negotiate it with more success than do the critics above. The "topless towers of Ilium" is a whispered repetition in Margaret George's historical novel *Helen of Troy* (2006) as Helen sees and hears her story in the future.[39] Yeats invokes "those topless towers" as a shorthand for Troy in "When Helen Lived" (1969: 124) and Terry Pratchett changes it, with comic irony, to "toppleless towers" (2000: 96). Mark Haddon titles his radio play *A Thousand Ships* (2002) but deliberately omits the phrase in his script. Margaret Atwood turns the phrase round, applying it to Penelope and changing the unit of measurement from ships to women. When Atwood's Penelope anticipates Odysseus' return, she images him praising her economic acumen and success in increasing his estates: "'You're worth a thousand Helens', he would say. Wouldn't he?" (2005: 89). (The anxious rhetorical interrogative at the end shows the difficulty of replacing female beauty with domestic economy as a source of male admiration.)

The thousand ships of Marlowe's line are cited pictorially in the 1955 Warner Brothers film. We see a single white sail against an azure bay and a cloudless sky. The camera pans back and the frame fills with a thousand ships. Andrew Waterman's poem "What's in a Name?" (1990) presents the infatuation of a student for his beautiful tutor, Helen, introducing her in the first line as "a face to launch a thousand ships!" Hugh MacDiarmid takes Marlowe's metaphor literally when his monarch launches her maritime namesake, the Queen Mary. MacDiarmid answers Marlowe's rhetorical question with an emphatic negative: "Was *this* the face that launched a thousand ships? / No! But it freighted one right smartly down the slips" (*Die Grenzsituation*, 1–2, italics original). Isaac Asimov is credited with inventing the unit of beauty known as the "milli-Helen"; if Helen of Troy represents the amount of beauty needed to launch a thousand ships, a "milli-Helen" is the amount needed to launch just one. Fractions of Marlowe's hyperbolic measurement are regularly invoked in discussions of beauty. *Salon* magazine found a smaller unit than a milli-Helen when it criticized the qualifications of Diane Kruger as a beauty to play Helen of Troy: "a Helen who couldn't launch a dinghy" (Zacharek 2004).

If Marlowe's mighty line has such a powerful afterlife, what about its pre-Marlovian existence? Marlowe clearly encountered the *ubi sunt* introduction in Lucian's "Dialogues of the Dead" 18, which also gave him the round number of a thousand ships: "Was it then for this that the thousand ships were manned from all Greece?" (1961: 23). Seneca too cites a thousand ships as a way of invoking a Greek armada in *Agamemnon* and *The Women of Troy*.[40] But it was the combination of beauty and naval launch that appealed to Marlowe in Lucian and that he made his own repeatedly. Lines in *2 Tamburlaine* anticipate those in Faustus: "Helen, whose beauty summoned Greece to arms / And drew a thousand ships to Tenedos" (*2 Tamburlaine*, 2.4.87–8). In *Dido, Queen of Carthage* the queen tells her sister:

> I never vow'd at Aulis' gulf
> The desolation of his native Troy,
> Nor sent a thousand ships unto the walls.
>   (5.1.202–4)

The lines, a translation of *Aeneid* 4.425–6, add "a thousand" to Virgil's generic noun *classis* (fleet).[41]

One might assume from Shakespeare's revision of Marlowe's line in *Troilus and Cressida* that by 1602 the Marlovian phrase had become standard: "[Helen] is a pearl / Whose price hath launched above a thousand ships" (2.2.81–2). That is far from the case. Although Michael Drayton uses "a thousand ships" in his poem *The Owl* (1604) to describe the Greek fleet ("a thousand ships stuffed with revengeful fire"; sig. F2v), it is 1622 before the Marlovian association of beauty with a thousand ships reappears. In Thomas May's comedy *The Heir* Philocles tells his beloved:

>   . . . a face not half so fair
> As thine, hath armed whole actions in the field
> And brought a thousand ships to Tenedos
> To sack lamented Troy.
>   (sig. E1v)

In Thomas Heywood's *2 The Iron Age* (1632) an aged Helen contemplates her "wrinkled forehead" in the mirror, questioning "[was] this the beauty / That launched a thousand ships from Aulis' gulf?" (sig. K4r). In more extreme fashion, Heywood's aged Helen in his long poem "The Dialogue of Ravisius Textor" (1637) tells how her "putrefied corpse . . . was after by a thousand ships re-sought" (381–2). In Heywood, the association between beauty and the Greek armada is twice reduced to war for a feature that must decay; nonetheless Heywood has identified the equation of beauty and effect in Marlowe. The equation was present in muted form in Lucian but it was Marlowe who developed it into a memorable hyperbole.

The line did not seem particularly memorable to his own age, however, failing to launch an avalanche of quotations or parodies. When the actor-dramatist William Mountfort adapted *Dr Faustus* in 1697 as a farce ("with the humors of Harlequin and Scaramouche"), he retained the Faustian occult plot (largely in Marlowe's words and lines) and treated it seriously, confining the farce to an invented subplot. Helen, who appears only in act 1, is given four sentences of stage time. In the first line Faust requests to see her (a paraphrase of the first scholar's request in Marlowe's 5.1). In the second he asks to kiss her (a prosaic paraphrase of Marlowe's 5.1.93: "Sweet Helen, make me immortal with a kiss"; Mountfort: "what would I give to gain a kiss from off those lovely lips"; sig. B3v). His third line begins "my soul is fled" (a prose summary of Marlowe's "her lips sucks forth my soul: see where it flies!" 5.1.94), then continues with what Mountfort felt to be Marlowe's most memorable poetry: "come Helen, come, give me my soul again." The beginning of the speech in Marlowe – "Was this the face . . ." – is excised.

Today most websites on beauty or Helen contain Marlowe's lines in an opening paragraph; often it is unattributed. Question and Answer pages on websites frequently post questions from surfers who know the phrase but not its source or even its subject. Like Helen and her clothing in Goethe's *Faust*, Helen herself vanishes but leaves textile/textual traces behind.

In 1979 Frederic Raphael wrote the screenplay for a short TV comedy, *Of Mycenae and Men* ("with six lines of additional dialogue specially written by Aeschylus"). A classically clever slave, Taramasalatopolis (Bob Hoskins), in the household of Menelaus, welcomes his master and mistress after an absence of ten years ("plus a day or two to avoid undue coincidence"). Diana Dors's Helen is an amply endowed matriarch who talks confidentially to the camera and with detached ennui to her husband. She is no more recognizable as the most beautiful woman in the world than the TV drama is as a Greek tragedy.

When a messenger enters, keen to deliver a messenger speech, he tells Dors that she does not "bear comparison with Helen," only to be corrected, "I *am* Queen Helen." Immediately he launches into the two lines of Marlowe's "Is this the face . . . ?" Helen approves of his poetry ("Nice one, messenger"), telling him "That is one for the record books" as she applauds appreciatively. The slave applauds too. Others in the cast stop to listen and applaud. From off-stage comes an unexpected sound: the sound of swelling applause. Helen comments, "The messenger has just entered

The Oxford Book of Quotations." Buoyed by his success, the messenger indicates a desire to continue with his original speech ("I have two hundred lines to go"), only to be cautioned "Quit while you're ahead." Marlowe's lines are considered the pinnacle of poetry.[42]

Jo Clifford (1950–)

Translation (as we saw at the beginning of this chapter) is a word whose meaning and practice have metamorphosed over the centuries. The title page of P. F.'s English Faust book advertises itself both as the Englishing of a German original and as a work that "amend[s]" the "imperfect matter" of the original when deemed appropriate ("in convenient places"). John Jones's 1994 edition of the English Faust book uses bold type to represent P. F.'s additions. Scarcely a page lacks bold type; some of the pages consist almost entirely of bold. This translation is a thoroughgoing revision.

Like translation, parody is a word that has lost its literal meaning as a song sung alongside (a para-ode), a work adjacent to another. When Neil Flax writes that Goethe's Helen in 2 *Faust* "arrives parodying classical Greek trimeters" (1983: 195), his participle has little of the modern reductive meaning; Helen is both positioning herself alongside ancient Greek poetry and trans-lating it (carrying it) and herself into eighteenth-century German.

Friedrich Schlegel (who corresponded with Goethe) was alert both to the positive cultural association of parody and its link with translation; in his notebook he wrote, "Die Parodie ist eine witzige Übersetzung": "parody is a witty translation" (Schlegel 1957: 118, fragment 1108).[43] Schlegel's parody pays tribute to an original (genre or work) that it carries across while simultaneously carrying that original further onwards or in a new direction. This complex interrelationship, of repetition and novelty, homage and critique, debt and independence, is summarized by Schlegel: "Zur echten Parodie gehört dasjenige selbst was parodiert werden soll" (true parody has within it the material that is being parodied; Schlegel 1957: 110, fragment 1021).[44] It is clear from this definition that parody needs a stable host-genre on which to ride.[45] If one is going to trans-late, it must be clear what one is trans-lating. The new work must have within it the old material.

Jo Clifford's 2006 translation of Goethe's *Faust: Parts One and Two* fits both the early modern notion of translation and the Romantic definition of parody. This innovative contemporary drama is, as Schlegel writes, a witty translation. When Clifford was commissioned by Mark Thomson, artistic director of the Royal Lyceum Theatre in Edinburgh, to translate

Goethe's *Faust*, he was an obvious choice: he had a long and impressive history of translating European classics (Calderon, Lorca, De Rojas) as well as works by Spanish, Portuguese, German, and Ivory Coast writers from the fifteenth century to the present day. His translations have been performed at venues from the National Theatre in London to the Edinburgh International Festival. He is one of Scotland's leading playwrights: his own plays have received productions and translations abroad.

Clifford's strong theatrical instincts and his understanding of translation as cultural *translatio* illustrate Jean-Michel Déprats' observation that if a translation is not "conducive to performance, it remains essentially unfaithful to the original" (1995: 347). There is some irony here inasmuch as Goethe's two-part original is generally considered unperformable (Goethe himself made no effort to stage it), although once Wagner's Ring cycle accustomed nineteenth-century audiences to mammoth productions, and the director Max Reinhardt's twentieth-century audiences to postnaturalism, *Faust* was, and continues to be, staged (Goethe/Luke 1987: xlviii–xlix). While recommending David Luke's poetically skilled translation to non-German readers, Clifford nonetheless "def[ies] anyone to stage it" (Goethe/Clifford 2006: xxxiv).

Until 2008 Clifford taught part-time at Queen Margaret University College in Edinburgh where his dual title reflected his skills as both actor and dramatist. He was "Professor of Theatre" and, as a prolific drama translator, "Fellow of Stage Translation." Stage translation, the second part of the title implies, is different from other kinds of translation. It must be, as Déprats writes, "conducive to performance."

In Clifford's *Faust: Part One*, Mephistopheles cynically corrupts an idealistic university student by redirecting her to Business Studies; Faust visits a Scottish tavern where the locals are watching a televised football match in which Scotland is losing to Uzbekistan; Goethe's witch's kitchen becomes a beauty parlor. In Clifford's *Part Two* Goethe's frame-figure, the male poet, changes gender. Wagner's creation of a new human being, the rational Homunculus, is now accompanied by a talking penis with whom he goes out on the town ("be sure to use a condom," cautions Wagner); and when the devil makes love to a boy angel he finds that, like the angels, he is now in possession of a penis and a vagina. This is clearly not a literal translation of Goethe. Although the title-page of the published text bills this as Goethe's *Faust*, and my local bookstore shelves it under "G," Clifford's online diary entry (www.teatrodomundo.com) for June 14, 2007, summarizes the previous working year in a sentence that distinguishes *Faust* from other translations: "I wrote *Faust Part One*, *Faust Part Two*, translated [the Duque de Rivas'] *The Force of Destiny*, . . ."

And yet Clifford's *Faust* is recognizably Goethe's, not least in the over-all premise: man's yearning for experience and the promise of fulfillment through the feminine Other. The last lines of Goethe's play are, "Eternal Womanhood / Draws us on high" (2 *Faust* 12110–12); Clifford's ends, "it's through the female / That the world's set free" (2006: 212). And the quest for the feminine within Faust provides a unifying theatrical thread for Goethe's episodic and "irrelevant" digressions. In Clifford's *Part One*, Mephistopheles introduces Faust to "pleasure specialists" whose appearance baffles Faustus: "Are they men or women?" "Believe me," says Mephistopheles, "It really doesn't matter" (48). Later in this scene, while Faust is both giving and receiving different kinds of penetrative sex, Clifford's Mephistopheles reflects on society's limited definitions of masculinity.[46] In his online diary for January 31, 2003, Clifford reflects on the "profoundly ridiculous" concept of masculinity lived out by Blair, Bush, and Saddam Hussein, a concept also "profoundly dangerous." "Trying to explore, trying to discover, trying to express different ways of being a man seems more important than ever just now." When Clifford's Faust sees in the mirror a beautiful female face (in Goethe it is unclear whether the vision is of Gretchen or of Helen), the Poet tells him "she is yourself. Your own lost self!" (64).[47] At the start of *Part Two*, the Poet changes from male to female. A curious Mephistopheles asks if she/he will change back into a man, only to be told "I'm not sure . . . You see, I think I've written myself out of the story. / Or perhaps the story's written itself out of me" (137). The story she/he rejects is that of culturally programmed and socially sanctioned gender roles.

In the Classical Walpurgis Night, Homunculus gives a trenchant mini-lecture about "the problematic interplay of male and female roles" in contemporary culture. In our "hyper-masculinised" society, "women are taking over the roles and clothing of men; but men are ignoring the roles and clothing of women. But we need both. Hence the need for our culture to revisit the female archetype" (147). This manifesto statement provides clear motivation for Goethe's material about Faust's visit to the Mothers. The Mothers are important in Clifford as females not (as in Goethe) as emblems of origin.

The visit to the Mothers leads to the Helen scenes, which are, in Clifford, seamlessly integrated. Mephistopheles, disguised (as in Goethe) as a Phorcyad (an old, ugly hag), explores his new gender role: "I feel a master of this element / Or mistress of this element" (164). Clifford exploits Mephistopheles' disguise not just as an emblem of absolute ugliness, an opposite to Helen's absolute beauty (as it functions in Goethe) but as an ugly old *female*. (In the German and English Faust books, as in Marlowe,

Mephistopheles is diabolically ugly – "thou art too ugly to attend on me" – but he has not yet been an ugly woman.) Clifford's Mephistopheles temporarily abandons diabolical and male ugliness to explore the equivalent female extreme. And it is this experience that triggers his decision to introduce Helen:

> I know exactly what to do
> And how to go about it.
> So now. Finally. Enter Helen.
> (164)

It comes as no surprise when Helen later reveals that Paris' effeminacy is one of his attractions for her. She sees his beauty both in body and mind, in contrast to the false masculinity of the warlike Menelaus (who laughs at Paris' effeminacy, 172).[48] In Clifford's classical world, gender is fluid: nymphs have beards (162) and warlike masculine Sparta shares a border with peaceful feminine Arcadia (173).[49]

But gender is only one of the unions Clifford's Faust is invited to explore. The problem of disharmony is stressed throughout when what should be complements function as opposites: language without thought (33), appearance without depth (35), intellectual knowledge without self-knowledge (87), humans who see themselves as a whole rather than as a part (36). This dissociation is dramatized in Homunculus. He is pure reason, academic life, detached (here physically) from sensual pleasures: accompanied by a separate dramatic character, Prick. As Homunculus explains, "I represent the ability to remove oneself from a given physical situation and thus reflect upon it," but the negative side effect of such cerebrality is that in sexual matters he can note technically only "a distinct dampness between the thighs" (149). Prick proudly announces this pleasure as his responsibility ("that was me coming. I'm good at that"). On the other hand, Prick acknowledges, without a brain you "can easily get it [the penis] into all kinds of trouble" (150). In the Classical Walpurgis Night the Sphinx and the Centaur, half human, half animal, represent the connection of heart and brain, instinct and analysis, which Faust lacks ("he understands with his brain . . . / But not with his heart"; 159). The play ends with Samaritana's peaceful assurance that Faust will "find himself one day," a liberation and a discovery that can happen only through the female.

Helen is also out of harmony with herself and seeks a means of finding and freeing her real self. This is partly expressed in the traditional Helen vocabulary of ontological confusion: "I no longer know if I'm illusion / Or if I'm truth" (171). But Clifford introduces a discussion about danger and blame: Helen "know[s] there is no harm in [her]," but Mephistopheles points out "the world does not. It never will" (169). The reason for his assurance is part of a new motif Clifford introduces: the judgmental attitudes of the world to sexual appearance.

Clifford's Helen and Gender Politics

The three Helen scenes correspond closely to those in Goethe. Helen and the Chorus talk poignantly of home, devastation, sacrifice, confusion, dread. As the action moves to the protection of the medieval castle, Helen protests that this is an action replay ("And so it starts again"; Clifford 2006: 170) of her Spartan and Trojan lives – guarded and regarded as a precious jewel. In two pages of monologue she tells her story, a story of beauty and brutality. Faust invites her to a different world, that of union ("heaven on earth, Arcadia") and a different kind of beauty:

> FAUST: Shall we try to explore its beauty?
> HELEN: In the outer world and in our own deep selves?
> FAUST: In the most profound and truthful language that there is.
> HELEN: The language loving bodies have.
>
> (174)

Goethe's depiction of love through rhyme is rejected, but its metaphoric relevance is retained: the couple share a "language" and in this physical language they find their "own deep selves." If Goethe's Faust consistently found himself short-circuited by semiotic systems, by the problems of language and representation, Clifford offers his Faust the linguistic transparency sought by Goethe's: sexual language is "truthful." The union of male and female is wordless; bodies provide their own version of Goethean rhyme. They form a couplet.

Mephistopheles-Phorcyas deflates the moment in a comic address to the audience. In deference to public desire for an unhappy ending, he takes us into Goethe's scene 13, the Euphorion scene (the son is here named Boy) where Clifford makes a significant change to Goethe (and to all Helen narratives). Helen realizes she must die. She has slept with every western male (in their dreams), "given and received every kind of sexual pleasure," and always been "some man's prize or treasure." She proposes to end this cycle (the cycle summarized earlier in "and so it begins again") by "vanish[ing] from the world / So there can be a new Helen and a new earth" (177). She here refers to herself not as a human but as a noun.[50] The noun encapsulates what she, as the embodiment of desired womanhood ("Helen of Troy"), participates in – a gendered dance with prescribed movements, a vicious circle of role-play, a hierarchy of coded sexual steps, a sequence of mindless assumptions and presumptions:

> I meet a powerful man and I am powerless.
> Without even thinking
> I make myself agreeable
> In the hope I will find him agreeable to me.
>
> (170)

The reverse logic of the last line is astounding. Helen makes herself agreeable not because she already finds the man agreeable but because, as a beautiful woman, she is defined sexually and is expected to pair. The line exposes the (as Helen herself says) "[un]thinking" stages of modern male–female relationships.

Mephistopheles' earlier observation now makes sense: being ugly (as Phorcyas is) is "not as hard as being beautiful." This is why Helen must use her power "to die." She uses her name as a proper noun for women and the society in which they live; she rejects sexualized stereotypes based on external aesthetic definitions of desirability in the hope of finding a "new Helen" and a "new earth."[51]

But Helen is not just a symbol: she is a loved woman whom Faust and the Chorus lose. Clifford's *Faust* begins with loss. At the beginning of *Part One* the Poet explains to the on-stage theater company who are awaiting his new play that

> Evil entered my life last year
> And destroyed one person I truly loved.
> I need to grieve. I need to understand.
> Understand how I can begin to live again . . .
> This strange old poem, Goethe's *Faust*, may help.
>
> (9)

Part Two begins with Faust having dreamt about Gretchen, the young woman he had loved and lost at the end of *Part One*: "I don't understand how I can go on / Now that she has gone" (129). The explosion that occurs when Faust tries to seize Helen at the end of act 1 of Goethe's *2 Faust* is here relocated to the start of the act, just a few pages into the play. Thus Faust experiences a double loss at the beginning, and is searching and grieving throughout. His words about Gretchen's loss at the beginning of the act (quoted above) are voiced by the Chorus when they face losing Helen at the end: "I've been with you so long / I can't imagine living with you gone" (178). Even Mephistopheles is affected by the human tragedy:

> What's this?
> Wetness! Ugh.
> Wetness at the corner of my eye!
> Loss. Humans and their loss.
> Away with it! Away with wetness!
>
> (178)

The quest of Goethe's Faust becomes less abstract in Clifford's play: it is now a quest for emotional wholeness after unbearable loss. These two motifs are present in Goethe; it is Clifford's insight to link them, thereby turning disconnected ideas in his source into theatrical and thematic unity.

To an unusual degree Clifford's personal circumstances shaped his work. Between the Lyceum's commission in summer 2003 and Clifford's starting work on the project in September 2004, his wife, his partner of 33 years and mother to their two daughters, the feminist writer Sue Innes, was diagnosed with an inoperable brain tumor; she died in February 2005. Clifford explains that he picked up Goethe's *Faust* in a "daze of outrage and grief" (Goethe/Clifford 2006: xxxi), and that the play had powerful emotional relevance. Mephistopheles' creed of pure destruction was something Clifford and his family were living with daily (xxxii). Faust's journey is not just a journey for total experience but a journey for a beautiful moment, for joy in life: Faust's suicidal despair at the start of the play is that of a heartbroken man who finds everything he has striven for to be valueless (17). Faust's articulation of his inability to carry on when he loses Gretchen, and the Chorus' similar statement when they face the loss of Helen, are clearly Clifford's.

Throughout their lives, Innes and Clifford had lived out their commitment to gender equality (McMillan 2005). When Innes died, Clifford had to become both mother and father, husband and wife in the amputated family, a gender wholeness explored in his version of *Faust*. His dual role was not just metaphorical. Clifford now allowed his transsexual identity/identities to be expressed. When Innes was dying, Clifford "realized that the female part of myself, of which I had always been so deeply ashamed and so profoundly fearful, was in fact a good energy. And that's when I started to become Jo" (Diary, June 15, 2007). His introduction to his translation of Goethe simply mentions *en passant* that he is "transgendered" (2006: xxxiii). But this exploration of dual identity, its ontological confusions ("It's not that I especially want to pass as a woman. But I HATE being mistaken for a man"; Diary, July 12, 2007), its teenage suppression, its wryly comic practicalities (if one wears a skirt yet possesses a penis, which lavatory does one use at the theater interval?[52]) is dominant in his creative writing (*God's New Frock* turns the Bible's patriarchal suppression of matriarchal religion into a play in which God is a closet queen), in his political ideology ("Our ideas of gender, of what it means to be male or female, are no longer adequate" is one of the mission statements of his "teatro do mundo"), and in his online personal Diary.

This last regularly explores ideas of male–female roles through his own experiences as, for example, when he notes men's embarrassment when they mistake him for a woman "because, in this misogynist world, there is no greater insult you can offer a man" (Aug. 2, 2007). His website has a page headed "transgender," and his learning to live again after the death of his partner is allied to learning to explore and express his sexualities. His observation that "the same old ways simply will not do" (Nov. 20, 2007) is a theme of *Faust*, expressed by the Poet in *Part Two* when she/he warns Mephistopheles that there will come a time

> When the old understandings
> Of who you are and what you do
> Simply won't make any sense.
>
> (138)

She explains how her understanding has developed:

> I wanted to change the world
> Change it through the power of the word.
> I spoke the word
> But nothing seemed to change.
> And I came to understand
> That the advice I so passionately wanted to give Faust
> Was advice I needed to take myself.
> "Make contact with your inner feminine."
>
> (137–8)

As in Goethe, words are seen as inadequate; but Goethe's vague replacement – "deeds" (*1 Faust* 215) – is turned into more explicit advice.

Faust's journey may be of help to Clifford, and Clifford's shapes his *Faust*, but this play is not simply autobiography or therapy. Clifford's account of his last moments with his wife, accompanied by the Burns song "Ae fond kiss, and then we sever" (June 18 and Aug. 26, 2007) is identical in tone to the parting of Faust and Helen in Goethe but is not part of Helen's farewell to Faust in Clifford's version. Helen simply vanishes. She makes a political speech about gender, not an emotional speech about love, leaving Faust "blankly / Uncomprehendingly / Holding onto her empty garment" (177–8). In a play about beauty – the search for beauty in life – the most beautiful woman in classical literature symbolizes the problems of gender politics because beauty (and what it represents: externals; ownership) is an obstacle to equality.

Beauty is not something Clifford's Helen wishes to represent. Neither does Goethe's: when the Chorus reminds her of her status as symbol, icon of beauty, she asserts her identity as an individual woman. But Clifford's play goes further. Helen vanishes as a necessary first step towards "a new Helen and a new earth" (177). She takes Mephistopheles' observation – "beauty is dangerous lady. It needs to be caged" – one step further, not just caging Helen of Troy but removing her altogether.

Scene 11's preparations for the sacrifice of Helen thus come to their intended conclusion, but with one difference: this is not sacrifice but self-sacrifice. It is an act of agency ("the only power left me is to die"; 177). Helen vanishes, not reluctantly with the "sorrowful farewell" of Goethe (2 *Faust* 9942) but powerfully. Faust cannot "stop" her, cannot "prevent" her going, and the emphasis is on her identification of a political need: "where I *need* to go," "that *must* end now," "I *need* to vanish" (my italics). The verbs of compulsion stress not Helen as victim or object but her identi-fication of a political structure that requires her intervention. We are close here to the material of chapter 4, of scapegoating and blasphemy, where for the semidivine Helen to volunteer to die is a gesture that has only one analogue: Christ. But in Clifford, Helen's gesture *is* an attempt to save the world – the secularized twenty-first-century world of imbalanced gender. Helen had to wait until 2006 to be given unequivocal agency and a strong political voice.

6

Parodying Helen

A story which, in its harmless variants, seems eminently suited for a comedy, if not a farce (Götz Schmitz, *The Fall of Women in Early English Narrative Verse*)

Laugh at Helen. Take her seriously and you end up with a few limp pre-Raphaelite paintings and some really bad films (Adrian Mourby, "Oh lord, it's hard to be Helen")

The more particular you get, the more universal you become (Derek Walcott in Robert Hamner, "Out of the Ordinary, Derek Walcott")

From Homer onwards, Helen's story has been difficult to tell. For a start, Helen has nothing to do. When, in the *Iliad*, she couples her biography with Agamemnon's or her feelings with Hector's death, it is a desperate attempt to assert herself in narrative. Shakespeare acknowledges this problem in *Troilus and Cressida*, offering us Helen in only one scene: it is a scene of "spectacular anti-climax" because "there is nothing for Helen to do in this play. She must simply *be*" (Rutter 2000: 232). But to portray mere being is difficult. Depicting her blankness leaves a narratological gap, yet filling this gap (by giving her emotions and desires) results in glibness – the reduction of the Trojan War to sexual willfulness. Often this willfulness is coupled, paradoxically, with passivity, as we see in the medieval Troy books or in Wolfgang Petersen's film *Troy* (2004). In *Troy* Diane Kruger's Helen desires helplessly: she simpers and sheds tears, and her attempts at personal tragedy reduce rather than enlarge the emotional scale. If Helen's essence is her unknowability, attempts to depict her as humanly knowable will be false, taking us further from, rather than closer to, who she is.

To portray Helen successfully, writers have to confront these problems head on: they have to transplant her, adapt her, or reinvent her so that she becomes a totally new Helen rather than a diluted form of the original. There are many ways of doing this but all involve taking her out of tragedy or epic. She can be translated generically into comedy/burlesque/satire (Greek satyr-plays; Offenbach's *opera-bouffe, La Belle Hélène*; Frederic Raphaël's TV film *Of Mycenae and Men*); she can become a modern Helen in a modern form: the novel (Jane Stanley's *A Daughter of the Gods* [1886]), Virginia Woolf's *Mrs Dalloway* [1925]); or she can be relocated ethnically, moving from ancient Greece to the Caribbean (Derek Walcott's *Omeros*). This chapter explores the generic afterlife of Helen.

In all the examples I discuss below, Helen's story is parodied. As we saw in chapter 5, "parody is a witty translation" (Schlegel 1957: 118, fragment 1108). It transforms a host text without obliterating it; the reader savors the transfer, recognizing both the indebtedness and the novelty. In this chapter Helen's story hovers behind and haunts the parodic resettings in Elizabethan fairy land, Victorian England, and the twentieth-century Caribbean. Helen's double is no longer a character but a genre; her *eidōlon* finds a home in generic rather than geographic relocation.

In offering parody as the theme of this chapter I do not mean that Helen is ridiculed, although comedy comes into several of my examples. The key elements in parody are an original text and its transfer to a new environment. The old and the new are in view simultaneously; it is the discrepancy between the two that makes parody, and if the discrepancy is large enough it makes comedy (e.g., epic style applied to an inappropriate subject). This doubleness or simultaneity is stressed by most writers on parody (indeed it is inherent in the Greek *para*, which means both "beside" and "opposite"). For Margaret Rose, "the work to be parodied is 'decoded' by the parodist and offered again (or 'encoded') in a 'distorted' or changed form"; the result is "two texts within one work" (Rose 1993: 39, 40). Florio describes parody as "a work grafted on another work," Isaac Disraeli as "the turning of another" (cited in Rose 1993: 28, 27). In this chapter we see authors turning, grafting, encoding, and distorting Helen.

Comedy

Helen's comic life begins early: she appears in both the Old and New Comedy of ancient Greece. We do not have the text of Cratinus' Old Comedy *Dionysalexandrus*, but its argument is preserved: Helen is abducted by a comic Dionysus who hides her in a bird basket (Lindsay 1974: 151–2). Helen is also a frequent figure in the satyr-drama of fifth-century BCE Athens. The tragic trilogies of the Athenian drama festivals were followed by a short satyr-play, a bawdy burlesque of the mythological material in the plays that had just been performed, written by the same author. (The Chorus in these plays was composed of satyrs; hence the name.) Only one satyr-play survives, Euripides' *Cyclops*, but there are fragments and the argument of others, and the titles of many more. One satyr-play, *The Satyric Marriage of Helen*, takes Helen as its main focus, in particular her first sexual encounter with Paris (Hughes 2005: 265), but she is the object of coarse sexual jokes in others even when she is not an on-stage character (see Euripides' *Cyclops*).

One critic has described satyr-drama as "tragedy-at-play" (Euripides/ Arrowsmith 1974: 28). The borders between comedy and tragedy have always been fluid, and marital infidelity has long been the subject of both. Edmund Spenser, the epicist of Elizabeth I's court, is not known for his sense of comedy, but in *The Faerie Queene* (1590) he places Helen in an Elizabethan satyr-play. Spenser's treatment is not just parodic but literally satyr-ical, for, abandoned by Paris, Helen sets up home with the satyrs.

The Faerie Queene *(1590)*

The Faerie Queene is a celebration of the virtues of Elizabeth's court. Each of the six books focuses on a specific virtue: Holiness, Temperance, Chastity, Friendship, Justice, and Courtesy. As these capitalized nouns indicate, the work is primarily allegorical. In book 3, the book of Chastity, we meet Elizabethan versions of Helen and Paris.

This, however, is not classical Greece but ancient Britain, and Spenser's characters are shrunken, trivialized descendants of their epic forebears. The beautiful wife is not Helen but a "second Helen, fair Dame Hellenore": her name is perhaps a homonym of "Helen o'er" (again) or "Helen whore". The abductor is not Paris but Paridell ("Paris-idle"?) and he proudly claims descent from the union of Paris and Oenone on Mount Ida.

Of these two Spenserian lovers, Paris' character is unambiguous: he is a selfish charlatan. He is epitomized by his attitude when he first arrives in canto 9. Denied entrance to the castle of the Menelaus figure, Malbecco, in a storm, he proposes sacking the castle and killing its owner (9.8.9).[1] When he meets Malbecco's wife, the beautiful and gracious Hellenore, he deliberately sets out to seduce her. The vocabulary of clandestine liaison recurs: close messages (9.27.9), close embassage (9.28.2), close signs, secret way (9.31.5), privily (9.52.8, 10.9.7–8; 10.35.9). He is a practiced seducer (9.29.8–9), contemptuous of wedlock (9.42.9; 10.35.9),[2] is motivated by lust, not love (10.35.7), and discards Hellenore once he has conquered her as he has discarded previous conquests. The two brief sentences that comprise one duodecimeter line convey the dispassionate conclusion to the affair: "He nould [would not] be clogged. So had he servèd many one" (10.35.9).

Although Spenser says, "of a wanton lady I do write" (9.1.6), the poem first introduces Hellenore's husband, Malbecco (whose name means wicked goat or cuckold). He is a personification of jealousy (in fact at the end of canto 10, living in a cave by the sea, eating toads and frogs, he "quite / Forgot he was a man, and Jealousy is hight [called]"; 10.60.8–9). He hides his young wife from sight, deprives her of recreational pastimes, and denies all visitors entrance lest they cuckold him. This obsessive suspicion is the opposite of the classical Menelaus' hospitality. In other respects, too, Malbecco is presented as different from Menelaus; he is "old and withered" (9.5.1) and the married couple are "unfitly yoked together" (9.6.2). Thus Hellenore is introduced as part of a January–May marriage. This is a genre familiar to us from fabliau tradition (Watkins 1995: 163), indeed from Chaucer's "Merchant's Tale" whose characters, January and May, give us our descriptive nomenclature. As readers, we know how to react to such a genre: we support the ingenuity of the young wife in cuckolding her husband. Even the negative comment about Hellenore's virtue being surpassed by her beauty reads benignly in such a tradition. The triangle is conventional.

But Spenser throws a spanner in the generic works. Malbecco is forced to give entrance to the visitors (because they prepare to destroy his gates) and they compel him to summon Hellenore to dinner, where she presides as a gracious hostess, much like Helen in Chaucer's *Troilus and Criseyde*. When Paridell embarks on his seduction, his campaign is presented very much as an assault on an innocent. He is a professional seducer ("a learned lover"; 10.6.1), and sets out to "beguile" Hellenore (10.5.4), "steal" her affection (10.5.8), ambush her feelings ("surprise her sprights [spirits]"; 10.8.3) with "false engines" (wiles), "sleights" [cunning tricks] (10.7.2–3), and "false nets" (10.9.6). He practices his "art" (a term with Ovidian associations; 10.5.1) and writes love messages in the spilt wine, as in Ovid's *Heroides* 16. He also consciously replays Virgil, relating the downfall of Troy at a banquet. Whereas Dido's love for Aeneas was an unanticipated consequence of his rhetoric, Paridell's narrative is intended to manipulate Hellenore (indeed he has earlier been glib about the fall of Troy: 9.33.1), and he supplements his speech with "many false belgardes" [amorous looks] (9.52.9).

> Thus finely did he his false nets dispred,
> With which he many weak hearts had subdued
> Of yore, and many had ylike misled:
> What wonder then, if she were likewise carrièd?
> (10.9.6–9)

The rhetorical question shows the poet's sympathy and lack of condemnation. The triangular relationship is complex: Hellenore bests Malbecco but Paridell beguiles Hellenore. Hellenore is the middle term, and the conventional fabliau attitudes (young wife manipulates old husband) do not apply because Hellenore is manipulated in her turn.

Having presented Hellenore as a victim – "through his trains he her entrappèd hath" (10.11.1) – the poet now shows her initiating the time and place for elopement (10.11.6–7). She collects part of her husband's treasure to carry away with her and sets fire to the rest. We do not know her motivation for this latter action, and Spenser foregrounds our lack of knowledge by offering alternatives: "the rest she fired for sport, or for despite" (10.12.6). Even diminished Helens are unknowable.

The text briefly follows Hellenore after Paridell has abandoned her. She is a "gentle lady" wandering forlorn in the forest, like the poem's earlier abandoned women, "withouten groom or guide" (10.36.1, 5), when the satyrs rescue her and take her home with them. There she lives as their housewife, milking goats, making cheese and bread. Only in the last line of this domestic stanza are we given surprising sexual information: "and every one as common good her handled" (10.36.9). Nor is this presented as victimization for "shortly she Malbecco has forgot, / And eke Sir Paridell, all were he dear" (10.37.1–2).

Malbecco, disguised as a goat, searches for his wife. He enters a forest that, we are told, threatens minotaurs (monsters unknown outside the tale of Theseus: all early modern references to the Minotaur are in the context of a Theseus narrative); Spenser's reference therefore recalls Helen's story even when he is narrating a different strand of the plot. Malbecco discovers Hellenore at home with the satyrs where, at night, one satyr has sex with her nine times. A surprising interlude in the book of Chastity, the stanza is both euphemistic and explicit. It is also pornographically prurient. Malbecco spies on his wife's sexual activities and although the poet tells us that this increases his torments – "all his heart with jealousy did swell" – the verb makes one wonder what other part of his anatomy might also be tumescent (10.48.6). Malbecco wakes his wife and promises her a fresh marital start ("All should be renewed / With perfect peace"; 10.51.3–4). She refuses, preferring to live among the "jolly satyrs" (10.44.3). This is satyr-drama with a vengeance.

Everything in this episode is diminished morally and parodically: characters, their motives, their names, events (as critics note, Hellenore's departure leads not to the burning of a city but of money). Hellenore's story is reduced to three encounters with lustful men: Malbecco is lustful and miserly; Paridell is lustful and selfish; the satyrs are pure lust.

Spenser's Britomart takes over the nonsexual aspects of Helen's story. Britomart is the heroine of book 3, a princess in disguise as a knight on a quest to find a husband whom she has seen in Merlin's magic mirror. She is androgynous; she is "the fairest woman wight that ever eye did see" (9.21.9); and her beauty has the effect that we observed in chapter 2: it makes hungry where most it satisfies (the male admirers feed "their hungry view" on Britomart "yet note [nor could] their hungry view be satisfied, / But seeing still the more desired to see"; 9.23.9, 9.24.1–2). Britomart is also actively desiring: she pursues a man but chastely, desiring wedlock, family, and the secure foundation of a kingdom. Unlike Helen, "her passion will create a nation, not destroy one" (Suzuki 1989: 155). She is "engaged imaginatively with her past, yet willing to heed its lessons" and "places herself in the service of history" (Suzuki 1989: 169–70). In this she contrasts with Hellenore, who simply repeats history in the form of her "literary models without any interesting differences; hence she trivializes them" (Suzuki 1989: 167). Suzuki's vocabulary of nationhood is analogous to the vocabulary of parody. Hellenore misunderstands parody – it is repetition with *difference* – and the result, as Suzuki writes, is trivialization.

Spenser here plays with parody on two levels. He depicts a character who simply emulates an originary text; but in depicting her doing so he provides an adaptation of the originary text his character slavishly imitates. Thus Spenser's two cantos have the twin effect that Virginia Woolf prescribes and describes in parodies: "First they make us laugh, and then they make us think" (Woolf 1987: 89).

George Peele, The Arraignment of Paris *(1584)*

The Faerie Queene was Spenser's compliment to Elizabeth I: like Elizabeth, from whom in the poem's mythological genealogy she is descended, Britomart is wedded to her people. A few years before *The Faerie Queene* was published in 1590 Elizabeth had received a similarly expansive tribute: George Peele's pastoral drama, *The Arraignment of Paris*. In this play Juno and Athena, aggrieved at the judgment of Paris, demand a retrial. During the retrial Paris glimpses Queen Elizabeth – before whom the play was performed – and awards the golden apple to his monarch.

Peele's *Arraignment of Paris* is not a comic play. In Louis Montrose's summary, "the play's setting is pastoral, its dramaturgy is spectacular, and its royal sentiments are fulsome" (1980: 433). Nor are the shows in act 2, scene 2, the Judgment of Paris, intended as burlesque. The Judgment of Paris was often interpreted allegorically as "a choice among life patterns faced by a young man on the threshold of maturity" (Montrose 1980: 434), a choice underlined here by the drama's pastoral mode: pastoral represents "the rejection of the aspiring mind" (Hallett Smith cited in Montrose 1980: 434). In this scene the three goddesses tempt Paris with bribes. Each of their speeches of persuasion is followed by a lavish mini-pageant illustrating the temptations described.

Juno is the first to tempt Paris, in 17 hyperbolically lyrical lines offering golden riches. The stage direction explains, "Hereupon did rise a tree of gold, laden with diadems and crowns of gold" (sig. B4v). Athena, who scorns Juno's "decaying wealth," now encourages Paris to "aspire" to greater things: wisdom, honor, victory. Her pageant is of nine martial knights (presumably the Nine Worthies). Venus is the last to speak. She promises Paris priority treatment in love, she offers him herself, and lastly she offers him "a face that hath no peer," a "lusty minion trull / That can give sport to thee thy bellyful." The stage direction tells us "Helen *entereth in her braverie, with 4 Cupids attending on her, each having his fan in his hand to fan fresh air in her face*" (sig. C1r).[3]

Venus' show consists of Helen's singing a song in Italian. The song has three anaphorically structured trios of lines in which Helen compares herself to Diana: "If Diana is a star in the heavens . . . / If Diana is a goddess in the underworld . . . / If Diana is queen of nymphs on earth . . . ," concluding with Helen's challenge to Diana in all three locations: "I am a rare and sweet Diana, / Who can make war with my eyes / On Diana in hell, heaven and earth" (C1r-v; my trans.). Helen's supremacy is already hinted at in the verse structure. Each of the three-line segments about Diana are structured abb, cdd, eff; Diana's beauty can create only a couplet. Helen's effects a triplet: ggg. Helen is more satisfying than Diana (at least aurally).

When Shakespeare's Globe Theatre staged the play in 2007, Helen sang in English (a last-minute decision, according to the music director) and performed Peele's lyrics as a torch-song. Rae Baker's tall brunette Helen was dressed in a red basque with a feather tail, black fishnet tights and boots, and carried two whips. Her backing group of two Cupids was unable to match her in dance skill, musical ability, or sex appeal. With wings clipped to their T-shirts, leaning backwards with the belts of their jeans provocatively open, they shuffled forward and back on their knees in hip-led movements with which they were clearly artistically and physically uncomfortable. Nonetheless they expended determined effort, looking self-consciously to each other and Helen for direction. Their conscientiousness was as comic as the eye-rolling scorn with which Helen reacted to their amateur ability as accompanists.

Music created comedy throughout this production. Mercury wants to talk to Oenone but can't work out when the band's reggae music will stop and enable him to do so. Vulcan performs musically with two hammers. "O Ida, O Ida, happy hill" becomes a show-stopping chorus in acts 1 and 5. The comic effect of the musical Helen was compounded by contrast when Rae Baker doubled the role of the shepherdess Thestilis. When Thestilis experiences rejection in love (3.5), she sings a blues number, "ain't no pain like disdain." (The modernization was not gratuitous: it picked up the two key nouns from Peele's text; sig. D1r.)

Peele's play is unlikely to have been as comic in 1584 as it was in 2007. But the Globe production showed an interesting side effect of comedy on Helen: in this setting – and aware of the bathos of her setting – Helen became more powerful dramatically, not less so. She stood outside the playworld, commenting as an actress on the indignity of exposing the iconic Helen to a theater that was unable to represent her environment with justice.[4]

Operetta

In the nineteenth century Jacques Offenbach took this tactic one stage further in *La Belle Hélène* (1864). The English translation at London's Adelphi Theatre in 1866 titled the operetta *Helen, or Taken from the Greek*. This punning title sums up the parodic nature of Offenbach's work. It is not just Helen but the subject itself that is trans-lated.

Offenbach's opera is multiply parodic: musically, politically, textually. Its macaronic music gives Paris a Tyrolean yodeling song, quotes Rossini and Meyerbeer, provides can-can music for Orestes and a waltz for Helen and Paris. Politically the opera satirizes the erotic and financial indulgences of Paris (the city) under Napoleon III. Calchas, the priest, is a corruptible clergyman; the Spartans and Greeks embody court society in the Second Empire and, in the original production, the high kings of Hellas were recognizable royal relations (Traubner 2006). Textually the plot parodies the classics (a complaint rather than a compliment for some outraged nineteenth-century reviewers). Orestes (a *travesti* role) keeps company with two women of easy virtue. Helen is a bored bourgeois housewife.[5] It was not just the classics but contemporary moral behavior that was stretched: Paris enters Helen's bedroom on stage and the couple make musical love – a scandalous intimacy permissible only because Helen thinks she is dreaming. Offenbach's first full-length operetta, *Orphée aux Enfers* (1858), was a hugely successful parodic mix; Offenbach here offers a successful repeat.

To these three levels of parody, the 2006 production at the English National Opera (ENO)[6] added visual parody: in the opening scene Helen retired to the marital bed with a sleeping pill and the TV remote control; in the seaside setting of act 3, Menelaus wore an Andy Capp cap, a visual shorthand for the kind of limited and misogynist husband of whom a wife might well be bored.[7] This modern-dress (1960s) English-language production emphasized its complex and multiple "trans-ferrences" (Thomas Heywood's Elizabethan term for translation). The libretto announces itself as a "translation / close adaptation of Agathe Melinand's dialogue," which was itself "after Meilach and Halévy," who were themselves "after classical mythology." Helen has been translated from nineteenth-century to twenty-first-century Paris and then from twenty-first-century French to English.

This production also extended the metamusical parody. Helen's plaintiff line "I can't remember the last time I saw Paris" is followed by Orestes helpfully humming Borodin's theme tune from the film Helen has accidentally cited. This production originally intended a song-contest parody for the act 1 finale: Dvořák's New World Symphony, Orff's *Carmina Burana*, Arne's "Rule Britannia," and Bach's Toccata in D create the four syllables Jacques-Orff-Arne-Bach (Jacques Offenbach). In production this was eschewed in favor of a simpler, and more thematically suggestive, Men-Age-A-Troy (ménage à trois).[8]

Such verbal charades are one of the hallmarks of the production's translator/adapter, Kit Hesketh-Harvey, who has international fame as both a musical and a verbal satirist. He has written screenplays, translated for opera and musical theater, and is an award-winning performer of his own satirical songs. His text of *La Belle Hélène* parodies Shakespeare's most famous classical text, transposing its rhetoric from Rome to Greece ("Friends, Achaeans, Countrymen"); it contains topical English references (notably to TV shows and journalism such as *Omega Kappa* [OK] magazine) as well as to commercial life and culture in the twenty-first century: a query about the two Ajaxes is explained as "buy one get one free." Calchas' solemn bass voice plays with and against a Hollywood reference:

> To the Augur Calchas shall appear
> A golden-headed shepherd, whom
> Great Aphrodite holds most dear
> And fitter than Orlando Bloom.

The reduced number of processional virgins of Sparta is explained as the result of cutbacks. Outrageous puns abound: "I'm a bit Homer-phobic"; "You almost got us Orested"; "Losing one's [Elgin] marbles"; "Often barking / Offenbaching." The libretto is given punning sexual innuendo ("we'll be dining at seven / my poires belle Hélène are heaven"); it is metatextual (cautioned to secrecy, the Chorus promises, "we'll sing it *ppp*"); and it exploits the bathetic comic effects of feminine rhymes in English ("Naughty Orestes, chasing crumpet / . . . / Daddy can like it, or he can lump it"). "Ooh la la!" is pressed into service as a gloriously all-purpose euphemism in Orestes' "Now it's up to bed for some ooh la la / . . . / Ow! I gotta head from the ooh la la!" Paying homage to his nineteenth-century French precursor, Hesketh-Harvey declines to translate "l'homme à la pomme." Clearly, "il y'à des choses qui ne se disent qu'en français." Throughout, the lambent dialogue and lyrics keep two schemes and genres in play simultaneously: then and now, historical material and local moment, serious story and ludic libretto.

Offenbach's Helen may be a bored housewife but she is a determinedly chaste one. Her premarital past is indeed past (alluded to in her aria about Helen of the golden tresses); and she tells Calchas that "I've tried hard to love him!" Although she falls in love with Paris, she conceals her physical attractions in shapeless clothing, avoids seeing him, and doubles the guards at her chamber lest he enter.

But Paris and Aphrodite conspire against her intentions. Act 1 ends with Calchas sending Menelaus to Crete, which Helen matter-of-factly accepts: "seems quite straightforward / Off to Crete then"; act 2 ends with Menelaus interrupting the dream love-making of Paris and Helen. Even so, Helen's reputation remains unblemished. The Chorus blames Menelaus: "I think it's time we called a halt here / For you are just as much at fault here." In a chorus that paves the way for Gilbert and Sullivan patter-songs, Menelaus is told:

> The husband, say
> Who's been away
> But then heads for
> His marriage-bed
> (Good sense dictates
> And foresight states)
> Should send some war-
> ning well ahead.

Act 3 sees Helen escaping to a seaside resort to recover from her heartache. It opens with the royal couple arguing and ends with a sail gliding in from Cythera. The boat contains Paris disguised as an Arch-augur of Aphrodite to take Helen away to appease Aphrodite who, angered at the rejection of Paris, has filled Greece with Dionysiac excess:

> We've husbands leaving spouses
> We have wives turning ex
> And the whole thing's all down to sex.

In a scene of Offenbachannalia, Helen enters (a stage direction tells us) "drunk as a skunk." Just as she made love with Paris in act 2 under the influence of a dream, here she allows herself to be captured while inebriated. She is sexually desiring throughout, comically so as in her earlier unconvincing protests at Paris' threat of abduction – "HELP! help! somebody help me! please!" – but she remains blameless.

This is something opera can achieve through its dual forms – music and text. It is able to present Helen's two sides as coexistent, not conflicting. Sublime music gives her divinity; ironic dialogue gives her a boulevard sexuality. When Helen and Paris sing in Helen's bedroom, it is the waltz music one remembers, not the marital infidelity. Opera, even operetta, puts her beyond accusation, beyond blame; the music remains uppermost.

Silent film

In 1927 Helen received her first film treatment in *The Private Life of Helen of Troy* (directed by Alexander Korda). The film advertises itself as an adaptation of John Erskine's 1925 novel of the same name. In fact it takes nothing from Erskine's novel except the title. Erskine's novel concerns Helen's afterlife in Sparta at the time when her daughter Hermione is approaching marriage. It is written in ironic, epigrammatic dialogue, and Helen is a clever conversationalist with deep powers of self-analysis (qualities and skills absent from her well-meaning but emotionally literal husband). The film preserves the tone of the novel and the characterization of the two protagonists but transfers the situation to the build-up to the Trojan War.

The film as broadcast was approximately an hour long. The British Film Institute (BFI) owns two fragments, totaling 29 minutes of playing time. (Fortunately these two reels contain the beginning and the end of the film, so it is possible to appreciate the overall structure – and the unexpected ending.) A third reel duplicates the second but with additional scenes that were cut from the final version.[9]

The film opens with Menelaus endlessly shaking soldiers' hands ("All day the king continued to give his right hand for his country").[10] Menelaus' passion is fishing; he finds royal duties, as well as his wife's planned social activities, tedious, and is constantly planning fishing trips. (As Helen later tells her maid, "Marriage is only exchanging the attention of a dozen men for the inattention of one.") A sequence of frames juxtaposes Menelaus' preparations for a relaxed night in with Helen's preparations for a social night out. Menelaus loosens his body armor; Helen slips into a sheath dress. Menelaus takes off a tight helmet; Helen dons a helmet-style 1920s hat. When Menelaus protests that he is tired and that Helen has already "seen that show," she retorts "yes, but not in this dress." Their debate concludes with the summary intertitle "The wife wanted to go to the theater. The husband did not. So they went to the theater." A glamorous evening, a sociable intermission, opportunity for Helen's wardrobe, hairstyle, and luminous face to be admired, are followed by an invitation to Paris to dine at the palace the next day: "The most important date in history – Helen's date with Paris." Their subsequent elopement is burdened by wardrobe trunks and boxes, forcing Paris to act as porter. Menelaus meanwhile is far from upset at Helen's departure: "Now we can go fishing!"

The Spartan soldiers have other ideas. Because Helen has strained the economy by buying all her clothes from Troy, they welcome war. "Now we can get even with them Trojan dressmakers." Menelaus suggests letting the Trojans keep Helen ("That'll be worse than war"), but the soldiers persuade him to take action while Eteoneus bitterly updates him on the fishing forecast.

Reel 2 opens with the fall of Troy. Menelaus welcomes victory, not because of the return of his wife but because of the opportunity it affords to go fishing. He believes he has made Helen "realize a wife's place"; indeed Helen announces her intention of doing some housework. Menelaus confidently assures an unexpected visitor, Telemachus, who has come to see the famed beauty of Helen, that "the face that launched a thousand ships could never do it again." Helen's entrance contradicts him: in a flapper mini-dress, pearls, and gold headband, she flirts with Telemachus, creating magic with her eyes, her pout, the wine she pours, and her dialogue. Menelaus' look of déjà vu changes from resignation to enthusiasm as he realizes the piscatory possibilities. Leaving Helen and Telemachus to amuse themselves, he tells Eteoneus: "Tomorrow we positively go fishing – for it looks as though Helen will be taking a little trip to Ithaca."

The film is not just comic but cartoonish. Everything in it is psychologically as well as visually black and white. Helen does not suffer from this, because everyone receives the same satiric treatment: the man dressmaker ("more dressmaker than man"), the maid Adraste ("a servant problem"), the theater-going husbands and wives ("Intermission – when husbands awaken and wives are forsaken"), the sartorially vain Trojan soldiers who welcome war as an opportunity to display their fashionable new uniforms. Clothing is both the star of the film and its constant satiric target. We see pictures of Spartan shop frontages with Trojan chitons and shoes; the Trojan War is reduced to a sequence in which its dress shops are attacked (these scenes were cut in the final version). Early on, when Menelaus orders Helen to stop wearing Trojan fashions or to wear none at all, she exploits the ultimatum: "the newest frocks from Troy are practically none at all." In Troy she acquires a wonderful new wardrobe. In one scene she puzzles over design details with her dressmaker; the soldiers' excited shouts "We're going to the front" direct her attention to the tailoring problem – the front has an insufficiently low neckline.

Maria Corda's Helen has a constantly changing filmstar wardrobe. This is the only film or stage Helen who looks convincingly like a divine creature. This is due not to Corda's dewy skin and heart-shaped face but to her exotic fashions: warrior-style in detail, and crowned with exotic, quasi-military headgear (hat, tiara, jewels, gold band) which are part Minerva, part Dior, this is both a classical and a screen goddess (see figure 10). The former can be burlesqued, but in the 1920s the latter must be taken seriously. Duality thus works here as it does in Offenbach: two semiotic systems coexist and one plays off the other, ensuring the harmony of the whole. Although opera adds a dimension and silent film removes one, the effect is the same: both media take Helen beyond what can be said. In opera the languageless element is music; in silent film it is design. Goethe's Helen may vanish leaving only her clothes behind, but Corda's designer-dressed Helen *is* her clothes. She thus capitalizes on a recognizable stage shorthand: the woman with the best wardrobe is the most beautiful woman.[11]

The Novel

When Helen reaches the novel, she has no shortage of narrators and ventriloquizers, all of them willing to grant her agency, to rescue her from blame, to put her at the center of her story, and, in many cases, to make her a first-person narrator. Historical novels about Helen quickly become tedious, however: they follow a familiar plot, a predictable chronology (the marriage of Helen, the arrival of Paris, the movement to war), and their primary interest becomes the subtlety of their deviations from the expected narrative – Agamemnon's abuse of Iphigenia in Cargill's *To Follow the Goddess* (1991) the invented character, Galanor (Helen's confidant) in George's *Helen of Troy* (2006). The most successful novels are those that use the Helen of Troy story distantly. Helen's story becomes a springboard, an analogue, an allusion, or an underpinning. Avoiding one-to-one correspondence, these novels do not retell Helen's story so much as remake it.[12] Two novels do this with ingenuity: Jane Stanley's *A Daughter of the Gods* (1886) and Virginia Woolf's *Mrs Dalloway* (1925).

Figure 10   *The Private Life of Helen of Troy* (1927). Maria Corda's Helen displays one of her many stunning designer outfits. This still has survived the loss of the original full-length film; it does not correspond to any footage in the fragment owned by the British Film Institute (London). Reproduced by kind permission of Getty Images.

Jane Stanley, A Daughter of the Gods *(1886)*

Jane Stanley is a Victorian novelist extraordinary in many respects, not least for having escaped critical notice in the twentieth century. In 1886 she published a 600-page novel, part psychological thriller, part romance. The novel's title, *A Daughter of the Gods,* refers to Helen of Troy and comes from Tennyson's "A Dream of Fair Women." Two lines from this poem (unidentified by author or poem) form the novel's epigraph: "A daughter of the gods, divinely tall, / And most divinely fair." In 1888 Stanley published a second two-volume novel, *A New Face at the Door.* This title also comes from Tennyson, from "The Death of the Old Year." Again the epigraph provides three lines from the poem (unattributed by author or title). Thereafter Stanley disappears from sight. She published no further novels nor is her activity in the 1880s noted by academic historians of the novel or of women's writing. She is unknown to John Sutherland's invaluable *Longman Companion to Victorian Fiction* (1982), to the *Dictionary of National Biography,* the *Dictionary of Literary Biography,* to the Victorian Web, or even to Google. The Bodleian Library acquired its copy of *A Daughter of the Gods* on May 15, 1886, its copy of *A New Face at the Door* on December 16, 1887. In 2007 every page of both novels remained uncut. The same was true in 2008 of all the pages of the British Library copy of *A New Face at the Door*; *A Daughter of the Gods,* however, had been cut. No copies of the novel have appeared on secondhand websites, nor has either been digitized by firms such as Kessinger's Rare Reprints, which specializes in "scarce and hard-to-find books." Stanley is a novelist who has simply disappeared. This is an accident of history rather than a reflection of quality: although the second novel is disappointing, that is only a relative reaction to the merits of the first.

Both of Stanley's novels are set in the 1880s and are full of domestic detail about upper middle-class life in central London and the countryside. *A Daughter of the Gods* depicts household management and decoration, dinners and dances, the difficulties for unmarried women, and the dangers of travel. One technically precise legal dialogue indicates the author's knowledge of law (whether generally or ad hoc). The characters and their narrator quote (without identifying) Tennyson, Walter Scott, Browning, Goethe, Longfellow, Thomas Moore, Shakespeare, Anne Marsh-Caldwell's *Emilia Wyndham* (1846), and Baron de La Motte Fouqué's *Sintram* (de la Motte Fouqué died in 1843); they refer to an unidentified "well-worn couplet" by Wordsworth and quote other snatches of poetry which I have been unable to identify. Sometimes the characters parody contemporary poets, adapting their lines to the situation at hand.[13]

Literary quotations and domestic realism are not unusual in Victorian romantic fiction, nor is the bigamy plot that propels this novel. But *A Daughter of the Gods* is distinguished by three things: plot control, witty dialogue, and its depiction of maternal love. The plot is narrated crisply, with the author in control of pace, economically conveying months in a paragraph yet simultaneously employing details that locate emotions with precision. The action is conducted mainly through dialogue, and the characters have an Austenesque sense of Augustan syntax (the heroine confesses to having read *Emma* six times; vol. 1: 267) coupled with ironic ripostes. Having heard James Grey's description of the heroine's extreme beauty, Kate Payn responds "as some slight set-off against such natural advantages does she at least dress badly?" (vol. 1: 88).

The novel explores motherhood as a love that is as painful as it is powerful; the power of her maternal love leads the heroine paradoxically to a feeling of powerlessness, compounded by the power others have over her because of her love for her child. Allied to this is a study of marital trust and deception, and a story of moral goodness, with the heroine's innocence being sincere rather than saccharine. It is difficult to convey the tone of a novel whose primary mode is dialogue, or to summarize a plot where five women aged between 20 and 35 seek the protection of marriage and one finds her past come back to threaten her. "Jane Austen meets Ibsen" is perhaps the most succinct description.

The novel begins with a short chapter depicting but not explaining antecedent action in Belgium, 1877; chapter 2 begins the story in France in 1882, and the novel ends in England in 1885. The heroine, 20-year-old Verena Dogan and her 28-year-old stepmother, Annette, nurse the consumptive Mr Dogan in their home in Boulogne, where they also look after Verena's stepsister, four-year-old Mara. Annette marries within four months of Mr Dogan's death; she and her new baby subsequently die after childbirth.

During Mr Dogan's last summer, a 50-year-old barrister from London, James Grey, holidays in France. Grey and Dogan had been friends in childhood, and the friendship is renewed. Grey's daily visits are prompted initially by sympathy, but subsequently by his attraction to Verena, who is 5 feet 8 inches tall, blonde, and exceptionally beautiful. "A woman without vanity," she dresses plainly in black, shuns ornaments, ostentation, and extravagance, wears a thick veil in public, and avoids society. She promises her father that she will accept Mr Grey if he proposes marriage, and after her father's death she does so. The plot moves to England, as do Verena and Mara.

Grey's Russell Square house is run by his unmarried 35-year-old sister, Emmeline, who is benignly resentful of the new mistress (Verena's "straightforwardness upset all her calculations"). Her social circle includes cousins Kate and Gertie, who are skeptically cordial to Verena. Gertie warms to Verena's intelligence but Kate is suspicious of her transparent goodness, feeling it "grafted on a good deal of original sin" (vol. 2: 211). The child Mara, who captures almost all hearts, prevents any of the undercurrent tensions erupting into confrontations, although her prominence in the household is a recurrent irritant to Emmeline. Similarly Emmeline's idle chatter is a constant trial to the contemplative Verena, who contrasts the mindless talk of her sister-in-law with that of her young stepsister: "the babble of an opening mind is very different from the babble of a mind that is never going to open" (vol. 1: 200–1).

Social routines, and the developing love between husband and wife, are disturbed by the arrival of Arthur Courtenay. The prelude in Ostend is now explained. As a schoolgirl, Verena had fallen in love with Courtenay and eloped. Their marriage at sea proved to be illegal for several reasons, not least of which was that Courtenay was already married. Discovering this within a week of the marriage, Verena fled home. Her subsequent pregnancy and childbirth were concealed and the baby brought up as Annette's. "The unhappy girl-mother was allowed to keep her treasure only on condition that she never claimed it as her own" (vol. 1: 293). Verena has promised her dying father to keep this secret from Mr Grey, a deceit that costs her enormous pain throughout the novel. Courtenay's arrival and his persistent persecution prompt her to tell her husband of the illegal marriage, but not until the child is drowned in a boating accident on the Thames does she reveal that she is Mara's mother. Her grief at the loss, and her husband's pain at her distress (and subsequent confession), a pain that he in turn conceals from her, are powerfully (because tersely) depicted.

James Grey visits Courtenay to put an end to his threats, and the novel ends with the birth of the Greys' daughter. Emmeline, who has never reconciled herself to Mara's charms but is ever keen to puncture Verena's quiet joys, now harnesses the dead Mara to her cause: she compares the new infant to Mara, to the former's disadvantage. The novel manages to conclude with both irony (the constant hierarchical one-upmanship of Emmeline) and domestic tenderness as her praise of the dead child only gladdens the hearts of the Greys.

Much about the novel advertises its indebtedness to Helen of Troy narratives. Courtenay is a Theseus figure, taking advantage of the schoolgirl Verena, and the product of their union is, like Iphigenia, transferred to a family member. Both Verena's sham husband and her legal spouse are mesmerized by her beauty. Courtenay finds her "the only beauty he had ever seen of whom the report did not outrun the reality" (vol. 2: 6–7), and

James Grey, declaring her beyond description, resorts to Tennyson's lines on Helen of Troy. Others comment on her unearthly quality (vol. 1: 284) and "*excessive* fairness" (vol. 1: 154, my italics).

On marriage, Verena's wardrobe changes from her preferred black to cashmeres and silks; but the sole dress described in detail is a Virgilian Helen of Troy yellow gown. Emmeline criticizes the fabric as having "too much yellow about it," but by the time it has been made into a ball gown it is "a most artistic combination of bronze velvet and pale yellow, embroidered in gold" (vol. 2: 96). When characters are discussed for a fancy dress ball, Kate suggests (referring to James's earlier Tennyson quotation) that, given her beauty, Verena should go as Helen. Her husband wonders if this casts him as Paris but Kate observes "you will find plenty of men ready to play Paris. Mr Courtenay, for instance" (vol. 2: 162–3). Verena refuses to play Helen (as she has done from the beginning of the novel, disguising her beauty and living quietly). She further rejects the suggestion that her husband play Menelaus and requests "a more domestic character." James wants Verena to be "some one who lived happy ever after"; she wants someone with "strict respectability" (vol. 2: 163, 164). That old stories are being revised is underlined in the next chapter when Verena frets over Courtenay's determination to destroy her: "that the old story should be sponged out and the unhappy heroine live happily afterwards – he would never, if he could help it, suffer that" (vol. 2: 176). Verena is set on revision. When she and James hunt for a house in the country, someone comments that "your townhouse won't see much of you then." Verena is adamant, "I have no intention of deserting my husband" (vol. 2: 71).

If Verena is Helen, she is a Helen without blame. The bigamous marriage is, in her eyes, legal. Her innocence is frequently stressed, by father and narrator, perhaps because Verena herself is so self-reproachfully conscious of the shadow over her life. Her life "was the expiation of a sin of which she was not guilty" (vol. 1: 115). Christian goodness structures her thoughts, her images come from Bunyan and the Bible, and she seeks out churches rather than society. Images that associate her with the heavens are designed to underline the effect of her beauty, but in the context of her daily feelings of guilt they elevate her beyond blame. When James pays homage to her, it is "the homage of a worshipper to a saint rather than the ardour of a lover" (vol. 1: 56).

Although the 21-year-old Verena marries her older suitor because she wants "no pretence of romance" (vol. 1: 104), she loves passionately: the novel redirects her emotions to her child. (It is her fondness for Mara that arouses Kate's suspicions about Verena.) Verena regularly reflects on her feelings for the child: "Other people did not pine and fall ill when they were separated from those they loved. Neither did they distract themselves with pictures of the accidents and sicknesses which might befall their dear ones in their absence. Other people loved reasonably" (vol. 1: 228). Despite such passion Verena is remote and unknowable. This is not because her emotions are unknown to us but because she must keep them concealed from other characters. The shadow in this novel is not an *eidōlon*, but the past (vol. 1: 285). Verena thus becomes a blank at the center of the characters' social circle. Kate tries hardest to read her; her husband tries both to read the blank and inscribe it, but acknowledges that he finds it hard to write upon the blank of her heart (vol. 2: 19).

When Verena rejects the fancy-dress persona of Helen, an alternative is proposed: Hypatia. A Greek scholar from Alexandria, born in the second half of the fourth century BCE, Hypatia became head of the Platonist school in Alexandria. She was a notable scholar who taught maths, philosophy, and astronomy. Verena's educational qualifications and intellectual abilities are frequently noted. In Boulogne, James observes her earnestness, her ability in modern languages, and the fact that she is "something more than well-educated": she has "a certain originality of thought" (vol. 1: 28–9). Verena is at ease with William Hamilton's *Lectures on Metaphysics* (1866) and George Henry Lewes' *History of Philosophy* (1845–6), which she undertakes to explain to Gertie (vol. 1: 170). When Verena meets her cousins-in-law, Kate observes critically, "you are quite a blue" (vol. 1: 170). Verena acquires legal knowledge in the course of the novel when she occupies herself with her husband's law books. This gives her a new authority when she encounters Courtenay, and she can tell him what his legal position is. In fact the newly confident Verena attracts Courtenay more than the sentimental 16-year-old he has betrayed (vol. 2: 11). This is Helen in the age of women's education (the 1880s saw the founding of women's colleges at Oxford, London, and Cambridge).

It is also Helen in the age of Ibsen. In *A Doll's House* (1879) Torvald, deeply in love with his younger wife, wishes he could prove his romantic feelings for her. He wants to be a knight on a white charger, to rescue her in a crisis. When the crisis comes, he fails miserably. Finding out his wife's secret – that she has forged a signature on a document for his benefit – he accuses her, thinks only of his own reputation, and the marriage collapses. Ibsen's view of male–female relations is sober: men fantasize about being women's savior, but when the crunch comes, they fail women.

Jane Stanley, writing seven years after *A Doll's House*, presents an optimistic view. Verena's revelation to her husband comes in two stages. The fake marriage to the scoundrel lover is something James Grey can cope with. When he and Courtenay meet in hostile circumstances, "it seemed for a moment as if the men would be in actual personal conflict, nor was the idea absolutely repulsive to Mr. Grey" (vol. 2: 13). To James, to be champion of his beautiful wife, is romantic. When Courtenay threatens to tell the whole story, Verena does not flinch – "a triumphant confidence in her husband's loyalty upheld her" (vol. 2: 15); "she believed that her husband would forgive her" (vol. 2: 16). This is also Nora's view in *A Doll's House*, but Verena's confidence is justified. James has already cleared one hurdle because of his love for Verena, the knowledge of Mr Dogan's debts, a fact that could shame him publicly if it were to become widely known. (Indeed one of his colleagues broaches the subject before marriage, but James takes it in his stride.)

However, when James finds out that Mara is Verena's child, his disillusion contrasts with Verena's relief. She feels "as Christian felt when the pack fell from his shoulders" (vol. 2: 272), but James feels "a glory had gone from the head he loved" (vol. 2: 269). Verena explains that she deceived him because her father thought James would not marry her if he knew. It is now James's turn to deceive by saying that he would have married her regardless, but he knows that it is not true. His disillusion is not permanent but neither is it fleeting.

> It was no fresh young girl whom he had married, but a woman who had suffered and died in her early life . . . Without that ruined life, his Verena might never have been born. Through all the storm of wounded love which tore him he realized that. (vol. 2: 270–1)

Stanley does not give us the exposé of male roles that Ibsen does, but neither does she give us unqualified romanticism.

Stanley can successfully rewrite the Helen story because its presence is so diffuse in her novel. For if Courtenay is the abductor Paris, he is also, given Verena's youth, a Theseus figure, and, in one startling image, he is Jove the rapist, making Verena both Helen and Leda. As Courtenay stalks Verena around London, Verena takes care to avoid him, but on one occasion her evasive action fails: "Courtenay had sprung from the earth, or fallen from the sky upon her" (vol. 2: 158).

Reviewers reacted positively to *A Daughter of the Gods*. *The Academy* observed that "the story moves smoothly, and is not without interest."[14] *The Daily News* (Oct. 2, 1886) appreciated the characterization, the style, and the empathy. The reviewer in *The Graphic* (June 12, 1886) praised the tragic writing in the accounts of Mara's death and Verena's sorrow. This reviewer, however, did not know his Tennyson, which made him unable to grasp the relevance of the title:

> The chief fault of the novel lies in the rank absurdity of its title – mostly an unimportant matter, except from a purely business point of view, but in the present case misleading, and irritating to readers who are sensitive about such things. The heroine was, we presume, made tall and fair to fit the quotation.

Failing to recognize the titular reference to Helen of Troy, he was consequently unable to see the way in which the novel continues the allusion. His knowledge of Tennyson did not improve in the next two years, for he made the same objection to the title of *A New Face at the Door* (*The Graphic*, Feb. 11, 1888).

Stanley's second novel was published within 18 months of the first. It lacks the sparkling dialogue format of *A Daughter of the Gods*, has a derivative Becky Sharpe-style antiheroine, and is overwritten. *The Glasgow Herald* said, "there is nothing strikingly original in this novel" (Dec. 15, 1887). The reviewer in *The Graphic* found it "not without interest" but damned with faint praise, "her story is certainly of the kind usually classified as 'readable' " (Feb. 11, 1888). The reviews were lukewarm rather than bad, and certainly contained nothing to deter a new novelist from further work. Nonetheless Stanley published no more novels after this. Uncovering her biography will almost certainly illuminate the matter, but Jane Stanley is not an unusual name and I have not yet identified Jane Stanley the novelist.

A woman called Jane Charlotte Stanley died on March 21, 1888; her funeral was reported in the *Belfast News-Letter* on March 27, 1888. This Jane Stanley was the wife of a Justice of the Peace (J. P.), Charles Stanley, and died at their upper middle-class home, Roughan Park in County Tyrone. Marriage to a J. P. might explain the legal detail in *A Daughter of the Gods*, and the lengthy trial that occupies volume 2 of *A New Face at the Door*. This Jane Stanley occupies the same social sphere as the characters in her two contemporary novels. However, she was 75 at the time of her death, and it seems unlikely that anyone would begin a career as a novelist in her eighth decade. The contemporary setting of the novels prevents our arguing that they were penned in youth and published later. A lady correspondent (or two lady correspondents) contribute(s) a "metropolitan gossip" column to the *Belfast News-Letter* (May 11, 1885) and a society column to the London *Daily News* (May 1, 1886). In these two columns the writer(s) covers the Royal Academy private views of 1885 and 1886: not the paintings but the fashions worn by those in attendance. In both columns the writer applies Tennyson's quotation about Helen of Troy to a beautiful woman. While this might seem an obvious comparison, the Poet Laureate being on everyone's lips, two facts suggest that this is more than coincidence: Tennyson's *Dream of Fair Women* was first published in 1833 and so not an obvious journalistic comparison in 1885–6; and electronic databases of Victorian periodicals do not provide any other instances of the lines being applied in this way in reviews. Verena's costumes in *A Daughter of the Gods* – cashmere dresses, ostrich feathers, ball gowns – are described as if by a fashion correspondent; the descriptions would be at home in the two newspaper columns and vice versa. The *Belfast News-Letter* column provides a tantalizing link with the Jane Charlotte Stanley of County Tyrone, but I doubt that this Stanley was traveling to the Royal Academy in her seventies.

Jane Stanley the novelist may not be the Royal Academy fashion reviewer. She may not be the occupant of Roughan Park. Nonetheless the coincidences between the milieu in Stanley's novels and three details in the life of Mrs Charles Stanley are helpful in suggesting explanations: the legal husband, the social class, and the date of her death. Anyone interested in Jane Stanley the novelist must wonder why a new Victorian novelist, published by a respectable press,[15] and well reviewed, suddenly stopped writing in 1888. Jane Stanley's death provides one explanation.

Virginia Woolf, Mrs Dalloway *(1925)*

Unlike Mrs Ramsay in *To the Lighthouse* (1927), who is described as "Greek, blue-eyed, straight-nosed" and called "the happier Helen of these days," Mrs Dalloway (Clarissa) is never explicitly compared to Helen of Troy, nor is she considered a great beauty. Clarissa herself reflects on her looks: "she had a narrow pea-stick figure; a ridiculous little face, beaked like a bird's" (1976: 11). Even Peter Walsh, in love with Clarissa from his youth, concedes "she was not beautiful at all" (68). Nonetheless Clarissa (like Helen) is magnetic to all who encounter her: "she came into a room; she stood . . . in a doorway with lots of people round her. But it was Clarissa one remembered" (68). The novel's phrase to describe her (through Peter Walsh's eyes) is "there she was." All Peter can do in the way of depicting her effect is to state that she exists. We are in the world of Camilla Paglia's beautiful goddesses depicted in the moment of "mere being."

Mrs Dalloway is structured round a classic (and classical) love triangle: the youthful Clarissa-Helen is loved by the stolid Richard-Menelaus and the romantic Peter-Paris. Clarissa chooses Richard. At the start of the novel we meet her, aged 50, after years of successful marriage. Nonetheless there is a fleeting moment of regret. After five years in India, Peter Walsh unexpectedly visits Clarissa, who is delighted to see him. When he bursts into tears, she kisses him. She feels "a tropical gale in her breast," holds his hand, and thinks "if I had married him, this gaiety would have been mine all day!" (43). Reflecting that "it was all over for her" (the narrow single bed which she occupies in the attic after her recent illness extends into an image of incarceration and solitude in a turret) she has a moment of uncharacteristic emotional impulse: "take me with you, Clarissa thought impulsively, as if he were starting directly upon some great voyage" (43). But it is only a moment: "next moment, it was as if the five acts of a play that had been very exciting and moving were now over and she had lived a lifetime in them and had run away, had lived with Peter, and it was now over" (43). Woolf collapses the traditional Helen of Troy story into one sentence.

In offering a maritally stable and monogamous Clarissa, Woolf thus offers a thorough revision of the Helen who, in myth and literature, is defined by one sexual act. The love triangle is resolved into a straight line in Clarissa's youth, and its reappearance (in Peter's return) is an emotional disturbance but not a major threat. Her husband remembers, "she had often said to him that she had been right not to marry Peter Walsh; which, knowing Clarissa, was obviously true" (104). Woolf's Clarissa-Helen not only rejects impulsive romance in favor of a reliable marriage; she is happy with her decision.

Like antiquity's Paris, Peter Walsh is an outcast (sent down from Oxford) and romantically impulsive. When we meet him at the age of 53, he is about to marry the 24-year-old wife of a major, still married, and with two children; Peter, also married, has come to England to see his lawyers about his own divorce (42). In Trafalgar Square his attention is caught by an attractive young woman whom he follows to a house off Great Portland Street, intending to invite her for an ice. He imagines her, Salome-like, shedding "veil after veil" (49); he envisions her whispering his name and opening her arms to him (48); he sees himself as "an adventurer, reckless . . . swift, daring, . . . a romantic buccaneer" (he repeats this last noun; 49). But Peter is a failed Paris. His Helen of Troy, Clarissa, rejected him.

In midlife, Peter is repeatedly haunted by this rejection: "Clarissa refused me, he thought. He stood there thinking, Clarissa refused me" (45). Furthermore she rejected him in favor of the traditionally limited Menelaus figure, Richard Dalloway. Menelaus' lack of intelligence is stressed throughout most Helen texts, and this one is no exception. Dalloway "was a thorough good sort; a bit limited; a bit thick in the head" (67). Sally Seton opines "that Richard would never be in the Cabinet because he had a second-class brain" (107–8). His intellectual limitations are several times contrasted with his public prominence as a Member of Parliament, yet Clarissa, "with twice his wits, . . . had to see things through his eyes – one of the tragedies of married life. With a mind of her own, she must always be quoting Richard" (69).

But it is Peter, not Clarissa, who sees this as marital tragedy. Clarissa gives parties for Richard, enjoys her "career" as a hostess, and her social life becomes a metaphor for living: it is flux, movement, people, interaction, the opposite of solitude and withdrawal. Clarissa defends her love of giving parties: "what she liked was simply life. 'That's what I do it for', she said, speaking aloud, to life . . . They're an offering" (108). When news of Septimus Warren Smith's suicide interrupts the joy of her party, "Oh! thought Clarissa, in the middle of my party, here's death" (162). The observation is not the complaint of a hostess for whom the tone of the evening has changed but a contrast between death and life.[16]

Despite her ability to draw others to her, Clarissa, like Helen, is repeatedly characterized as emotionally distant. "There was always something cold in Clarissa" (45); "this coldness, this woodenness; . . . an impenetrability" (55); "so calm, so cold . . . as cold as an icicle" (72). Peter Walsh observes that despite having known Clarissa for over 30 years, he only really has a "sketch" of her. These observations about distance and emotional frigidity – all Peter Walsh's observations – are not the biased bitterness of a rejected suitor: Clarissa herself acknowledges that she lacks warmth (30) and her emotional role model is Lady Bexborough, who opened a bazaar without any visible distress despite having just opened a telegram announcing her son's death in World War I (10).

The imagery that characterizes Clarissa is not just cold; it is sexually frigid: she is like a nun (the image occurs twice), she sleeps alone in a single bed, and "a virginity preserved through childbirth . . . clung to her like a sheet" (29). When Peter Walsh interrupts her sewing her dress, she tries to conceal the garment "like a virgin protecting chastity" (37). In the *Odyssey* Homer revirginizes Helen by comparing her to Artemis; here we have the *Odyssey*'s Artemis image writ large.

Woolf thus makes significant changes: she foregrounds the Helen character; she makes her faithful; she presents her in a *post*war setting; and she presents her in middle age. *Mrs Dalloway* is a Helen of Troy story in the loosest sense. Like Jane Stanley's *A Daughter of the Gods*, it uses Helen's story not as a plot straitjacket but as a springboard to female experience: Clarissa-Helen reflects on emotional choices made in youth, their consequences, and her current state of acceptance/happiness. This interiority is not just unusual for a Helen narrative; it is unusual for the novel. Woolf makes Clarissa-Helen's interiority the defining feature of a new genre: stream-of-consciousness.

Unlike Stanley's novel, Woolf's narrative is consistently Homeric in language and image. Stream-of-consciousness repetitions recur like Homeric formulae, only here they provide not a metrical mnemonic or a thematic cross-reference but a poetic lyricism: "all because she was coming down to dinner in a white frock to meet Sally Seton!" (32); "Lady Bruton, . . . whose lunch parties were said to be extraordinarily amusing" (28); "So utterly taken aback to have Peter Walsh come to her unexpectedly in the morning" (37).

Like epic, the novel begins *in medias res* and is episodic. It parodically uses classical images. Taking Mrs Dalloway's parasol, her maid "handled it like a sacred weapon which a goddess, having acquitted herself honourably in the field of battle, sheds, and placed it in the umbrella stand" (28). The question "Well, and what's happened to you?" in the conversation between Peter Walsh and Clarissa after Peter's five-year absence is presented as a military overture: "So before a battle begins, the horses paw the ground; toss their heads; the light shines on their flanks; their necks curve. So Peter Walsh and Clarissa, sitting side by side on the blue sofa, challenged each other" (41). Like Helen of Troy, Mrs Dalloway sews. Like Helen of Troy, she has one daughter, Elizabeth. Much is made of Elizabeth's exotic Chinese eyes, her Mongol looks, and her great beauty. Beauty, in fact, is the focus of both Septimus Warren Smith's thoughts and those of Peter Walsh. Walking to Clarissa's party, Peter intuits, "that he was about to have an experience. But what? Beauty anyhow. Not the crude beauty of the eye . . . Absorbing, mysterious, of infinite richness, this life" (144–5). Sitting in Regent's Park, the shell-shocked Septimus listens and observes, "Beauty, the world seemed to say" (63). Beauty in this novel is not the absolute beauty of Helen of Troy, but the beauty of life and the concomitant ability to live in the moment.

As these examples show, Woolf is not interested in a consistent and classical correspondence. The Warren Smiths belong to another classical world: Septimus has a Latin name, and Lucrezia's is that of the Roman heroine who is Helen's opposite. And if Clarissa is a Helen figure, she is also a Penelope: sewing while her husband is absent, and refusing an opportunistic suitor, Peter. Her father is an accidental Agamemnon: Clarissa's loss of belief in classically plural, indifferent gods is caused by the death of her young sister, an Iphigenia figure "on the verge of life" for whose death her father is to blame: "to see your own sister killed by a falling tree (all Justin Parry's fault – all his carelessness) before your very eyes" (70). Woolf's predecessor in revising classics for the novel was James Joyce in *Ulysses* (1922), a novel Woolf read without much enjoyment. *Ulysses* has reasonably consistent and tight representations of modern characters and episodes with Homeric characters and episodes.[17] In *Mrs Dalloway* Woolf offers a macaronic alternative to Joyce. Here is the episodic structure of epic, its military images, its linguistic formulae, and its characters. But the character correspondences are inconsistent, the temporal sequence is twice revised (Menelaus-Richard and Paris-Peter appear simultaneously, and the narrative is recalled from the perspective of middle age) and epic's omniscient point of view is abandoned in favor of multiple perspectives: our information about Clarissa-Helen comes both from the men who love her and from herself.

Woolf could have removed the Helen character – as she does in her next novel, *To the Lighthouse*, where Mrs Ramsay dies halfway through the novel – and she at one stage intended to do so (Clarissa was to commit suicide at the end). Instead Woolf's Clarissa-Helen rejoins life. Even so, she is left, as is typical of Helen characters, as is characteristic of this stream-of-consciousness novel (and of stream-of-consciousness novels in general), in the moment: "there she was" (172). The novel ends with Peter's inability to render Clarissa-Helen's charms in language (an inability, as we have seen, common to Helen narratives).

In this chapter Helen has moved from epic to comedy and from poetry to the novel. One more narrative innovation awaits her: she changes color, from white to black, with the Caribbean Helen of Derek Walcott's *Omeros*.

Caribbean Helen: Derek Walcott, *Omeros* (1990)

This 64-chapter poem, divided into seven books, covers four continents and nearly four hundred years. It begins and ends in St Lucia where two village fishermen, Achille and Hector, compete for the love of the local beauty, Helen. A pig-farmer (a retired white Englishman, Major Dennis Plunkett) and his Irish wife, Maud, employ (and subsequently dismiss) Helen as a maid. The locals in Ma Kilman's "No Pain Café" include the fisherman Philoctete (who suffers from a festering leg wound) and an old blind sailor, Seven Seas (also identified with Homer). A narrative "I," whose biographical details overlap with those of Walcott, travels from St Lucia to Boston, Lisbon, Dublin, and London. Achille too makes a journey when, in a sunstroke-induced vision, he travels to Africa, the land of his ancestors.

Walcott's poem, like other epics from Homer through Ovid and Virgil to Milton, is an account of origins. The narrator's literary journey, prompted by the ghost of his father, Warwick Walcott, explores the European cities of writers, a pilgrimage that eventually encourages him to return home and love his island "for its green simplicities" (36.3.59).[18] Both Achille, the fisherman, and Major Plunkett, who has made St Lucia his home after World War II, are on quests to find their ancestors and understand their own identity. In Achille's hallucinatory journey he meets a distant relative, Afolabe,[19] and witnesses the slave raid that brought his family to the West Indies. Plunkett journeys through the record books, where he comes across a young midshipman with the same surname who was killed in 1782. He invents a family tree to connect them despite the fact that the midshipman died without issue. Ma Kilman too journeys towards roots, literally: she climbs the hillside in search of a herb of African origin with which to cure Philoctete's wound.

The characters' quest for origins is framed by a larger myth of origins: that of the dying/reborn vegetation god. The poem begins with the felling of St Lucia's trees to make canoes. The three sunrises which function as a Proem are both local and primordial: "Sunrise bespeaks the pristine, the moment when light first floods across the void and gives the formless form" (Austin 1999: 29). The green island, like Maud Plunkett's orchid garden or the green space of her native Ireland, is both pagan – the Golden Age – and biblical – "like Adam and Eve . . . / Before the snake. Without all the sin" (10.3.58–9).

Throughout the poem Homeric echoes remind us of the story's epic ancestry. Achille's heel is twice caught by a forest vine, his vulnerability naturalized to a forest threat. The gods, in their only appearance, create a hurricane (Cyclone and Ma Raine); the cyclone is simultaneously a Cyclops, giving nuance to the phrase "eye of the storm." The characters have Homeric names (Helen, Hector, Achille, etc.) and Achille and Hector compete in an *Iliad*ic running race. From the poem's first publication, reviewers have debated its genre. Walcott rejects attributions of epic but claims the epical: "a natural element is more challenging than an army. You can perhaps face an army. You cannot face a hurricane. And that's more epical" (Walcott 1997: 244). In another interview he points out that the poem lacks epic battles. But it has combat of a different kind: a struggle for survival. And this struggle (like the poem) is both Antillean and Greek, modern and ancient.

At the center of Walcott's poem, like the center of Homer's, is absence – in this case, the absence of name, history, home, identity. The classical names have as much to do with slave heritage as classical inheritance. It was customary for slave owners to assign mythological or biblical names to their slaves, erasing their African identity. When Achille travels to Africa, his forebear Afolabe is surprised that Achille does not know the "meaning" of his name: "A name means something . . . / Unless the sound means nothing. Then you would be nothing" (25.3.28, 32). Walcott explains that "for somebody not to know the meaning of the sound of his or her name is to be nameless, not to have an identity" (Walcott 1997: 238). A variant of this ontological problem is depicted in chapter 2 when the fishermen are gathered in the early morning light: Hector, Theophile,

Chrysostom, Philoctete – "In this light, / they have only Christian names" (2.1.1–2). These are *pagan* names yet they are, as Norman Austin realizes, Christian names "in that they are not surnames" (Austin 1999: 36–7). Names thus reflect the characters' divided heritage, and their quest is how to resolve their dual identity: culturally and physically black and white (like the narrator, who has white ancestry), African and Caribbean, classical and Christian (like the poem). This quest is as applicable to the white characters as it is to the black. The English Plunkett is disconcerted to discover that his ancestors are Scottish, and when his car is involved in a road accident, the other car's occupants offend him by calling him "honky" (a pejorative term for "white," inapplicable to his 20-year residency on the island; 51.1.34–8). It is this hybrid identity that makes Plunkett, who initially seems an easy expatriate target, such a sympathetic character.

The poem's exploration of divided identity is reified in its generic ambiguity: is it or is it not epic? What does it mean to "be" something without being it wholly? To be epical without being epic?

Like the black fishermen, Plunkett has a form of a classical name: Dennis, from the French form *Denis*, means a follower of Dionysus. The poem's names, like the characters, have multiple signifieds, caught in cultural crossroads. As critics often note, Omeros is Greek for Homer, but it is modern Greek, far removed from the oral poet. Homer is also the surname of the American artist Winslow Homer, whose *Storm at Sea* the narrator observes in book 20, and it is homonymically related to Dustan St Omer, Walcott's friend characterized as Gregorias in *Another Life* (Thieme 1999: 155). And as *Omeros* itself tells us,

> *O* was the conch-shell's invocation, *mer* was
> both mother and sea in our Antillean patois,
> *os*, a grey bone, and the white surf as it crashes.
> (2.3.10–12)

To which of these cultures does the name Omeros/Homer belong? What does it "mean"? In this context, Achille is justified in not knowing the meaning of his name.

Achille's onomastic ignorance is further justified in that there is no meaning to know. Norman Austin explains that Achille is not a name "but an absence of a name, being a marker for the name that was taken from him" (Austin 1999: 31). Walcott's *Omeros*, like all Helen narratives, is a story of abduction but what is taken away is black identity, black history, black autonomy – all encapsulated in the removal of the African name and its replacement by European labels.

Structured round the absent name, *Omeros*, like the *Iliad*, is structured round other absences, symbolized repeatedly by images of blankness (white snow, white pages). Plunkett embarks on his history of the island because of the absence of St Lucia and her people from official history books. There are genealogical absences: Plunkett's and Achille's histories. Midshipman Plunkett lies unnoticed in the record books for two hundred years before Major Plunkett claims him. The omnipresent sea is absent at a critical time: during Plunkett's service in the Sahara against Rommel in World War II (Leithauser 1991: 92). As everywhere in Helen narratives, we are faced with the problem of filling the blank. In *Omeros* that means: How to remember one's cultural history without being its victim? How to turn competition and struggle (the *Iliad*ic theme) and the journey (the *Odyss*ic theme) into a poem of homecoming (the *Nostoi*)?

Through this poem of pain and healing ("affliction is one theme / of this work" explains the narrator, 5.2.20–1) floats Helen. Walcott's Helen initially seems a familiar figure from classical Helen narratives. She is aloof, self-contained, remote, both emotionally and narratologically ("she functions independently of the other characters' fates"; Minkler 1993: 273). Like Virgil's Helen, she wears a yellow dress. This dress was stolen from, or given her by, Maud Plunkett – an ambiguity never resolved in the poem, thereby relocating the familiar question from antiquity about her guilt or innocence. Plunkett wonders, "What did she [Helen] want? For History to exorcize her / theft of the yellow frock?" (10.3.50–1). (His question summarizes a literary challenge across 28 centuries.) Helen is fought over by Achille and Hector, a quarrel that leads indirectly to the death of Hector. Her beauty halts the action: in her first appearance, as she makes her confident, feline way up the beach, her beauty causes all to stop and stare. Later, when Plunkett catches her in the act of stealing a bracelet, it is he not she who freezes: "he was fixed by her glance" (18.1.39). And she is unknowable. "Who is that?" inquires the narrator, in admiration. The waitress's response does not answer the question: "She? She too proud" (4.3.27).

Walcott's use of myth eschews programmatic correspondence. Legends, like names, "are not oars / that have to be laid side by side" (62.2.21–2). In interview Walcott has said, "every new myth has screwed up the one preceding it, gotten it wrong, including Christianity. They got it wrong – and then they started something" (Walcott 1997: 242). (This is a description of myth but it is also a description of parody.) His Helen is not simply a variant of Homer's – a black Helen – but a totally new creature. When Minkler writes, "she [Helen] belongs to no-one" (1993: 274), we are in the familiar territory of the absolute. But we are also in a new territory of black identity. As Walcott explains in a different context, one problem for black people is the problem of comparison:

> when you live in this country [USA] . . . you have to continually draw comparisons like "Lou Gossett is as good an actor as somebody else." That's the process and horror of living in this country, continually saying that the Black thing is as good as the White thing. (Walcott 1997: 232)

This statement helps illuminate his repudiation of the "epic" label: "the parallel, in its attempt to ennoble, actually demeans" (Breslin 2001: 242). Viewing *Omeros* as a Caribbean *Iliad* or *Odyssey* "say[s] to the Caribbean Sea, 'You must think of yourself as a second-rate Aegean' " (1997: 232). Walcott's Helen represents transcendence of categorization (like the poem in which she features). She is herself. She is not a Black version of a White Helen; she is Helen and she is black. She is not an Antillean version of a Homeric Helen; she is Helen and Antillean. Perhaps the greatest testimony to this independent identity comes in Robert Hamner's book *Epic of the Dispossessed*, where Helen is given two entries in the index: "Helen (of Troy)" and "Helen (of Antilles)." The former has 9 references, the latter 87. Helen of Troy is eclipsed by a totally new creature. It is perhaps relevant that Walcott's Helen is based not on a disembodied ideal but on a real woman he saw on the bus. And Walcott has none of Zeuxis' difficulty in painting Helen: he has done so three times (figure 11).

It may be helpful here to state what Walcott's Helen is not: she is not a victim. None of the Helens in this chapter are victims and it is no coincidence that the revised/parodied versions all concern a postwar Helen. These are stories of growth not of abduction, of home not exile (cf. Minkler 1993: 272). These are stories with Helen as agent. Walcott's Helen leaves Achille, moves in with Hector, returns to Achille – all actions of her own volition; indeed the point is that they are *actions*. We know nothing about Helen's feelings[20] and we do not know the father of her child but we know much about her action and its consequence for the two rivals, both of whom go to great efforts to keep or attract her (Achille dives for shipwrecked treasure; Hector gives up fishing to drive a taxi, an occupation that ultimately kills him). As in other Helen narratives, Helen's beauty is depicted by its effect. But there is a crucial difference between Walcott's Helen and the traditional Helen. Previous Helens launch a thousand ships; this Helen is herself a ship: "a beauty / that left, like a ship, widening eyes in its wake" (4.3.24–5). Independence from Marlowe signals the height of literary independence for any Helen.

Figure 11 Derek Walcott, "Ideal head: Helen / *Omeros*" (1998). Walcott's watercolor depicts his Helen from *Omeros* wearing the yellow dress she received (or stole) from Maud Plunkett. Reproduced by kind permission of Derek Walcott and the University of New York at Albany, Museum of Art.

This independence of spirit and being, free from any anxiety of Homeric or Marlovian influence, represents the black identity the narrator and Philoctete claim when they become proud inhabitants of St Lucia rather than diminished descendants of Africa. Helen is a character but also symbolizes the island (as, in the work of an earlier writer confronting colonial shackles, Yeats's Helen stands for Ireland). St Lucia has long had the moniker "Helen of the West Indies" both because of its beauty and because it was fought over. (It has changed hands 13 times, as Walcott recounts in the poem.) When Major Plunkett, in love with Helen from a distance, decides to write her history, he writes a history of the island. The island's history begins in the history books only when the French cede the island to the British in 1782. "Skirting emotion / as a ship avoids a reef" (18.1.29–30), the standard history signifies "the non-European . . . only as absence – if he or she is signified at all" (Williams 2001: 280). Plunkett's revisionist historical intention is the intention of all Helen writers from the epic cycle onwards: he wants to rescue Helen from the margins, to put her center stage, to make it her story: "Helen needed a history, / . . . / Not his, but her story. Not theirs, but Helen's war" (5.3.46, 48).

Plunkett abandons his attempt however, because he comes to realize – or feel – that a chronicle of this kind constitutes patronizing objectification, an example of the colonial ownership of which he is ashamed and that he is trying to correct. Plunkett had begun by forging correspondences between the Trojan War and the Battle of the Saints in 1782. This is his – and history's – version of Walcott's explaining "the Black thing" in terms of "the White thing." Every writer wants to use Helen; and historical narrative is a form of use. Plunkett realizes Helen's right, as woman and island, to be herself, independent of the meanings imposed by history and narrative.

When we first meet Helen, she is singing the Beatles song *Yesterday*. But yesterday has no place in Helen's story or identity. (Similarly Achille realizes that St Lucia, not Africa, is his home.) Walcott demythologizes her: "she was not a cause or a cloud, only a name / for a local wonder" (61.3.19–20). And it is as a local wonder, not a symbol, that he depicts her.

In its carrying across cultures, *Omeros* is an example of *translatio*. And in not being an exact fit – in being a parody – it is closely aligned with the concerns of this chapter. Walcott's classical references, as Oliver Taplin observes (picking up a metaphor from the poem), are "dug in like manure" (Taplin 1991: 219). Achille is not Achilles but is alongside him. *Omeros* is not Homer but works alongside him (and, as we have seen, alongside Winslow Homer and St Omer). The identity of this poem, like the characters in it, is multilayered.

This is true too of the poem's form. Dante provides the tercet structure and the insertion of a narrative "I" on a personal quest (*Omeros'* action is un-Homerically interior). The Caribbean provides patois, colonial education, the *Hamlet* structure (the ghost of Warwick Walcott who visits his son). Calypso is both classical and Caribbean. This "eclectic textual procedure . . . articulates a poetics of migrancy" (Thieme 1999: 158); it also embodies the structure of myth and of parody: tradition and innovation (Baugh 2006: 187).

Above all there is ludic spirit in both content (the many puns, the misspelling of Achille's boat name: In God We Troust) and rhyme. Walcott's rhyming ingenuity is well analyzed by Brad Leithauser: triple rhymes, visual rhymes, pararhymes, anagrammatic rhymes, apocopated rhymes, macaronic rhymes, off rhymes, apheretic rhymes. Leithauser reserves his final comment however for Walcott's use of feminine rhymes ("outlandish pairings of a sort usually reserved for light verse").

When [Walcott] rhymes "panther" with "and her" or "altar" with "halt. Her" or "Florida" with "worried her" or "hunter" with "front of her," we are closer to W. S. Gilbert or Ogden Nash than to Milton or Spenser. We are perched right at the teetering edge of parody – which is where he wants us (1991: 93).

Leithauser's invocation of parody, farce, and light verse are all apropos. Given Walcott's "life-long goal of realizing St Lucia on the printed page" (Thieme 1995: 177) and his macaronic, ludic, compassionately satirical epic of voyage, we might characterize this poem as both lucianic and literally Lucianic.

At Maud Plunkett's funeral, the narrator tells us "the fiction of her life needed a good ending" (53.2.15). This is, as we have seen from the start of this book, true of all Helen narratives. Walcott closes Helen's story by leaving it open; and he leaves it open by dividing it. Helen has two successors. The first is Ma Kilman's niece, Christine, who comes to work at the No Pain Café: a new local wonder, "a new Helen" (63.1.9). This is in keeping with Walcott's emphasis on continuity with variation (which is both the pattern of the sea, which anchors this poem, and the structure of myth itself). But Helen also provides her own successor in the form of her unborn child. This is the only Helen to be pregnant (Faust's pregnant Helen is an illusion) and *Omeros* leaves her in pregnancy. Her fertility becomes a metaphor for the Helen parodies explored throughout this chapter: two entities in one, functioning temporarily alongside but ultimately independently of each other.

*

When Isocrates finished his *Encomium*, he revealed that "far more has been passed over than said" (vol. 3, 1945: 97). The same applies to this book. Many poems, several novels, and one screenplay have been omitted; political and religious uses of the Helen myth have been ignored; stage histories of plays and their Helen actresses have been sidelined.[21] The vast number of texts about Helen in every period illustrates the hold she has on writers' imaginations; and it illustrates, like Walcott's pregnant Helen, the fecundity of this classical creature (or creation).

When Maud Plunkett dies in *Omeros*, the narrator is aware that he is attending the funeral of a character he has created. From Euripides to Goethe (and between and beyond) Helen herself is similarly aware that her existence is literary. But Maud's literary life assumes a tangible reality – with pianos, embroidery, orchids, maids – and her biography can be plotted from

Ireland to St Lucia. So too can Helen's, from Sparta to Troy (and, in the hands of some writers, back again to Sparta). It is this journey that I have attempted to chronicle, in a book that is both a literary biography (an account of Helen's development in literature) and a biography of a literary character.

In Shakespeare's *Midsummer Night's Dream* Theseus and Hippolyta discuss the story the four lovers tell about their transformative nocturnal experience in the Athenian wood. Theseus is skeptical, arguing that lovers' minds are like those of madmen and poets: they imagine things, they create fictions. For example, a lover will see "Helen's beauty in a brow of Egypt". Hippolyta counters that something permanent has arisen from the lovers' perceived experience: their story "grows to something of great constancy" (5.1.11, 26).

However, while Theseus argues against Hippolyta, he inadvertently proves her case, for this disbeliever in "antic fables" (preposterous; or possibly antique, ancient tales) is nothing more than an antique fable himself, one who assumed sufficient "constancy" to be adopted by Athens as a historical hero. Accidentally reinforcing this point, he talks about another antique fable, Helen – one whose existence is tied to his – as if she were a real person. Furthermore Theseus' argument against the poetic imagination is that the poet's pen "gives to aery nothing / A local habitation and a name" (5.1.16–17); but although he means to stress literature's insubstantial origins in "aery nothing," the structure of the line gives the last word to "local habitation and a name" and thereby leaves the corporeality of the poet's creation as the uppermost impression. The metrical movement reinforces this, with the enjambed trochaic "nothing" ceding terminative emphasis to the iambic "a name." Thus Theseus repeatedly supports Hippolyta's conclusion, that the poet's invented character (his "local habitation and a name") assumes a reality. He himself is living (literary) proof of this point.

Helen of Sparta may have started literary life as an anthropomorphization of a goddess, a causal explanation, or an excuse for war, but her exact origin does not matter in literary terms. She has, like Theseus, assumed a life of her own; her literary presence across the centuries is so large that a book like this is not only possible but necessary. And when Theseus – a fictional-real character – invokes Helen – another fictional-real character – we see the power of narrative to grow to "something of great constancy."

Notes

Introduction: *Ab ovo*

1 Dares' account is known only in a sixth-century Latin translation based on a lost first-century Greek original; for Dictys' fourth-century Latin text we have a first-century Greek fragment. For the dates, texts, and identities of Dares and Dictys see Frazer 1966: 3–15.

2 The anonymous *Siege of Troy* is the exception to this narrative pattern, moving rapidly over the Argonaut material and the abduction of Helen to get to the poem's titular subject.

3 Zeus tormented Prometheus as a punishment for his championing mankind and because of his refusal to reveal the prophecy concerning Thetis. He chained Prometheus to a rock, where an eagle gnawed his liver each day; because Prometheus was immortal, his liver renewed itself each night.

4 An alternative genealogy has Aphrodite born from the foam (*aphros*) of the sea. I give here the Greek names of the goddesses. In Roman mythology Hera is known as Juno, Pallas Athena is Minerva, and Aphrodite is Venus.

5 In the presentation of the play at Shakespeare's Globe in 2007 it was Paris' melancholy looks that comically provided evidence of his experience of love.

6 For accounts of the Judgment of Paris see Lucian *Dialogues of the Gods* 20, translated as "The judgement of the goddesses" (1969: 384–409), and Lydgate's *Troy Book* 2.2369–92. Lydgate's Paris refuses to judge the goddesses unless they appear naked (2.2747–54). Medieval literature, with its love of dream visions, frequently presents the Judgment of Paris not as a real event but as a vision dreamed by Paris (see e.g. Dares in Frazer 1966: 138–9). The Judgment is also a dream in American TV's *Helen of Troy* (2003), where Paris retires to a cave to escape the midday heat and falls asleep, and in Eric Shanower's graphic novel *Age of Bronze: A Thousand Ships* (2005). The retrial in Peele's *Arraignment* ends harmoniously when the goddesses catch sight of Queen Elizabeth I (for whom the play was first written and performed) and are content to acknowledge the monarch's superior beauty.

7 On being twin sister to a woman of Helen's beauty see Eva Salzman's poem "Helen's Sister" (2004).

8   Malcolm Bull reprints a Renaissance painting of *Leda and the Swan* in which "the eggs are helpfully stamped with the names of their occupants" (2005: 169 and plate VIIIb).

9   In the *Cypria* (in Hesiod 1977: 499) Helen is Nemesis' third child after Castor and Pollux. Helen's birth is the result of Nemesis' rape by her father, Zeus. Isocrates also names Nemesis as Helen's mother (1894, vol. 1, §59: 304). A scholiast on Pindar notes that Hesiod "makes Helen the child neither of Leda nor Nemesis, but of a daughter of Ocean and Zeus" (*Catalogues of Women* in Hesiod 1977: 191).

10   Both Hughes (2005) and Schmitz (1990), from whom Hughes clearly takes her information, are incorrect in describing Helen as eight years old in this poem; presumably they were misled by the unexpected collocation "eight score moneths" (Trussell in Shaaber 1957: 425 [43]).

11   Pausanias attributes the story to Stesichorus (Pausanias vol. 1, 2.22, in 1918: 365–7). If Helen gave birth to Iphigenia, this gives us an indication of her age when Theseus raped her: old enough to bear children. It is possible that this story is the slander on Helen for which Stesichorus was punished with the loss of his eyesight (Adams 1988: 116).

12   We can read about the suitors' oath in fragments from Hesiod and Stesichorus, and in Euripides' *Iphigenia in Aulis* (in Euripides 1972: 368–9); see Spentzou 1996: 305 n12. The oath may have been Hesiod's invention: he is the first to relate it (Adams: 1988: 99–100).

13   Quintus of Smyrna tells this story in his *Post Homerica* (*The War at Troy*).

14   The anonymous *Gest Hystoriale* describes a sacrifice in Aulis but not of Iphigenia (TLN 4655–61). Hesiod reports that Diana turned Iphigenia into Hecate (*Catalogues of Women* in Hesiod 1977: 205). In Herodotus, book 4 (1965: 276) the Taurians identify Hecate as Iphigenia; but in Euripides' *Iphigenia among the Taurians* she is "merely priestess of the goddess" (editor's note in Hesiod 1977: 205).

15   Peter Jackson's recent study of the Indo-European roots of the Trojan War myth cautions that it would be "naive to assume that Stesichorus invented the phantom story *ex nihilo*" (2006: 85).

16   The variant was well known to the Renaissance (see Roche 1964: 152–67).

17   George A. Kennedy (1987: 16) has a total of 17, of whom the last (in a twentieth-century play by Eric Linklater) is Voltaire!

18   This is also the name given to Paris' son with Oenone, so Dictys may be confused here.

19   Paris was also known as Alexander which means "defender." In Ovid's *Heroides* he explains, "When I / Was hardly grown to man's stature I regained / Our herds by killing an enemy. / For that I received the name I proudly bear" (Ovid 1990: 160).

20   William Morris's Helen imagines three possible methods of death the Greeks might inflict on her: burning at the stake, slaughter by a knife, or being thrown (in a sack) from the cliffs into the sea (1915: 4).

21 She also commits suicide in Thomas Heywood's *2 Iron Age* (1632), but at a later stage and for a different reason: old age has destroyed her beauty. In John Gould Fletcher's "On a Moral Triumph" (1925) she hangs herself when called a "wrinkled harridan" by children, "first taking care to leave behind a note, in which she laid all the blame on Menelaus and his fits of bad temper" (1925: 97).

22 The "Envoy" to Maurice Hewlett's "Helen Redeemed" (1913) parallels Helen's beauty with Achilles' strength and sees their union as "the marriage of true minds."

Chapter 1: Narrating Myth

1 This is a strong position in narrative terms, the final elegy, although its strength seems partly undercut by its sentiment – Hector was kind *"even to Helen"* (Willcock 1976: 276, my italics) and by its change of tone and subject from heroic paean to solipsistic concern: "I mourn for you [Hector] in sorrow of heart and mourn myself also and my ill-luck" (24.773–4). However, Helen's self-pity is not unusual; Colin Burrow notes that in Homer sympathy regularly "lead[s] to the reaffirming of one's own grounds for sorrow" (1993: 21).

2 The parallels between weaving and narrative are long attested. See for example Clader 1976: 5–9, 33; Heilbrun 1990: 103–4, 111; Bergren 1980: *passim*; *Ion* in Euripides 1973: 47. Homer twice gives Helen the opportunity to tell her own story: in the *Iliad* (book 3) she does so with weaving, in the *Odyssey* (book 4) with words. On Achilles with his lyre and Helen with her tapestry as two forms of the poet see Austin 1994: 38 and 38, n21. Isocrates relates how Helen came to Homer at night and ordered him to compose a Trojan epic. Helen is thus responsible for the *Iliad*: "partly owing to the genius of Homer, but *chiefly through her*, his charming poem of universal renown was composed" (1894: §65, my italics). On Horace's depiction of Helen as a poet see Putnam 2006: 92. Andrew Lang's "Palinode" (the octave of which is addressed to Helen, the sestet to Homer) presents Helen as a poet (Lang 1923). In "Helen at the Loom" George Lathrop depicts Helen's relief at being in control of her material (in both senses).

3 Shakespeare's Cleopatra is similarly concerned with artistic afterlife in the dominant seventeenth-century genre of drama: "Some squeaking Cleopatra" shall "boy my greatness" (*Antony and Cleopatra* 5.2.250). Whereas Homer's Helen is concerned about the effect of (mis)representation on her reputation, Shakespeare's Cleopatra is concerned about the effect of (mis)representation on her regality.

4 Nor does he think about regaining Helen when he does fight, even though this is technically the reason for the war.

5   For a good account of this absent material, and Homer's knowledge of it, see Lattimore 1961: 20–8. Some of the absent material is probably purposeful omission of details familiar to Homer's audience; some, however, comprises post-Homeric additions.

6   Analyzing "abruptness," "jolts," and "partially undigested" material in Homer, Burrow observes that "the Homeric poems are generously capacious: they leave later writers space to invent motives" (1993: 11–12).

7   The epic cycle additions are extant only in fragmentary summaries; they are available in a Loeb parallel-text edition of Hesiod (1977). For an analysis of the epic cycle see Burgess (2001).

8   Quintus' association with Smyrna, long considered doubtful, has been reexamined and accepted by the poem's most recent translator, Alan James.

9   In the BBC film version of *Troilus and Cressida* (1981) Helen is a silent presence in 2.2, the scene in which the Trojan council debate whether to return her to Greece. In the 2008 Cheek by Jowl production of the play in London, she is on stage "throughout the battles, reminding us that she is the ultimate provocation of war" (Billington 2008). Poetry too inserts Helen – through metaphor. As Martin McKinsey points out, Eumaeus' complaint that Helen "has been the death of many a good man" (*Odyssey* book 14, p. 209) reads literally that Helen "cut the legs from under troops of men"; similarly, in Yeats's "No Second Troy," Helen "is credited . . . with having burned Ilium much as if she had wielded the torch herself" (McKinsey 2000: 187 n5).

10 This in fact is how all perception works. In hearing, auditors do not receive every sound transmitted by the speaker but fill in gaps according to logic (deafness is when the gaps outnumber the received words, making the auditor incapable of completing the sense). In night driving, the brain connects remarkably little visual data into a road, a bend, a hill.

11 For an extended analysis of this aspect of Helen see Gumpert 2001.

12 In Homer the aim is simply to regain her. Revenge is a later addition, first implied in the epic cycle (in the *Little Iliad*; in Hesiod 1977: 519). There is no evidence that female adulteresses were ever punished by death in the fifth century BCE (see Patterson 1998; Cohen 1991: ch. 5).

13 On both occasions the Greek simply reads, "thus he spoke."

14 The same Sanskrit root leads to Latin *gnavus/navus* = "diligent," "assiduous"; i.e., working for knowledge.

15 Part of the word's negative, fearful meaning comes from its punning association with the River Styx (which means hateful, something that makes you shudder), as Hesiod explains, "And there dwells a goddess who makes the immortals shudder, awful Styx, eldest daughter of Oceanus" (*Theogony* in Hesiod 1988: 26).

16 On the relation between these two texts see Maguire 2007: 91–109.

17 Henry Rider Haggard and Andrew Lang convey this more overtly in their novel *The World's Desire* when Helen lifts her veil to the Sidonian. "When he saw her loveliness he stopped suddenly as one who is transfixed by a spear" (1894:

233). The simile is telling: an image of disaster, of death. In the seventeenth century Daniele Bartoli notes Nicostratus' reaction to Zeuxis' painting of Helen: he was mesmerized "as though he had seen not the head of Helen, but that of Medusa, he remained as though of stone" (cited in Colantuono 1997: 161). For images of petrification in the rhetoric of Renaissance art see Cropper 1991. Even children's literature adheres to this: climbing a wall to glimpse Penelope through a window, Tony Robinson's Odysseus "froze. He knew at once who it was: she was thirteen or fourteen and she was incredibly beautiful. It was Helen" (1987: 18).

18 I am indebted to Ben Morgan for this reference.

19 The causes of the several destructions are varied: internal conflict; fire; earthquake; external attack; fire again. The nine numbered Troys (I–IX) subdivide into 47 phases of construction/habitation (Wood 2005: 19; Latacz 2004: *passim*).

20 The parallels between Pandora and Helen are overt in Hesiod's *Works and Days*, where the phrase used to describe Pandora – "fearfully like the immortal goddesses" – is Homer's description of Helen in *Iliad* 3.158. West's translation (1988: 39) reads dilutedly, "model upon the immortal goddesses' aspect the fair lovely form of a maiden."

Ericthonius, son of Vulcan by Athena or by Earth, was hidden by Athena in a chest and given to Cecrops' daughters to guard without opening. They disobeyed, were horrified by its contents (something serpentine) and leapt from the Acropolis to death.

The beautiful Feather Woman fell in love with the beautiful Morning Star and was taken from earth to live in the sky. She spent her days gardening but was told not to dig up the Great Turnip (which plugs the hole between sky and earth). Curious, she disobeyed and brought death and unhappiness into the world.

21 In seasonal myths the earth-mother divides into two characters, a mother and a daughter (as in the Demeter-Persephone myth) to "express the stages of summer-fullness and of spring rebirth after the wintry death" (Lindsay 1974: 186). The story of Demeter-Persephone has exact parallels in Sumerian myth in the story of Dunuzi and Geshtines (see Armstrong 2005: 52).

22 At other times myth copies its model precisely. The stories of Moses and Jesus offer what Plutarch would call "parallel lives." Each is threatened with death as a baby by tyrannical fiat. (Moses' story here parallels other birth stories from the ancient Near East. For example, the mother of King Sargon of Akkod protected him by putting him in a box of reeds which she set afloat on the Euphrates; Reinhartz 1998: 5). Each delivers the law of their respective religion (Moses in the Ten Commandments, Jesus in the Sermon on the Mount). For each a new spiritual identity is heralded by water (the crossing of the Red Sea; baptism in the River Jordan). Each spends a period of 40 days or years in the wilderness. The story of Moses is itself modeled on creation myths in which a god splits water to create the world. The narrative innovation in the Moses myth is that "what is being born is not a cosmos but a nation" (Armstrong 2005: 96).

23 As Mercea Eliade notes, "symbolism does not depend on being understood" (1958: 450).
24 Throughout Greek myth, gods shine and dazzle. They wear shining clothes, have gleaming hair, are associated with light. In Luke's Gospel, when two men in dazzling clothes appear inside Jesus' empty tomb, we are meant to understand from this sartorial semiotics that they are angels. When Jesus is transfigured, the four Gospels agree in telling us that his face *shone*. On the ways in which Christianity harnessed Homer see Coupe 1997: 106.
25 The story is told by Herodotus 1965: 381.
26 Herodotus describes a shrine of Helen at Therapnae (1965: 381), Pausanias a temple of Menelaus. Isocrates says both Menelaus and Helen were worshiped there as gods, not as heroes (1894: §63).
27 Other narrative innovations – such as hanging – are also likely to be anthropomorphizing adaptations of a tree goddess religion. Pausanias relates that Helen was hanged at Rhodes by a vengeful widow of the Trojan War. The specific location, Rhodes, suggests that this is a variant of the *Helen dendritis* tradition. The parallel ends of the sisters Phaedra and Ariadne – both hanged from a tree – suggest the origin of each as a tree-goddess (Clader 1976: 70). The power of the tree-goddess structures the opening of Miranda Seymour's novel *The Goddess* (1979); Helen as matriarchal deity is the subject of Linda Cargill's *To Follow the Goddess* (1991).
28 Most editors emend the folio's "a fear" to "afeared," including the RSC Shakespeare, which is an edition of the Folio text.
29 Penelope in the *Odyssey* is similarly nostalgic, reminiscing about Odysseus' leadership – "if ever there was such a man" (book 19, p. 295).
30 In Homer Odysseus and Diomedes steal the Palladium from Troy.
31 In Thucydides' analysis Agamemnon was power-hungry (1972: 39–40).
32 On the importance of the Trojan War to subsequent literary and political narratives see Waswo 1997.
33 Derek Walcott writes, "ten years' war was ... an epic's excuse" (*Omeros*, 56.3.11; p. 284).
34 In the London version this ending to act 1 was replaced by a dialogue between Cassandra and Helen.

Chapter 2: Beauty

1 The Latin reads: "primo Helenam speciositate nimia refulsisse" (delle Colonne Griffin 1936: 83).
2 John Pollard similarly refers to Helen as a woman "whose only fault was that she was *too* beautiful" (1965: 145, my italics). Cf. Ovid's Paris in the *Heroides* who tells Helen "I find more now than I was promised by the goddess and you exceed by far that promise" (1990: 152–3).
3 The production was directed by Sam Mendes; Helen was played by Sally Dexter.

4   The antistrophe can be found in *Helen* in Euripides 1973: 179, but the translation smoothes over the textual difficulties. Austin (1994: 177–82) provides a literal translation, indicates the lacunae, and chronicles the difficulties in reconstructing and interpreting.

5   Helen, in John Erskine's novel *The Private Life of Helen of Troy*, defines the central problem of beauty as insufficiency, not the insufficiency of an individual but of beauty itself: "In the presence of great beauty all men seem to be inexperienced. There isn't enough of it, I suppose, to get used to" (1926: 36).

6   In literature Helen regularly talks of her beauty as a curse. In Ovid's *Heroides* she laments, "I wish beauty had passed me by" (1990: 172). In *The Private Life of Helen of Troy*, Helen observes, "They always said I was beautiful, but the only effect I could notice was that they treated me as if I weren't a human being" (Erskine 1926: 140). Disguised as a commoner, Linda Cargill's Helen enjoys the "novel sensation" of guards "glancing at me indifferently" (1991: 23). Mark Haddon's Helen (2002) bonds with her newborn daughter because "it was the first time I had ever been loved by someone who did not care what I looked like" (this replays, in stronger form, her fascination with her ataraxic suitor, Menelaus: "he looked through me. It was the first time in my life I had ever felt invisible"). Sara Teasdale's Helen talks of her beauty as the gods' "cruel gift" (1937: 9). Delmore Schwartz's Klymene pities one "chained to so beautiful a body" (1979: 115). Only the Chorus in Goethe's *2 Faust* does not see beauty as a bane: "For supreme good fortune is yours alone / In the fame of beauty, excelling all" (8516–17). In Sonnet 6 of John Erskine's sequence about Paris, it is Paris who feels the pressure of Helen's beauty (1922: 137).

7   Shakespeare will later express the pivotal moment between knowing you should conclude with Helen and being unable to do so in the adversative conjunction "yet." In *Troilus and Cressida* Hector offers 27 lines of axiological argument as to why Helen should be returned to the Greeks, but concludes in favor of retaining her: "yet ne'ertheless / I propend to you / In resolution to keep Helen still" (2.3.193–6). The contrasting conjunction "yet" is unspoken in Aeschylus but the hinge is there. The Chorus cannot articulate Helen's beauty (because, as they realize, it cannot be articulated: "beauty no thought can name") and yet they cannot stop themselves trying to do so. Their subsequent four lines are chrestomathic clichés. Helen herself encounters this problem in Goethe's *Faust* when she meets the absolute of ugliness: Mephistopheles/Phorycas. She tries to describe her/it before conceding "Yet I waste breath; for ever vainly words attempt / To recreate and recompose the forms we see" (*2 Faust* 8692).

8   Faced with a more prosaic extreme in *Vanity Fair*, that of the hangover of Joseph Sedley from too much rag punch at Vauxhall Gardens, Thackeray also employs the tactic of omission: "agonies which the pen refuses to describe" (1977: 95).

9   A parallel episode of transferred representation occurs in art history in Apelles' (c. fourth century BCE) complaint about a student artist who had

lavished gold on his painting of Helen: "Because you knew not how to paint her fair, you have made her rich." The incident, first reported by Clemens Alexandrinus, is narrated by Franciscus Junius (librarian to the Earl of Arundel) in *The Painting of the Ancients* (1638, book 2, ch. 6, §2, sig. Q4r; the Latin edition is 1637).

10   The frequency with which Butler sees landscapes "in terms of painters he liked" perhaps recalls his own abandoned ambition to be a painter (Butler 1970: 264n).

11   My informal survey of editions of *Tristram Shandy* in libraries, second-hand bookstores, and private collections has so far revealed only one reader (John Scholar) who has accepted Sterne's invitation.

12   I am grateful to David Summers for this reference. On the absent or off-stage representations of God and the godlike see Taylor 2001 and Daileader 1998.

13   In 1576 Thomas Rogers took Zeuxis to task for his presumption in painting Helen when "neither Homer by eloquence, nor any man by imagination, should conceive the like" (sig. U4r).

14   For Helen figures in the novel, see ch. 6. For Homeric echoes and structures in both *To the Lighthouse* and *Mrs Dalloway* see Hoff (1999) and Wyatt (1973).

15   In his *Iconologia* Cesare Ripa uses a naked woman as the emblem of beauty (first Italian ed. 1593).

16   On the early modern equation of nakedness with "absence or deficiency of language" see Neill 2000: 411–12.

17   Variants of this phrase occur in Ibycus, Sappho, Plutarch, Pindar, Hesiod, and Homer. Later literary tradition consistently portrays Helen as blonde. In the medieval *Gest Hystoriale* we read, "[t]he here of hir hede, huyt as the gold, / Bost out uppon brede bright on to loke" (TLN 3021). Shakespeare's Pandarus tells us that Cressida's hair is "somewhat darker than Helen's" (*Troilus and Cressida* 1.1.41–2). There is nothing unusual about this in terms of beauty. Paris is traditionally blond, almost every medieval heroine is blonde, and in Marlowe's *Dido Queen of Carthage* blond is the Trojan norm: Aeneas' description of the sack of Troy includes "virgins half-dead dragg'd by their golden hair" (2.1.195).

18   Heroines and gods in Greek drama such as Alcestis in Euripides' *Alcestis* (1974: 38) and Dionysus in his *Bacchae* (Euripides 1973: 206) also have curls. Ciliary curls are attributed to both Aphrodite and Medea in Hesiod's *Theogony*.

19   See e.g. Fra Angelico, Jacques-Louis David, Evelyn de Morgan, William Morris, Antonio Canova. Curls had a long reign as the capillary desideratum for both men and women. Chaucer's Pardoner's blond hair is deemed ugly partly because it refuses to curl (General Prologue 675–9). Cf. Sir Andrew Aguecheek in *Twelfth Night*, whose hair "will not curl by nature"; 1.3.98–9 (Theobald's emendation for F's "coole my nature" is universally accepted, including by the RSC Shakespeare editors whose copy text is the Folio). Absalon has curly golden hair in Chaucer's "Miller's Tale." Curly hair is praised in *Gest Hystoriale* TLN 3968, 3757 and in Lydgate's *Troy Book* 2.4550. A French manuscript of the fifteenth century (an illustration from the *Works of*

Christine de Pisan) depicts Paris with blond curls (BL Harley MS 4431, fol. 129).

20 It is this tradition that Shakespeare mocks in Sonnet 130: "I never saw a goddess go, / My mistress when she walks, treads on the ground."

21 Since Achanes is a child, this may mean no more than that Cupid imitated his childlike gait. But since Cupid is himself a child, the inference holds: the divine paediatric gait is different from mortal childlike movement.

22 In his essay "On Beauty" Francis Bacon considers movement more important than features (1985: 189).

23 The fake female in Aristophanes' *The Poet and the Woman* (*Thesmophoriazusae*) wears a yellow dress and perfume. When later called upon to play Helen, he says that he is appropriately dressed for the role. This may mean no more than that he is dressed as a woman; but it may refer to the color of the dress he is wearing. In Derek Walcott's *Omeros* (1990) Helen is characterized throughout by a controversial yellow dress. When Verena, the Helen character in Jane Stanley's novel *A Daughter of the Gods* (1886), attends a ball, her dress is "a most artistic combination of bronze velvet and pale yellow, embroidered in gold" (1886, vol. 2: 96). (For Walcott and Stanley see chapter 6.)

24 Clothes, like their wearers, shine, as in Penelope's "shining veil" in *Odyssey* book 16, p. 252. See Hughes (2005: 106–7) on the saturation of clothes with olive oil to create this luminous effect.

25 What is true of humans and gods is true of other sites of beauty too: effect is more illustrative than description. Sidney's *Arcadia* tells us "we can better consider the sun's beauty by marking how he gilds these waters and mountains" (1977: 63). This tradition is Platonic in origin: beauty is the reflected splendor of the divine countenance (see Rogers 1988: 67, citing Ficino's commentary on Plato's *Symposium*).

26 Later writers developed this reaction, not just comparing the beautiful woman to a goddess but mistaking her for one. We see this in the *Gest Hystoriale* (TLN 13808), in Lydgate's *Troy Book* 2.3653–4, and in Shakespeare's romances.

27 *Laud Troy Book* TLN 3067–76; *Gest Hystoriale* TLN 3538–64; Lydgate's *Troy Book* 2.4296; *Siege of Troy* TLN 664–5; Caxton's *Recuyell* 1894, vol. 2: 538–9.

28 Hecuba anticipates Menelaus' change of heart in Euripides' *The Women of Troy*. She tries to dissuade Menelaus from returning to Sparta in the same ship as Helen because she knows his thoughts of vengeance will evaporate when he gazes on Helen's beauty.

29 The translator marks Lampito's Spartan dialect with Scottish forms. Dictys narrates another version of this. Achilles first plans to kill Helen in public (Frazer 1966: 84). After the sack of Troy, it is Ajax who proposes killing Helen. Menelaus' love for Helen is such that he petitions for her life (unmotivated by her appearance: neither she nor her breasts are in sight). It is the intercession of Odysseus with persuasive speech that saves Helen's life.

30 Joseph's source for this episode was the anonymous *Excidium Troiae*.
31 In Lady Mary Wroth's *Urania* (1621) Philargus suspects his wife of infidelity, and repeatedly threatens her with death: by drowning, by burning, by being dragged naked through thorn bushes. But when he catches sight of her breast ("a most heavenly breast"), he stands stock-still in admiration and offers his wife a two-day reprieve to confess (1995: 13).
32 For Stopford Brooke, "only one passage, that about the breasts of Helen and the sword, seem to me awkward in conception" (1900, vol. 1: 137). In Ben Jonson's *The Staple of News* it is Hermione who has beautiful breasts, and Helen is praised "for a mouth!" (4.2.9). Jonson may have read *Gest Hystoriale*, which describes Helen's lovely lips ("lippus full luffly, as by lyn wroght"; TLN 3049). The author of *Gest Hystoriale* takes his description from Guido, with one silent editorial omission: that Helen's lips "ad oscula auidis affectibus inuitabant" (sig. d4r; Curry 1916: 66 n2).
33 The poem, as Stopford Brooke first realized, is Roman rather than Greek in ambience. Lucretius' devotion is to duty (stern, rigid) rather than to beauty, and "the sense of the beautiful as a part of life does not appear in the poem" (1900, vol. 1: 136). Consequently Helen's beauty is not presented holistically.
34 This tradition is recorded by Pliny (1968, vol. 33, §23: 63) among others. The tradition was later eroticized: Henri II of France (1519–59) complimented his mistress, Diane de Poitiers, by modeling his drinking goblet on the size of her breast (Yalom 1997: 68).
35 The noun in Greek, *malon*, is the word for apple or any other tree fruit (pomegranate is another common translation) and is a common metaphor for breasts. Here the sequence of lines means literally "don't despise the young girls, for softness resides in their tender thighs, and blossoms in their apple/breast/pomegranate."
36 Duffy here overlaps "beauty" and "sex symbol" but they are not always complementary categories. In fact the latter is defined by a focus on breasts rather than on facial beauty; breasts draw attention away from the face. I am grateful to Elisabeth Dutton for this observation. However, in Marlowe's *Dr Faustus* outstanding female beauty is compared to the breasts of Aphrodite (1.1.161–2).
37 That Canova was perfectly capable of distinguishing male from female is apparent from his sculpture of Napoleon (large, strong, with rippled muscles) and his head of a female dancer (with flowers in her hair), both in Astley House, London.
38 I am grateful to Kathryn Loveridge for this reference.
39 This, at least, is the general meaning but it is a difficult image, perhaps best glossed as "and you look pretty good in drag too."
40 The phrase was used in Offenbach's *La Belle Hélène* (at the ENO in London's Coliseum, 2006) where it describes Paris, a young Toby Spence (in the ENO casting) to Felicity Lott's Helen (25 years Spence's senior); but it is equally applicable to the gender-fluid Helens of this section. Not in Hesketh-Harvey's

original typescript, the pun was clearly added or ad libbed in the course of rehearsal or performance.

41 A poem to Sir John Salusbury on the occasion of his marriage compares him to Paris, to the latter's disadvantage. Paris is "beautiful," "manlike," "with face so feminate," but Salusbury is even more so; consequently "Helen revives to love sweet Salusbury" (XXI, 25, 27, 21, 30; 1914: 30, 29). I am grateful to Katherine Duncan-Jones for this reference.

42 Lyly's detail was clearly not an error; when he revised his text, he kept this paragraph intact. *Euphues* first appeared in 1578; a revised edition appeared in 1579.

43 A character called Dares appears in the *Iliad* (5.9ff).

44 For Hector's lisp see Barbour's Bruce (Curry 1916: 73). For Hector's stammer see Lydgate 2.4648.

45 Curry (1916: 48) identifies the first qualification of Briseis' monobrow as a defect in Tzetzes (1150), followed a decade later by Benoît.

46 The verbal portraits are accompanied by illustrations, although the scale is too small to represent details such as Helen's scar. Sylviane Messerli points out (personal communication) that Helen's portrait on folio 25r is separate from those of the women (which begin on folio 28r). Helen's portrait is followed by the men; Briseis effects the transition from warriors to women.

47 This personal feature contrasts with the gap teeth of Chaucer's Wife of Bath, which "becam [her] weel" (Chaucer 1987: *Wife of Bath's Prologue*, line 603). In Richard Brathwaite's commentary on the Wife of Bath's prologue (1665: sig. I5v), Brathwaite links the Wife of Bath's gap teeth with Venus' mole: the former "became her well, even as Venus' mole made her more lovely." This is the same Richard Brathwaite who cited Helen's scar in a poem in 1621 (*Nature's Embassy*); he is clearly taken by the notion of a defect enhancing beauty (a topic I shall explore in the next section).

48 In Shakespeare's *Troilus and Cressida* Thersites enters with the rhetorical question "Agamemnon, how if he had boils, full, all over, generally?" (2.1.2). Curry (1916: 76–7) suggests that in Lydgate's case the King of Persia's warts are a misunderstanding and mistranslation of Guido's *faciem lentiginosam* (sig. E2v) and *lentignosa facie* (sig. E2r).

49 If Lyly foregrounded the scar tradition, Thomas Heywood foregrounded the dimple. Alone of all the later revisers John Masefield picks up this issue and gives his Helen neither a scar nor a beauty spot but a monobrow (1923: 35).

50 For extended discussion of this material I am indebted to my colleague and former student, Ben Morgan. In particular, in the second part of this section his assistance comes closer to co-authorship.

51 Hence our habit of using gods' names adjectivally – martial, venereal – because they are the essence of the category.

52 The same linguistic dilemma obtains in *Antony and Cleopatra* where Enobarbus cites Cleopatra's emotional exudations as inimical to metaphor: "we cannot call her winds and waters sighs and tears; they are greater storms and

tempests than almanacs can report" (1.2.147–9). If Enobarbus sees Cleopatra as an absolute of woman and therefore beyond language, Cleopatra sees Antony as the absolute of men; in her attempts to describe him, comparison becomes recursively redundant. He is a "man of men" (1.5.72) and "lord of lords" (4.8.16). Consequently metaphor "devolves upon itself to become mere tautology" (Bates 2002: 200). The *Laud* Troy poet anticipates this tautology when he introduces King Cilydis, the most beautiful man alive: "His fairnes might no man discryve, / No man myght his fairnes say" (TLN 5260–1). The second line duplicates the first; faced with beauty it cannot describe, language is reduced to repeating its inability.

53   Almost all commentators on Chaucer's Criseyde and Shakespeare's Cressida agree that Criseyde's/Cressida's situation is an action replay of Helen's, *mutatis mutandis.*

54   Lord Bonavida's speech reveals Heywood's medieval reading here in which Helen is only the most beautiful woman in *Greece*; it is *Polyxena* who is the most beautiful woman in Troy. Some medieval versions (the anonymous *Siege of Troy*, Caxton's *Recuyell*, the *Laud Troy Book*) offer the alternative tradition – the tradition which was to become the dominant one – that Helen is the most beautiful woman in the world.

55   This is true of all forms of beauty – poetry, for instance. In Ian McEwan's *Saturday*, a violent intruder is stopped in his tracks by the poetic beauty of Arnold's "Dover Beach," which his victim recites to him (2005: 217–24).

56   I am grateful to Jonathan Gil Harris for this suggestion.

57   These examples occur in the dedicatory letter to Sir William West prefaced to the 1597 edition of *The Anatomy of Wit*. I am grateful to Leah Scragg for drawing this to my attention.

58   This is the view of Henry Fielding in *Joseph Andrews* (1742) when he describes Fanny Price, the 19-year-old previously dismissed by Mrs Slipslop "on account of her extraordinary beauty" (1977: 65). When Fielding later details Fanny's beauty, his details include innumerable flaws; e.g., two small-pox scars, and teeth that, though white, "were not exactly even" (1977: 155).

59   This work is a translation from Plutarch and others, but this observation seems to be Grant's addition. I am grateful to Kirsty Milne for this point and for the reference to Grant.

60   Pliny reports that Helen had a cosmetic to combat old age; he identifies it as helenium. When mixed in wine, this same herb banishes sorrow (1969, vol. 21, §91: 273–4). Homer's Helen is seen to possess such a herb in the *Odyssey* book 4 (see also Edwin Muir's poem "The Charm"). But it is poets not cosmetics that defeat age, as Chiron observes in Goethe's 2 *Faust*: "The poets freely choose her changing face. / She never need grow up, grow old, / Or lose her looks" (7429–31).

61   Without naming her, Wilfred Owen invokes Helen in "The Kind Ghosts" (1918), which contrasts the equanimity of the sleeping Helen with the generosity of the permanently sleeping boys who died for her.

62 The unfinished story was published in 1966, along with the comments of Green and Fowler.

63 The transformation of Elfine in *Cold Comfort Farm* (1932) creates the most frequent effect of beauty: love. Richard Hawk-Monitor realizes "not that Elfine was beautiful, but that he loved Elfine" (Gibbons 2006: 158).

64 The heavy mythological superstructure, cumbersome allegory, and antiquated language are partly responsible for the novel's failure. For the *National Observer*'s devastatingly bad review of the novel see Green 1946: 134.

65 John Ogle had anticipated them in 1594 when he described Helen as "Beauty's existence" (sig. D2v).

66 Katy Littlewood offered a version of this in 2004 when she directed a student production of Euripides' *Helen* at Magdalen College, Oxford. Three actresses were chosen to play the role of Helen. The triple casting was partly a practical response to the size of the role, partly an aesthetic response to the Diane Kruger problem outlined above, and partly an embodiment of the production's keynote question blazoned on the poster campaign: "The most beautiful woman in the world – who does she think she is?" Delmore Schwartz approached the casting challenge in the same way in his theatrical poem of 1941, "Paris and Helen: An Entertainment." In his projected cast of characters he alternately cast four actresses as Venus: Greta Garbo, Myrna Loy, Hedy Lamarr, and Dame May Whitty (Schwartz 1979: 105). To him a convincing representation of Venus was obviously more difficult than that of Helen, whose role is confidently assigned to Madeleine Carroll. One quarter of his Venuses, Hedy Lamarr, later played Helen in the film *L'Amante de Paride* (1954). Coincidentally this Helen was also a quartered role: Lamarr's character has four reincarnations of which Helen is one.

67 He has also commented on her stature in *Memoirs* 1972: 40.

68 Oliver Taplin explains how the *Iliad* "became a nationalist epic" from the fifth century CE onward (1992: 110). Austin relates this to the nationalist plot of Euripides' *Helen*, designed "to remove Helen's body from all foreign beds once and forever" (1994: 143).

69 Similarly the Greeks in Quintus of Smyrna's account, when they see Helen/home, forget their previous reviling and see in her only perfection.

70 The goddess Circe manipulates nostalgia in the opposite way, encouraging Odysseus to forget his fatherland.

71 Delmore Schwartz's poem "Paris and Helen" is structured round nostalgia. The Dioscuri, dead in their native land, contrast with the exiled Helen who is fearful that Venus will take her "further from home" (Schwartz 1979: 123) and with the "expatriate American," never mentioned by name (Ezra Pound), who "puts old Greek into modern English" (115), "speaking Greek / Perception, and Greek passion" (116). "Nostalgia is the easiest emotion, / Helen must suffer it, despite her beauty" (115). Schwartz's view of the past parallels Theodore Weiss's view of Helen: both renew themselves in poetry. "How the past / Once in a poem, has more lives than a cat!" (Schwartz 1979: 116); "Helen,

it seems, is more herself the more she's reproduced" (Weiss 1988: 953, lines 37–8).

72 Talking of nationalism, Schwyzer explains that the "project of bringing a nation into being" has as "one of its prerequisites . . . the *absence* of a fully realized nation" (2004: 75).

73 For Schiller (1967: 5) beauty is a mystery and that is its attraction. (Hence Paglia's – or Western art's – equation of beauty with the mysterious smile.) George Santayana (1955: 19) and Northrop Frye (1970: 66) agree. The technical phrase for this mystery in seventeenth-century continental philosophy is the *je-ne-sais-quoi*; see Bouhours (1960) and Scholar (2006).

Chapter 3: Abducting Helen

1 Briseis lost her husband and three brothers on one day (19.282–30) in the same campaign in which Andromache lost her father and brothers, also slain by Achilles (6.414–24).

2 Medieval narrative combines or confuses the two rhyming females, Briseis and Chryseis, with a new character, Criseyde, who becomes the lover of the Trojan prince Troilus.

3 It is not the loss of Briseis that pains and angers him so much as the personal insult to his valor and status. As he later explains, he and Agamemnon are equals; to have his "prize of honor" confiscated is to be treated like a "dishonored vagabond" (16.53, 54, 59).

4 *Bia* implies unwillingness, but unwillingness need not imply force. In classical thought, force (*bia*) is commonly opposed to persuasion (*peithō*) and trickery (*dolos*), which are the other means of getting an unwilling person to do something. The contrasts or parallel with Helen's abduction – which was accompanied by persuasion (of Helen) or trickery (of Menelaus) or force (of Helen) is an interesting one. The respective value of each method is a matter of controversy (explored by Gorgias; see chapter 4). I am grateful to Florence Yoon for the points in this paragraph.

5 Phoenicia was a collection of city states, organized along Greek lines, occupying the area known in the Bible as Canaan and today as Lebanon, Syria, Israel, and the Palestinian territories.

6 In Herodotus, value, and how value is determined, is a practical rather than ethical activity. Long notes that the Phoenicians, bargaining people, are "peculiarly accustomed to fixing values and prices" (1987: 47).

7 For the ancient Greek belief that women experience greater sexual pleasure than men and therefore can never be unwilling see Walcot 1978: 141.

8 The participial phrase (my italics) is designed to prevent us viewing Helen's information as special pleading. She is speaking to Hecuba, Queen of Troy, who is surely in a position to contradict this information were it false.

9 Chaucer himself suffered – or benefited – from the ambiguity of the category *raptus* in the accusation brought against him by Cecily Champaigne. A summary of this case might read, she thought he raped her (in the modern sense of the word); he thought she consented (Ackroyd 2004: 83–6; Chaucer 1987: xxi–xxii).

10 I am indebted to Marion Turner for drawing my attention to this passage and the passage on incest in book 3, and for invaluable discussion on their implications.

11 This is the action that Shakespeare's Cressida will later present as submission to prevent rape: "upon my back to prevent my belly" (*Troilus and Cressida* 1.2.260).

12 T. E., the author of *The Law's Resolution of Women's Rights* (1632), could be glossing this episode when he talks of rapists' arguments that "a careless liberty in [women's] behaviour" was "an infallible argument of sensuality," and therefore an invitation to violence (390). Although T. E. wishes he could persuade women not to behave in such ways, his censure is directed at those who misinterpret this behavior.

13 The atmosphere in the BBC film (directed by Jonathan Miller) was threatening throughout, as the manipulative verbal treatment threatened to become physical: Cressida was forced into a semisupine position in her tent, with Diomedes pressing towards her, leaning over her, physically restraining her. A similar atmosphere of constraint was created by the set in the RSC production of 1990, directed by Sam Mendes. Cressida's tent was represented by steel ladders, and she looked as if she were behind prison bars.

14 For extended discussion of this in Shakespeare see Maguire 2007: 78–119. For rape in *Romeo and Juliet* see Watson and Dickey (2005).

15 See Kahn and Hutson 2001, Sheen and Hutson 2005, Hutson 2007, and Thompson 2008.

16 For an excellent account of consent in T. E. and in Shakespeare see Sale (2003).

17 For an explanation of the contexts of statute change ("each had its own story and a reason for being told") in Elizabeth's parliaments see Dean 1996: xiii and passim. The abduction debate is part of Parliament's concern "with ordering the household" and "punishing those who challenged the stability of the household" (16).

18 Sir Simonds D'Ewes records the readings in his journals (D'Ewes 1682: 551, 552, 555).

19 The will (National Archives PROB 11/89) was written on Jan. 3 and proved on Feb. 3 and proved again (? or entered in the PCC?) on Mar. 14. Stoite describes himself as being "aged and weak of body yet of perfect mind and memory" in January; a month later he was dead.

20 Alice's abductor, Donnington, was tried and acquitted in London; what happened to him at the assizes in Dorset I have not yet discovered. Alice was returned to her family in Dorset and whom she subsequently married is unknown (the Dorset records do not begin until 1651).

21 Cf. *Measure for Measure* in which Angelo asks Isabella to agree to her own violation.
22 In Homer et al. the name is often used both for the country and for the city.
23 I am grateful to Robert Parker for this reference.
24 One of his variants, "Helen ye pearle of Greece," may have caught Shakespeare's eye for use in *Troilus and Cressida* (2.2.81).
25 A later Thomas Watson (d.1686) has a "Helen Graeco" in a Latin marginalium about beauty in *Heaven Taken by Storm* (1670).
26 Without using the specific collocation, Faustus too associates Helen with Greece rather than Troy, promising the students that they will see "that peerless dame of Greece."
27 Given Menelaus' injunctions to Helen not to struggle in Morris's *Scenes from the Fall of Troy*, this poetic drama may also end with rape.

Chapter 4: Blame

1 Ovid's *Heroides*, by contrast, presents Helen's ambivalence as a flirtatious technique.
2 Pollard notes that Eve, Pandora, and Helen are judged by the "repercussions on others," not "by their degree of personal guilt" (1965: 161–2).
3 The earliest MS is ninth century CE but the original was probably written sometime between the fourth and sixth centuries CE (Atwood and Whitaker 1944: xv).
4 The Latin dialogue is of such banal simplicity that one can only imagine it being used as a textbook for language tuition (Anon / Atwood and Whitaker 1944: xviii).
5 In 1909 Alfred Williams's Helen suggests that the Greeks are more to blame "who for one feeble woman, drew / With one consent a world to strife" (111).
6 In English, "faultless" can be a reference to Helen's flawless beauty or her faultless actions. In Greek the word is *amōmētos* (a variant of the more usual *amymōn*) whose primary meaning is blameless, although in Quintus, who uses the word three times, it always refers to physical beauty (see Parry 1973: 83). I am grateful to Florence Yoon for talking me through the Greek complications here.
7 Different versions of Helen's story present her attendant as the mother of Theseus or as a totally separate character who just happens to share a name with Theseus' mother. Homer's designation of Aethra as "Pittheus' daughter" leaves no room for doubt (3.144).
8 Maionia is an old name for Lydia, in the centre of Asia Minor.
9 This is an instance where narrative logic (not a high priority in epic) is sacrificed to emotional need: the father was killed in book 5 (Willcock 1976: 152). He is here resurrected when his son is slain so that we can share his anguish.

10 For a discussion of doubled episodes in the *Odyssey* (which unfortunately, does not include this one) see Fenik 1974.

11 "Guilt" is clearly a term with Christian connotations; the Greek reads, "Helen . . . is the cause of many evils for Greece."

12 Despite the gap of five hundred years Pollard's point is essentially the same as Caxton's in his *Recuyell*; Helen's problem, Caxton states, is a general female problem: curiosity. Having heard of Paris' great beauty, Helen *"after the custom of women . . .* had great desire to know by experience if it were truth that she heard speak of" (Caxton 1894: 530, my italics).

13 This is a Latin translation of Benoît's *Roman de Troie*, although Guido says it comes from Dares and Dictys.

14 The phantom myth is believed to originate with Stesichorus' "Palinode," a poem we know only from Plato's quotation of it in *Phaedrus* §243a–b. For a reinvestigation of the relationship between Plato's quotation and its alleged origin in Stesichorus, see Wright 2005: 83–90, 99–105, who argues that Plato's argument is full of spurious references. We might note here that Stesichorus' (alleged) palinode, in which he recants his slander of Helen (for which he had been struck blind) and in which he rehabilitates Helen's reputation through the *eidōlon* story, is a double exculpation: he rescues himself from blindness and Helen from blame.

15 "Defense," like "encomium," is a technical generic term: the latter is a eulogy, the former an argument of vindication. Despite its title, Gorgias' work is a defense, not an encomium (although its playful nature perhaps makes it a *mock* encomium).

16 He makes this point again later when he lists the "blessings" of the Trojan War, of which the greatest is Greek national independence.

17 When Chaucer refers to his source in Dares, he means Joseph of Exeter (Joseph/Roberts 1970: ix).

18 Bate (Joseph/Bate 1986: 168) suggests an analogue in Dido's banquet for Aeneas.

19 Bate interprets this phrase as premature ejaculation. Kennedy (1987: 9) views it as a euphemism for fellatio.

20 When Helen is reunited with Menelaus, the poet replays the line of her meeting with Paris: 'Ether kyssid oder and were acord" (TLN 1902).

21 This is a version of Guido delle Colonne's *Historia Destructionis Troia*.

22 This complaint recurs in most medieval Troy books. It is reinforced in the weavers' song in Thomas Deloney's later prose narrative *Jack of Newbury* (1626) where the weavers, naturally, approve of Penelope's spinning, and conclude that disaster would have been averted "had Helen then sat carding wool" (sig. F2r).

23 The book was sold in the Houghton sale at Christie's of London on June 11 and 12, 1980, lot 362, for £14,000.

24 Bullen edited the poem in the nineteenth century; he collated both the 1589 and 1604 texts. I quote from Bullen's text because it has the convenience of line numbers. Where variants between the two printed versions are an issue, I quote the two versions separately, relying on Bullen's representation of the

1604 text. However, as will be evident below, Bullen's edition is not reliable in all details.

25   1589: "will be no better rulde"; 1604: "will not be oreruled."

26   I retain the edition's italic and modernize spelling.

27   The apparent paradox is rooted in the difference between blame and responsibility. Those texts (e.g., the *Iliad*) that point the finger of responsibility at the gods view them as agents of action, not as figures of blame. To say the gods are responsible is a fact, not an accusation. In Greek mythology gods behave badly, not immorally.

28   In a self-defeating circularity typical of early modern revenge tragedy he says (four times) that he now must take revenge for Hector's death.

29   Contrast the sacrifice of Iphigenia.

30   As McKinsey notes (2002: 182), this unfulfilled form reflects the unfulfillment of the poet.

31   It is notable that at the time Shakespeare was revising women's roles in myth – a project he pursues in the problem plays with Isabella replaying Lucrece's predicament (but refusing to become a martyr, a role for which her position as novice nun admirably equips her) and with Helen and Cressida's reputations being recuperated in *All's Well That Ends Well* and *Troilus and Cressida* – he was simultaneously exploring how one might escape "being." Troilus and Cressida are aware of their roles as historical lovers, destined to betray and be betrayed. Yeats's question "What could she have done, being what she is?" applies to Cressida.

32   Agnes Latham betrays an anachronistically twentieth-century sensibility when she glosses "Helen's face, but not her heart" in *As You Like It* as follows: "few if any of Shakespeare's audience would pick up the reference and know that he was saying Rosalind was as beautiful as Helen but more chaste" (3.2.140).

33   The respective texts are Greene, *Ciceronis Amor*; Lodge, *An Alarm Against Usurers*; Fenne, *Fenne's Fruits*; Parry, *Moderatus*.

34   Little St Helen's, now called St Helen's Place, is one street north of Great St Helen's, the street in which John Crosby in Heywood's *1 Edward 4* desires his last resting place: "In Little St Helen's will I be buried" (sig. D3r).

35   This reference occurs in a scene that textual critics attribute to Shakespeare's collaborator (possibly George Peele). John Stow invokes "Helen, mother to Constantine" in his *Chronicles* of 1589, as does Lodowick Lloyd in 1590 (*The Consent of Time*), Antoine de la Faye in 1599 (*A Brief Treatise*), Henry Timberlake in 1603 (*The Travails of Two English Pilgrims*), and John Wilson in 1608 (*English Martyrology*). In 1612 Michael Drayton repeats the formula three times in *Polyolbion*.

36   We recall the "rolling eye" of Helen in ch. 45 of the English Faust book.

Chapter 5: Helen and the Faust Tradition

1   The English translator is known only by his initials, "P. F"; John Jones (1994: 26–34) makes a convincing case for identifying him as Paul Fairfax, an Englishman who had traveled in Germany.

2   Goethe changes Faust's pact with the devil to a wager between God and Mephistopheles. Although in scene 7 Faust enters into a contract with Mephistopheles, its terms are vague ("sometime later / Wages in the same kind will then fall due"; 1658–9). David Luke comments that this bargain "seems to be an artistically necessary concession by Goethe to the old Faust tradition" and "its importance is immediately played down" (Goethe/Luke 1987: 555 n33).

3   The earliest extant English edition is dated 1592, but an Oxford inventory of late 1589 contains what is almost certainly an English edition of the Faust book (Fehrenbach 2001).

4   All references are to John Jones's 1994 edition and are by through-line numbers. For convenience, I also provide chapter numbers.

5   This quotation is P. F.'s addition to his original.

6   This detail is P. F.'s addition to his German original.

7   There is tautology here in the English. The EFB reads "suddenly the globe opened and sprang up in height of a man: so burning a time, in the end it converted to the shape of a fiery man" (115–17, ch. 2). Since the grammatical subject is consistently the globe, the sentence must mean (awkwardly): the globe became a burning man then a fiery man. In German the man-height stream of fire extinguishes itself and then reforms as a fiery man (Anon. 1988: 17).

8   These encouragements are P. F.'s additions.

9   This chapter is considerably expanded by P. F. from the German. He adds animal details (e.g., the specificity of hog, worm, and dragon), extends the list of animal forms in which the devils appear, adds new dialogue between Faust and Lucifer about shape and transformation, and describes the emotional and physical effects on Faust of the therioform devils.

10   The terror and the two-hour time scheme are P. F.'s addition.

11   The A-text reads "*Enter* [MEPHISTOPHELES] *with a* Devil *dressed like a woman, with fireworks*" (2.1.151SD, my italics). The B-text reads "*He fetches in a* woman Devil" (2.1.146SD, my italics). The A-text thus explains how the B-text effect is achieved.

12   This pedagogical promise is P. F.'s addition.

13   P. F. omits a phrase from the German, which reads "fair *and rosy-cheeked* like milk and blood mixed" (omission in italics).

14   As in Marlowe, Faustus seems not to know what to ask for. Marlowe's Mephistopheles appropriately promises Faustus "more than thou hast wit to ask" (A-text and B-text, 2.1.47).

15   P. F.'s endearing explanatory literalism occasions one of his additions here: the pregnant Helen is only pregnant "to his [Faustus'] *seeming*" (2668, ch. 55, my italics). As devils are incapable of creation, pregnancy is a technical imposs- ibility. The pregnant Helen is doubly an illusion.

16   On function: the German Faust Book informs us that Faustus prefers to walk rather than ride (on horseback or in a carriage). The EFB adds an explana- tion for Faustus' preference: on foot "he could ease himself when he list" (2392–3, ch. 46). "Ease himself" can mean either urinate or defecate (Jones glosses it as the latter). Either way it is a supererogatory insertion in narrative terms but consistent with P. F.'s interest in the body.

17   The Duchess of Anholt is the only "real" female character. The wife in act 1 and Helen in acts 2 and 5 are devils; the alewife is a stock caricature.

18   Even Goethe's Faust indulges a momentary libidinous impulse when he first sees Helen.

19   Damnation, then, as defined by Mephistopheles, would seem to have attrac- tions: "Hell hath no limits" (2.1.124). Hell in short is a metaphysicians' (or at least a Faustian) paradise.

20   By the end of the play, however, in an unsurprising theophobic volte-face, Faustus will be begging for the reimposition of limits: "Oh God, / . . . / Impose some end to my incessant pain. / Let Faustus live in Hell a thousand years, / A hun- dred thousand, and at last be saved. / No end is limited to damned souls" (5.2.98, 101–4).

21   Productions rarely attempt a realistic Helen, opting instead for devils in drag or property objects. In the 1974 RSC production, directed by John Barton, Helen was a puppet with a blonde wig, manipulated by Mephistopheles; in the 1970 RSC production, directed by Gareth Morgan, a straw wig on a mop represented Helen. Often the devil who represents the wife in 2.1 represents Helen of Troy at the end.

22   See Riggs 2004: 318–19 for a discussion of the Dutch Church libel in which controversial views, posted on the wall of the Dutch churchyard in London, were signed "Tamburlaine."

23   On the autobiographical relevance of both Faust and Homunculus to Goethe see Goethe/Luke 1994: xxxiv–xxxvii.

24   To avoid confusion, I refer to Goethe's texts as *1* and *2 Faust*; I call Clifford's *Part One* and *Part Two*. References to Goethe are by through-line number; references to Clifford are by page number. For an interesting joint exploration of Marlowe and Goethe see Keefer 2004.

25   A version of Shakespeare's *Hamlet*, corresponding in many respects to the text of Q1 (1600), survives in a German edition of 1781.

26   Lyric, epic, opera, operetta, masque, procession, allegory, choral ode, folk tale, and comedy are just some of the many forms incorporated in *Faust*.

27   Cf. Hatfield 1987: 77: "a remarkably irrelevant scene."

28   In conversation with Johann Eckerman, Goethe's secretary and live-in com- panion during his last decade, Goethe said that poetry should be both frag-

mentary and difficult (Goethe/Luke 2 *Faust* 1994: xvii; 1 *Faust* 1987: xlvi). Eckerman published his *Conversations* after Goethe's death.

29   The philosopher James Kirwan offers an explanation of the relationship between time and ecstasy, which is transferable to *Faust*: "Paradise is never here and now, for one cannot be conscious of being entirely happy; the moment I become absolute, in ecstasy, the 'I' disappears; such a moment is timeless, but the 'I' that wanted ecstasy no longer exists. Thus time, as finitude, separates us from paradise now, yet time causes paradise to come into being – then" (Kirwan 1999: 68). This explains why Goethe's devil loses the wager.

30   "Das Heidenvolk geht mich nichts an" – literally, "Heathen folk don't do it for me" (Goethe 1949: TLN 6209).

31   The Astrologer voices two of the topics of ch. 2: Helen is not beautiful, but is beauty itself; and her beauty is associated with excess.

32   One of Goethe's early subtitles for the Helen fragment written in 1800 was "Helena in the Middle Ages" (Goethe/Luke 1994: xli). In becoming a medieval knight Goethe's Faust fulfils the ambition of Marlowe's Faustus ("I will . . . wear thy colours on my plumèd crest"; 5.1.98–101).

33   In German the nouns are "Sage," "Märchen": tale, fairytale.

34   Goethe critics agree that the references to Helen and Paris as Luna and Endymion refer to an engraving by Le Sueur.

35   There is similar acoustic self-consciousness when Heywood's Helen moves between rhyme and blank verse in 1 *Iron Age* (1632).

36   In *Omeros* (1990) Derek Walcott describes rhyme as "language's desire to enclose the loved world in its arms" (13.3.14–15).

37   Euphorion is an allegory of Byron, revealed Goethe, although this identification was an afterthought. His name is the Greek form of the Latin "Faustus."

38   <http://clem.mscd.edu/~holtzee/odyssey/helen.html > accessed June 7, 2008.

39   In her afterword George reverts to the mode of the critics cited above when she talks of Helen's story as "culminating" in Marlowe's "famous" line, the "ultimate description of Helen" (2006: 608).

40   "A thousand" is used as a round figure for a large number in Virgil's *Aeneid*, as in book 2's description of "death in a thousand forms" (1981: 62).

41   Cf. the use of "a thousand" in *Dido* 2.1.175, 185; 5.1.39.

42   In 1909 Arthur Symons, questioning whether prose could compare with poetry as being "the best words in the best order" (1927), used Marlowe's lines as a test case for comparison (challenging the conclusion of W. J. Courthorpe, Oxford professor of poetry, who had used the same lines for the same purpose).

43   In this paragraph I take my lead from Flax's explanation of romantic parody in McMillan 1987: 43–4. The Schlegel quotation is cited by Flax.

44   I have modernized Schlegel's spelling.

45   The generically fluid nature of modern fiction means that parody has left the novel for other more traditional genres. Journalism is probably our last stable

genre; hence the British satirical newspaper *Private Eye* can flourish, piggy-backing as it does on journalistic staples from the tabloid press to the parish magazine.

46   He acknowledges wryly that "from a professional point of view I should rejoice in this. / Machismo is such a useful tool. / The destructiveness it causes is beyond belief" (49).

47   The conversation is replayed on p. 68 before the appearance of Gretchen, the innocent young girl with whom Faust falls in love.

48   Paris' effeminacy is often ridiculed by male characters in twentieth- and twenty-first-century texts, while being an attraction for Helen (see Drew 1912: 11; Drew 1924: 24SD; Haddon 2002).

49   Although this geographic boundary occurs in Goethe, it is not made relevant to the thematically liminal as it is in Clifford.

50   Helen is used as a sexual noun in Schiller's *Mary Stuart*, where it functions as an insult to Mary – she is "a Helen." As we shall see, this is exactly the synecdoche that Clifford's Helen seeks to overturn.

51   This rejection of gender stereotypes applies even in the Witch scenes, where Faust is surprised that the witches' spells do not sound like those in Shakespeare's and Middleton's *Macbeth*. "You mustn't believe all the stuff you see on the commercials, dearie. / It doesn't rhyme," a witch explains (Clifford 2006: 67). The Hollywood film *The Truth about Cats and Dogs* (1996) had similarly used Helen's name as a shorthand for the damage caused by over-valuing female beauty in male–female relations. Dr Abby Barnes (Janeane Garofalo), a vet with a call-in radio show, falls in love with one of her callers, Brian, yet convinces herself he would not be attracted to her were he to see her. When Brian suggests a meeting, she arranges for her tall blonde neighbor (Uma Thurman) to stand in for her. Asked for the truth at the height of the confusion, Abby expostulates: "The truth is Helen of Troy! Helen of Troy!" The 15-year-old protagonist of Mark Schultz's play *A Brief History of Helen of Troy* (2005) feels similarly burdened by the beauty of her dead mother. In Tom Stoppard's *The Invention of Love* (1998) the recently deceased textual critic A. E. Housman feels no such pressure. Arriving in the underworld, he expresses interest in meeting Benjamin Hall Kennedy, the classical scholar after whom Housman's academic Chair was named. Charon remarks that this is not usually the first request of the newly dead. "Who *is*?" inquires Housman naively. The response: "Helen of Troy" (1998: 2–3).

52   Diary, Aug. 2, 2007. Marjorie Garber analyzes the segregated lavatory as the key site of gender difference in *Vested Interests: Cross Dressing and Cultural Anxiety* (1992).

Chapter 6: Parodying Helen

1 Since my discussion concerns only book 3, I omit the preliminary 3 from all canto references.
2 Hamilton (9.42.9n) notes that this comment about Aeneas' regret of his marriage is added by Paridell to his Virgilian source.
3 Marlowe's *Dr Faustus* later halves the number of Cupids: "*Enter* HELEN *again . . . passing over between two Cupids.*" (This stage direction exists only in the B-text, 5.2.93.)
4 When performed by boys, as in the original Elizabethan production, this effect might have been more (or less) obvious.
5 In his poem *La Belle Hélène* (1878), about attending a performance of the opera, Edgar Fawcett resigns himself to Offenbach's opera as the lesser of two evils: better to parody the classics than to forget them.
6 The production was directed by Laurent Pelly; Kit Hesketh-Harvey provided the English translation/adaptation.
7 The director, Laurent Pelly, also designed the costumes.
8 Coincidentally Offenbach had originally planned a musical parody of Wagner's *Tannhäuser* but was overruled by his librettists (Traubner 2006). For a lucid account of the development of the opera see Traubner 2003: 45–50.
9 I have not found any copies of this film in American libraries, although the Library of Congress owns a two-page synopsis. According to the synopsis, the missing material includes the Judgment of Paris (the goddesses are listed as Aphrodite, Hera, and Thetis, although the attached cast list correctly offers Athena instead of Thetis); Helen's disillusion with Paris who snores just like Menelaus; Paris' irritation at Helen's sartorial extravagance; Helen's attempts to end the war (thwarted by the Trojans); and the wooden horse. Two stills, available on the Web and copyrighted to Getty Images, show episodes not in the BFI fragments.
10 The film won an Oscar for its intertitles in the first year of the Academy Awards.
11 Elisabeth Dutton, personal communication.
12 See Wilfrid S. Jackson's *Helen of Troy, New York* (1904) and Mrs Burton Harrison's *The Story of Helen Troy* (1881), for examples. Jackson's novel was made into a musical comedy by Bert Kalmar in 1923, titled *Looking for the Happy Ending* (but sometimes also known by the title of Jackson's novel).
13 Kate Payn teases the heroine Verena about her aversion to being photographed, revising Scott's lines from "Lady of the Lake" for the purpose (vol. 1: 235). In vol. 2: 213 Kate reassures her mother, who is losing her in marriage, that she has another daughter; Tennyson's lines from "The May Queen," pressed into service here, do not include Kate's comments about curling tongs and female hairstyles. The novel is in two volumes; all references are to volume and page number.

14 This review is quoted in an advertisement for the book in *The Daily News* of May 26, 1886.
15 Hurst and Blackett specialized in popular novels, publishing the work of Mary Braddon (author of *Lady Audley's Secret*), Mrs Oliphant, and "John Halifax, Gentleman," for example. Stanley's novels were also published and widely publicized in the USA.
16 For the parallels between Clarissa's parties as an "offering" and Septimus Warren Smith's suicide as a Girardian sacrifice, see Wyatt 1973. On the Homeric world of the novel generally, see Hoff 1999.
17 I am grateful to John Scholar for observations on Woolf and Joyce in this paragraph and throughout this section.
18 References to *Omeros* are in the form: chapter/section/line.
19 John van Sickle sees in the name of Achille's ancestor, Afolabe, a Greek etymology: *apo* = from, away, and *labē* = take (1999: 23). Afolabe's name means "taken away," even before he is captured as a slave.
20 Although this is typical of Helen narratives, it is unusual in *Omeros*, where everyone's interiority is examined at length. The poem's events are primarily emotional.
21 Boswell's *Past Ruined Ilion* provides wide coverage of Helen poems, but the list has expanded considerably since 1982. In addition to the novels cited in endnotes throughout this book, see Nye (1980), McLaren (1996), Franklin (1998), Pollard (2004), and Elyot (2005); in 1956 Warner Brothers released a book of the film: *Helen of Troy – The World's Greatest Love Story*. For a screenplay (adapted from his stageplay) see Miller (2003). Political and religious uses of Helen are at their height in the early modern period: see Rainold 1563: Gir–v; Buchanan 2004: 79; and Fuller 1799: 153–4 (a late-eighteenth-century transcript of a seventeenth-century speech delivered by Charles I). I am grateful to Thomas Roebuck for these three references. For religious uses see Pikeryng's *Horestes*, lines 538–601 (where the satire is conveyed by using the tune of a popular song about Mary Queen of Scots to words about Clytemnestra and Helen; Axton 1982: 158) and Bridges (1587) where Helen is compared to the Roman Catholic mass. For philosophy and politics see Camus (2000).

References

Abbott, H. P. (2002) *The Cambridge Introduction to Narrative*. Cambridge University Press, Cambridge.

Ackroyd, P. (2004) *Chaucer*. Chatto & Windus, London.

Adams, A. M. (1988) "Helen in Greek literature: Homer to Euripides." PhD thesis. University of Aberystwyth.

Adams, T. (1615) *The Black Devil* (STC 107). London.

Aeschylus (1968) *Agamemnon* in *The Oresteian Trilogy*, trans. Vellacott, P. Penguin, Harmondsworth.

Alemán, M. (1623) *The Rogue* (STC 289). London.

Allott, R. (1599) *Wit's Theatre* (STC 381). London.

Andreas, B. (1858) *Historia Regis Henrici Septimi*, ed. Gairdner, J. Longman et al., London.

Anon (1968) Review of Dr Faustus. *Reading Evening Post*, June 28.

Anon. *Excidium Troiae*. See Atwood and Whitaker.

Anon. *The "Gest hystoriale" of the Destruction of Troy*. See Panton and Donaldson.

Anon. *The Siege of Troy*. See Wager.

Anon. (1594) *A Pleasant Conceited History, Called The Taming of a Shrew* (STC 23668).

Anon. (1601) *The Death of Robert, Earl of Huntington* (STC 18269).

Anon. (1956) *Helen of Troy – The World's Greatest Love Story* (Beverley Books of the Film). Beverley Books, London.

Anon. (1988) *Historia von D. Johann Fausten*. Phillip Reclam jun. GmbH, Stuttgart.

Anon. *The Laud Troy Book*. See Wülfing.

Aristophanes (1978) *The Assemblywomen* in *The Knights and Other Plays*, trans. Barrett, D. and Sommerstein, A. H. Penguin, Harmondsworth.

Aristophanes (1973) *Lysistrata* in *Lysistrata and Other Plays*, trans. Sommerstein, A. H. Penguin, Harmondsworth.

Aristophanes (1964) *The Poet and the Women* in *The Frogs and Other Plays*, trans. Barrett, D. Penguin, Harmondsworth.

Armstrong, K. (2005) *A Short History of Myth*. Alfred A. Knopf, Toronto.

Atwood, E. B. and Whitaker, V. K. (eds.) (1944) *Excidium Troiae*. Medieval Academy of America, Cambridge, MA.

Atwood, M. (2005) *The Penelopiad*. Canongate, Edinburgh.

Austin, N. (1994) *Helen of Troy and her Shameless Phantom*. Cornell University Press, Ithaca, NY.

Austin, N. (1999) "Homer and the sunrise in Derek Walcott's *Omeros*." *Classical World* 93, 29–42.

Axton, M. (ed.) (1982) *Three Tudor Classical Interludes: Thersites, Jacke Jugeler, Horestes*. D. S. Brewer, Cambridge.

Bacon, F. (1985) *The Essays*, ed. Pitcher, J. Penguin, Harmondsworth.

Baines, B. J. (1998) "Effacing rape in early modern representation." *ELH* 65, 69–98.

Barthes, R. (1975) *The Pleasure of the Text*, trans. Miller, R. Hill & Wang, New York.

Barthes, R. (1982) "Introduction to the structured analysis of narratives." In *Image-Music-Text*, repr. in Sontag, S. (ed.), *A Barthes Reader*. Hill & Wang, New York, pp. 251–95.

Bashar, N. (1983) "Rape in England between 1550 and 1700." In *The Sexual Dynamics of History: Men's Power, Women's Resistance*. (No editor.) Pluto Press, London, pp. 28–42.

Baswell, C. C. and Taylor, P. B. (1988) "The 'faire Queen Eleyne' in Chaucer's *Troilus*." *Speculum* 63, 293–311.

Bate, J. (1993) *Shakespeare and Ovid*. Oxford: Clarendon Press.

Bates, C. (2002) "Shakespeare's tragedies of love." In McEachern, C. (ed.), *The Cambridge Companion to Shakespearean Tragedy*. Cambridge University Press, Cambridge, pp. 182–203.

Baugh, E. (2006) *Derek Walcott*. Cambridge University Press, Cambridge.

Beaumont, F. (1969) *The Knight of the Burning Pestle*, ed. Hattaway, M. Ernest Benn, London.

Beaumont, F. and Fletcher, J. (1968) *The Maid's Tragedy*, ed. Norland, H. B. Edward Arnold, London.

Bellori, G. P. (1968) "The idea of the painter, sculptor and architect, superior to nature by selection from natural beauties." In Panofsky, E. (ed.), *Idea: A Concept in Art Theory*, trans. J. J. S. Peake. Columbia University Press, New York, pp. 154–75.

Benét, S. V. (1920) "The first vision of Helen." In *Heavens and Earth*. Henry Holt, New York, pp. 3–18.

Benoît de Ste-Maure (1904) *Le Roman de Troie*, vol. 1, ed. Constans, L. Firmin Didot et Cie, Paris.

Benson, C. D. (1980) *The History of Troy in Middle English Literature*. D. S. Brewer, Woodbridge, Suffolk.

Bergren, A. L. T. (1979–80) "Helen's web: time and tableau in the *Iliad*." *Helios* 7, 19–34.

Bergren, A. L. T. (1981) "Helen's 'good drug': *Odyssey* IV: 1–305." In Kresic, S. (ed.), *Contemporary Literary Hermeneutics and Interpretation of Classical Texts.* University of Ottawa Press, Ottawa, pp. 201–14.

Billington, M. (2008) Review of *Troilus and Cressida.* May 29, 2008, <http://www.guardian.co.uk>. Accessed May 31, 2008.

Blenerhasset, T. (1578) *The Second Part of the Mirror for Magistrates* (STC 3131). London.

Blount, C. (1680) *The Two First Books of Philostratus, Concerning the Life of Apollonius Tyaneus* (STC Wing P 2132). London.

Boswell, J. (1982) *Past Ruined Ilion.* Scarecrow Press, London.

Bouhours, D. (1960) "The je ne sais quoi" from *The Conversations of Aristo and Eugene (1671).* In Elledge, S. and Schier, D. (eds.), *The Continental Model: Selected French Critical Essays of the Seventeenth Century, in English Translation.* Carleton College, Minneapolis, MN, pp. 228–38.

Bourdillon, F. W. (1893) "Helen." In *Sursum Corda.* T. Fisher Unwin, London, pp. 19–21.

Brathwaite, R. (1614) *The Poet's Willow* (STC 3578). London.

Brathwaite, R. (1621) *Nature's Embassy, or the Wild Man's Measures Danced Naked by Twelve Satyrs* (STC 3571). London.

Brathwaite, R. (1665) *A Comment upon the Two Tales of our Ancient, Renowned, and Ever-Living Poet Chaucer . . . The Miller's Tale and The Wife of Bath* (STC Wing B4260). London.

Breslin, P. (2001) *Nobody's Nation: Reading Derek Walcott.* University of Chicago Press, Chicago.

Bridges, J. (1587) *A Defence of the Government Established in the Church of England for Ecclesiastical Matters* (STC 3734). London.

Brooke, R. (1918) "Menelaus and Helen." In *The Collected Poems.* Sidgwick & Jackson, London, pp. 92–3.

Brooke, S. A. (1900) *Tennyson: His Art and Relation to Modern Life.* Isbister, London.

Buchanan, G. (2004) *A Dialogue on the Law of Kingship among the Scots,* ed. and trans. Mason, R. A. and Smith, M. S. Ashgate, Aldershot, UK.

Bull, M. (2005) *The Mirror of the Gods: Classical Mythology in Renaissance Art.* Allen Lane, London.

Bulwer Lytton, Sir E. (1866) "Bridals in the spirit land." In *The Lost Tales of Miletus.* Bernhard Tauchnitz, Leipzig, pp. 217–26.

Burgess, J. S. (2001) *The Tradition of the Trojan War in Homer and the Epic Cycle.* Johns Hopkins University Press, Baltimore.

Burnett, A. P. (1971) *Catastrophe Survived: Euripides' Plays of Mixed Reversal.* Clarendon Press, Oxford.

Burrow, C. (1993) *Epic Romance: From Homer to Milton.* Clarendon Press, Oxford.

Burton, R. (1621) *The Anatomy of Melancholy* (STC 4159). London.

Butler, S. (1970) *Erehwon,* ed. Mudford, P. Penguin, Harmondsworth.

Callaghan, D. (2007) *Shakespeare's Sonnets*. Blackwell Publishing, Oxford.

Calasso, R. (1994) *The Marriage of Cadmus and Harmony*. Vintage, London.

Camden, W. (1605) *Remains* (STC 4521). London.

Camus, A. (2000) *The Myth of Sisyphus*. Penguin, London.

Cannon, C. (2001) "Chaucer and rape: uncertainty's certainties." In Robertson, E. (ed.), *Representing Rape in Medieval and Early Modern Literature*. Palgrave, New York, pp. 67–92.

Cargill, L. (1991) *To Follow the Goddess*. Cheops Books, Charlottesville, VA.

Catty, J. (1999) *Writing Rape, Writing Women in Early Modern England: Unbridled Speech*. Macmillan, Basingstoke.

Caxton, W. See Le Fèvre.

Chatman, S. (1978) *Story and Discourse: Narrative Structure in Fiction and Film*. Cornell University Press, Ithaca, NY.

Chaytor, M. (1995) "Husband(ry): narratives of rape in the seventeenth century." *Gender and History* 7, 378–407.

Chaucer, G. (1987) *The Riverside Chaucer*, ed. Benson, L. D. Houghton Mifflin, Boston, MA.

Chedzgoy, K. (2004) "Marlowe's men and women: gender and sexuality." In Cheney, P. (ed.), *The Cambridge Companion to Christopher Marlowe*, pp. 256–61.

Cheney, P. (ed.) (2004) *The Cambridge Companion to Christopher Marlowe*. Cambridge University Press, Cambridge.

Churchyard, T. (1596) *A Musical Consort of Heavenly Harmony* (STC 5245). London.

Clader, L. L. (1976) *Helen: the Evolution from Divine to Heroic in Greek Epic Tradition*. E. J. Brill, Leiden.

Clifford, J. (2006) *Faust, Parts One and Two by Goethe*. Nick Hern Books, London.

Clifford, J. <http://www.teatromundo.com>. Accessed Jan. 24, 2008, and May 28, 2008.

Coetzee, J. M. (2004) *Elizabeth Costello: Eight Lessons*. Vintage, London.

Cohen, D. J. (1991) *Law, Sexuality and Society: The Enforcement of Morals in Classical Athens*. Cambridge University Press, Cambridge.

Colantuono, A. (1997) *Guido Reni's* Abduction of Helen*: The Politics and Rhetoric of Painting in Seventeenth-Century Europe*. Cambridge University Press, Cambridge.

Colie, R. (1966) *Paradoxia Epidemica: The Renaissance Tradition of Paradox*. Princeton University Press, Princeton, NJ.

Colonne, Guido delle (1936) *Historia Destructionis Troiae*, ed. Griffin, N. E. Medieval Academy of America, Cambridge, MA.

Colonne, Guido delle (1974) *Historia Destructionis Troiae*, trans. and ed. Meek, M. E. Indiana University Press, Bloomington, IN.

Combellack, F. See Quintus of Smyrna.

Cornford, F. M. (1934) *The Origins of Attic Comedy*. Cambridge University Press, Cambridge.

Coupe, L. (1997) *Myth*. Routledge, London.

Cropper, E. (1991) "The petrifying art: Marino's poetry and Caravaggio." *Metropolitan Museum Journal* 26, 193–208.

Curran, J. V. (2000) "Goethe's Helen: a play within a play." *International Journal of the Classical Tradition* 7, 165–76.

Curry, W. C. (1916) *The Middle English Ideal of Personal Beauty*. J. H. Furst, Baltimore, MD.

Daileader, C. R. (1998) *Eroticism on the Renaissance Stage: Transcendence, Desire, and the Limits of the Visible*. Cambridge University Press, Cambridge.

Danzig, A. (1967) "The contraries: a central concept in Tennyson's poetry." *PMLA* 77, 577–85.

Dares [= Dares Phrygius]. See Frazer.

Dares (1873) *Daretis Phrygii de excidio Troiae historia*. B. G. Teubner, Leipzig.

Dasent, J. R. (ed.) (1903) *Acts of the Privy Council of England, Volume 27: 1597*. HMSO, London.

Dean, D. (1996) *Law-Making and Society in Late Elizabethan England: The Parliament of England, 1584–1601*. Cambridge University Press, Cambridge.

De la Faye, A. (1599) *A Brief Treatise* (STC 24216). London.

De la Marche, O. (1569) *The Travelled Pilgrim* (STC 1585). London.

Deloney, T. (1626) *Jack of Newbury* (STC 6560). London.

De Pisan, C. *The Works of Christine de Pisan*. BL MS Harley 4431.

Déprats, J.-M. (1995) "Translating Shakespeare for the theatre." In Klein, H. and Maguin, J.-M. (eds.), *Shakespeare and France*. Edwin Mellen Press, Lewiston NY, pp. 345–58.

D'Ewes, S. (1682) *The Journals of All the Parliaments During the Reign of Queen Elizabeth*, rev. Bowes, P. London.

Dictys [= Dictys Cretensis]. See Frazer.

Dictys, Cretensis (1825) *De Bello Trojano . . . Accedunt Josephi Iscani De Bello Trojano Libri Sex*. A. J. Valpy, London.

Donaldson, I. (1982) *The Rapes of Lucretia*. Clarendon, Oxford.

Drant, T. (1566) *A Medicinable Moral, That Is, the Two Books of Horace's Satyres* (STC 13805). London.

Dowden, E. (1914) "Helena." In *Poems*. J. M. Dent, London, pp. 33–6.

Drayton, M. (1604) *The Owl* (STC 7211.5). London.

Drayton, M. (1612) *Polyolbion* (STC 7226). London.

Drew, B. (1912) "Helen." In *Helen and Other Poems*. A. C. Fifield, London, pp. 9–13.

Drew, B. (1924) *Helen of Troy: A Play*. Selwyn & Blount, London.

Duffy, C. A. (2002) "Beautiful." In *Feminine Gospels*. Picador, London, pp. 8–14.

Dunsany, E. Lord (1938) "An interview." In *Mirage Water*. Putnam, London, p. 61.

Eliade, M. (1958) *Patterns in Comparative Religion*. Sheed & Ward, London.

Elyot, A. (2005) *The Memoirs of Helen of Troy*. Crown Publishers / Random House, New York.

Erskine, J. (1922) "Paris, Helen's lover." In *Collected Poems 1907–22*. Duffield, New York, pp. 132–7.

Erskine, J. (1926) *The Private Life of Helen of Troy*. Eveleigh, Nash & Grayson, London.

E. T. See T. E.

Euripides (1972) *Andromache* in *Orestes and Other Plays*, trans. Vellacott, P. Penguin, Harmondsworth.

Euripides (1989) *Alcestis*, trans. Arrowsmith, W. Oxford University Press, Oxford.

Euripides (1972) *Iphigenia in Aulis*. In *Orestes and Other Plays*, trans. Vellacott, P. Penguin, Harmondsworth, pp. 363–427.

Euripides (1963) *Electra*. In *Medea and Other Plays*, trans. Vellacott, P. Penguin, Harmondsworth, pp. 105–52.

Euripides (1972) *Orestes*. In *Orestes and Other Plays*, trans. Vellacott, P. Penguin, Harmondsworth, pp. 297–361.

Euripides (1973) *The Bacchae*. In *The Bacchae and Other Plays*, trans. Vellacott, P. Penguin, Harmondsworth, pp. 191–244.

Euripides (1973) *Helen*. In *The Bacchae and Other Plays*, trans. Vellacott, P. Penguin, Harmondsworth, pp. 135–89.

Euripides (1973) *Hippolytos*, trans. Bagg, R. Oxford University Press, Oxford.

Euripides (1973) *Ion*. In *The Bacchae and Other Plays*, trans. Vellacott, P. Penguin, Harmondsworth, pp. 41–88.

Euripides (1973) *The Women of Troy*. In *The Bacchae and Other Plays*, trans. Vellacott, P. Penguin, Harmondsworth, pp. 89–133.

Euripides (1974) *Alcestis*, trans. Arrowsmith, W. Oxford University Press, Oxford.

Fawcett, E. (1878) "La belle Hélène." In *Fantasy and Passion*. Roberts Brothers, Boston, MA, pp. 141–3.

Fawcett, E. (1903) "Helen, Old." In *Voices and Visions*. Eveleigh Nash, London, p. 118.

F. P., Gent. (= P. F.) See Jones.

Fehrenbach, R. J. (2001) "A pre-1592 English Faust book and the date of Marlowe's *Doctor Faustus*." *Library* 2, 327–35.

Fenik, B. (1974) *Studies in the Odyssey*. Franz Steiner, Wiesbaden.

Fenne, T. (1590) *Fenne's Fruits* (STC 10763). London.

Ficino, M. (1985) *Commentary on Plato's Symposium on Love*, trans. Jayne, S. Spring Publications, Dallas, TX.

Fielding, H. (1977) *Joseph Andrews*, ed. Brissenden, R. F. Penguin, Harmondsworth.

Fielding, H. (1978) *Tom Jones*, ed. Mutter, R. P. C. Penguin, Harmondsworth.

Fineman, J. (1991) *The Subjectivity Effect in Western Literary Tradition*. MIT Press, Cambridge, MA.

Flax, N. M. (1983) "The presence of the sign in Goethe's *Faust*." *PMLA* 98, 183–203.

Flax, N. M. (1987) "Goethe and Romanticism." In McMillan, *Approaches*, pp. 40–7.

Fletcher, J. (1966) *The Woman's Prize or the Tamer Tamed*, ed. Ferguson, G. B. Mouton, The Hague.

Fletcher, J. G. (1925) "On a moral triumph." In *Parables*. Kegan Paul, Trench, Trubner, pp. 96–7.

Ford, J. (1606) *Honor Triumphant*. (STC 11160). London.

Forsyth, N. (1987) "Heavenly Helen." *Etudes de Lettres*, 4th ser., 10, 11–21.

Fradenburg, L. O. (1992) " 'Our owen wo to drynke': loss, gender, and chivalry in *Troilus and Criseyde*." In Shoaf, R. A. (ed.), *Chaucer's Troilus and Criseyde, "Subgit to alle Poesye": Essays in Criticism*. Medieval & Renaissance Texts & Studies, Binghamton, NY, pp. 88–106.

Franklin, S. B. (1998) *Daughter of Troy*. HarperTorch, New York.

Frazer, R. M. (1966) *The Trojan War: The Chronicles of Dictys of Crete and Dares the Phrygian*. Indiana University Press, Bloomington, IN.

Frye, N. (1970) "On value-judgments." In *The Stubborn Structure: Essays on Criticism and Society*. Methuen, London, pp. 66–73.

Fuller, J. (1799) *The History of Berwick upon Tweed*. Edinburgh.

Garber, M. (1992) *Vested Interests: Cross Dressing and Cultural Anxiety*. Routledge, New York.

Gataker, T. (1619) *On the Nature and Use of Lots* (STC 11670). London.

George, M. (2006) *Helen of Troy*. Viking Penguin, New York.

Gibbons, S. (2006) *Cold Comfort Farm*. Penguin, Harmondsworth.

Gillies, A. (1957) *Goethe's Faust: An Interpretation*. Basil Blackwell, Oxford.

Girard, René (2000) *A Theatre of Envy*, orig. 1991. Gracewing/Inigo, Leominster and New Malden, Surrey.

Girard, René (2005) *Violence and the Sacred*. Continuum, London.

Giraudoux, J. (1955) *Tiger at the Gates*, trans. Fry, C. Methuen, London.

Goethe, J. W. (1949) *Faust: Eine Tragödie. Zweiter Teil*. Benno Schwabe, Basel.

Goethe, J. W. (1987) *Faust: Part One*, trans. Luke, D. Oxford University Press, Oxford.

Goethe, J. W. (1994) *Faust: Part Two*, trans. Luke, D. Oxford University Press, Oxford.

Goethe, J. W. (2006) *Faust, Parts One and Two by Goethe*, trans. and adapt. Clifford, J. Nick Hern Books, London.

Golding, A. (trans.) (1567) *The XV books of P. Ovidius Naso, entitled Metamorphoses* (STC 18956). London.

Gorgias (1982) *Encomium of Helen*, ed. and trans. MacDowell, D. M. Bristol Classical Press, Bristol.

Grange, J. (1577) *The Golden Aphroditis* (STC 12174). London.

Grant, E. (1571) *A Precedent for Parents* (STC 20057.5). London.

Green, R. L. (1946) *Andrew Lang: A Critical Biography*. Edmund Ward, Leicester.

Greene, R. (1589) *Ciceronis Amor* (STC 12224). London.

Greene, R. (1590) *Greene's Mourning Garment* (STC 12251). London.

Greene, R. (1621) *Greene's Groatsworth of Wit* (STC 12248). London.

Greene, R. (1963) *Friar Bacon and Friar Bungay*, ed. Seltzer, D. Edward Arnold, London.

Griffin, N. E. (1907) *Dares and Dictys: an Introduction to the Study of Medieval Versions of the Story of Troy*. J. H. Furst, Baltimore, MD.

Gumpert, M. (2001) *Grafting Helen: The Abduction of the Classical Past.* University of Wisconsin Press, Madison, WI.

Habernhern, M. (1987) "The Romantic revolution." In McMillan, *Approaches*, pp. 101–3.

Habinek, T. (2005) *The World of Roman Song: From Ritualized Speech to Social Order.* Johns Hopkins University Press, Baltimore, MD.

Haddon, M. (2002) *A Thousand Ships.* BBC Radio 4 Broadcast, Jan. 28.

Haggard, H. R. and Lang, A. (1894) *The World's Desire.* Longmans, Green, London.

Hamner, R. D. (1997) *Epic of the Dispossessed: Derek Walcott's* Omeros. University of Missouri Press, Columbia, MS.

Hamner, R. D. (2005) "Out of the ordinary, Derek Walcott." *Callaloo* 28, 1–6.

Hardy, T. (1978) *Tess of the D'Urbervilles*, ed. Skilton, D. Penguin, Harmondsworth.

Harrison, B. Mrs (1881) *The Story of Helen Troy.* Sampson Low, Marston, Searle & Rivington, New York.

Hartley, T. E. (ed.) (1995) *Proceedings of the Parliaments of Elizabeth I, Volume III: 1593–1601.* Leicester University Press, London.

Hatfield, H. (1987) "Two roads to *Faust*." In McMillan, *Approaches*, pp. 77–80.

Healy, T. (2004) "*Doctor Faustus*." In Cheney, P. (ed.), *The Cambridge Companion to Christopher Marlowe*, pp. 174–92.

Hedreen, G. (1996) "Image, text, and story in the recovery of Helen." *Classical Antiquity* 15, 152–84.

Heilbrun, C. G. (1990) *Hamlet's Mother and Other Women.* Columbia University Press, New York.

Herodotus (1965, orig. 1954) *The Histories*, trans. de Sélincourt, A. Penguin, Harmondsworth.

Hesiod (1977) *The Homeric Hymns and Homerica*, trans. Evelyn-White, H. G. Harvard University Press, London.

Hesiod (1988) *Theogony* and *Works and Days*, trans. West, M. L. Oxford University Press, Oxford.

Hewlett, M. (1909) *The Ruinous Face.* Harper & Brothers, London.

Hewlett, M. (1913) *Helen Redeemed and Other Poems.* Macmillan, London.

Heywood, T. (1599) *1 and 2 Edward 4* (STC 13341). London.

Heywood, T. (1609) *Troia Britannica or Great Britain's Troy* (STC 13366). London.

Heywood, T. (1613) *A Marriage Triumph* (STC 13355). London.

Heywood, T. (1625) *The Fair Maid of the Exchange* (STC 13318). London.

Heywood, T. (1632) *1 and 2 The Iron Age* (STC 13340). London.

Heywood, T. (1636) *A Challenge for Beauty* (STC 13311). London.

Heywood, T. (1637) "The dialogue of Ravisius Textor betwixt Earth and Age." In *Pleasant Dialogues and Dramas* (STC 13358). London, sigs. D4r–E3r.

Heywood, T. (1963) "Oenone and Paris." In *Elizabethan Minor Epics*, ed. Donno, E. S. Routledge & Kegan Paul, London, pp. 127–54.

Hoban, R. (1975) *Turtle Diary.* Jonathan Cape, London.

Hoff, M. (1999) "The pseudo-Homeric world of Mrs Dalloway." *Twentieth-Century Literature* 45, 186–209.

Homer (1961) *The Iliad of Homer*, trans. Lattimore, R. University of Chicago Press, Chicago, IL.

Homer (1991) *The Odyssey*, trans. Rieu, E. V., rev. trans. Rieu, D. C. H. Penguin, Harmondsworth.

Hughes, B. (2005) *Helen of Troy: Goddess, Princess, Whore*. Jonathan Cape, London.

[Hughes, T.] "An Old Boy." (n.d.) *Tom Brown's Schooldays*. Ward, Lock, London.

Hutson, L. (2007) *The Invention of Suspicion*. Oxford University Press, Oxford.

Irwin, M. E. (1990) "Odysseus' 'hyacinthine hair' in 'Odyssey' 6.231." *Phoenix* 44, 205–18.

Iser, W. (2006) *How to Do Theory*. Blackwell Publishing, Oxford.

Isocrates (1894) "Helen." In *The Orations of Isocrates*, trans. Freese, J. H. George Bell & Sons, London, vol. 1, pp. 289–306.

Isocrates (1945) "On Helen." In *Isocrates*, trans. Norlin, G. and van Hook, S., 3 vols., William Heinemann, London, vol. 3, pp. 53–97.

Jackson, P. (2006) *The Transformations of Helen: Indo-European Myth and the Roots of the Trojan Cycle*. J. H. Röll, Dettelbach, Germany.

Jackson, W. S. (1904) *Helen of Troy, New York*. John Lane, New York.

Jankélévitch, V. (1974) *L'Irréversible et la Nostalgie*. Flammarion, Paris.

Jones, J. H. (ed.) (1994) *The English Faust Book*. Cambridge University Press, Cambridge.

Jonson, B. (1890) *Masques and Entertainments*, ed. Morley, H. Routledge, London.

Jonson, B. (1968) *Volpone*, ed. Brockbank, P. A. & C. Black, London.

Jonson, B. (1988) *The Staple of News*, ed. Parr, A. Manchester University Press, Manchester.

Jonson, B. (2000) *Poetaster, or, The Arraignment; Sejanus his Fall; The Devil is an Ass; The New Inn, or, The Light Heart*, ed. Kidnie, M. J. Oxford University Press, Oxford.

Joseph of Exeter (1970) *Frigii Daretis Ylias*. In Gompf, L. (ed.), *Joseph Iscanus: Werke und Briefe* (vol. 4 of Mittellateinische Studien und Texte). E. J. Brill, Leiden.

Joseph of Exeter (1970) *The Iliad of Dares Phrygius: De Bello Trojano*, trans. and ed. Roberts, G. A. A. Balkema, Cape Town.

Joseph of Exeter (1986) *Trojan War I–III*, ed. and trans. Bate, A. K. Aris & Phillips, Warminster.

Junius, F. (1638) *The Painting of the Ancients* (STC 7302). London.

Kant, I. (1964) *Critique of Judgment* in Hofstadter, A. and Kuhns, R. (eds.), *Philosophies of Art and Beauty*. Random House, New York.

Keefer, M. (2004) " 'Fairer than the evening air': Marlowe's gnostic Helen of Troy and the tropes of belatedness and historical mediation." In Shepard, A. and Powell, S. D. (eds.), *Fantasies of Troy: Classical Tales and the Social Imaginary in Medieval and Early Modern Europe*. CCRS, Toronto, pp. 39–62.

Kennedy, G. A. (1987) "The story of Helen: myth and rhetoric." Washington University, St. Louis, MS.

Kesey, K. (1977) *One Flew Over the Cuckoo's Nest*, ed. Pratt, J. C. Penguin, Harmondsworth.

Kirwan, J. (1999) *Beauty*. Manchester University Press, Manchester.

Kirwan, M. (2005) *Discovering Girard*. Cowley Publications, Cambridge, MA.

Landor, W. S. (1847) *The Hellenics*. Edward Moxon, London.

Lang, A. (1882) *Helen of Troy*. George Bell & Sons, London.

Lang, A. (1923) "Helen of Troy" and "Palinode." In *The Poetical Works of Andrew Lang*, ed. Mrs. Lang. 4 vols., Longmans, Green, London, vol. 4, pp. 5–204, 221.

Lanyer, E. (2000) "Salve Deus Rex Judaeorum." In Clarke, D. (ed.), *Renaissance Women Poets*. Penguin, Harmondsworth, pp. 228–74.

Latacz, J. (2004) *Troy and Homer: Towards a Solution of an Old Mystery*, trans. Windle, K. and Ireland, R. Oxford University Press, Oxford.

Latham, A. See Shakespeare, *As You Like It*.

Lathrop, G. P. "Helen at the loom." In *Rose and Roof-Tree: Poems*. <http://www.fullbooks.com/Rose-and-Roof-Tree>. Accessed July 27, 2008.

Lattimore, R. (1951) *The Iliad of Homer*. University of Chicago Press, Chicago, IL.

Le Fèvre, R. (1894) *The Recuyell of the Histories of Troy*, trans. Caxton, W., ed. Sommer, O., 2 vols. Published for the Early English Text Society, David Nutt, London.

Leggatt, A. (1973) "Tamburlaine's sufferings." *The Yearbook of English Studies* 3, 28–38.

Leithauser, B. (1991) "Ancestral rhyme." *The New Yorker*, Feb. 11, pp. 91–5.

Levinson, M. (1986) *The Romantic Fragment Poem*. University of North Carolina Press, Chapel Hill, NC.

Lewis, C. S. (1966) "After ten years." In *Of Other Worlds: Essays and Stories*, ed. Hooper, W. Geoffrey Bles, London, pp. 127–45.

Lindsay, J. (1974) *Helen of Troy*. Constable, London.

Lloyd, L. (1590) *The Consent of Time* (STC 16619). London.

Lodge, T. (1584) *An Alarm Against Usurers* (STC 16653). London.

Long, T. (1987) *Repetition and Variation in the Short Stories of Herodotus*. Athenäum, Frankfurt am Main, 1987.

Lucian (1905) *Hermotimus*. In *The Works of Lucian of Samosata*, trans., Fowler, H. W. and Fowler, F. G., 4 vols. Clarendon Press, Oxford, vol. 2, pp. 41–90.

Lucian (1961) "Dialogues of the dead," trans. MacLeod, M. D. In Loeb Classical Library, *Lucian*, vol. 7. William Heinemann, London, pp. 1–175.

Lucian (1969) "The judgement of the goddesses," trans. Harmon, A. M. In Loeb Classical Library, *Lucian*, vol. 3. William Heinemann, London, pp. 384–409.

Lydgate, J. (1906) *Lydgate's Troy Book A.D. 1412–20, Part 1*, ed. H. Bergen. Published for the Early English Text Society by Kegan Paul, Trench, Trübner, London.

Lydgate, J. (1908) *Lydgate's Troy Book A.D. 1412–20, Part 2*, ed. H. Bergen. Published for the Early English Text Society by Kegan Paul, Trench, Trübner, London.

Lydgate, J. (1910) *Lydgate's Troy Book A.D. 1412–20, Part 3*, ed. H. Bergen. Published for the Early English Text Society by Kegan Paul, Trench, Trübner, London.

Lyly, J. (1578) *Euphues* (STC 17051). London.

Lyly, J. (1579) *Euphues*, 2nd ed. (STC 17053). London.

Lyons, C. P. (1964) "The trysting scenes in *Troilus and Cressida*." In Thaler, A. and Sanders, N. (eds.), *Shakespearean Studies*. University of Tennessee Press, Knoxville, TN, pp. 105–20.

MacDiarmid, H. (1978) "Die Grenzsituation." In Grieve, M. and Aitken, W. R. (eds.), *Complete Poems Vol. II: Hitherto Uncollected Poems Contributed to Books and Periodicals (1920–1976)*. Martin Brian & O'Keeffe, London, p. 1331.

McEwan, I. (2005) *Saturday*. Jonathan Cape, London.

McGrath, C. (2004) "Brad Pitt's big fat Greek toga party." *New York Times*, May 9, sect. 2A.

McKinsey, M. (2002) "Classicism and colonial retrenchment in W. B. Yeats's 'No Second Troy'." *Twentieth-Century Literature* 48, 174–90.

McLaren, C. (1996) *Inside the Walls of Troy*. Simon Pulse / Simon and Schuster, New York.

MacLeish, A. (1917) "Our Lady of Troy." In *Tower of Ivory*. Yale University Press, New Haven, CT, pp. 1–21.

McMillan, D. J. (ed.) (1987) *Approaches to Teaching Goethe's Faust*. Modern Language Association of America, New York.

McMillan, J. (2005) "Sue Innes, writer and feminist campaigner." *Scotsman*, Mar. 3.

Maguire, L. (2007) *Shakespeare's Names*. Oxford University Press, Oxford.

Malalas, J. (1831) *Chronographia*. Weber, Bonn.

Marlowe, C. (1976) *Complete Plays and Poems*, ed. E. D. Pendry and J. C. Maxwell. J. M. Dent & Sons, London.

Marlowe, C. (1989) *Dr Faustus*. A programme/text with commentary by Simon Trussler. RSC/Methuen, London.

Marlowe, C. (1993) *Doctor Faustus, A- and B-texts*, ed. Bevington, D. and Rasmussen, E. Manchester University Press, Manchester.

Marlowe, C. (2005) *Dr Faustus with the English Faust Book*, ed. Wootton, D. Hackett Publishing Co., Indianopolis, IN.

Marston, J. (1963) "The metamorphosis of Pygmalion's image." In Donno, E. S. (ed.), *Elizabethan Minor Epics*. Routledge & Kegan Paul, pp. 244–52.

Marston, J. (1606) *Sophonisba* (STC 17488). London.

Masefield, J. (1923) *The Taking of Helen*. Macmillan, New York.

Maveety, S. (1973) "'A second fall of cursed man': the bold metaphor in *Richard II*." *Journal of English and Germanic Philology* 73, 175–93.

May, T. (1622) *The Heir* (STC 17713). London.

Meagher, R. (1995) *Helen: Myth, Legend, and the Culture of Misogyny.* Continuum, New York.

Melchiori, G. (1978) *The Whole Mystery of Art: Pattern into Poetry in the Work of W. B. Yeats*, orig. 1961. Greenwood Press, Westport, CT.

Meres, F. (1634 [1598]) *Wit's Commonwealth [Palladis Tamia]* (STC 17835). London.

Middleton, T. (2007) *The Old Law* in Taylor, G. and Lavagnino, J. (eds.), *The Collected Works.* Clarendon Press, Oxford.

Middleton, T. *The Revenger's Tragedy.* See Tourneur.

Miller, J. W. (2003) *Helen of Troy: Paris and Helen's War. A Play and a Screenplay.* Xlibris: USA (no further publication details).

Milton, J. (1979) *Paradise Lost*, ed. Fowler, A. Longman, London.

Minkler, J. A. (1993) "Helen's Calibans: a study of gender hierarchy in Derek Walcott's *Omeros.*" *World Literature Today* 67, 272–6.

Montrose, L. A. (1980) "Gifts and reasons: the contexts of Peele's *The Araygnment of Paris.*" *English Literary History* 47, 443–61.

Morris, W. (1915) "Scenes from the fall of Troy." In *The Complete Works of William Morris*, intro. Morris, M., vol. 24. Longmans, Green, London, pp. 3–51.

Mountfort, W. (1697) *The Life and Death of Doctor Faustus* (STC Wing M 2975). London.

Mourby, A. (2006) "Oh lord, it's hard to be Helen." Program article for ENO, *La Belle Hélène.*

Muir, E. (1984) "The charm." In *Collected Poems.* Faber & Faber, London, pp. 218–19.

Nashe, T. (1592) *Pierce Penilesse his Supplication to the Devil* (STC 18373). London.

Natanson, M. (1979) "Phenomenology, anonymity and alienation." *New Literary History* 10, 533–46.

Neill, M. (2000) *Putting History to the Question.* Columbia University Press, New York.

Norris, P. (1998) *The Story of Eve.* Picador, London.

Nye, R. (1980) *Faust.* Book Club Associates and Hamish Hamilton, London.

Ogle, J. (1594) *The Lamentation of Troy for the Death of Hector. Whereunto is Annexed an Old Woman's Tale in her Solitary Cell.* London.

Olson, S. D. (1989) "The stories of Helen and Menelaus (*Odyssey* 4.240–89) and the Return of Odysseus." *American Journal of Philology* 110, 387–94.

O'Neill, M. (2005) "Romantic forms: an introduction." In Roe, N. (ed.), *Romanticism: An Oxford Guide.* Oxford University Press, Oxford, pp. 275–91.

Orton, J. (1993) *What the Butler Saw.* In *The Complete Plays.* Methuen, London.

Oswald, E. (1905) *The Legend of Fair Helen as Told by Homer, Goethe and Others.* John Murray, London.

Ovid (1567) *Metamorphoses*, trans. Golding, A. (STC 18956). London.

Ovid (1955) *Metamorphoses*, trans. Innes, P. Penguin, Harmondsworth.

Ovid (1982) *The Erotic Poems*, trans. and ed. Green, P. Penguin, Harmondsworth.

Ovid (1990) *Heroides*, trans. and ed. Isbell, H. Penguin, London.

Owen, W. (1963) "The kind ghosts." In Day Lewis, C. (ed.), *The Collected Poems of Wilfred Owen*. Chatto & Windus, London, p. 102.

P. F. [Paul Fairfax?]. See Jones.

Paglia, C. (1991) *Sexual Personae: Art and Decadence from Nefertiti to Emily Dickinson*. Penguin, New York.

Panton, G. A. and Donaldson, D. (eds.) (1869 and 1874) *The "Gest hystoriale" of the Destruction of Troy*. Published for the Early English Text Society by N. Trübner, London.

Parker, P. (1996) *Shakespeare from the Margins*. University of Chicago Press, Chicago, IL.

Parry, A. (1973) *Blameless Aegisthus: A Study of Amumon and other Homeric Epithets*. E. J. Brill, Leiden.

Parry, R. (1595) *Moderatus, the Most Delectable and Famous History of the Black Knight* (STC 19337). London.

Paster, G. K. (1987) "'Leaky vessels': the incontinent women of city comedy." *Renaissance Drama* 18, 43–65.

Pater, W. (1986) *The Renaissance*. Oxford University Press, Oxford.

Patterson, C. (1998) *The Family in Greek History*. Harvard University Press, Cambridge, MA.

Pausanias (1918) *Description of Greece*, trans. Jones, W. H. S., vol. 1 (bks. 1 and 2). William Heinemann, London.

Pausanias (1926) *Description of Greece*, trans. Jones, W. H. S. and Ormerod, H. A., vol. 2 (bks. 3–5). William Heinemann, London.

Peacham, H. (1638) *Valley of Variety* (STC 19518). London.

Peele, G. (1584) *The Arraignment of Paris* (STC 19530). London.

Peele, G. (1589) *A Farewell Entituled To the Famous and Fortunate Generals of our English Forces: Sir John Norris & Sir Francis Drake Knights ... Whereunto is annexed: a Tale of Troy* (STC 19537). London.

Peele, G. (1888a) *The Arraignment of Paris*. In Bullen, A. H. (ed.), *The Works of George Peele*, 2 vols. J. C. Nimmo, London vol. 1, pp. 1–73.

Peele, G. (1888b) *The Beginning, Accidents and End of the Fall of Troy*. In Bullen, A. H. (ed.), *The Works of George Peele*, 2 vols. J. C. Nimmo, London vol. 2, pp. 231–65.

Peele, G. (1952) *Volume One: The Life and Minor Works of George Peele*, ed. Horne, D. H. In Prouty, C. T. (gen. ed.), *The Life and Works of George Peele*, 3 vols. Yale University Press, New Haven.

Peterson, H. (1883) "Helen, after Troy." In *Poems*. J. B. Lipincott, London, pp. 45–9.

Pettie, G. (1576) *A Petite Palace of Pettie's Pleasure* (STC 19819). London.

Philaretes (1602) *Work for Chimney Sweepers* (STC 12571). London.

Phillips, S. (1915) *Panama and Other Poems*. John Lane, London.

Pikering, J. (1982) *Horestes*. In Axton, M. (ed.), *Three Tudor Classical Interludes*. D. S. Brewer, Cambridge, pp. 94–158.

Plato (1973) *Phaedrus and Letters VII and VIII*, trans. and ed. Hamilton, W. Penguin, Harmondsworth.

Plato (1997) *Complete Works*, ed. Cooper, J. M. Hacket Publishing, Indianapolis, IN.

Pliny (1968) *Natural History*, trans. Rackham, H., vol. 9. William Heinemann, London.

Pliny (1969) *Natural History*, trans. Jones, W. H. S., vol. 6. William Heinemann, London.

Poe, E. A. (1882) *The Poetical Works of Edgar Allan Poe*. Moxon, London.

Pollard, J. (1965) *Helen of Troy*. Robert Hale, London.

Pollard, J. H. (2004) *Helen, Queen of Sparta*. Athena Press, Twickenham.

Pollard, T. (ed.) (2004) *Shakespeare's Theater*. Blackwell Publishing, Oxford.

Pope, A. (1963) *The Poems of Alexander Pope*, ed. Butt, J. Methuen, London.

Porter, J. A. (1979) *The Drama of Speech Acts: Shakespeare's Lancastrian Tetralogy*. University of California Press, Berkeley, CA.

Pratchett, T. (2000) *Eric*. Victor Gollancz, London.

Proctor, T. (1866) *The Triumph of Truth*. In Collier, J. P. (ed.), *Illustrations of Old English Literature*, vol. 2. Privately printed, London.

Proctor, T. (1578) "The reward of whoredom by the fall of Helen." In *A Gorgeous Gallery of Gallant Inventions* (STC 20402). London, sigs L1r-v.

Pseudo-Dionysius (1897) *Works*, trans. Parker, J. James Parker, London, Online ed.: <http://www.ccel.org/ccel/dionysius/works>. Accessed Mar. 22, 2008.

Putnam, E. J. (1971) "Helen in Egypt." In *Candaules' Wife and Other Old Stories* (orig. 1926). Books for Libraries Press, NY, pp. 79–119.

Putnam, M. C. J. (2006) *Poetic Interplay: Catullus and Horace*. Princeton University Press, Princeton, NJ.

Quintus of Smyrna (1968) *The War at Troy: What Homer Didn't Tell*, trans. Combellack, F. M. University of Oklahoma Press, Norman, OK.

Quintus of Smyrna (2004) *The Trojan Epic: Posthomerica*, trans. James, A. Johns Hopkins University Press, Baltimore, MD.

Rainold, R. (1563) *A Book Called the Foundation of Rhetoric* (STC 20925a.5). London.

Reckford, K. J. (1981) "Helen in *Aeneid* 2 and 6." *Arethusa* 14, 85–99.

Reinhart, K. (1968) "Goethe and antiquity: the Helen Episode of Goethe's *Faust*." In Lange, V. (ed.), *Goethe: A Collection of Critical Essays*. Prentice-Hall, Englewood Cliffs, NJ, pp. 99–109.

Reinhartz, A. (1998) *"Why Ask My Name?" Anonymity and Identity in Biblical Narrative*. Oxford University Press, Oxford.

Richards, I. A. (1926) *Principles of Literary Criticism*. Kegan Paul, Trench, Trübner, London.

Riggs, D. (2004) *The World of Christopher Marlowe*. Faber & Faber, London.

Ripa, C. (1602) *Iconologia*. Milan.

Robinson, T. and Curtis, R. (1987) *Odysseus, the Greatest Hero of Them All*. BBC/Knight Books, London.

Roche, T. P. (1964) *The Kindly Flame*. Princeton University Press, Princeton, NJ.

Rogers, M. (1988) "The decorum of women's beauty: Trissino, Firenzuola, Luigini and the representation of women in sixteenth-century painting." *Renaissance Studies* 2, 47–89.

Rogers, T. (1576) *A Philosophical Discourse entitled The Anatomy of the Mind* (STC 21239). London.

Rose, M. A. (1993) *Parody: Ancient, Modern, and Post-Modern.* Cambridge University Press, Cambridge.

Rutter, C. C. (2000) "Designs on Shakespeare: sleeves, gloves, and Helen's placket." In Ioppolo, G. (ed.), *Shakespeare Performed: Essays in Honor of R. A. Foakes.* University of Delaware Press, Newark, DE, pp. 216–39.

Sainte-Maure, B. de. (1904) *Le Roman de Troie*, ed. Constans, L. Firmin, Didot et Cie., Paris.

Saker, Austin (1580) *Narbonus* (STC 21593). London.

Sale, C. (2003) "Representing Lavinia: the (in)significance of women's consent in legal discourses of rape and ravishment and Shakespeare's *Titus Andronicus.*" In Woodbridge, L. and Behler, S. (eds.), *Women, Violence, and English Renaissance Literature.* Arizona Center for Medieval & Renaissance Studies, Tempe, AR, pp. 1–27.

Salusbury, J. and Chester, R. (1914) *Poems by Sir John Salusbury and Robert Chester*, intro. Carleton Brown. Published for the Early English Text Society by Kegan Paul, Trench, Trübner and Oxford University Press, London.

Salzman, E. (2004) *Double Crossing.* Bloodaxe Books, Tarset, Northumberland.

Santayana, G. (1955) *The Sense of Beauty, Being the Outline of Aesthetic Theory*, orig. 1896. Dover Publications, London.

Sappho (1955) *Poetarum Lesbiorum Fragmenta*, ed. Lobel, E. and Page, D. Clarendon Press, Oxford.

Scarry, E. (2000) *On Beauty and Being Just.* Duckworth, London.

Scherer, M. (1967) "Helen of Troy." *Metropolitan Museum of Art Bulletin* 25, 367–83.

Schiller, F. (1967) *On The Aesthetic Education of Man: In a Series of Letters (1795)*, trans. Wilkinson, E. M. and Willoughby, L. A. Clarendon Press, Oxford.

Schlegel, F. (1957) *Literary Notebooks, 1797–1801*, ed. Eichner, H. University of London, Athlone Press, London.

Scholar, R. (2006) *The Je-Ne-Sais-Quoi in Early Modern Europe.* Oxford University Press, Oxford.

Schmitz, G. (1990) *The Fall of Women in Early English Narrative Verse.* Cambridge University Press, Cambridge.

Schultz, M. (2005) *A Brief History of Helen of Troy, or Everything Will Be Different.* Oberon Modern Plays, London.

Schwartz, D. (1979) "Paris and Helen: an entertainment." In *Last and Lost Poems of Delmore Schwartz*, ed. Phillips, R. Vanguard Press, New York, pp. 105–33.

Schweitzer, C. E. (1987) "The structure of *Faust.*" In McMillan, *Approaches*, pp. 70–6.

Schwyzer, P. (2004) *Literature, Nationalism and Memory in Early Modern England and Wales*. Cambridge University Press, Cambridge.

Segal, C. (1971) "The two worlds of Euripides' *Helen*." *Transactions of the American Philological Society* 102, 553–614.

Seymour, M. (1979) *The Goddess*. Michael Joseph, London.

Shaaber, M. A. (1957) "*The First Rape of Faire Hellen* by John Trussell." *Shakespeare Quarterly* 8, 407–48.

Shakespeare, W. (1975) *As You Like It*, ed. Latham, A. Methuen, London.

Shakespeare, W. (1997) *The Riverside Shakespeare*, gen. ed. Blakemore Evans, G. Houghton Mifflin, Boston, MA.

Shakespeare, W. (2007) *The Complete Works*, ed. Bate, J. and Rasmussen, E. Macmillan, Basingstoke.

Shanower, E. (2005) *Age of Bronze, Volume 1: A Thousand Ships*. Image, Berkeley, CA.

Sidney, Sir P. (1973) *The Countess of Pembroke's Arcadia (The Old Arcadia)*, ed. Robertson, J. Clarendon Press, Oxford.

Sidney, Sir P. (1977) *The Countess of Pembroke's Arcadia*, ed. Evans, M. Penguin, Harmondsworth.

Singerman, A. J. (1976) "Helen and Troïlus: war and allegory in Giraudoux's 'La Guerre de Troie n'aura pas lieu'." *French Review* 49, 669–75.

Spenser, E. (1977) *The Faerie Queene*, ed. Hamilton, A. C. Longman, London.

Spentzou, E. (1996) "Helen of Troy and the poetics of innocence: from ancient fiction to modern metafiction." *Classical and Modern Literature* 16, 301–24.

Spinoza, B. (1910) *Ethics and De Intellectus Emendatione (1677)*, trans. Boyle, A. Dent, London.

Sprague, R. K. (ed.) (1972) *The Older Sophists*. University of South Carolina Press, Columbia, SC.

Stanley, J. (1886) *A Daughter of the Gods*. Hurst & Blackett, London.

Stanley, J. (1888) *A New Face at the Door*. Hurst & Blackett, London.

Sterne, L. (2003) *The Life and Opinions of Tristram Shandy*, ed. New, M. and New, J. Penguin, Harmondsworth.

Stewart, S. (2005 [1993]) *On Longing: Narratives of the Miniature, the Gigantic, the Souvenir, the Collection*. Duke University Press, Durham, NC.

Stockholder, K. (1988) "'Within the massy entrails of the earth': Faustus' relation to women." In Friedenreich, K., Gill, R. and Kuriyama, C. B. (eds.), *"A Poet and a Filthy Play-maker": New Essays on Christopher Marlowe*. AMS Press, New York, pp. 203–20.

Stoppard, T. (1997) *The Invention of Love*. Faber & Faber, London.

Stow, J. (1589) *Chronicles* (STC 23333). London.

Sundwall, M. (1975) "Deiphobus and Helen: a tantalizing hint." *Modern Philology* 73, 151–6.

Sutherland, J. (1982) *The Longman Companion to Victorian Fiction*. Longman, London.

Suzuki, M. (1989) *Metamorphoses of Helen: Authority, Difference and the Epic*. Cornell University Press, Ithaca, NY.

Symons, A. (1906) "Faustus and Helen." In *Poems by Arthur Symons*, vol. 2. William Heinemann, London, pp. 219–27.

Symons, A. (1927) "The Romantic movement in English poetry." In Archbold, W. A. J. (ed.), *Twentieth-Century Essays and Addresses*. Longmans, Green, London, pp. 14–33.

T. E. (1632) *The Law's Resolution of Women's Rights*. London.

Taplin, O. (1991) "Derek Walcott's *Omeros* and Derek Walcott's Homer." *Arion* 1, 213–26.

Taplin, O. (1992) *Homeric Soundings: The Shaping of the Iliad*. Clarendon Press, Oxford.

Taylor, G. (2001) "Divine [ ]ssences." *Shakespeare Survey* 54, 13–30.

Teasdale, S. (1937) *The Collected Poems of Sara Teasdale*. Macmillan, New York.

Telotte, L. E. (1989) "'Fire, water, women, wind': *Tristram Shandy* in the Classroom." In New, M. (ed.), *Approaches to Teaching Sterne's* Tristram Shandy. Modern Languages Association of America, New York, pp. 118–22.

Tennyson, A. (1936) *Poems of Tennyson, 1830–1870*, ed. Warren, T. H. Oxford University Press, London.

Thackeray, W. (1977) *Vanity Fair*, ed. Stewart, J. I. M. Penguin, Harmondsworth.

Thieme, J. (1999) *Derek Walcott*. Manchester University Press, Manchester.

Thomas, S. (2005) "The fragment." In Roe, N. (ed.), *Romanticism: An Oxford Guide*. Oxford University Press, Oxford, pp. 502–13.

Thompson, P. S. W. (2008) "'Our doubtful author': concepts and practices of interpretation in the Poets' War and its aftermath, 1600–1610, with particular reference to plays by Jonson, Marston and Shakespeare." DPhil thesis, University of Oxford.

Thucydides (1972) *History of the Peloponnesian War*, trans. Warner, R. Penguin, Harmondsworth.

Timberlake, H. (1603) *The Travails of Two English Pilgrims* (STC 24079). London.

Tourneur, C. (1967) *The Revenger's Tragedy*, ed. Gibbons, B. Ernest Benn, London.

Traubner, R. (2003) *Operetta: A Theatrical History*. Routledge, NY.

Traubner, R. (2006) "Helen, or taken from the Greek." Program article for ENO *La Belle Hélène*.

Trevelyan, R. C. (1934) *Poems*. Macmillan, London.

Tuchman, B. W. (2005) *The March of Folly: From Troy to Vietnam*. Abacus, London.

Tydeman, W. (1984) *Doctor Faustus: Text and Performance*. Macmillan, Basingstoke.

Tynan, K. (1984) *A View of the English Stage, 1944–1965*. Methuen, London.

Van Sickle, J. B. (1999) "The design of Derek Walcott's *Omeros*." *Classical World* 93, 7–27.

Vellacott, P. (1975) *Ironic Drama: A Study of Euripides' Method and Meaning*. Cambridge University Press, London.

Virgil (1981) *The Aeneid*, trans. Knight, W. F. J. Penguin, Harmondsworth.

Vivante, P. (1991) *The Iliad: Action as Poetry*. G. K. Hall, Twayne Publishers, Boston, MA.

Wager, C. H. A. (ed.) (1899) *The Siege of Troy*. Macmillan, New York.

Walcot, P. (1978) "Herodotus on rape." *Arethusa* 11, 137–47.

Walcott, D. (1990) *Omeros*. Faber & Faber, London.

Walcott, D. (1997) "Reflections on *Omeros*." *South Atlantic Quarterly* 96, 229–46.

Walker, G. (1998) "Rereading rape and sexual violence in early modern England." *Gender and History* 10, 1–25.

Waswo, R. (1997) *The Founding Legend of Western Civilization: from Virgil to Vietnam*. University Press of New England, Hanover, NH.

Waswo, R. (1988) "The history that literature makes." *New Literary History* 19, 541–64.

Waterman, A. (1990) "What's in a name?" In *In The Planetarium*. Carcanet Press, Manchester, pp. 44–5.

Watkins, J. (1995) *The Specter of Dido: Spenser and Virgilian Epic*. Yale University Press, New Haven, CT.

Watson, R. N. and Dickey, S. (2005) "Wherefore art thou Tereu? Juliet and the legacy of rape." *Renaissance Quarterly* 58, 127–56.

Watson, T. (1582) *Hekatompathia* (STC 251181). London.

Watson, T. (1670) *Heaven Taken by Storm* (STC Wing 1128). London.

Wegner, H. (1987) "In search of Goethe's *Faust* from without: a dramatic approach." In McMillan, *Approaches*, pp. 87–91.

Weil, S. (1951) "Forms of the implicit love of God." In *Waiting for God* (1950), trans. Craufurd, E. New York: G. P. Putnam's Sons, pp. 137–215.

Weiss, T. (1988) "The ultimate antientropy." In *The Norton Anthology of Modern Poetry*, 2nd ed. Norton, New York, p. 953.

West, M. L. (1975) *Immortal Helen*. Bedford College, London.

White, H. (1987) *The Content of the Form: Narrative Discourse and Historical Representation*. Johns Hopkins University Press, Baltimore, MD.

Willcock, M. M. (1976) *A Companion to the Iliad: Based on the Translation by Richmond Lattimore*. University of Chicago Press, Chicago, IL.

William, J. (1628) *Perseveria Sanctorum* (STC 25727). London.

Williams, A. (1909) *Songs in Wiltshire*. Erskine Macdonald, London.

Williams, J. R. (1983) "Faust's classical education: Goethe's allegorical treatment of Faust and Helen of Troy," *Journal of European Studies* 13, 27–41.

Williams, T. 2001: "Truth and representation: the confrontation of history and mythology in 'Omeros'." *Callaloo* 24, 276–86.

Wilson, J. (1608) *English Martyrology* (STC 25771). London.

Wood, M. (2005) *In Search of the Trojan War*. BBC Books, London.

Woolf, V. (1976) *Mrs Dalloway*. Granada, London.

Woolf, V. (1987) *The Essays of Virginia Woolf*, ed. McNeillie, A., 3 vols. Vol. 2. New York, Harcourt.

Woolf, V. (1992) *To the Lighthouse* in *Three Great Novels: Mrs Dalloway, To the Lighthouse, The Waves*. Harmondsworth, Penguin.

Worman, N. (1997) "The body as argument: Helen in four Greek texts." *Classical Antiquity* 16, 151–203.

Wright, L. (1589) *Summons for Sleepers* (STC 260343). London.

Wright, M. (2005) *Euripides' Escape Tragedies: A Study of* Helen, Andromeda, *and* Iphigenia among the Taurians. Oxford University Press, Oxford.

Wroth, M. (1995) *The First Part of the Countess of Montgomery's Urania*, ed. Roberts, J. A. Renaissance English Text Society / Medieval and Renaissance Texts and Studies, Binghamton, NY.

Wülfing, J. E. (ed.) (1902) *The Laud Troy Book*. Published for the Early English Text Society by Kegan Paul, Trench, Trübner, London.

Wyatt, J. M. (1973) "*Mrs Dalloway*: literary allusion as structural metaphor." *PMLA* 88, 440–51.

Wynne-Davies, M. (1991) "'The swallowing womb': consumed and consuming women in *Titus Andronicus*." In Wayne, V. (ed.), *The Matter of Difference*. Cornell University Press, Ithaca, NY, pp. 129–51.

Yalom, M. (1997) *A History of the Breast*. Alfred A. Knopf, New York.

Yeats, W. B. (1925) *A Vision: An Exploration of Life Founded upon the Writings of Giraldius and upon Certain Doctrines attributed to Kustan Ben Luka*. Werner Laurie, London.

Yeats, W. B. (1937) *A Vision*. Macmillan, London.

Yeats, W. B. (1955) *Autobiographies*. Macmillan, London.

Yeats, W. B. (1969) *Collected Poems*. 1st ed., 1933. Macmillan, London.

Yeats, W. B. (1972) *Memoirs*, ed. Donoghue, D. Macmillan, London.

Zacharek, S. (2004) "*Troy*." <http://www.salon.com>. Accessed May 1, 2006.

Filmography

The Private Life of Helen of Troy (1927) dir. Alexander Korda.

Helen of Troy (1955) dir. Robert Wise.

Helen of Troy (2003) dir. John Kent Harrison.

Troy (2004) dir. Wolfgang Petersen.

Raphael, F. (1979) *Of Mycenae and Men*, dir. Hugh David.

The Truth about Cats and Dogs (1996), dir. Michael Lehmann.

Index

Abbott, H. P.   10, 19, 26
absence   12–15, 79–80, 81–2, 83–4,
    90–2, 134, 137, 199, 201,
    220n72
Achilles
    absent   12, 209n4
    anger   11
    heel   12
    marriage to Helen   9, 157–8,
        209n22
Adams, T.   70, 139
Aeschylus   13, 18, 27, 38, 39, 50,
    110
Alcidamas   5
Alemán, M.   106
Allott, R.   139
L'Amante de Paride   219n66
Andreas, B.   40
Angelico, Fra   214n19
Apelles   213–14n9
Aristophanes   52, 55, 119–20,
    215n23,n29
Armstrong, K.   26, 28, 211n21,n22
Asimov, I.   161
Atwood, M.   31, 53, 83, 98, 161
Austin, N.   18, 20, 118, 120, 200,
    209n2, 213n4, 219n68

Bacon, F.   215n22
Baines, B.   98
Bashaw, N.   84, 101

Baswell, C. C. and Taylor, P. B.   92,
    93, 96
Bate, A. K.   223n18,n19
Bate, J.   143
Beaumont, F. and Fletcher, J.   28–9
beauty
    as absolute   65–9
    and androgyny   56–9
    and breasts   55, 216n31, 216n36
    of Briseis and Polyxena   61, 62
    as clothing   74, 185, 215n24
    as compensation   110, 112–13,
        131
    of Criseyde   62, 64
    and curly hair   214n18,n19
    details   37, 67–9, 158
    effect of   11, 20, 22, 49–51, 137,
        178, 201, 215n25
    and eyebrows   62, 217n45,n49
    and height   47–8
    insufficiency and excess   35–6,
        212n2, 213n5, 227n31
    and language   38, 39, 45, 65–7,
        121–2, 218n52
    and longing   79
    and movement   215n21,n22
    in Mrs Dalloway   197
    and narrative   37, 67–9, 158:
        see also narrative, shudder in
    and nostalgia   78–81, 219n70,n71
    and objectivity/subjectivity   74–8

LaVergne, TN USA
02 March 2010
174364LV00002BA/17/P